Globalisation and Migratio

This book critically examines some of the new issues and the new politics surrounding migration in the era of globalisation from a majority world perspective. It examines the current shifts in the global political economy and the effects it has on the movement of people. When and how does development lead to migration? We need to examine the complex ways in which migration is cut across and impacts on the generation of racism and xenophobia in the west. The issue of remittances by migrants to the 'developing' nations needs careful study as does the controversial issue of 'brain drain' versus 'brain gain' through migration. The growing importance of trafficking for forced labour has now been taken up by various international bodies but is it the new normality or simply an unfortunate side effect of globalisation to be overcome through legislation? Migration is becoming increasingly gendered in terms of its composition and flows but also in the receiving countries where men and women carry out very different jobs. We can predict the increasing racialization and gendering of migration but how will the state and society respond to these shifts? Migration is increasing in importance along with globalisation; this book seeks to explain why and its impact on the majority world.

This book was published as a special issue of *Third World Quarterly*.

Ronaldo Munck is based at Dublin City University and is a well-known specialist on labour in the era of globalisation.

Thirdworlds

Edited by Shahid Qadir, *University of London*

THIRDWORLDS will focus on the political economy, development and cultures of those parts of the world that have experienced the most political, social, and economic upheaval, and which have faced the greatest challenges of the postcolonial world under globalisation: poverty, displacement and diaspora, environmental degradation, human and civil rights abuses, war, hunger, and disease. **THIRDWORLDS** serves as a signifier of oppositional emerging economies and cultures ranging from Africa, Asia, Latin America, Middle East, and even those 'Souths' within a larger perceived North, such as the U.S. South and Mediterranean Europe. The study of these otherwise disparate and discontinuous areas, known collectively as the Global South, demonstrates that as globalisation pervades the planet, the south, as a synonym for subalterity, also transcends geographical and ideological frontiers.

Globalisation and Migration

New Issues, New Politics

Edited by Ronaldo Munck

Routledge
Taylor & Francis Group

LONDON AND NEW YORK

Transferred to digital printing 2010
First published 2009 by Routledge
2 Park Square, Milton Park, Abingdon, Oxon, OX14 4RN

Simultaneously published in the USA and Canada
by Routledge
270 Madison Avenue, New York, NY 10016

Routledge is an imprint of the Taylor & Francis Group, an informa business

© 2009 Edited by Ronaldo Munck

Typeset in Times by Value Chain, India

British Library Cataloguing in Publication Data
A catalogue record for this book is available from the British Library

ISBN10: 0-415-46832-9 (hbk)
ISBN13: 978-0-415-46832-9 (hbk)

ISBN10: 0-415-59087-6 (pbk)
ISBN13: 978-0-415-59087-7 (pbk)

CONTENTS

CONTENTS

NOTES ON CONTRIBUTORS

Ronaldo Munck is Theme Leader for internationalisation, interculturalism and social development at Dublin City University and Visiting Professor of Sociology at the University of Liverpool. He has written widely on development (including *Critical Development Theory: Contributions to a New Paradigm*, Zed, 1999) and on Latin America (most recently *Contemporary Latin America*, Palgrave Macmillan, 2008). His recent work has focused mainly on the impact of globalisation in *Globalisation and Labour: The new 'Great Transformation'* (Zed Books, 2002); *Globalization and Social Exclusion: A Transformationalist Perspective* (Kumarian Press, 2005) and *Globalization and Contestation: The new great counter-movement* (Routledge, 2007). He is currently working on globalisation and migration in Ireland and edits the journal *Translocation: Migration and Social Change* (www.translocations.ie).

Piyasiri Wickramasekara is a Senior Migration Specialist in the International Migration Programme of the International Labour Office (ILO). Previously he served as a senior development economist in ILO technical teams in Bangkok and New Delhi and he was a senior lecturer in the Department of Economics, University of Peradeniya, Sri Lanka, 1968–84. Recent publications include 'Skilled labour mobility: the resurgence of the "brain drain" debate', in *Development Perspectives: Growth and Equity in Sri Lanka* (eds SMP Senanayake, W Wimalaratna & A de Silva, 2008) and *Afghan Households and Workers in Iran: Profile and Impact* (with J Seghal et al, 2006).

Pauline Gardiner Barber is Associate Professor in the Department of Sociology and Social Anthropology, cross-appointed to International Development Studies, at Dalhousie University. Her research interests include globalisation, culture and political economy, gender, citizenship and Philippine migration and development. She has published in various books and co-edited publications, for example *Focaal European Journal of Anthropology and Anthropologica*, and is a co-editor for the Ashgate series *Gender in a Global/Local World*.

Nicola Piper is Senior Lecturer at Swansea University, Department of Geography and Associate Director of the Centre for Migration Policy Research. Her most recent edited book is *New Perspectives on Gender and Migration: Livelihoods, Rights, and Entitlements* (2008) and she recently coauthored *Critical Perspectives on Global Governance: Rights and Regulation in Governing Regimes* (with Jean Grugel, 2007).

Hein de Haas is Senior Research Officer at the International Migration Institute of the University of Oxford. He previously held researcher and lecturer positions at

Radboud University, Nijmegen and the University of Amsterdam. His research focuses on the reciprocal linkages between migration and broader development processes. Recent publications include 'International migration and regional development in Morocco: a critical review of the literature', *Journal of Ethnic and Migration Studies* (forthcoming) and *Migration, Remittances and Social Development* (2007).

Nicos Trimikliniotis is Assistant Professor of Law and Sociology and Director of the Centre for the Study of Migration, Inter-ethnic and Labour Relations, University of Nicosia. He has researched on ethnic conflict, migration and gender, racism and discrimination. Recent works include *Irregular Migration, Informal Labour and Community: A Challenge for Europe* (with E Berggren et al, 2007); and special issues of the Cyprus Review on 'Reconciliation in Cyprus' (19 (1), 2007) and 'Migration, Racism and Multiculturalism in Cyprus' (20 (2), 2008).

Steven Gordon is a Tutor at theUniversity of KwaZulu-Natal, Durban. He researches on immigration policy, patterns of undocumented migration and the trade union responses to migrant workers in post-apartheid South Africa, which formed part of his MA dissertation.

Brian Zondo is a Tutor at the University of KwaZulu-Natal, Durban and an MA candidate in the Social Policy Program there. His research is based on working conditions in the development of shopping malls in black townships. He is also a social activist with the Social Movement Indaba, the Socialist Student Movement and the Democratic Socialist Movement.

Oliver Bakewell is a Senior Research Officer at the International Migration Institute, in the Department of International Development at Oxford University. His research focuses on changing patterns of migration, both forced and voluntary, across Africa. Recent publications include 'In Search of the Diasporas within Africa.' *African Diaspora* 1(1), 2008 and 'Research beyond the categories: the importance of policy irrelevant research into forced migration.' *Journal of Refugee Studies* 21(4), 2008.

Raúl Delgado Wise is Director of the Doctoral Program in Development Studies at the University of Zacatecas and Executive Secretary of the International Migration and Development Network. He is author/editor of 14 books and more than 100 essays. His recent publications include *Migración y Desarrollo: Perspectivas desde el Sur,* (as editor with Stephen Castles, 2007) and *Contribuciones al análisis de la migración internacional y eldesarrollo regional en México* (as editor with Beatrice Knerr, 2005).

Humberto Márquez Covarrubias is a Researcher/Professor at the Development Studies Institute at the University of Zacatecas. He has published several articles in refereed journals and book chapters around the problematic of development and migration. His research focus is the political economy of development.

Marianne H Marchand is Professor of International Relations at the University of the Americas, Puebla, where she also co-ordinates the PhD programme in

International Relations and directs the Canadian Studies programme. She is a member of the National System of Researchers (SNI). Her most recent research focuses on the migration–development nexus. From 2007 to 2008 she was vice-president of the International Studies Association.

Rahel Kunz is a Research and Teaching Assistant at the Political Science Department of the University of Lucerne. She is currently finalising her doctoral thesis on the migration–development nexus. Her latest and forthcoming publications include 'The migration–development nexus in EU external relations', *Journal of European Integration* 30:3 (with Sandra Lavenex, 2008) and a chapter in the second edition of *Gender and Global Restructuring: Sightings, Sites and Resistances* (eds M Marchand & AS Runyan, forthcoming 2010).

Tine Davids is Senior Lecturer at the Centre for International Development Issues (CIDIN), Radboud University, Nijmegen. Her research areas are globalisation and gender; deprived urban youth and regionalism; transnationalism; and remigration. Related publications include T*he Gender Question in Globalization* (2007) and *Urban Youth: Actors of Change* (2007).

Marieke van Houte is a PhD candidate at CIDIN. Her publications include *Towards a Better Embeddedness? Monitoring Assistance to Involuntary Returning Migrants from Western Countries* (2008) and (with Tine Davids) 'Remigration, development and mixed embeddeness: an agenda for qualitative research?', in *Contemporary Challenges in Return: In Theory and in Practice* (ed JP Cassarino, 2008).

Ben Rogaly is Senior Lecturer in Human Geography at the University of Sussex, UK, and a member of the Sussex Centre for Migration Research. He has published a series of reports and journal articles on migrant workers in agriculture in India and the UK, and co-edited (with Arjan de Haan) a special issue of the *Journal of Development Studies* entitled Labour Mobility and Rural Society. His most recent book (co-authored with Becky Taylor) is *Moving Histories of Class and Community: Identity, Place and Belonging in Contemporary England* (Palgrave Macmillan, 2009).

Martin Baldwin-Edwards is co-founder and co-Director of the Mediterranean Migration Observatory, Panteion University, Athens and a Research Associate of the International Centre for Migration Policy Development (ICMPD), Vienna. He is currently scientific co-ordinator of an advisory project for the European Commission on regularisation of illegal immigrants in the EU, and the country expert on Greece and Cyprus for the ICMPD PROMINSTAT project on migration statistics. In recent years he served as a consultant on migration issues for the East-West Institute, the IOM, the Global Commission on International Migration, the Migration Policy Institute (USA), UNECE and the governments of Greece and Italy. His latest publications include: 'La migración en África subsahariana y el Magreb', *Vanguardia Dossier* (2008); 'Navigating between Scylla and Charybdis: Migration policies for a Romania within the European Union', *South East European and Black Sea Studies* (2007); 'Between a Rock and a Hard Place: North Africa as a region of emigration, immigration and transit migration', *Review of African Political Economy* (2006).

Globalisation, Governance and Migration: an introduction

RONALDO MUNCK

As Stephen Castles put it recently at a migration futures workshop, 'Never before has international migration been so high on the political agenda'.[1] A token of this importance was the establishment in 2003 of the Global Commission on International Migration (GCIM) to place international migration on the global governance agenda. Much of the state attention on migration has been negative, especially after the '*evénements*' of September 2001 in the USA. It is thus fitting that this introductory overview begins with a consideration of migration and security to unpack the dominant discourse of migrant as security threat. The other major way in which migration is approached today is as a governance problem. The International Organisation for Migration (IOM) argues that. 'Despite the prominence of migration on international agendas for more than a decade now, efforts to achieve global consensus on its governance have proven elusive'.[2] We thus end this introductory survey with a consideration of managing migration as global governance problem, but also by articulating the alternative prospect of open borders.

To refer to a 'Southern' perspective on migration and development might seem perverse in the era of globalisation when such binary divisions are supposedly overcome. At best it might appear as a crude appeal to a geographical Thirdworldism long since forgotten in a global order where flows and hybridity prevail. Yet most (all?) of the contributors to this collection show in different ways how the globalisation and migration debate now opening up is over-determined by the perspectives and the interests of the rich countries. As Raúl Delgado Wise and Humberto Márquez Covarrubias put it succinctly, 'there is as yet no theoretical–conceptual framework that takes into account the point of view and particular interests of the underdeveloped countries, which, at this point, are seasoned exporters of cheap qualified and unqualified workforce'.[3] What is, indeed, a global issue is invariably studied from the perspective of the receiving countries, with little or no understanding of the political economy of development which caused the migratory flows in the first instance. The dominant paradigm thus studies migration in a somewhat decontextualised manner, with a sometimes heavy tinge of ethnocentrism as well as methodological nationalism.

We could argue that adopting a Southern perspective is in fact a first step towards a holistic global approach to the interlinked processes of migration and development. It is not really a question of reversing the receiving country perspective to become a sending country outlook. Rather, it is a question of developing a paradigm through which a specific process (or set of processes) can be properly contextualised and, for that matter, placed in a historical perspective. The North–South divide continues as an overarching feature of the global system and is the inescapable context within which international migration today needs to be set.[4] The uneven development of global capitalism sets the parameters of both migration processes and development prospects in the South or Third World. Unidirectional and un-dialectical treatments of the migration–development nexus (seen not least in the burgeoning literature on economic remittances) will not provide us with the analytical tools to understand (let alone change) the world around us. Migration studies should be embedded within the broader debates around the political economy of globalisation and its implications for development.

Migration is not, of course, a topic or a process which can be studied in isolation. Migration studies have hitherto been somewhat of a self-contained problematic in the academic as well as policy milieus. We need to consider carefully, based on the evidence, what it means to say we live in 'The Age of Migration'. It is also important to consider why existing theories of international migration have such difficulty in explaining a complex, if not chaotic, socioeconomic and intercultural process. One of the major elements of this complexity is that of gender, race and class, which breaks with a common underlying assumption that migration is a unified process. Clearly the transnational flows of the business class traveller cannot be equated with the situation of those trafficked across national borders for the purpose of sexual or labour exploitation. Finally, and most appropriately for this journal, we turn to an engagement with migration and development, where sustained international attention is now being paid to this complex problematic. We need to go beyond simple theories of a 'brain drain' from dependent countries to understand much more about remittances and their development impact.

The Age of Migration?

The globalisation of migration is usually taken to refer to 'the tendency for more and more countries to be crucially affected by migratory movements at the same time'.[5] International migration is, in short, seen to be part of a revolutionary globalisation process which is reshaping economics, political systems and our whole cultural parameters. There is also a common belief that 'the current flows of migrant labour are now fundamentally different from earlier forms of mass migration'.[6] Such is the complexity of current population movements that existing explanatory frameworks are seen as inadequate. John Urry, in theorising the new 'global complexity', refers to 'massive, hard-to-categorise, contemporary migration, often with oscillatory flows between unexpected locations', which can only be seen as 'a series of turbulent waves, with a hierarchy of eddies and vortices, with globalism a virus that stimulates resistance.'[7] The migrant—from this 'globalisation as revolution' perspective—becomes more or less a symbol of the fluidity, impermanence and complexity in an era of time–space compression.

The actual increase in the numbers and, more importantly, proportions of those migrating has not actually expanded that dramatically. The IOM points out that all 190 or so sovereign states in the world are either migrant sending, receiving or transit points and that there are some 190 million people now living outside their country of birth.[8] That figure is double what it was as recently as 1980 and equivalent to the population of Brazil, the world's fifth most populous country. However, this is still less than 3% of the world's population, up only slightly from the 2.5% of the total world population who in 1960 were classified as international migrants. What this means is that we need to see migration in context as just one element in the global process of capital accumulation and labour exploitation (not that all migrants are workers of course). Migration theories perhaps need to examine more closely not only why people move, but why (preponderantly) they do not, the factors inducing immobility as well as mobility, centripetal socioeconomic factors as well as centrifugal ones.

What is particularly interesting is to examine the broad flows of migrants, in terms of the North–South divide, insofar as international migration is often just assumed to be a flow from the South to the North. With due regard to the limitations of the data, current global migration flows can be presented as in Table 1.

TABLE 1. International migration by region, millions and percentage (2000)

	From OECD countries	From rest of the world	Total
To OECD countries	22.2 (16.2)	34.1 (24.9)	56.3 (41.1)
To rest of the world	2.5 (1.8)	77.9 (57.0)	80.4 (58.8)
Total	24.7 (18.0)	112.0 (81.9)	136.7 (100.0)

Source: A Harrison, T Britton & A Swanson, *Working Abroad: The Benefits Flowing from Nationals Working in Other Economies*, Paris: OECD, 2004, p 4.

3

It is immediately apparent from this table that only a quarter of international migrants go from the global South (non–OECD countries) to the global North (OECD countries), while not quite two-thirds of migrants move within the global South. This reflects the reality of globalisation as an uneven process with poles of development within the South promoting migration. Certainly media attention is focused almost entirely on the 16% of migrants who move across the South–North divide, giving a quite unbalanced feeling to the resultant understanding of migration as a global process.

Since the era of mass migration began researchers and policy analysts have sought to explain it. However, these efforts have not been particularly successful, with knowledge acquisition and theory building not being cumulative. Rather, as Joaquín Arango puts it 'theorising about migration takes the form of a string of separate, generally unconnected theories, models or frameworks'.[9] The main economic explanation for migration has been the 'push-pull' theory in its various manifestations. This approach was and is one-dimensional, based at it is on a reductionist, neoclassical model of the rational individual. This model cannot explain why more people do not move in pursuit of higher wages or better welfare systems, nor does it tell us why there is more migration from some countries. The political economy model which developed in the 1970s clearly brought in the missing political element but, despite its radical intent, tended to be quite economistic. Based on an understanding of the world system, pitting an industrialised North against a dependent agrarian South, the structuralism of this approach had a similar 'water-pump' approach to migration to the push-pull theories, except that the units of analysis were social classes and not the neoclassical rational individual.

Most recently the theory of 'migration networks' has tended to dominate in critical thinking about migration. The relations between migrants and their friends/relatives at home act as an information network; this also builds social capital and facilitates further migration. Migration can thus become cumulative and self-perpetuating over and above any particular push-pull factors operating in a given situation or period. There is also increased attention currently being paid to the family or household theory of migration. The focus here is on the household as relevant decision-making unit rather than on the individual. Migration can thus serve as a strategy to diversify income and spread the risk across a household.[10] Gender relations in the household and in relation to migration can be foregrounded in this approach. A third alternative seeks to move beyond both the simplistic push-pull theories and the dualism of structure/agency explanations of its rivals. The emphasis is very much on flows and on cultural hybridity, on diasporas and the complex turbulence of migration. Whether the implicit underlying chaos theory is an alternative paradigm, or is even meant to be one is, I would say, a moot question.

If we accept that no new paradigm for the overall understanding of migration is about to crystallise, where does that leave us, in terms of a proactive critical understanding of the Age of Migration? We probably need to turn away from the compulsion to 'explain' the causes of migration in some semi-scientific manner. While, at one level, migration is a complex process, it is quite simple to understand the actual processes involved. What might be better than using migrants as metaphors for global movement (as good or bad thing) would be to bring together the various middle-level theories out there, but also to dig deeper into the regional dimension sometimes subsumed by the attention to the global/local divide. This knowledge-building exercise will by definition be interdisciplinary and it will also involve diverse forms of knowledge, from the scientific, to the policy domain, to the personal. We then need more detailed attention on the different aspects of migration, such as the gender and race dimensions. The 'old' debate on migration and development interactions now takes on a new shape in the era of globalisation. By unpacking the general debates in the era of globalisation, we might better reveal the empirical complexity and social dynamic of the overall process of people movement.

Migrants and security

The GCIM, set up by the United Nations to construct a global governance approach, declares in the midst of its generally progressive tenor that: 'In a number of destination countries, host societies have become *increasingly fearful* about the presence of migrant communities, especially those with unfamiliar cultures that come from parts of the world associated with extremism and violence".[11] There is fear (in the West) over people coming from parts of the world (in the South) where there is violence. The culture of these peoples is unfamiliar (to the West) giving rise to unease and uncertainty, fear and rejection. Migration is thus clearly not a purely economic process dictated by market forces but is also a key element in shaping the contemporary politics of culture and the culture of politics. The social construction of migration as endangering the security of the nation-state has a profound impact on the whole discourse around migration, which is always over-determined by the securitisation drive and the will to mastery on the part of the state. Of course, securing national borders in an era in which they become permeable in so many other ways will be a state priority.

Since the events around what the US state calls '9/11' the securitisation of migration has take on new dimension. While migration had previously been an issue of societal security, it was now squarely a key priority for state security along with drugs and weapons. The IOM dedicates a whole chapter of its 2005 report to 'managing migration in the wake of September 11: implications for a cost–benefit analysis'.[12] The reasons for investing in improving migration management would include, of course, the reduction of irregular movement across borders but also to 'reduce security weaknesses in the migration sector'.[13] The 2001 events in the USA—and the absolute prioritisation of US national security since then—have prompted a new global approach in which the dominant rationale was state security. Security has become the main modality of governance, thus creating a generalisation of insecurity for the population at large. This is because, as KM Fierke puts it, 'far from a clear distinction between secure citizens and insecure migrants, or insecure citizens and threatening migrants, a generalised environment of fear emerges'.[14] On the one hand, the distinction between the police (internal security) and the army (external security) is blurred, but so also both migrant and citizen are securitised.

Security has increasingly become the dominant prism through which migration is viewed in the West. Figures deployed by the international migration managers include the supposed five million irregular migrants in Europe, out of the total of 56 million, with 500 000 undocumented migrants arriving in Europe every year, while there are supposedly 10 million irregular status migrants in the USA, with 50% of the Mexican-born population having irregular status.[15] Not surprisingly the state apparatus deploys a security paradigm to understand and respond to this phenomenon. To contest this paradigm on the basis of the contribution that all migrants make to the Western economies is simply beside the point and does not contest its hegemony. The securitisation of migration has much deeper roots than the rise of right-wing parties or of the new racism. The framing of the state as a body endangered by transgressive migrants is a political narrative which, as Didier Bigo puts it, 'works as a political demonology through which politicians construct a figure of the enemy to generate a counter-subversive discourse and a law-and-order program'.[16]

Migrants in the heated securitisation atmosphere become the bearers of all things bad and dangerous. They transport drugs in their bodies, smuggle guns across borders and inflict themselves on others on spurious grounds of persecution. They are also deemed the bearers of illness. As one critical security analyst has said: 'The more frequent movement around the globe ... serves to transport diseases to all new parts of the world in ever-greater quantities'.[17] Of course, there are political and practical difficulties in discriminating between the potentially dangerous immigrant and the innocent tourist or returning national (all being potential carriers of illness). There are deep roots to this type of thinking, going back to the Black Death in Europe, supposedly delivered via imported goods from the Orient. Today, it is AIDS/HIV and avian flu or any other pandemic which might emerge through the movement of people, goods or animals that make headlines. Symbolically migration acts as the Other in relation to 'good' movements, such as those represented by the internet, knowledge transfer and financial markets, seen as some of the main benefits brought about by increased internationalisation. The migrant, on the other hand, is often associated with the 'dark' side of globalisation: disease, drugs, death and destruction.

Migrants can be and are also viewed as a threat to cultural identity and security. Where a nation is defined by ethnicity, then minority ethnic groups must supposedly assimilate into the dominant group or run the risk of being marginalised or, ultimately, be subject to 'ethnic cleansing'. At the very least, national citizenship will only be granted to the migrant under carefully controlled guidelines. More often the migrant will be deemed a 'guestworker', a 'non-national', or will number among what Robin Cohen has called the 'new helots' (the undocumented, the overstayers, the asylum seekers).[18] There is currently a resurgence of interest in 'cultural identity' in Western Europe and the USA, not least as a bulwark against the unwanted (yet economically necessary) Other. The arrival of migrants may prompt a sudden rediscovery of 'national identity' and 'cultural traditions' which are brushed down and rejuvenated. Citizenship tests—which many of the state's own nationals would have difficulty in passing—are now being created to weed out the undesirable alien while allowing 'in' those who fit in, can be assimilated and therefore deemed 'one of us'.

The flow of migrants across geographic, political and cultural space can be seen both as a natural consequence of globalisation and as a perceived threat to order, security, and identity. According to Roxanne Dotty, 'Anti-immigrantism is a significant contemporary practice of statecraft and like most practices of statecraft it is motivated by a desire for order'.[19] It is that element of desire (so often sublimated) in relation to order and security, identity and belonging, which explains why migration often rises to the top of the political agenda. The term neo-racism barely captures the complexity of this reaction, which goes far beyond traditional xenophobia too, in making the foreigner the source of all our ills. It is in many ways a reaction to the insecurities created by globalisation, with its increased social and geographical levels of inequality, and to the displacement of traditional notions of time and place created by the time–space compression, which is also at the heart of what we call globalisation.

Gender, race and class

Migrants are not, of course, an undifferentiated human flow and, at the very least, we need to unpack migration's gender, race and class differentials. Today almost half of international migrants are women and yet the gendered dynamics of migration are barely understood. There is somewhat of a dual labour market situation for migrant women. As the GCIM notes, 'Migration can be an empowering experience for women ... Regrettably, however, migration can have the opposite effect.'[20] Some women get to earn more money and gain decision-making power through migration. Many more, however, migrate into domestic labour or the sex industries, where they suffer isolation and extreme forms of exploitation. It is also clear, given the prevailing gender division of labour, that migrant women are more likely to remain outside the formal labour market and will have difficulty gaining the language skills and accessing the social networks necessary to achieve social inclusion in their new homes.

Migration processes are clearly patterned along gender lines in the same way that national labour markets are segmented along gender lines. In the sending countries the encroachment of free market commodification on the household economy has driven many women out of employment. Thus there are considerably more women migrants than men in both Latin America and Russia, where the neoliberal onslaught was most severe. These women are most likely to be working in the labour-intensive manufacturing sectors and the lower end of the services sector. As Spike Peterson remarks, 'The shift to an informational and service economy generates jobs that are polarised in terms of skills and work conditions, especially in big cities'.[21] Women enter both the top end of this spectrum—accentuating the so-called 'brain drain'—but also the devalorised bottom end that is both racialised and gendered in terms of which migrants enter the sector and how they do so. Migration in and of itself of course shifts and restructures traditional gender divisions of labour, the nature of the household and of the community. Shifting places can lead to shifting identities and new, complex forms of gender, race/ethnicity and communal belongings, forms of identity and repertoires of struggle.

In regard to race, as Philip Marfleet puts it simply and clearly: 'Immigration control, racism and exclusion are inseparable'.[22] Globalisation theories have, by and large, neglected race and ethnicity in their accounts of the making of the new global order. While racism and anti-immigrantism are certainly not synonymous by any means, the racialisation of migration debates has to be noted, analysed and acted upon. Racist and (the sometimes quite distinct) xenophobic discourses are not atavistic and timeless notions of difference and simply motives for exclusion. We need rather to explore the particular processes of making and unmaking of racisms in an era of flux and insecurity. In the specific area of immigration control, at the national borders where the writ of human rights barely applies, race, ethnicity and national categories are explicitly deployed to filter out the undesirable, the unclean and the unworthy. Today the most clearly differentiated is the Muslim 'Other' seen as bearer of the most retrograde social customs, cultural norms and terrorist impulses.

The racial geography of globalisation is clearly closely related to the history of colonialism and imperialism, even if this is not usually made explicit in globalisation theory. Likewise the ways in which race and ethnicity are key elements in global migration are not always made explicit. Certainly these divides do not map on to migration patterns as clearly or as visibly as do wealth and poverty differentials. If we accept that there is no such thing as a truly global labour market, then it is bound to be segmented, even segregated, along race/ethnicity lines among others. If the history of empire was the story of race, so the unfolding history of globalisation and its discontents (and resistance to them) must be written in the grammar of race and ethnicity. However, the dominant labour market model of migration does not really assist us in critically deconstructing this process. As Caroline Knowles argues, 'Mapping the trajectories of human mobility and the conditions in which they are produced is an urgent task in the analysis of globalisation's racial and ethnic grammar and the race making that produced it'.[23] This is a complex task that cannot be substituted by facile critiques of 'the racist state' as though that was sufficient as critique and alternative to the status quo.

Where social class is concerned, it is very easy from a globalisation theory perspective to become beguiled by the mobility of the new transnational capitalist and professional classes. The business class traveller for whom 'the world is my oyster' is, indeed, a growing phenomenon and at its higher levels there is a genuine global market emerging. However, as the International Labour Organisation (ILO) and others have pointed out, the era of globalisation has also been marked by a return of coerced labour that for some analysts is tantamount to a new slavery.[24] In its *Stopping Forced Labour* report of 2001 the tripartite ILO has declared that 'Although universally condemned, forced labour is revealing ugly new faces alongside the old.

8

Traditional types of forced labour, such as chattel slavery and bonded labour are still with us in some areas, and past practices of this type haunt us to this day. In new economic contexts, disturbing forms such as forced labour in connection with trafficking for human beings are now emerging *almost everywhere*.[25] Leaving aside the somewhat problematic past/present binary division the ILO is clearly locating the issue of unfree labour as a major characteristic of the new global labour market. Forced labour is defined in the IOM convention as 'all work or service that is exacted from any person under the menace of any penalty and for which the said person has not offered himself [sic] voluntarily'; using this broad definition, it is estimated that there are 12.3 million people submitted to forced labour worldwide, of which 2.45 million are trafficked for forced labour.[26]

Growing in importance as a form of unfree labour today is trafficking for forced labour (TFL), increasingly the subject of legislation—national, European and international—and of research.[27] It is estimated that nearly half of these cross-border flows of unfree labour are for commercial sexual exploitation, one third are for labour exploitation and the rest are mixed mode exploitation.[28] Trafficking for forced labour is classified as a criminal activity in its own right, this classification only recently having moved beyond the prohibition of the sex trade traffic. Trafficking involves transportation, its means includes force, coercion, fraud or deception and its purpose will be for exploitation. The Trafficking Protocol defines exploitation as 'at a minimum, the exploitation or the prostitution of others ... forced labour or services, slavery or practices similar to slavery' but it does not clearly define these terms.

The dominant interpretation of trafficking for forced labour and other coerced migration modalities is that it represents an unfortunate anomaly, part of the 'dark' side of globalisation as it were. But in reality forms of unfree labour not only survive, but are reproduced and even expanded while the capitalist mode of production (and thus free wage labour) becomes dominant. The capitalist relations of production have never been universal and they certainly do not emerge automatically through text book economics mechanisms. Unfree labour has played, and continues to play a role in the development of global capitalism. David Harvey has argued recently in this regard that we are living through a new 'primitive accumulation' (that gave rise to capitalism) that he calls 'accumulation by dispossession'.[29] Agriculturalists are driven off the land by agri-business, corporate fraud dispossesses small savers, biopiracy has become rampant and the manipulation of the foreign debt has left whole populations in debt bondage. Unfree labour emerges when 'normal' wage labour relations break down (as a result of indebtedness for example) or they coexist with free labour in a symbiotic relationship. In these circumstances, which may coexist in varying combinations, we can agree with Miles who says that 'unfree labour is an anomalous necessity'.[30]

Migration and development

Policy makers are paying increasing attention to the relationship between migration and development, not least in relation to migrant remittances, now widely seen as more important to development than official aid. The so-called migration–development nexus points to a number of areas where these problematics intersect. Questions now being asked, particularly from an EU perspective, include the ways in which aid might be targeted to reduce the number of asylum seekers, whether aid can prevent or at least reduce migration by promoting development, and how migrants might be mobilised to promote development and assist conflict resolution. The migration–development nexus is clearly highly significant given the importance of these issues, for both sides of the equation. However, from the start we should probably recognise with Sriskandarajah that, from a broad global development perspective, 'development is marginal to migration' insofar as the Northern integration and economic impact agenda dominates and that conversely 'migration is marginal to development' in terms of all the various factors determining development.[31]

It seems clear that the 'costs and benefits' of migration cannot be read as a zero-sum game. In principle migrants may create openings in the sending economy, contribute to development through economic remittances and bring back capital, skills and social networks when they return. However, they also represent a drain on the educational services that trained them, remittances may diminish and most migrants do not return, rather they create a 'culture' of migration. The verdict of the policy makers is that both sending and receiving countries can benefit from migration, but the actual data to support the verdict is still patchy. Thus a study conducted for the IOM has concluded *inter alia* that data on the impact of remittances on growth, poverty and inequality remain vague, and that, while the potential benefits of diasporas is clear, the precise way their transnational networks and capital flows operate is less so; there is also little evidence on the prevalence of return migration and its impact while, finally, there are still very few sustained accounts on the direct and indirect impacts of migration on poverty and inequality in the so-called developing countries.[32]

Recent Western governmental concern with the development potential (positive and negative) of migrants is often a thinly disguised move against migrants in their own countries. Thus there has been recent EU-level concern to stimulate the 'development potential' of migration through the encouragement of circular or temporary migration, somewhat conflating these two distinct categories. This is presented as a win-win situation, with the sender country not being hit through the 'brain drain' and the receiving country having a more flexible labour supply at its disposal. The Western political audience is reassured that the tap of migration can be turned off if necessary. However, not only is this argument dubious in its own terms because revolving-door policies rarely work in practice but, as Hein de Haas points out, 'this is somehow reminiscent of the failed attempts in the 1970s and 1980s to stimulate the return of European "guest workers"'.[33] The *Gastarbeiter* are a constant reminder of the probably apocryphal tale of the Western employer who said in relation to migrants that 'we asked for hands and we got people'.

Without doubt the most salient issue being debated today in this field is the role of migrant remittances in the development process. We are told that in

2004 global formal remittances amounted to $150 billion, with informal remittances amounting to perhaps double that figure.[34] A country like Mexico is estimated to receive $16 billion per annum from its migrant remittances. Formal remittances alone are worth three times the total amount of official development aid to the South. While their volume is not in doubt, the precise ways in which remittances affect development is less clear. But it is evident that remittances are a significant source of income and foreign exchange earnings for many countries. They are usually less volatile than aid programmes and they often reach parts of society not touched by development aid. For a small country with a large diaspora, remittances are clearly very important indeed. Yet, for much of sub-Saharan Africa, remittances are currently not that significant. In terms of their impact on inequalities within countries, the evidence is mixed: in some cases, predictably, they increase inequalities but there are cases when they become more generalised and act as an equaliser.[35]

Migrants do much more than send money home in terms of their impact on socioeconomic development. Peggy Levitt and Ninna Nyberg-Sørensen have referred in this regard to the role of 'social remittances', by which they mean 'the ideas, behaviours, identities and social capital that migrants export to their home communities'.[36] Social remittances can be over-whelmingly positive, introducing notions of democracy, accountability and gender equality, but they can also be negative in the sense of encouraging a sense of individualism over community. Luis Goldring has also referred to 'political remittances' and in particular the new tendency towards collective remittances, as when funds are transmitted by a group to a particular community in the sending country.[37] If migration is a complex and multidimensional process, then clearly remittances cannot be reduced to their economic dimension and we should consider, not least, how they (re)shape political identities. In brief, the 'remittances' that migrants make involve a set of interlocking spheres including funds, ideas, knowledge, skills, social networks, technology, political influence and political strategies.

We can conclude by considering Hein de Haas's argument that 'migration and development are functionally and reciprocally connected processes'[38] or, more simply, that migration is both cause and effect of a broader development process. As capitalism expands its reach to all parts of the world and extends the wage–labour relationship, so population movements from rural to urban areas will accelerate not least in the rapidly developing major economies of China, India and Brazil. However, as we saw above, most migration happens *within* the so-called developing world. Then it is the better equipped of these migrants who make the longer and more fraught journeys to the North. Migration is not some unwanted by-product of this process of capital accumulation and social dispossession but is, rather, an integral element of it. Internationalisation in social, economic and political terms will have as an effect the increasing movement of people. International migration, in its turn, will in practical and symbolic terms accentuate this process of global integration from which it itself resulted.

Managing migration?

That migration needs to be 'managed' is now an article of faith in most Western policy-making circles. In part this is because of the securitisation of migration, discussed above, which points towards tightening border controls. It is also, however, because international migration is now widely seen as a global issue much like 'global warming', which necessitates a global governmental response. The GCIM argues that 'the very nature of transnational migration demands international cooperation and shared responsibility. Yet, the reality is that most states have been unwilling to commit fully to the principle of international cooperation in the area of international migration.'[39] That is because controlling who enters the state and who does not is one of the few remaining powerful attributes of national sovereignty. It is also, as the Commission notes, 'a very sensitive public issue, and one that has as a result of recent terrorist attacks, become increasingly associated with threats to public security'.[40]

Pro-market development economist Jagdish Bhagwati argues that 'the world badly needs enlightened immigration policies and best practices to be spread and codified'.[41] and for over a decade he has been arguing for the creation of a World Migration Organisation which would synchronise Western immigration policies and effectively 'manage migration' as it does trade. The GCIM has for its part called for the creation of an inter-agency Global Migration Facility, which is effectively the same thing without putting it on a par with the World Trade Organization. The governance deficits in regard to international migration are thus widely recognised but progress towards doing something about them has been slow. For Stephen Castles the main reason for this is 'essentially due to the fear of labour-recruiting countries that regulation will increase the costs of migrant labour and put social obligations on receiving countries'.[42] It seems likely that in practice we will continue to see some piecemeal attempts at transnational co-ordination but a predominance of national states continuing to decry the 'smugglers and traffickers' while themselves continuously criminalising the human movement they simultaneously require for their economic survival.

Most of the empirical evidence points to the difficulties of 'managing' migration, something we might expect from our perspective that migration is a direct result of global development. Hein de Haas has argued that the whole notion of 'managing' migration is overly optimistic and that 'restrictive immigration policies fail since they ignore and cannot address the root causes of migration'.[43] While global development continues—and its uneven character deepens—so will the tendency for migration to increase. The nature of transnational migration networks today makes their management, let alone control, extremely difficult. Even a decade or more ago a major study of cross-national immigration controls could find that:

> Despite significant increases in immigration control efforts and the tightening of entry restrictions, and monitoring of unauthorised foreign workers already working in other countries ... [there is] less confidence today among officials that they could effectively regulate immigration flows and employment to unauthorised foreign workers, than there was fifteen years ago.[44]

Managing migration seems like a commonsense proposal: who would advocate unmanaged, unchecked and unbalanced flows of people across borders? When discussing these matters with Irish migration and integration policy makers, I am rapidly reminded that 'there is such a thing as national interest'. But from a global development perspective, can we really leave things at that? Mobility is the order of the day—whether it is in terms of ideas, images, investments or human beings—and national frontiers are porous at best. There is no economic logic to promoting labour mobility within the boundaries of a political border but restricting it when it steps over that frontier. There are thinly disguised racist arguments which seek to restrict population movements from certain regions or social categories. There are also 'caring' arguments about the so-called 'brain drain' from the South or the plight of the unskilled local workers who might be 'displaced'. But the specialist literature really does not provide much support for this argument. Ultimately, we can perhaps understand why Milton Friedman, early guru of the neoliberal paradigm, is supposed to have said: 'about immigration the least said the better'.

Current immigration policies in the North are essentially a form of what used to be called national manpower planning. They are part of the tendency towards national protectionism which persists (and can even be accentuated) under globalisation. Managing migration is a project of the dominant states which favours their relatively affluent populations and not the global majority. If, instead of protectionism to defend the privileges of a minority, the free flow of labour was allowed, what would its economic impact be? There is now considerable empirical evidence that international labour restrictions are very costly. We should equally ask what the economic gains might be from liberalising national labour market regulations. One recent comprehensive economic study found that 'the estimated efficiency gains from the liberalisation of global immigration controls have actually increased over time, relative to GNP—more than 15 percent (15–40%) in all (adjusted cases). In all cases, these gains exceed current levels of official foreign and foreign direct investment in the developing world.'[45] Certainly not all (or even most) of these gains would go to the South, but we should always bear in mind that the lack of mobility of labour was crucial to the original emergence of the development/under-development divide. The free movement of people would be the most dramatic way to signal a commitment to reversing underdevelopment.

Another compelling argument for open borders is the clear fact that 'Human rights are at their weakest in the vicinity of frontiers ... Injustices gather like vultures around frontiers'[46], as argued by Bob Sutcliffe, who shows how national borders are a particularly acute site for the violation of human rights in the era of globalisation. If the UN Universal Declaration of Human Rights grants the right to migrate as a fundamental and undeniable basic human right, why is the right to immigrate so restricted? From a human rights and global development perspective, we can only support the free movement of people. The lines between citizen and foreigner, local and global, national and transnational are rapidly blurring. The capitalist nationalism underlying border controls—and the relative silence of much progressive political opinion around them—will find itself under intensified pressure in the decades to come. Managing migration from a global governance perspective is of course one answer to this dilemma; another would be a renewal of a transnationalism from below that creates human bonds across artificial national and other barriers to forge a universal interest.

This volume

This special issue of *Third World Quarterly* seeks to address many of the above problematics from a wide range of perspectives, both disciplinary and regional.

Piyasiri Wickramasekara provides us with a broad overview of international labour migration in the era of globalisation, from the perspective of migrant workers' rights. While the stock of the world's transnational (as against internal) migrants almost doubled between the mid-1960s and 1990, only a small proportion of the world's population—around 3%—live elsewhere than their country of birth. The question is, what rights these international migrant workers have and what protection they are afforded. While rules for trade and capital flows across borders have developed as internationalisation intensified in the 1990s, the same cannot be said for people who cross borders. Globalisation has accelerated labour migration by accentuating income disparities between nations, but it has not (yet?) sought to establish clear governance rules. While praising the convergence between the ILO and other recent global initiatives, such as the GCIM, the author recognises the large unfinished agenda before us in making migration work for development and in providing a fair deal to migrant workers.

Pauline Gardiner Barber develops a transnational perspective to grasp the complexities of contemporary migration dynamics through a case study of gendered class subjects in Philippine–Canada migration. Her article takes issue with overly optimistic developmentalist readings of migration, but also with unduly negative views based on the rigidity of historically structured global inequalities. The labour market and the domain of citizenship in Canada is clearly racialised and gendered, but we must also attend closely to the agency of migrants. Filipino migration has produced commodified labour for export since the original development of capitalism in that country. Migration has become so central in the Philippines that it shapes people's experience in culturally normative ways. Particular emphasis is placed on the 'invisibilisation' and 'marketisation' of women migrants in border and citizenship policies in Canada. The article clearly exposes the complex reality behind the common belief of Philippine migrants as the 'ideal immigrant', known for their flexibility, hard work and pliability. Agency must always be foregrounded in a critical analysis of migration.

Nicola Piper addresses the until recently somewhat neglected aspect of migration's gendered nature. It is now quite evident that women and men experience migration differently, in complex ways not even captured by the term 'feminisation of migration'. Gender differentials need to be set in conjunction with national ethnic, skill level and legal status differentials.

What the gender focus provides is an emphasis on the broad social factors influencing women's and men's roles and their access to resources in the migration process. While much of the literature on the migration–development nexus focuses on the economic aspects—such as remittances—a gendered perspective directs us to the crucial social dimensions and the often buried considerations of equality. Through a detailed study of the linkages between migration and development in Asia in relation to the feminisation of inter-regional migratory flows this article contributes to our understanding of these broader issues.

Hein de Haas takes up what he calls the 'inconvenient realities' of African migration to Europe, thus challenging the widely promulgated image of 'invasion' to which the 'Fortress Europe' project must respond. The popular imagination and that of many policy makers is seemingly focused on the traumatic crossings of the Mediterranean and to the Canary Islands of African migrants seeking the elusive El Dorado of 'Europe'. This image conveniently ignores the structural demand for cheap migrant labour (especially in the informal sector) which fuels migration from North Africa in particular. Nor are current concerns within the EU to promote 'stay at home' development in Africa through return migration likely to lead to any significant decline in migratory flows. Indeed, development (as conventionally understood) most often fuels migration and not the opposite. Restrictive immigration policies and border controls in Europe are thus unlikely to have an impact on migration, any more than they have done at the US–Mexican border, subject of another contribution to this volume (see below).

Nicos Triminkliniotis and co-authors examine critically the relationship between globalisation, regionalisation and migration in the 'new' post-apartheid South Africa. The emergence of xenophobia and racism in relation to migrants from other southern African countries has been a shocking but under-researched issue. Here was a powerful and iconic liberation movement supporting free trade, but not the free movement of people. For the migrant worker entering South Africa little seems to have changed compared with the apartheid era, when a well oiled machine operated a regional labour market—both formal and informal—to the benefit of the settler regime. The authors argue that the 'new' South Africa is treating the question of free movement, migration and integration more or less following the example of the European Union. The trade unions in South Africa—a key component of the liberation movement—have initially reacted defensively towards migration but are now increasingly organising migrant workers, a strategy which, ironically, could benefit from the experience of (some) European trade unions.

Oliver Bakewell turns our attention to the ambivalent relationship between development and migration in Africa, thus delving behind many common yet simplistic preconceptions. At the core of these lies a very particular understanding of development from the optic of population stability, leading to a view of migration as symptomatic of development failure. Even the recent enthusiasm for a focus on the so-called development–migration nexus has failed to challenge the assumption that 'staying at home' is or should be the norm. Most development theories—including radical dependency theory—tend to share the modernist perspective and Western illusions about 'progress' as and unquestioned and unquestionable lodestar. There is a growing 'post-development' literature—not least around the work of Arturo Escobar—but it has had a limited impact on the practice of development as against critical discourses. What we need, argues Bakewell, is a radical re-conceptualisation of development for a mobile world.

Raúl Delgado Wise and Humberto Márquez Covarrubias take up the case of Mexican labour migration to the USA in the context of the ongoing capitalist restructuring process. The creation of the North American Free Trade Area (NAFTA) in 1994 was the first move towards free trade across a North–South border. Thus Mexican migration to the USA might serve as a paradigmatic case to explore the relationship between migration and development in the context of capitalist restructuring under the aegis of neoliberal globalisation. Through a detailed case study the authors conclude that capitalist restructuring results in forced migration towards developed countries. Migrants contribute simultaneously to capitalist restructuring in the global North and to the deepening of precarisation in socioeconomic terms in the global South. This critical political economy approach also points us towards the non-inevitability of this situation. An alternative development strategy needs to be developed urgently to address in a holistic way that goes beyond methodological nationalism the needs of migrants, and of development in the era of globalisation.

Marianne Marchand tackles the very violent reality of the migrant experience from the crossing of frontiers through almost every interaction they and their families have with the quaintly dubbed 'host societies'. While the state has been assiduously constructing a potential migrant/security threat nexus since the events of 2001 in the US and across the majority world, the actual security of migrants has been increasingly compromised. Based on a study of the critical Mexico/United States interface between North and South, Marchand traces carefully the diverse and interlocking forms of insecurity which migrants are subject to very much from the perspective of the migrant. This is, of course, a perspective which varies according to gender, age and other characteristics. But this is not primarily an enriching or uplifting cultural experience as some starry eyed proponents of 'crossing borders' seem to imply. Migrants experience bodily what the 'securitisation' of migration by the state means in practice: that is more risk, more insecurity and more unnecessary deaths.

Rachel Kunz tackles the topical yet controversial issue of migrant remittances from a gender perspective. While migrants have always been sending economic remittances back to their country of origin, this is now of particular interest to policy makers. The vast sums involved have impressed this sector and migrants can now be made somehow responsible for development. The issue is one of how remittances can be harnessed for development. While ostensibly gender-neutral, this emerging discourse is clearly making many gendered assumptions. A gender perspective allows us to delve beneath simplistic notions of remittances as simple economic transfers. Rather remittances are embedded within a complex web of negotiations within and between households and between the diasporas and the country of origin. These are all gendered social realities and thus gender relations need to be foregrounded in any critical and contextualised analysis of economic migrant remittances in the era of globalisation.

Marieke van Houte and Tine Davis take up a crucial aspect of the migration–development nexus, namely the issue of return migration, now being promoted by a number of Northern governments. But, while the policy of returning migrants is widely seen as a means to promote sustainable development, little is known about its effects on the ground. Even when return to the sending country is viable and sustainable for the individual migrant, it is unclear whether it does actually promote development as conventionally defined. Based on detailed research the authors show how not all returnees are successfully (re)embedded. Return migration of involuntary returning asylum seekers, for example, is not sustainable. 'Going home' is never a simple or automatically positive experience. Restrictive migration policies and migrants' rights cannot be compensated for by an ill-thought out return policy. While the objective is seen to be development, the reality is more often an added burden on the household in the sending country.

Ben Rogaly carries out a critical analysis of the ILO's Global Alliance Against Forced Labour through an analysis of temporary migration for agricultural work as forced labour in India and the UK. The theoretical framework is provided by the new geographical emphasis on the 'politics of scale' in terms of household, local, regional and national scalar boundaries. There appears to be a disjuncture in the ILO analysis between forced labour seen as a form of debt bondage (in the global South) and as trafficking (in the global North). Migrant workers seem to be categorised differently according to the geographical region from which they migrate. By examining the employment of rural migrant workers at particular socially constructed scales the author exposes important and productive contradictions and tensions. One particular argument worth pondering on is whether the contemporary liberal discourse on slavery and forced labour slips into a politics of sympathy which obscures the more complex causal mechanisms lying behind unfree labour relations.

Martin Baldwin-Edwards provides a theoretical and historical focus on 'illegal migration' too often taken for granted as a commonsense concept. While at one level it is simple to define as migration outside the law, in reality it covers a range of social phenomena from overstaying a visa to fraudulent entry. When examined from the perspective of state management of migratory flows it is clear that illegal migration is in fact socially constructed. It is precisely the politicisation of immigration management since the 1970s which has created illegal employment and illegal migration as fundamental structural components of contemporary capitalism. It is this structurally embedded reality which produces the flow of migrants across the borders of the richer countries. We could argue that unpacking the seemingly simple category of illegal migration uncovers some of the fundamental contradictions at the core of the globalised system we all live under.

Finally Gerard Boucher carries out a detailed deconstruction of several major recent statements on migration, such as the report by the GCIM. His main argument is that contemporary global policy discourses on managing migration all converge on a number of similar policy themes and outcomes. At one level they are quite lucid in discerning the responsibilities of globalisation for the current contradictions around globalisation and migration, for example in relation to development. Yet they also draw the line at calling this capitalism or referring to anything inherent in it as a mode of production which might generate these contradictions. It is most often far-right politicians and popular xenophobia in the North which is blamed for restrictionist immigration policies, and thus the rise in illegal or irregular migration. This is a technocratic view whereby the managers of globalisation seek to become incidental to politics and do not consider the inherent contradiction of neoliberal globalisation which preaches the free movement of investment, finance and ideas but not of people.

Conclusion

In their influential book *Empire* Hardt and Negri declared that 'A spectre haunts the world and it is the spectre of migration'.[47] Migration is seen by them as an act of refusal, of insecurity, violence, starvation and of a desire for peace, freedom and prosperity. Migrants can be seen as both the product of globalisation and its expression insofar as they treat the globe as a common space. There is a definite strain of romanticism in Hardt and Negri's rendering of migration and we should beware of translating the necessity to move directly into the desire for freedom. Nor should we mirror the irrationality of the actually-existing 'Empire', which views every traveller to its homeland as a potential if not actual terrorist. However, there is a great deal of truth in Hardt and Negri's later uncovering of the great irony (or should it be contradiction?) whereby 'the great global centres of wealth that call on migrants to fill a lack in their economies get more than they bargained for, since the immigrants invest the entire society with their subversive desires'.[48] In this it is like the employers prone to say: 'We wanted hands and we got people' when they consider the *Gastarbeiter* who did not want to go 'home'.

As a subject, writes Saskia Sassen, 'the immigrant filters a much larger array of political dynamics than its status in law might suggest'.[49] Immigration can be used as a sharply focused lens to understand the contradictions of contemporary nation-states in the era of globalisation. Denied the rights of citizenship which are accorded to the national, the immigrant becomes an alien in law or, to use a term deployed unselfconsciously by many today, a non-national. This dualism places in sharp relief the tensions of nation-states partaking willingly of globalisation in all its glory, while seeking to maintain or even reinforce the rigid control of their boundaries *vis-à-vis* the mobile person (unless they are clearly part of the new transnational managing or information classes). Migration is also a barometer of development, though not in a simplistic way, as we have seen above. It is a challenge for global governance, which is where we began this analysis. But above all migration policy tells us a lot about the quality of democracy in a given territory: for which other sections of the population do basic equality and justice principles not apply so shamelessly? Which other group so lacking in security is deemed a threat to national security and sovereignty?

Notes

1 S Castles, 'In the next 50 years … what will be the shape of politics, policy and governance in respect to international migration?', *CGIM Migration Futures Workshop*, Oxford University, p 14.
2 International Office of Migration (IOM), *World Migration 2005: Costs and Benefits of Migration*, Geneva: IOM, 2005, p 368.
3 R Delgado Wise & H Márquz Covarrubia, 'Towards a new theoretical approach to understanding the relationship between migration and development', *Social Analysis*, forthcoming.
4 See G Arrighi, B Silver & B Brewer, 'Industrial convergence, globalization, and the persistence of the North–South divide', *Studies in Comparative International Development*, 38 (1), 2003, pp 3–31.
5 Castles, 'In the next 50 years', p 7.
6 N Papastergiadis, *The Turbulence of Migration: Globalization, Deterritorialization and Hybridity*, Cambridge: Polity Press, 2000, p 6.
7 J Urry, *Global Complexity*, Cambridge: Polity Press, 2000, p 62.
8 IOM, *World Migration 2005*, p 13.
9 J Aranjo 'Explaining migration: a critical view', *International Social Science Journal*, 165, 2000, p 283.
10 R Cohen, *Migration and its Enemies: Global Capital, Migrant Labour and the Nation-State*, Aldershot: Ashgate, 2006, p 132.
11 Global Commission on International Migration (GCIM), *Migration in an Interconnected World*, Geneva: GCIM, 2005, p 8. Emphasis added.
12 IOM, *World Migration 2005*, pp 351–357.
13 *Ibid*, p 353.
14 KM Fierke, *Critical Approaches to International Security*, Cambridge: Polity Press, 2007, p 165.
15 GCIM, *Migration in an Interconnected World*, p 85.
16 D Bigo 'Security and immigration: towards a critique of the governmentality of unease', *Alternatives*, 27, 2002, p 69.
17 P Hough, *Understanding Global Security*, London: Routledge, 2004, p 156.
18 R Cohen, *The New Helots: Migrants in the International Division of Labour*, London: Avebury, 1987.
19 R Dotty, *Anti- Immgrantism in Western Democracies: Statecraft, Desire and the Politics of Exclusion*, London: Routledge, p 14.
20 GCIM, *Migration in an Interconnected World*, p 49.
21 S Peterson, *A Critical Rewriting of Global Political Economy: Integrating Reproductive, Productive and Virtual Economies*, London: Routledge, 2003, p 67.
22 P Marfleet, *Refugees in a Global Era*, Basingstoke: Palgrave, 2006, p 289.
23 C Knowles, *Race and Social Analysis*, London: Sage, 2004, p 124.
24 See K Bales, *Disposable People: New Slavery in the Global Economy*, Berkely, CA: University of California Press, 2004.
25 International Labour Office (ILO), *Stopping Forced Labour*, Geneva: IOM, 2001, p 5.
26 B Andeers, *Forced Labour and the Linkage to Trafficking in Human Beings*, Geneva: ILO Special Action Programme to Combat Forced Labour, 2006.
27 See F Laczko & E Gozdziak (eds), 'Data and research on human trafficking: a global survey', *International Migration*, 43 (1/2), 2005, pp 5–16.
28 Andeers, *Forced Labour and the Linkage to Trafficking in Human Beings*.
29 D Harvey, *The New Imperialism*, Oxford: Oxford University Press, 2003, ch 4.
30 R Miles, *Capitalism and Unfree Labour: Anomaly or Necessity?*, London: Tavistock, 1987, p 222.
31 D Sriskandarajah, 'Migration and development', at www.gcim.org, p 28.
32 M Farrant, A MacDonald & D Sriskandarajah, *Migration and Development: Opportunities and Challenges for Policymakers*, Geneva: IOM Migration Research Series, 22, 2006, p 45.
33 H de Haas, 'Turning the tide? Why development will not stop migration', *Development and Change*, 38 (5), 2007, pp 819–841.
34 GCIM, *Migration in an Interconnected World*, p 85.
35 Farrant *et al*, *Migration and Development*, p 19.
36 P Levitt & N Nyberg-Sørensen, 'The transnational turn in migration studies', *Global Migration Perspectives*, 6, 2004, p 8.

37 L Goldring, 'Family and collective remittances to Mexico: a multi-dimensional typology', *Development and Change*, 35 (4), 2004, pp 799–840.
38 De Haas, 'Turning the tide?'.
39 GCIM, *Migration in an Interconnected World*, p 66.
40 *Ibid*.
41 J Bhagwati, *In Defence of Globalization*, Oxford: Oxford University Press, 2004, p 218.
42 Castles, 'In the next 50 years', p 19.
43 De Haas, 'Turning the tide?'.
44 W Cornelius, P Martin & J Hollifield (eds), *Controlling Immigration: A Global Perspective*, Stanford, CA: Stanford University Press, 1994, p 4.
45 J Moses & B Lettnes, *The Economic Costs of International Labor Restrictions*, Helsinki: WIDER, 2002.
46 B Sutcliffe, 'Freedom to move in the age of globalisation', in D Baker, G Epstein & R Pollin (eds), *Globalisation and Progressive Economic Policy*, Cambridge: Cambridge University Press, 1998, pp 331–333.
47 M Hardt & A Negri, *Empire*, Cambridge, MA: Harvard University Press, 2000, p 133–134.
48 *Ibid*.
49 S Sassen, *Globalisation and its Discontents: Essays on the New Mobility of People and Money*, New York: Free Press, p 294.

Globalisation, International Labour Migration and the Rights of Migrant Workers

PIYASIRI WICKRAMASEKARA

International migration has been high on the global agenda in recent years with considerable attention being paid to its linkages with development. The discourse has highlighted the role of remittances, return migration and circular migration, and of transnational communities as major factors in promoting development benefits in countries of origin. There have been widespread calls for integrating migration issues into national development and poverty reduction strategies.[1]

While this shift of emphasis in the global migration debate from its earlier negative perception as an asylum-seeker and refugee problem is to be welcomed, the paper argues that there is a large gap between promise and delivery in actual practice—much more political will and action would be needed to go beyond lip service to making migration work for development.

There is general consensus that the challenge for policy is to maximise the positive aspects of migration while minimising the negative aspects. It is important to note at the outset that gains from migration and protection of migrant rights are inseparable. Migrant workers can make their best contribution to economic and social development in host and source countries when they enjoy decent working conditions, and when their fundamental human and labour rights are respected. Yet the negative aspects of the balance sheet of global migration leave little room for complacency. There are a number of the challenges associated with current migration patterns and trends: rampant abuse and exploitation of migrant workers; growth of irregular migration, especially trafficking in persons and smuggling of human beings; brain drain from developing countries, including heathcare workers; limited avenues for migration of low-skilled workers; poor integration of migrants and their families in host societies; growing racism and xenophobia; lack of credible migration polices; and poor ratification of, and compliance with, international normative standards.[2]

The paper cannot address all these wide-ranging issues. The focus will be on selective admission policies of destination countries, which have obvious consequences for irregular migration flows, migrant rights, brain drain from developing countries and development benefits of migration.[3] It will briefly consider whether recent interest in temporary migration programmes and other regional and global initiatives offer much scope for meeting these challenges.

The paper makes a case for more neutral terms in international migration discourse. Since labour is not a commodity, the terms 'export' and 'import' should not be used in relation to movements of human beings or workers. All workers have skills—migrant workers are no exception—which can range from low skills to high skills. Thus the term 'low-skilled' is more appropriate than 'unskilled'. There is also international acceptance of the terms, 'irregular migration' and 'migrant workers in irregular status' in place of 'illegal migration' and 'illegal migrant workers'. The former terms do not criminalise migrants and are also more comprehensive in capturing different dimensions of irregularity.

International migration is mainly a decent work and labour market issue

The UN Population Division estimated that there were 191 million migrants in the world in 2005, defined as persons living outside their country of birth.[4] The number of the world's migrants has more than doubled since 1960 but they still account only for about 3% of the global population. Female migrants constitute about half of the migrant stock (49.6%), and their share has not changed much between 1965 and 2005.

This global estimate includes migrants for employment, their families, asylum seekers and refugees. The number of refugees is relatively small and has decreased from 18.5 million in 1990 to 13.5 million in 2005. Annual asylum seekers in recent years (2004–07) have ranged from 300 000 to 400 000 only.[5] The balance is made up of migrant workers—the economically active population among global migrants—and their families. The International Labour Office (ILO) estimated the total number of migrant workers in the world to be around 86 million for 2000,[6] and the 2005 figure to reach about 94 million.

Thus the bulk of global migrants are migrant workers—those who migrate for employment—and their families, and international migration is, therefore, a decent work and labour market issue—less an asylum-seeker, refugee or security issue.[7] The former UN Secretary General echoed a similar view:

> The vast majority of migrants are industrious, courageous, and determined. They don't want a free ride. They want a fair opportunity. They are not criminals or terrorists. They are law-abiding. They don't want to live apart. They want to integrate, while retaining their identity.[8]

While there has been greater integration of global markets for goods, services and capital across borders, its impact on the cross-border movement of people and labour remains much more restricted, regulated by a complex web of immigration laws and policies that uphold the principle of state sovereignty. Moses has described international migration as 'globalisation's last frontier',[9] while Pritchett characterises the present process as 'the globalisation of everything but labor'.[10]

The Universal Declaration of Human Rights recognises the right of every person to leave any country, including his/her own, and the right of every person to return to the home country. But there is no corresponding right to enter or stay or work in a third country, since no state has surrendered that right under any international treaty. This makes the mobility of persons from one state to another quite restricted, and vastly reduces the scope of the above human rights.[11]

Mostly the backdoor option for low-skilled workers

There is mounting evidence of large gains to the global economy through liberalisation of migration, especially of less skilled workers. The Global Commission on International Migration (GCIM) holds that the world would benefit substantially from a well regulated liberalisation of the global labour market.[12] The World Bank carried out a simulation of a 3% modest addition (14.2 million workers, of whom 9.7 million were low-skilled) to the global labour force through migration over 2001–2025.[13] It predicted overall gains of US$356 to the global economy—higher than what could be achieved through trade liberalisation. The study concluded that development gains from low-skilled emigration were clear cut, while high-skilled emigration had more complex effects. A more recent analysis of removal of trade and migration barriers by Anderson and Winters has predicted even higher gains.[14] A number of researchers have also argued the case for letting 'the huddled masses' into developed countries to meet labour market needs and reap the development benefits of migration.[15]

Today's restrictive immigration policies, however, place many barriers on the migration of low-skilled workers. Such policies do not reflect actual labour market needs, being built on the myth that the demand is temporary or seasonal. Yet there is increasing demand for 'low-skill, hard-core non-tradables', primarily in services. The US Department of Labour projections show that more than 50% of new jobs in the top 25 occupations will occur in this category.[16] Similarly EU projections of labour demand show that the demand is not short-term or temporary.[17] The strong demand for care work or health workers cannot be considered temporary in an ageing Europe. At the same time many native workers shun certain occupations as incomes and living standards rise, making them immigrant-dependent sectors: agriculture, construction, cleaning, catering and other hospitality services, tourism, care work, domestic service, and the entertainment industry. The fact is that the demand for low-skilled workers cuts across all skills categories. The European Commission (EC) Policy Plan on Legal Migration clearly recognised this fact:

> With regard to economic immigration, the current situation and prospects of EU labour markets can be broadly described as a 'need' scenario. Some Member States already experience substantial labour and skills shortages in certain sectors of the economy, which cannot be filled within the national labour markets. This phenomenon concerns the full range of qualifications— from unskilled workers to top academic professionals.[18]

Yet the Policy Plan ignored this in the formulation of policy measures, and focused on skilled worker admissions. A recent OECD study pointed out: 'As shortages and mismatches across the skills spectrum intensify, recognizing the human capital of all immigrants so as to employ it more smartly, even strategically, must become a priority'.[19]

The high demand for low-skilled workers partly arises from demographic trends—population ageing and population decline. The Eurostat demographic projections indicate that in the EU25 the share of population of working age in the total population will decrease from 67.2% in 2004 to 56.7% in 2050, a fall of 52 million.[20] The former UN Secretary-General hit the nail on the head on demographic imperatives in Europe when he stated:

> The message is clear. Migrants need Europe. But Europe also needs migrants. A closed Europe would be a meaner, poorer, weaker, older Europe. An open Europe will be a fairer, richer, stronger, younger Europe—provided you manage migration well.[21]

Current policies also fail to take into account the essential complementarity between low-skilled and high-skilled activities. Skeldon observes:

> However, skilled migration systems are not independent of unskilled systems. Skilled migrants create unskilled jobs. Skilled IT engineers require packers, transporters and shippers of the hardware and software they create. Bankers and other financial experts require office cleaners, restaurateurs and valets.[22]

The Secretary-General's report for the UN High Level Dialogue on international migration and development emphasised the need for states to develop forward-looking policies that take realistic account of their long-term structural demand for both low-skilled and highly skilled workers.[23] The GCIM found the traditional distinction between 'skilled' and 'unskilled' workers to be an unhelpful one, and concluded that, while they may have different levels of educational achievement, all of them could be legitimately described as 'essential workers'.[24]

The general policy bias against the admission of low-skilled workers in major destination countries is partly a legacy of the experience of guest worker programmes of the 1960s in western Europe, which resulted in a sizeable number of temporary workers settling down. However, the global situation has changed much since then. Cheap and fast modern travel and communications mean that people can commute easily between home countries and destination countries, with no pressures for settlement.[25] A recent Institute for Public Policy Research (IPPR) study found that more than half of recent Eastern European migrants from new accession countries to the UK had returned home, and new arrivals were falling.[26] Fear of settlement also fails to consider the long-standing successful temporary or seasonal worker programmes of Gulf countries, Singapore or of Canada and Europe.[27] Destination countries now also have access to a wide array of tools involving biometrics, electronic surveillance systems, and 'e-borders', which can track overstayers easily and ensure returns.

The selective migration policies of new immigration countries such as Australia, New Zealand, Canada and the USA, favouring skilled migrants, have served to accentuate this policy bias. The number of highly educated emigrants from developing countries residing in OECD countries doubled from 1990 to 2000, compared to only about a 50% rise in the number of developing country emigrants with only a primary education.[28] The USA offers only 5000 visas per year to low-skilled persons with no relatives in the country,[29] in contrast to the annual 65 000 H1-B visas for skilled migrants.

A major effect of this policy is to reduce the poverty-alleviating impact of migration, since low-skilled persons come from relatively poor families.[30] The background report for the UN High Level Dialogue stated: 'Low-skilled migration has the largest potential to reduce the depth and severity of poverty in communities of origin'.[31] Nigel Harris has emphatically pointed out the results of this policy of restricted immigration:

> In the relationships between the developed North and the developing South, the biggest failure has not been the decline in aid programmes, which are trivial in the sum of things, or the failure to open markets quickly enough, or transfer technology, but in consistently denying the right to work to the willing and eager workers of the developing countries. In doing this, the developed countries have reduced the prosperity both of their own people and the Third World.[32]

Pritchett goes even further:

> The primary policy pursued by every rich country is to prevent unskilled labor from moving into their countries. And because unskilled labor is the primary asset of the poor world, it is hard to even imagine a policy more directly inimical to a poverty reduction agenda or to 'pro-poor growth' than one limiting the demand for unskilled labor (and inducing labor-saving innovations).[33]

He argues for adding wider access for low skilled labour to rich countries to the development themes of fairer trade, better aid and debt relief.[34]

The lack of legal avenues for low skilled workers results in channelling of large migrant flows to irregular migration, trafficking and smuggling.[35] This is taken up in the next section.

Irregular migration—bugbear of immigration policy in developed nations

Irregular migration has emerged as a central concern in the management of international migration in major destination countries. It has been blown out of proportion in migration debates and policies, ignoring the complex factors behind its growth. The RSA Migration Commission correctly observed that: 'Irregular migration is the growth within each country of the global labour market'.[36] The image that destination countries project of themselves as 'victims' of irregular migration sounds hollow because it is the direct result of their restrictive immigration policies.

The numbers of migrants in irregular status are anybody's guess, but there is no doubt that the figures quoted are sometimes exaggerated or presented out of context. Duvell points out that the presence of four to seven million migrants in irregular status should be seen in the context of the 83 million regular immigrants in Europe. He concludes that migrants in irregular status represent only a tiny share of the total stock of regular migrants or of international traffic of persons.[37] The share of immigrants in irregular status in the total population is 3.6% in the case of the USA, but less than 2% in most other OECD countries.[38] Hein de Haas has challenged the myth of invasion of Europe by uncontrollable waves of West African migrants and boat people.[39] Yet most immigration policies in the West are driven by the spectre of non-stoppable waves of migrants in irregular status.

As seen above, the closing of doors to low-skilled workers in the face of strong demand is a prime factor in the growth of irregular migration. The EU Justice Commissioner Frattini has admitted that the near certainty of finding so-called 'illegal' work in EU member states is the main driving force behind irregular immigration.[40] The UN Special Rapporteur on the human rights of migrants states:

> Denial of demand is an important issue as it is one of the main factors that leads to irregular migration, a situation at the core of much of the abuse and numerous human rights violations suffered by migrants.[41]

Intense competition under globalisation forces some enterprise to cut corners and go underground. The GCIM has referred to the growth of informal and undeclared work in destination countries, and the resulting demand for cheap and flexible labour.[42] Enterprises in low-skilled sectors attempt to survive on the basis of cheap labour and avoidance of taxes and social protection, often relying on migrant workers in irregular status. About 7%–16% of GDP in the European Union is said to arise from the shadow economy.[43] Schneider found the shadow economy in 21 OECD countries to comprise about 15% of GDP in 2004.[44]

The phenomenon of irregular migration is also traceable to outsourcing of production operations under globalisation forces. In the process 'labour brokers' have emerged who supply the needs of different enterprises. Munck adds: 'The fact is that irregular migrants in Europe are not just working in dark alleys hidden in damp cellars; they are often working for major enterprises, not least through subcontracting relationships'.[45] The surge in subcontracting and a high level of privatisation has had profound effects on the labour market generally. Migrant workers are particularly vulnerable as victims of disguised employment relationships. As Bustamante has rightly pointed out: 'The practice of subcontracting migrant labour can also be a gateway for the impunity for abuse of and violations against migrant workers'.[46]

There is no doubt that irregular migration poses a number of problems for both origin and destination countries, and for migrant workers themselves. Above all, irregular migration is a protection problem, since migrant workers become vulnerable to extreme violations of their human and labour rights. The UN High Commissioner for Human Rights maintains that 'Migrant workers face the gravest risks to their human rights when they are recruited, transported and employed in defiance of the law'.[47] Fear of detection may keep migrant workers away from even legitimately available services. Migration governance also becomes very difficult when large migrant populations are in irregular status, which undermines the credibility of legal migration programmes. It is a problem of unfair competition as well, with advantages going to enterprises using workers in irregular status at cheap wages.

There is tacit tolerance of the presence of migrant workers in irregular status on the part of many governments during economic booms, and to sustain large informal sectors in their economies, while officially they aim to be seen as 'combating' or 'fighting' irregular migration. Madame Ramphele has pointed out that 'the world's more prosperous states bear a significant degree of responsibility for the forces which have prompted and sustained the movement of irregular migrants from one country and continent to another'.[48]

While it is desirable to prevent or minimise irregular migration, the policy approaches focusing on intensified control measures and militarised borders have proved ineffective. Such polices do not address the real causes of migration, they ignore the demand side of the issues, and often result in criminalisation of irregular migration and gross violations of human rights.

Security concerns and the so-called 'war on terror' have made migrants convenient scapegoats. As Sutcliffe observed: 'human rights are at their weakest in the vicinity of frontiers'.[49] There is ample evidence to show that controls have rarely succeeded in preventing irregular migration: it can only be made more costly and dangerous.[50] Castles has commented in relation to recent European migration policies: 'Building walls (between the USA and Mexico) and increasing naval patrols (between the EU and Africa) increases the death rate and the smugglers' profits, but does not solve the problem'.[51]

According to Cornelius, the fortified US–Mexican border has, during nine years of operation, been ten times deadlier to Mexican migrants (with 2750 reported deaths crossing the border) than was the Berlin Wall was to East Germans during 28 years (with 239 deaths while attempting to cross the wall).[52] He pointed out that the main consequences of 10 years of tighter US border control have been redistribution of irregular entries; increased cost of irregular entry; more permanent settlement in the USA; higher mortality among irregular entrants; and an increase in anti-immigrant vigilante activity. While cyclical (circular) migration leads to developments benefits, particularly in source countries, stricter border controls in the USA have led to an unintended consequence in ending such cyclical patterns and to more permanent settlement of unauthorised populations.[53]

Yet lessons of history seem to be easily forgotten. One extreme response was the unsuccessful attempt at criminalisation of undocumented migrants in the US legislation, and making an estimated 10–12 million migrant workers active in the US labour market 'criminals' at one stroke of the pen.[54] The UN Special Rapporteur has argued that irregular migration should be treated as an administrative offence rather than a criminal offence.[55] The US House and Senate approved a $1.2 billion Secure Fence Act in September 2006, which called for 700 more miles of 15-foot high double-layered fencing along the US–Mexico border in addition to the existing 100 miles of fencing.[56]

Amnesties and regularisations for migrants in irregular status have been a common approach in Europe, especially southern Europe. This is also recommended as a good practice in international instruments, although they have not set any guidelines for regularisation programmes. Spain carried out a bold regularisation exercise in 2005 which gave 700 000 undocumented workers regular status. However, the current French EU presidency is proposing measures to prevent member states from using 'mass regularisation' programmes, as part of its proposed common European Pact on Immigration and Asylum.[57]

Many host countries fail to recognise that migrant workers in irregular status also have fundamental rights as human beings as well as workers, recognised in ILO and UN international instruments. The International Convention on the Protection of the Rights of All Migrant Workers and their Families (ICMW), 1990 spells out their basic rights, while they should also benefit from the eight ILO core conventions (against forced labour and child labour, and for freedom of association, and non-discrimination). Moreover, the ILO position is that all labour standards apply to migrant workers in the workplace regardless of their status.[58] The ruling of the Inter-American Court of Human Rights on the juridical condition and rights of undocumented migrants (17 September 2003) is a reiteration of international acceptance of this position. It clearly upheld that the migratory status of a person cannot constitute a justification for depriving him/her of the enjoyment and exercise of his/her human rights, including those related to work.[59]

Focus on skilled migration—brain drain

While developing countries have a surplus of low-skilled labour eager to secure work abroad, developed countries have liberalised policies for attracting mostly their skilled workers. The exodus of critical skills from developing countries, or brain drain, is one of the main collateral problems associated with the process of globalisation.[60] This has been called 'cherry picking' in the sense of attracting the 'best and brightest' from poor countries, thereby depriving them of heavy investments made in education and human capital, often at public expense. A World Bank study found that 77 countries had experienced a loss amounting to 10% or more of their skilled persons (tertiary educated), while 28 countries had a 30% or more loss in 2000. It is also estimated that 56% of the highly educated migrants in OECD countries originate in developing countries. Smaller Caribbean countries have more than 60% of their skilled persons abroad. For countries such as China and India, with a large educated workforce, the outflow is not significant as a share of the local skilled labour force.[61]

The problem is best illustrated in the case of health worker migration. The cumulative impact of the medical brain drain is that foreign-trained health professionals now represent more than a quarter of the medical and nursing workforces of Australia, Canada, the UK and the USA.[62] The worst affected region is the African continent. The unethical nature of African health worker recruitment is highlighted by the fact that Africa's share of global diseases is 25%, while its share of the global health workforce is only 3%. In contrast South and North America combined have only 10% of global diseases but command 37% of the global health work force.[63] In the Philippines it is reported that the cumulative migration of doctors and nurses to higher-paying jobs abroad has forced the closure of as many as 1000 private hospitals in the past five years.[64]

The World Health Organisation (WHO) rightly pointed out that countries with the lowest relative need have the highest numbers of health workers.[65] 'Ghana, with 0.09 physician per thousand population, sends doctors to the United Kingdom, which has 18 times as many physicians per capita'.[66] The quality of health services is declining just as needs are increasing in regions such as sub-Saharan Africa with the HIV/AIDS crisis, resurgence of malaria, and falling life expectancies. The WHO has identified 57 countries with critical shortages across the globe which are struggling to achieve Millennium Development Goals related to health.[67] The GCIM has stated:

> Countries that are active supporters of the health and education objectives included in the UN's Millennium Development Goals are nevertheless recruiting personnel from hospitals and schools in low-income countries that are unable to offer basic health and education services to their own citizens.[68]

Movements of health personnel have been described as fatal flows compared with other movements, since health workers save lives.[69] Codes of conduct for ethical recruitment of health workers have been limited and not particularly effective.[70]

Revival of guest worker programmes—too little, too late?

The question posed here is whether temporary and circular migration programmes currently being promoted represent a credible option to address the above issues, and contribute to promoting development benefits of migration. Several international agencies have called for expansion of legal migration opportunities through such programmes.[71] Principle 5 of the ILO Multilateral Framework states: 'Expanding avenues for regular labour migration should be considered, taking into account labour market needs and demographic trends'.[72] The GCIM has argued for 'carefully designed temporary migration programs as a means of addressing the economic needs of both countries of origin and destination.[73] The World Bank has also come out clearly in favour of such programmes in its Global Economic Prospects, and the study of Eastern Europe.[74] The conclusions of the first Global Forum on Migration and Development (GFMD) claim to have 'enabled a shift of the migration and development paradigm by promoting legal migration as an opportunity for development of both origin and destination countries, rather than as a threat'. It added:

> Temporary labor migration can be a flexible way of meeting labor surplus and shortage across countries. Assuring legal access to a varied labor market, protecting the basic rights of migrants, especially women, and assuring temporariness of the migration are key to maximizing the mutual benefits of such migration.[75]

There is also rising interest in circular migration. The ILO had earlier highlighted its potential in the context of policy options to address skilled migration.[76] The intuitive appeal of the option is not in doubt. Source countries do not lose skills or human capital permanently, while promoting brain circulation and ensuring regular remittance inflows. It can allay fears of developed countries about the risk of permanent settlement or the problems of integration. Circulation programmes contribute to poverty alleviation since it is low-skilled workers who are most likely to benefit.[77]

The support for temporary and circular migration programmes accords well with the emerging global consensus on the need to expand legal opportunities for migration to potential migrants, especially the low-skilled workers, from developing countries. The European Commission has taken a number of parallel initiatives in recent years to deal with the issues of opening more legal avenues for migration and promoting migration and development linkages with third countries. These include the EC Policy Plan on Legal Migration and the Circular migration and mobility partnerships between the European Union and third countries.[78]

Yet the proposals fall short of these claimed objectives, especially relating to their development orientation, because they focus on skilled workers, thus reinforcing the brain drain in origin countries. Only seasonal workers are covered under the four directives of the Policy Plan on Labour Migration (which forms the basis for other initiatives). At the same time the Plan is silent about the large presence of migrant workers in irregular status already inside the European Union, and on their exploitation and limited rights. The Communication on circular migration and mobility partnerships promises legal migration opportunities in EU for third countries provided they commit to 'fighting illegal migration', and facilitating reintegration of returnees.[79] Out of nine conditions to be met by third countries, eight relate to effective border management, preventing irregular migration and readmissions. The ninth covers efforts by third countries to reduce migration pressures. Thus the impact on freer mobility or development is limited given that source countries with limited resources do not have a high degree of control over migration or the capacity to manage borders effectively.

The European Commission's latest directive on the 'Blue Card' marks the aggressive entry of the EU into the global competition for talent, which may accelerate brain drain from poor countries. With Europe needing 20 million skilled workers in the next two decades, the European Commission President Jose Manuel Barroso states: 'With the European blue card, we send a clear signal: highly-skilled workers from all over the world are welcome in the European Union'.[80]

The optimistic conclusions of the GFMD about promoting legal migration as an opportunity for development of both origin and destination countries have not been borne out by subsequent experience because there have been few concrete measures to that effect by member states up to now. Although the first Forum meeting established a 'marketplace' mechanism to allow countries to 'market' their needs in connection with migration and development and to find partners who could assist with these, there were apparently no offers of legal migration opportunities by destination countries, which was one of the concrete results expected.[81]

The limited progress on development of credible and concrete options for promoting low-skilled migration seems to suggest that most destination states and employers may prefer to keep the status quo, and continue to rely on workers in irregular status as an exploited and marginalised second-class category of workers to meet their labour market needs.[82] The failure of President George Bush's proposal for a guest worker scheme for Mexicans in the USA lends support to this generalisation.

The other major issue is the rights to be accorded to temporary migrant workers. Development benefits from migration are directly related to the protection of migrant rights and conditions of work which determine their potential contributions to both countries of origin and destination.[83] It is a matter for concern that the first GFMD decided that the rights issue was not a priority on the basis of a survey of member states. The second Forum in Manila has put it on the agenda, but the co-ordination of the Roundtable on rights by a country with no track record on migrant rights, and divergent interests of destination and origin governments do not augur well for any major breakthroughs.

Ruhs and Martin have raised the issue of a trade-off between numbers and rights in temporary migration programmes for low-skilled migrant workers, arguing that increasing the numbers of low skilled migrants would be possible only at the expense of their rights.[84] The idea that source countries can expand overseas employment of their nationals by agreeing to reductions in their rights is morally unacceptable, and indeed violates international norms. All migrant workers have basic rights as human beings and workers which cannot be traded-off.[85] Their view corresponds to 'viewing migrants as commodities, rather than as persons with rights and duties afforded to them through the international human rights framework'.[86] The argument seems to boil down to saying that source countries can 'market' more of their workers by offering bigger discounts on their rights (price or cost to employers). The example cited of Gulf countries with large numbers of migrants with low rights is to some extent misplaced, because these are non-democratic societies where even national workers do not enjoy many workplace rights. It is the political system which largely determines rights for both national and foreign workers, not only the numbers. Moreover, international instruments do not provide absolute rights for temporary workers. There are restrictions on job mobility, social security and family unification rights depending on the length of employment and residence. Since labour laws in most countries apply equally to national and non-national workers (including those in irregular status as in the USA), the authors seem to be arguing that employers can and do violate national labour laws with impunity. New temporary migration programmes introduced in Malaysia, Thailand and the Republic of Korea clearly state that national labour laws apply equally to migrant workers. What seems to matter more than numbers is the nature of the political regime and status of migrant workers, since employers will exploit migrant workers in irregular status whether they are large or small in numbers. The challenge before the international community is not to justify or condone the status quo of limited rights, but to search for ways and means to advance the rights agenda under temporary schemes, which can enhance the development benefits of migration.

Global governance of international migration—mission impossible?

Given the above trends, it is important to assess whether some progress has been or can be made at the international level to deal with the pressing challenges of international migration. A global regime or new international order for migration would need to address issues of international co-operation and policy coherence on major issues such as liberalising the global labour market, maximising the development benefits of migration while minimising its negative consequences, and promotion and protection of the rights of all migrant workers.

There are obvious gaps in the existing international institutional architecture, with no single agency having a comprehensive mandate on issues of international migration, as highlighted by the Doyle report.[87]

The International Labour Organisation (ILO) has a clear mandate on labour migration and protection of migrant workers based on tripartite co-operation. The United Nations High Commissioner for Refugees (UNHCR) deals with forced migrants—asylum seekers and refugees. The UN Office of the High Commissioner for Human Rights (UNOHCHR) looks after the human rights of migrants. The International Organisation for Migration (IOM)—an intergovernmental body which is outside the UN system—has expanded its mandate, which nevertheless does not include protection. Other agencies, such as the World Bank, the World Trade Organization (WTO) and the UN Department for Economic and Social Affairs, also deal with specific aspects of migration only.[88]

While there are a number of options for a global migration regime, the most effective option would be to create a new agency with a clear mandate—a 'World Migration Organisation' (WMO). Bhagwati has long advocated the creation of a WMO.[89] However, states, especially the major destination countries, are unlikely to agree to this option for financial and even more for political reasons because it may erode part of their sovereignty over immigration. As the former UN Secretary-General observed: 'There is no appetite for a World Migration Organization'.[90] Timothy Hatton also analysed the feasibility of establishing a WTO-type model for international migration, and concluded that there was no basis for WTO-style negotiations over migration.[91]

The second option is to mandate an existing agency—either one of the existing UN agencies (eg ILO or UNHCR) or an intergovernmental agency (IOM). The GCIM in fact considered this as a long term option via the merger of IOM and UNHCR or a global agency for economic migration such as IOM. An expanded role for IOM, including normative elements, is hardly likely find favour with its member states, including its major funders, as well as those reliant on its services.[92]

International standards on governance of migration and protection of migrant workers already exist,with three international migrant worker cnventions defining an international charter of rights and obligations covering all stages of the migration process: the ILO Migration for Employment Convention (Revised), 1949 (No 97); the ILO Migrant Workers (Supplementary Provisions) Convention, 1975 (No 143); and the International Convention on the Protection of the Rights of All Migrant Workers and Their Families (ICMW). Seventy-nine countries in the world have ratified at least one of these instruments, which is no mean achievement. The problem is that some major destination countries are reluctant to ratify them or to enforce their provisions even where ratified. None of the major destination countries have ratified the ICMW except Libya. Given the reluctance of states to ratify binding conventions and effectively enforce their provisions, international agencies can promote non-binding frameworks: this is the rationale behind the ILO Multilateral Framework on Labour Migration produced through tripartite negotiations and adopted in 2006. It provides a rights-based approach to labour migration covering four objectives: promoting international co-operation, governance of migration, protection of migrant workers, and strengthening migration–development linkages.[93] Yet its non-binding nature means that countries have no obligation to define migration policies and practices in terms of its principles and guidelines.

Another soft option would be to establish a global consultative forum consisting of major agencies working on different aspects of migration. The Global Migration Group was established by the United Nations Secretary-General in early 2006 based on a GCIM recommendation. Its aim is to promote good governance of migration through wider application of relevant instruments and norms, and provision of more coherent and co-ordinated leadership. The membership has now been expanded to 13 UN agencies and the IOM. Its current focus is on exchange of information through regular consultations. There is not much evidence that it has been effective in its co-ordination function or in promoting operational programmes, given the diverse interests of the membership and the fact that it is not a decision-making body.

The establishment of a Global Forum on Migration and Development was proposed by the UN Secretary-General at the UN General Assembly High Level Dialogue on International Migration and Development in September 2006. Contrary to initial intentions, the Forum was established outside the United Nations system as a state-driven process, and has no direct link with the GMG either. The goals of the GFMD are to enhance inter-state dialogue and co-operation, and to foster practical outcomes on international migration and development issues. The Belgian government organised the first meeting of the GFMD in Brussels on 9–11 July 2007; the second one will be organised by the Philippines government in October 2008 in Manila. The state-led process does not involve civil society stakeholders directly, although the Forum arranges for separate civil society deliberations. The divergent interests of source and destination countries, and its informal consultative nature, act as major constraints on the functioning of the GFMD and on achieving concrete outcomes in promoting migration and development.

At the regional level there are several consultative forums—the Inter-governmental Consultations on Migration, Asylum and Refugees, the Pueblo Process, the Budapest Process and the Bali Process, among others.[94] But these have primarily been initiated to address irregular migration and combat trafficking, focusing on security concerns. They are mostly confined to state-driven processes, and are not very transparent.

Thus there has been very limited progress on concrete multilateral initiatives for a new international migration order. Most destination countries are not willing to move beyond non-binding, voluntary and informal consultative processes and groupings. Despite the lack of concrete achievements, there is an emerging convergence of views in recent global initiatives in several areas: enhanced international co-operation, expanding legal avenues for migration, promoting migration–development linkages, particularly in the area of remittances, protection of migrant rights, gender-sensitive migration policies, and creation of decent work opportunities in home countries to reduce migration pressures. Yet the machinery and co-operation mechanisms at the international and regional levels to promote these understandings are lacking, leaving major challenges of migration yet to be addressed.

By way of conclusions

There is a large unfinished agenda before the international community in making migration work for development, and in providing a 'fair deal' to migrant workers. While there has been no poverty of words and lip service on these issues by many countries at global and regional summits and forums, there is indeed poverty of action and of genuine commitment. The Nigerian proverb, 'Fine words do not produce food', seems an apt description of the current state of affairs on international migration policies and practices.

The Chair of the first GFMD raised the issue of whether, 20 years from now, we might be wondering why countries were spending so much resources on controlling immigration—often with so little success—and of whether we are trying to build fences in a globalising labour market.[95] Limited progress in global labour mobility, despite intense globalisation in the past two decades or so is indeed evidence of developed countries attempting to build fences through a globalising labour market. The challenge before the international community is to build bridges, not fences, to promote international mobility for all workers, ensuring protection of their rights, and to move towards a truly global labour market that can deliver the promised win-win scenarios.

Notes

1 Global Commission on International Migration (GCIM), *Migration in an Interconnected World: New Directions for Action*, Geneva: GCIM, 2005, at http://www.gcim.org/attachements/gcim-complete-report-2005.pdf; International Organisation for Migration (IOM), *World Migration 2005*, Geneva: IOM 2005; United Nations, *International Migration and Development: Report of the Secretary-General*, A/60/871, New York: United Nations, 2006; World Bank, *Global Economic Prospects 2006: Economic Implications of Remittances and Migration*, Washington, DC: World Bank, 2006; Global Forum on Migration and Development (GFMD), *Summary Report*, Brussels: GFMD, 2007, at http://www.gfmd-fmmd.org/en/system/files/Rapport+GFMD_EN+_3_.pdf and International Labour Office (ILO), *International Labour Migration and Development: The ILO Perspective*, Geneva: International Migration Programme, ILO, 2007, at http://www.ilo.org/public/english/protection/migrant/download/mig_brief_development.pdf.
2 ILO, *A Fair Deal for Migrant Workers in the Global Economy*, Report VI, 92nd Session, International Labour Conference, Geneva: ILO, 2004, at http://www.ilo.org/public/english/standards/relm/ilc/ilc92/pdf/rep-vi.pdf; and World Commission on the Social Dimension of Globalization (WCSDG) & International Labour Office, *A Fair Globalization: Creating Opportunities for All*, Geneva: WCSDG/International Labour Office, February 2004, at http://www.ilo.org/public/english/wcsdg/docs/report.pdf.
3 Royal Society for the Encouragement of Arts, Manufactures & Commerce (RSA) Migration Commission, *Migration: A Welcome Opportunity—A New Way Forward*, London: RSA, 2005, at http://www.migrationcommission.org/publications.htm.
4 United Nations Population Division (UNPD), *Trends in Total Migrant Stock: The 2005 Revision*, New York: Department for Social and Economic Affairs, UNPD, February 2006.
5 United Nations High Commissioner for Refugees (UNHCR), *Asylum Levels and Trends in Industrialized Countries 2007*, Geneva: UNHCR, 2008.
6 ILO, *A Fair Deal for Migrant Workers in the Global Economy*.
7 ILO, *International Labour Migration and Development*.
8 Kofi Annan, Address to the European Parliament upon receipt of the Andrei Sakharov Prize for Freedom of Thought, Brussels, 29 January 2004, at http://www.europa-eu-un.org/articles/sk/article_3178_sk.htm.

9 J Moses, *International Migration: Globalisation's Last Froniter*, London: Zed Books, 2006.

10 L Pritchett, *Let their People Come: Breaking the Gridlock on Global Labor Mobility*, Washington, DC: Center for Global Development, 2006.

11 P Wickramasekara, 'Protection of migrant workers in an era of globalization: the role of international instruments', in R Blanpain (ed), *Comparative Labour Law and Industrial Relations in Industrialized Market Economies*, Dordrecht: Kluwer, 2007, pp 239–274.

12 GCIM, *Migration in an Interconnected World*.

13 World Bank, *Global Economic Prospects 2006*.

14 K Anderson & LA Winters, 'The challenge of reducing international trade and migration barriers', *Discussion Paper Series No. 6760*, London: Centre for Economic Policy Research, 2008.

15 Moses, *International Migration*; Pritchett, *Let their People Come*; P Legrain, *Immigrants: Your Country Needs Them*, Princeton, NJ: Princeton University Press, 2007; J Dayton-Johnson *et al*, *Gaining from Migration: Towards a New Mobility System*, Paris, OECD, 2007; and S Castles, 'Guestworkers in Europe: a resurrection', *International Migration Review*, 40 (4), 2006, pp 741–766.

16 Pritchett, *Let their People Come*.

17 Castles, 'Guestworkers in Europe'.

18 European Commission, *Policy Plan on Legal Migration*, COM(2005) 669 final, Brussels, 21 December 2005.

19 Johnson *et al*, *Gaining from Migration*.

20 European Commission, *Green Paper on Confronting Demographic Change: A New Solidarity between the Generations*, COM(2005) 94 final, Brussels, 16 March 2005.

21 Annan, Address to the European Parliament.

22 R Skeldon, *On Migration and the Policy Process*, Sussex: Sussex Centre for Migration Research, Working Paper T20, August 2007, at http://www.migrationdrc.org/publications/working-papers/WP-T20.pdf.

23 United Nations, *International Migration and Development*.

24 GCIM, *Migration in an Interconnected World*.

25 G Hugo, 'Circular migration: keeping development rolling?', *Migration Information Source*, New York: Migration Policy Institute, 2003, at http://www.migrationinformation.org/Feature/display.cfm?ID=129.

26 N Pollard *et al*, *Floodgates or Turnstiles: Post-EU Enlargement Migration Flows to (and from) the UK*, London: Institute for Public Policy Research, 2008.

27 Pritchett, *Let their People Come*.

28 F Docquier & A Marfouk, 'International migration by educational attainment, 1990–2000', in C Ozden & M Shiff (eds), *International Migration, Remittances, and the Brain Drain*, Washington, DC: World Bank/Palgrave Macmillan, 2005, pp 151–199.

29 Legrain, *Immigrants*.

30 N Harris, *Thinking the Unthinkable: The Immigration Myth Exposed*, London: IB Tauris, 2002; Dayton Johnson *et al*, *Gaining from Migration*; and Pritchett, *Let their People Come*.

31 United Nations, *International Migration and Development*.

32 Harris, *Thinking the Unthinkable*.

33 Pritchett, *Let their People Come*.

34 *Ibid*.

35 RSA Migration Commission, *Migration*.

36 *Ibid*, p 22.

37 F Duvell, 'Illegal immigration in Europe: patterns, causes and consequences', talk given at Stockholm University seminar on 'Irregulars, sans papiers, hidden, illegal and black labour', 29 November 2006.

38 OECD, *International Migration Outlook*, Paris: OECD, 2007.

39 H De Haas, *The Myth of Invasion: Irregular Migration from West Africa to the Maghreb and the European Union*, Oxford: International Migration Institute, 2007.

40 European Commission, 'Towards a comprehensive European Migration Policy: cracking down on employment of illegal immigrants and fostering circular migration and mobility partnerships', press release IP/07/678, 16 May 2007, at http://ec.europa.eu/justice_home/news/intro/news_intro_en.htm.

41 J Bustamante, *Specific Groups and Individuals: Migrant Workers*, Report of the Special Rapporteur on the Human Rights of Migrants, E/CN.4/2006/73, Commission on Human Rights, Geneva, 66nd session, 30 December 2005, at http://daccess-ods.un.org/access.nsf/Get?Open&DS=E/CN.4/2006/73&Lang=E.

42 GCIM, *Migration in an Interconnected World*.

43 European Commission, 'Towards a comprehensive European Migration Policy'.

44 F Schneider, 'Shadow economies and corruption all over the world: new estimates for 145 countries', *Economics: The Open-Access, Open-Assessment E-journal*, 1 (9), 2007, at http://www.economics-ejournal.org/economics/journalarticles/2007-9/version_1/count.

45 R Munck, 'Irregular migration and the informal labour market: the "underside" of globalisation or the new norm?', in E Berggren *et al* (eds), *Irregular Migration, Informal Labour and Community: A Challenge for Europe*, Maastricht: Shaker Publishing, 2007, pp 51–65.

46 Bustamante, *Specific Groups and Individuals*.

47 United Nations, *International Migration and Development*.

48 M Ramphele, presentation to the 88th session of the IOM Council on 'International Dialogue on Migration: Valuing Migration—the costs benefits, opportunities and challenges of migration', Geneva, 30 November–3 December 2004.

49 Cited in Munck, 'Irregular migration and the informal labour market'.

50 Harris, *Thinking the Unthinkable*.

51 Castles, 'Guestworkers in Europe'.

52 WA Cornelius, 'Controlling "unwanted" immigration: lessons from the United States, 1993–2004', *Journal of Ethnic and Migration Studies*, 31 (4), 2005, pp 775–794.

53 A Portes, *Migration and Development: A Conceptual Review of the Evidence*, CMD Working Paper #06-07, Princeton, NJ: Center for Migration and Development, Princeton University, 2006, at http://cmdprinceton.edu/papers/wp0607.pdf.

54 See HR 4437: The Border Protection, Antiterrorism and Illegal Immigration Control Act of 2005 passed by the US House of Representatives on 16 December 2005.

55 Bustamante, *Promotion and Protection of all Human Rights, Civil, Political, Economic, Social and Cultural Rights, including the Right to Development*, A/HRC/7/12, report of the Special Rapporteur on the Human Rights of Migrants, Human Rights Council, Geneva, Seventh Session, 25 February 2008.

56 'Congress, Senate, House, CBO', *Migration News*, 12 (4), 2007, at http://migration.ucdavis.edu/mn/more.php?id=3221_0_2_0.

57 Cited in Open Europe, *Briefing Note: The French EU Presidency 2008—What to Expect*, London: Open Europe, 2008.

58 ILO, *ILO Multilateral Framework on Labour Migration: Non-binding Principles and Guidelines for a Rights-based Approach to Labour Migration*, Geneva: ILO, 2006, at http://www.ilo.org/public/english/protection/migrant/download/multilat_fwk_en.pdf.

59 Inter-American Court of Human Rights, 'Juridical condition and rights of the undocumented migrants', Advisory Opinion OC-18/03, 17 September 2003, at http://wwwl.umn.edu/humanrts/iachr/series_A_OC-18.html.

60 WCSDG & International Labour Office, *A Fair Globalization*.

61 Docquier & Marfouk, 'International migration by educational attainment'.

62 F Mullan, 'The metrics of the physician brain drain', *New England Journal of Medicine*, 353, 2005, pp 1810–1818.

63 World Health Organisation (WHO), *World Health Report 2006: Working together for Health*, Geneva: WHO, 2006.

64 '1000 hospitals closed down by doctors' exodus', *Manila Times*, 5 December 2005, at http://www.abs-cbnnews.com/storypage.aspx?StoryId=22798.

65 WHO, *World Health Report 2006*.

66 LC Chen & JI Boufford, 'Fatal flows: doctors on the move', *New England Journal of Medicine*, 353 (17), 2005, pp 1850–1852.

67 WHO, *World Health Report 2006*.

68 GCIM, *Migration in an Interconnected World*.

69 Chen & Boufford, 'Fatal flows'.

70 Connell, 'Review of codes of practice and memoranda of understanding on the international role of skilled health workers', mimeo, WHO, Geneva, 17 October 2007.

71 GCIM, *Migration in an Interconnected World*; IOM, *World Migration 2005*; ILO, *ILO Multialteral Framework on Labour Migration*; and World Bank, *Global Economic Prospects 2006*.

72 ILO, *ILO Multilateral Framework on Labour Migration*.

73 GCIM, *Migration in an Interconnected World*.

74 World Bank, *Global Economic Prospects 2006*; and A Mansoor & B Quillin (eds), *Migration and Remittances: Eastern Europe and the Former Soviet Union, Europe and Central Asia Region*, Washington, DC: World Bank, 2007.

75 GFMD, *Summary Report*.

76 P Wickramasekara, 'Policy responses to skilled migration: retention, return and circulation', *Perspectives on Labour Migration 5E*, Geneva: ILO, 2003, at http://www.ilo.org/public/english/protection/migrant/download/pom/pom5e.pdf.

77 GFMD, *Summary Report*; and S Vertovec, *Circular Migration: The Way Forward in Global Policy*, Working Paper 4, Oxford: International Migration Institute, Oxford University, 2007.

78 European Commission, *Policy Plan on Legal Migration*; and European Commission, *On Circular Migration and Mobility Partnerships between the European Union and Third Countries*, COM(2007) 248

final, Brussels, 16 May 2007, at http://ec.europa.eu/commission_barroso/frattini/doc/2007/com_2007_248_en.pdf.

79 European Commission, *On Circular Migration and Mobility Partnerships*.

80 European Commission, 'Making Europe more attractive to highly skilled migrants and increasing the protection of lawfully residing and working migrants', press release IP/07/1575, 23 October 2007, at http://europa.eu/rapid/pressReleasesAction.do?reference=IP/07/1575.

81 GFMD, *Summary Report*.

82 Castles, 'Guestworkers in Europe'.

83 ILO, *International Labour Migration and Development*.

84 M Ruhs & P Martin, 'Numbers vs rights: trade-offs and guest worker programmes', *International Migration Review*, 42 (1), 2008, pp 249–265.

85 ILO, *ILO Multilateral Framework on Labour Migration*; and UNOCHR, *Migration and Development: A Human Rights Approach*, Geneva: Office of the United Nations High Commissioner for Human Rights, 2006, at http://www2.ohchr.org/english/bodies/cmw/docs/HLMigration/Migration DevelopmentHC'spaper.pdf.

86 Bustamante, *Promotion and Protection of all Human Rights*.

87 M Doyle, 'Report to the Secretary-General on migration', Migration Working Group, New York, 20 December 2002 (access restricted).

88 *Ibid*; and GCIM, *Migration in an Interconnected World*.

89 J Bhagwati, 'Letter to the Editor: working towards a World Migration Organization', *Financial Times*, 26 July 2002.

90 UN Secretary-General, Address to the Ibero-American Summit, SG/SM/10715, Department of Public Information, New York, 3 November 2006.

91 TJ Hatton, 'Should we have a WTO for international migration?', *Economic Policy*, 22 (50), 2007, pp 339–383,

92 Doyle, 'Report to the Secretary-General on migration'.

93 ILO, *ILO Multilateral Framework on Labour Migration*.

94 IOM, *Regional Consultative Processes*, Geneva: International Organization for Migration, 2008, at http://www.iom.int/jahia/Jahia/pid/386.

95 GFMD, *Final Conclusions and Recommendations of the Chair*, Brussels: Global Forum on Migration and Development, 10–11 July 2007, at http://www.gfmd-fmmd.org/en/system/files/Summary+ Conclusions+.pdf.

The Ideal Immigrant? Gendered class subjects in Philippine–Canada migration*

PAULINE GARDINER BARBER

Contemporary globalisation has seen a proliferation of research in migration studies, accompanied by debates over the historical antecedents to the current forms of transnational mobility for people and capital.[1] Neoliberalism, evidenced in variously applied interlocking reforms in the political and economic structures of nation states,[2] is also associated with hyper-mobility for capital and for certain people with the right social and cultural attributes.[3] The vast majority of the people in the global South have experienced neoliberalism through the rise of a new international division of labour, along with flexible, geographically decentred production regimes, and the casting of certain nationals as particular kinds of immigrant labour. Together with the innovations in capital's mobility there has been concerted effort by Western states to attract the right kinds of immigrants to address demographic needs and labour shortages. The Philippines, with its extensive history of political and economic instabilities, represents a significant example of these processes: the movement of capital to labour and of labour (racialised, deskilled and feminised) to capital. The second of these processes comprises the focus for this paper, which employs a transnational perspective to explore contemporary features of Philippine migration, now constituted as both culturally normative and politically palatable, a safety valve in times of political crisis and/or a contribution to national development, despite its questionable social and economic effects. A transnational perspective is considered essential to grasping the complexities of contemporary migration dynamics and the linking of migration/emigration/immigration scenarios beyond the binary and container models seen in some migration literature.[4] Methodological nationalism in earlier generations of migration studies has been challenged for the failure to consider sending and receiving nation dynamics, and migrants' perspectives.[5]

Further, the paper raises questions about the singularity of interpretations as either positive, as argued by proponents of migration as a form of development, or solely as negative in terms of a socially deterministic review of the rigidity of the historical structuring of global inequalities, an account which condemns emigrants to strategies of accommodation within exploited global labour markets in the Philippines and beyond. Instead, the paper highlights the complexities of contemporary Philippine migration and emigration through an examination of how emigrants arrive in Canada as different kinds of migrants. Although gendered racialised labour market and citizenship scenarios inevitably structure the emigration and reception process, it remains important to theorise the complexities of migration through more attention to the agency of emigrants, albeit an agency constrained by limited choices, elsewhere described in terms of a Janus metaphor.[6]

Commencing with a brief review of contemporary migration statistics, the first section outlines the paper's main themes, especially relative to migration and class. This section concludes with a discussion of the research context informing the paper, which shapes a methodological argument about migrant agency and 'economic subjectivities'. This is followed by a more thorough discussion of Philippine migration history. The following sections then review recent research results analysing the different ways Philippine emigrants are currently entering Canada, revealing a marked tension between the structuring of immigration policy attentive to the needs of capital, and the agency of the immigrants themselves.

Migration, class and gender in transnational perspective

Ranked in the top three source countries for international migrants (after China and India),[7] the Philippines is a prototypical labour export country with Manila, the national capital, serving as an important hub in global migration circuits.[8] In 2006 the Philippine Overseas Employment Administration (POEA) processed contracts for a record high of over one million Filipinos, deployed in foreign labour markets on land and sea, in a remarkable global sweep of 179 countries.[9] This translates into an average of 3000 persons leaving the country each day, with around 30% of the land-based migrant workers headed for gendered jobs in household service employment. Not surprisingly given this statistic, in a pattern established in the mid-to-late 1980s, 60% of those who took on new contracts in foreign labour markets in 2006 were women.[10] In this same year the top 10 destination countries for deployed Filipino workers represented diverse regions covering the Middle East, Asia and Europe.[11] Remittances received from Filipinos living abroad in 2006 were reported by the Central Bank of the Philippines to be over US$12 billion; moreover, remittances comprise roughly 12% of the gross domestic product, constituting the largest single item. Given the gendered nature of contemporary Philippine migration, particularly relative to women's employment in demeaned service jobs, this is a significant contribution to the national economy. As is the case elsewhere in the migration literature, debate continues over whether migrant remittances constitute 'productive investment'.[12]

Feminist literature on gendered migration has proliferated as demands for women's labour have increased. We know a good deal about how some migrants are faring (generally poorly for systemic reasons) in particular kinds of domestic service labour markets. But the class effects of Philippine gendered migration flows require much more attention. Class was not prioritised in the first wave of feminist post-structural research on commoditised reproductive labour and migrant agency. Influenced by Foucault, this work analysed the mechanics of power and discipline in live-in service work, avoiding the significant challenge of (re-)writing class into domestic spaces.[13] Interdisciplinary research tackled the deprivations of commoditised domestic labour variably cast through a range of spatial scales, working outwards from embodiment and disciplined bodies,[14] to gendered, sexualised global divisions of labour and domestic servitude.[15] Some research skirted a tendency to 'victimise' women migrants but the debates shaped current understandings of global structures of commoditised social reproduction.[16]

Much less is known about how migrants appraise global labour markets to stage their migration journeys. Nor has there been much research on the transnational exchanges of information that enable migrants to adjust to changing policy conditions attending the migration process. As countries such as Canada and the USA adjust their immigration strategies to address labour market challenges, policies are being translated across borders to migrants-in-waiting. Multiple sources of information are relied upon, including other migrants and actors in the ever-expanding migration-related industries. Taking the case of Philippine migrants departing the country for permanent settlement abroad in Canada's migration streams, who are differentiated by entrance qualifications, labour market categories and levels of capital required to launch the emigration–migration–immigration process, this paper explores the implications not only of border crossings of actual migrants but also their information sources, as well as the citizenship policy regimes, national and transnational, that migrants accommodate themselves to and vice versa. What this approach demonstrates is continuities and changes in the social, political and economic context for Philippine labour migration and Filipino gendered migration practices.

To summarise, the paper addresses the class complexity and nimbleness of Filipino emigrants in adjusting their migration strategies to the shifting priorities of neoliberal citizenship regimes. Such complexity is rendered visible through a transnational perspective analysing sending and receiving contexts. Further, class complexity is here explained by an argument about how state policies enable capital to be mobilised in migration to serve the interests of sending and receiving countries. Sometimes this appears to benefit the better resourced migrants but it also produces deeper class cleavages between migrants in different streams and those who remain behind. For reasons having to do with the history of Philippine migration, Filipinos seem to be able to draw advantage from even apparently subtle shifts in Canadian immigration policy. In this, encouraged by Philippine and Canadian state policies, they constitute *the ideal immigrant*, but to what effect?

The research context

Migration research tends to address migrants in either their home or their destination countries rather than as a total social process. This paper draws upon multi-sited collaborative research to explore the class implications of current migration flows in relationship to changing international labour markets and national and international citizenship policies.[17] Our primary concern is to question how migration creates new class identities and subjectivities in migrant sending and receiving communities. Class identities both shape and are shaped by the migrant workers' negotiations of the hurdles they meet in the journey to work. Migrant workers typically move from low-waged and surplus labour slots to in-demand slots in distant labour markets. National citizenship and immigration policies smooth over the tension between labour export and import while attending to national and international security concerns.

Ethnographic research methods, primarily open-ended interviews, examine how potential migrants prepare for and experience migration. In the process of fitting themselves into available labour market niches they must present themselves as having particular identities, foregrounding what they have learned to be desirable qualities (their gender, cultural identity, age, place of origin, education, religion, connections), while playing down less desirable ones (but in precisely the same categories). For example, Filipina cultural stereotypes present women who seek work as nannies as family minded, yet what of their own family commitments? If they are doctors and nurses seeking lower skilled work, we ask how they negotiate the skill shift. We label such negotiations as 'performances of subordination' and, we contend, how such performances are prepared for remains an empirical question, as do migrant sources of information.

Often, however, the processes we seek to illuminate remain as statistical aggregates in migration summaries. This enables the perpetuation of stereotypical characterisations of South–North gendered migration flows to feed public policy debates in immigrant receiving countries, where population decline and labour shortages loom large. Discussions in Europe, Australasia and North America are patterned, with some variations, on consistent themes defying ready categorisation between perspectives from political left- and right-wing parties. Such themes include whether immigration is necessary at all, even though demographic and labour market projections insist that it is; and which immigrants are the most desirable, and why, a question that lends itself to racial and cultural stereotyping that takes on a different form in Europe, the USA and Canada.[18]

In Canada recent debates over immigration flare up around issues of border protection and the meanings ascribed to certain citizenships, particularly with regard to transnational practices. For example, Israel's attack on Lebanon in 2006 provoked an ongoing contentious debate over dual citizenship and transnationalism. Economic issues loomed large in the debate because of the significant costs, projected at around Can$94 million,[19] associated with the evacuation of 15 000 Canadian citizens, some of whom were permanent residents of Lebanon. Further issues have arisen as a result of the harmonisation of US–Canada border practices insisted upon by the Bush administration's homeland security agendas. Recent research on Canadian–US border securitisation exposes the flawed yet pernicious logic of these measures.[20] Securitisation can be linked to the 'marketisation, racialisation and the invisibilisation and/or instrumentalisation of women' in citizenship regimes, for example Britain's and Canada's.[21] Hence deeply entrenched discourses of racialising alterity remain an essential component of citizenship and immigration policies, in Canada and elsewhere. These realities attend the border crossings of the respective flows of migrants in our research. So how are Philippine migrants in 2008 scripting their migration performances? And, given the structural constraints in the political economy of migration, combined with the neoliberal individualising conditions in global labour markets and immigration policies, how are they faring?

Philippine migration histories

Historically migration linked Filipinos to global labour markets and the spread of capitalism. Filipino migration as commodified labour is present from the Age of Capitalism—roughly the mid-19th century to the First World War.[22] With the shift from Spanish to US colonisation (1898) Filipinos were recruited for work in Hawaii's sugar plantations as indentured labour and to the US navy. Throughout the history of Filipinos departing for work overseas there has been a maritime dimension for a significant number of male migrants. Even today Philippine statistics record overseas contract workers as land- or sea-based.

Philippine migration scholars have identified three waves of migration.[23] The first wave, from 1900 to the early 1940s, placed Filipinos in a variety of labour markets throughout the USA—such as agriculture, food processing and services. During this period colonial rulers also introduced an English-based educational system which continues in the 21st century to distinguish

Filipinos from most other Asian migrants, particularly in countries where English is privileged as a first or second language. The second wave occured after the granting of independence in 1946 to the early 1970s, when a more class-diversified stream of Filipinos departed for the USA, including military personnel and their families, medical professionals and skilled technical workers. This was a period when bilateral agreements recognised the strategic importance of the Philippines to US security concerns in Southeast Asia. But in this period Filipino labour was also employed in various regional contract labour markets. By the time of the Marcos administration's declaration of martial law in 1972,[24] political instability and economic uncertainty again compelled out-migration, evidenced by a 671% increase in applicants wanting to work abroad.[25]

A third wave of migration saw Filipinos become more visible and more researched in global labour markets. This period commenced in the mid-1970s with the devastating effects of increases in the prices of crude oil. Within the Philippines the oil crisis further exacerbated economic hardships associated with colonisation and the mismanagement of the economy during the Marcos years. Filipinos were yet again eager to fill in-demand slots in Middle Eeastern oil-exporting nations flush with petro-dollars. The Marcos regime also recognised the political advantages of facilitating overseas contracts as a means to control the potential for social unrest associated with high rates of poverty and landlessness.[26] So during this period we see the drawing of the contemporary contours of labour export as a key feature of Philippine development policy and diplomacy.

Overall four trends can be discerned in the patterns shaping Philippine international migration: an overwhelming majority of Filipinos leave the country for temporary work rather than permanent residence abroad; Asia surpasses the Middle East as the primary work destination for Filipinos in the 1980s and 1990s; at this time, male-dominated migration gives way to feminised streams; and, in the same period, the skill composition of migrant workers shifts from production, transport and construction to service workers, particularly domestic workers.[27] Space does not permit the further detailing of the complexities of labour market deployment of Filipinos who continue to seek gendered jobs as contract workers basically all over the world.[28] By 2002 over 800 000 Filipinos were reported to be exiting the country annually to work in between 130 and 180 countries, the estimates varying with the source of the information. As always it needs to be noted that, although official statistics report migrants leaving the country with authorised documents, including exit visas and labour contracts, many thousands leave each year without such papers, typically declaring themselves as tourists, or travelling to visit relatives working abroad. During 1994–2001 there was a decline in the number of employed Filipinos, with more people receiving jobs overseas than there were new jobs created locally. Underemployment and youth unemployment are also characteristic of Philippine labour markets.[29]

Perhaps the most striking feature of the steady rise in Philippine overseas employment is its gendered character. The number of women working abroad continued to grow throughout the 1980s. This flow cannot be disarticulated from historical patterns of women's migration from rural to urban jobs, in classed streams, within the Philippines. Women in poor peasant and working class households have a long tradition of migration to work in better-off households as 'helpers', a pattern or labour they were socialised into through religious and cultural idioms valorising the contributions of daughters to family social reproduction and livelihoods.[30] In 1975 men comprised 70% of the deployed overseas contract workers, sea-based and land-based. However, in the 1980s women surpassed male migrants in overseas work, in part a function of the increase in global demand for commoditised domestic labour to replace the labour of women entering paid employment.[31] But other factors also contributed, including the decline in male gendered jobs in the Middle East. As noted, when Philippine women and other domestic service workers became more prominent in the global economy, feminist scholars and political advocates began to analyse the exploitative nature of contracts and the subordination, power dynamics and vulnerabilities associated with live-in care work.[32] To a lesser extent questions were also posed about political activism and mobilisation associated with gendered migration.[33]

However, the degradations and deprivations of women's work abroad are well known in the Philippines through the iconic representations of abused migrants whose devastating stories have been broadcast in Philippine media. Public discussion about the benefits not just the risks of overseas work is threaded through the discursive shifts of successive administrative regimes. By 2006 marketing campaigns had achieved the target, established in 2003–04, of deploying one million workers abroad per year, in an ever-expanding range of countries. Overseas workers are truly prime commodities for export.[34] Currently the POEA estimates that eight million Filipinos are living and working overseas under temporary, permanent and irregular contract arrangements. Given a total population of 80 million, 10% of Filipinos are overseas, with over 17% of Filipino families estimated to contain at least one family member living abroad.[35]

The reproduction of migration

What this brief overview of Philippine migration history highlights is that, despite the relatively recent attention accorded Philippine migrants as global workers with particular reputations, most recently in racialised gendered service jobs, contemporary migration has a long and relatively complex history associated with developments in the articulations of global capital and marked by class and gender differentiation. Further, that history reveals Filipinos adapting to various labour markets as gaps and closures occur, yet attentive to political and economic conditions within the Philippines. Because migration is so fundamental to people's experience, it has become culturally normative, initially for men, but now particularly so for women. The significance of women's migration has provoked a debate over the impact of migration on the Philippine family and for children with absent mothers.

Some argue that the material benefits combined with the provision of support from extended kin, culturally sanctioned by religion and custom, outweigh the disadvantages. Others suggest a greater emotional cost is borne by all concerned, as evidenced by familial 'breakdown', husbands taking up with other women while living on remittances, and so forth.[36] Either way there is little doubt that migration is fuelling consumption and that this feeds new wants and indebtedness, producing a scenario whereby migration is reproducing migration in the next generation—as evidenced in about 80 qualitative migrant interviews I have conducted in two regions of the Philippine over a 15-year period. One way this happens is through women's remittances funding education for migrants' children or the children of relatives. Recognising that education adds value to migration, female children, particularly first-born or those with scholastic aptitude, are often encouraged by teachers, parents and other relatives to take on the 'mission' to be economically helpful to their families. Migration overseas is one of the primary routes to economic improvement for Filipinos with a wide variety of skill sets. Hence migration feeds further migration.

Reliance upon migration as a significant component of household livelihoods and social reproduction remains a key element to what can be described as Filipino economic subjectivities within a culture of migration that has a strong historical and material basis. Migration reproduction has been reinforced through a sequence of government policy shifts. These date from the Marcos regime's promotion of labour export, through Corazon Aquino's efforts to halt migration in the absence of bilateral measures to better protect Filipinos abroad, to the Ramos government's valorisation of overseas workers as heroes and heroines, forced into this position during an election year in the face of national rage over the brutal treatment of migrants abroad.[37] Repeated calls for greater protection for migrant workers since this time have paradoxically produced a state response of firmer commitments both to protecting overseas workers and to labour export. Such manoeuvres are seen by many observers as instrumental to the state's desire to sustain migration for political and economic purposes.[38] Neoliberalism has been fundamental to state agendas dating to the imposition of structural adjustment policies during the Marcos years.[39] I now turn to Canadian migration streams illustrating the flexibility of Filipinos in positioning themselves in foreign labour markets.

Canada's 'caregivers' and Filipino global service work

First, a note about terminology is necessary. The changing gendered character of Philippine migration in the 1980s and 1990s has meant that commoditised domestic service workers, 'caregivers' to Citizenship and Immigration Canada, are perhaps the most described group of overseas workers. Filipinos used to call caregivers DHs, short for domestic helpers, but they are also referred to as 'maids' or 'nannies' in the literature, depending upon the national context of the research. In 2008 the POEA website refers to 'household service workers'.[40] This new (replacement) terminology suggests a further discursive move to placate critics of the state's reliance on labour export. The change is perceived by some Filipinos as conveying more dignity to the global workforce. But it also serves to better situate the skills of Philippine women and men within the dispassionate language of migration statistics and policy, while at the same time severing the workers from Philippine social and cultural history. This detachment is probably unproblematic for researchers concerned to understand the transnational historical context of Philippine migration and its politics, but it also encourages a tendency seen in earlier studies of women migrants theorised through a post-structural lens, to individualise migrant experience and eschew their political activism.[41] The shift in the discourse would, however, be popular because Philippine women travellers are often offended by stereotypical readings of their journeys that place them as 'global maids', regardless of their ages, class backgrounds, destinations, occupations, etc. Yet again, their migration is smoothed over by the Philippine state.[42]

We turn now to Canada's live-in caregiver programme (LCP), an anomalous component in Canada's temporary foreign worker stream and politically controversial with feminist activists in Canada.[43] Until very recently most other 'unskilled' temporary foreign workers had to leave Canada at the expiration of their contract but caregivers can apply for permanent residence and then citizenship. The programme is controversial mainly because of the two year live-in restriction and the prohibiting of other forms of employment during the worker's time off. In 2007 an amendment allowed workers to complete the two years of full-time work over a three year period. This adjustment means that, should caregivers terminate their employment in the first two years, they have additional time to locate a suitable replacement position without having to leave the country. Canada's extension of the unemployment gap contrasts with Hong Kong, where the turn around time for seeking new employment is a very restrictive 14 days. The Canadian changes were criticised by caregiver advocates, who argue for the removal of the live-in requirement on the grounds that it denies citizenship rights.[44] A further concern raised by LCP critics, such as SIKLAB[45] and the National Alliance of Philippine Women in Canada, is that processing delays for work permits erodes the 36-month period, limiting the options for workers who typically leave employment for legitimate reasons associated with exploitation and oppressive workplace conditions. As these groups point out, policy reforms seem more responsive to employer concerns over recruitment delays than to the constrained rights of LCP workers.[46] An ongoing critique of the LCP has been that many caregivers have deliberately deskilled themselves, a particularly contentious issue for registered nurses unable to gain entry to work as nurses.[47] Critics correctly argue that the policy encourages such deskilling through specifying set levels of education, training or appropriate job experience.[48]

Research shows that this issue becomes more complicated in a comparative perspective. Canada is such a desirable destination because. unlike many contract-only global labour markets for commoditised domestic service workers, it allows permanent migration. Hence Canada's caregiver positions are highly sought after. An unpublished report on the LCP prepared in Manila 2005 speaks of the 'tremendous' increase in applications. The language of 'legitimacy' of applications in the report confirms the line of critique about concern for employers driving programme changes noted above:

> Neither the legitimate processing demands nor the legitimate demands of Canadian employers are currently being met due to the numbers involved. The sheer numbers have resulted in substantially increased waiting times for interviews, increased representations from employers and Members of Parliament, increased incidences of fraud and misrepresentation, increased anti-fraud and quality assurance measures being executed, and increased involvement on the part of Manila visa officers to deal with HRSD [Human Resources and Social Development] issues.[49]

The rise in applications is accompanied by growth in the recruitment sector tailored to the Canadian market. The report goes on to record phenomenal growth in the number of caregiver training programmes, numbering 10 in 1999, to more than 800 in 2005. Almost 80% of these schools commenced operations during the period 2002–03. Since the LCP requires a specified amount of training and employment experience, promotions by agencies for targeted employment in Canada have encouraged increased levels of formal education as well. This contributes to a proliferation of educational institutions offering health-related education to potential applicants (as we shall see below), and many well educated women have been prepared to deskill to enter Canada as caregivers, again as affirmed in advocacy group challenges to the programme.

The valorisation of skill (even if temporarily suspended through the exploitative conditions of the caregiver contract), is in marked contrast to the experience of women working in similar jobs in regional labour markets such as Hong Kong, Taiwan and Singapore. My research with applicants preparing to leave for contract work in those destinations reveals a pattern of migrant self-awareness about the need to downplay their skills, sexualities and class identities. 'Performed subordination' was apparent in migrants' self-representation as properly demure, subordinate, maids, capable of contributing English education to employer's children but not so educated and worldly that it might be difficult for the employers concerned to tightly control their live-in 'maids'.[50] Working days in these countries are typically protracted at the whim of employers, even when they may be compelled by labour regulations to provide a set number of hours off per week, for example 12 hours in the case of Hong Kong. In a number of studies, women reported working from early in the morning until employers retired for the night, routinely 16–18 hour days. Many slept in confined quarters and attended to small children during the night.[51] Looked at from the Philippines then, work in Canada, while still subject to labour code violations, seems relatively less exploitative in comparison.

From the point of view of Canadian immigration policy, the specification that caregivers entering Canada must have a certain level of education is one component of the policy that acts to screen out less desirable potential immigrants, namely those who will not fare as well in Canadian labour markets as permanent residents. Controversies and comparisons aside, caregiving is no longer providing a primary immigration pathway to Canadian citizenship, as it has in the past. Today 90% of caregivers arriving in Canada are women, with the Philippines remaining the main sending country. However, waiting times for processing visas through the 'normal channels' have increased to between 12 and 18 months (as of March 2008). This means that, without a considerable amount of pre-planning, or the appropriate social networks in the Philippines, Canadian employers seeking 'nannies' for their children are likely to be frustrated in their recruitment efforts. Similarly the long waiting times facing a significant number of women migrants renders them more vulnerable to exploitation by unscrupulous immigration consultants and recruiters, despite regulatory efforts to monitor these industries. Not surprisingly, given these conditions, around 50% of new caregivers are destined for employment in the households of family members.

In 2007 there were around 6276 applicants. Some 50% of these were declined for reasons having to do with the language requirement, inappropriate experience, or because unscrupulous recruiters had not secured verifiable employers. In the last instance, the recruiter might attempt to bring Filipinos into Canada and 'warehouse' them until employment could be confirmed. Canadian border officials might identify such irregular migrants through a failed answer to a screening question about employment, for example residence address or the name of the person meeting them at the airport. This suggests that class as well as gender is a factor in screening out applications. Further, when caregiver applications are reviewed for legitimacy in the Philippines, 10% to 15% of such applicants are declined because there is insufficient evidence that the employer has the means to pay the caregiver, or there is some other feature of the caregiver profile that does not ring true. For example, a male applicant, an engineer with teenage children, applied as caregiver to a relative's younger children. This applicant's 'relevant experience' was questioned on the assumption that he had previously held a skilled job unrelated to childcare. From the applicant's point of view, assuming he met the age requirements, the skilled worker stream would have provided the most obvious pathway to Canada, but with a minimum waiting time of five years.

Indeed, the 2005 Embassy report cited above speculates about a possible inter-relationship between an increase in caregiver visa applications and the introduction of the Immigration and Refugee Protection Act in mid-2002 which introduced and ranked categories of occupational skill, making it harder for some potential applicants to qualify for skilled worker visas. Further, in 2008 HRSDC, which in Canada oversees temporary foreign worker programmes, has insufficient resources to provide a 'proper' means test for caregiver employers, or to assess kinship relations between applicants and employers to establish whether applicants are inappropriately 'fast tracking' family members who will not be put to work in caregiving duties. Doubtless some irregularities do occur, despite the efforts of Embassy staff in Manila. The 2005 report also noted that in applicant interviews, some applicants (mis)spoke of their employers as sponsors. Further, a survey of 154 Canada-destined caregivers, undertaken in a pre-departure counselling session in November/December 2004, revealed that none was then currently employed as a caregiver, despite the visa stipulation of education and/or experience. So while the evidence points to Filipinos hedging their chances at immigrating to Canada, many other women and men seeking emigration as caregivers will be frustrated in their efforts. The same is true for potential 'legitimate' employers. And, of course, it needs to be pointed out that Filipino-Canadian families have the same kinds of legitimate needs for family caregivers as other Canadians. Discerning the differences between legitimate immigrants and what public discourse calls 'queue-jumpers' is, nonetheless, posing challenges to maintaining the status quo of screening processes.

This dramatic shift in the employer profiles for caregivers is also not surprising given that direct hire recruitment is the most efficient means of securing a caregiver, that is, not utilising a recruitment agent, the route that Canadians would follow in the absence of Philippine networks. Already one of the top three source countries, Philippine–Canada migration is increasing, through a combination of factors. There is the previously mentioned advantage in Canada's English-speaking provinces, the Philippine state is aggressively promoting the qualities of Filipinos in various global labour markets, and immigrant receiving countries such as Canada are receptive to 'Brand Philippines'. As one Canadian immigration official suggested, Filipinos are seen as 'the ideal immigrant', but this is paradoxical when viewed in transnational perspective. For example, in interviews with skilled workers in Manila preparing to depart for Canada (in February 2008), the most common response to my question about why Canada should be interested in Filipino workers produced a listing of stereotypical adjectives: Filipinos are 'hard-working, compliant, grateful, and patient'.[52] Yet Philippine media reports propose that Filipino workers have insufficient discipline to inspire confidence in their work abroad.[53] What these contradictory discourses reveal is the tension between structure, agency and the economic subjectivities of Philippine migrants as classed social subjects in diversified migration flows.

Flexible Filipinos and border policy translation

Canada's Citizenship and Immigration policy has quietly diversified how immigrants enter Canada. In keeping with neoliberal agendas of privatisation the state has created conditions for private actors, including employers, to manipulate the terms of entry to Canada.[54] Resourceful Filipinos seem well positioned to take advantage of these changes and they are doing so with remarkable speed, particularly with regard to two relatively new policy translations. I use the word translation deliberately because the policies I will now summarise—the provincial nominee programmes (PNPs) and the

50

temporary foreign worker programme (TFW)—were developed separately, the former being relatively new to all provinces but Quebec, the latter being longstanding but used today in new ways, particularly it seems by employers and brokers of Filipino immigrants. Policy translation is demonstrated by the way in which Filipinos manage to shift from the temporary classification to the permanent immigration stream.

The PNPs are a recent innovation developed primarily in response to concerns over declining fertility rates and labour market shortages, combined with extensive processing wait times for economic migration streams, including skilled workers and professionals, and family reunification. Under individually tailored agreements with the federal government, provinces are accorded a quota of immigrants they can then pre-select in accord with designated streams designed to their needs. Depending upon their access to information and personal financial resources, the PNPs now provide the most flexible and perhaps malleable option for immigrants to enter Canada. Flexibility also occurs in the investor, entrepreneur and self-employed persons stream—which essentially enables immigrants to 'buy' their immigration status. For those without the resources to access the investor stream, the PNPs provide 'fast tracked' immigration to Canada. This is because applicants with appropriate skills are processed much more quickly. Further, PNPs are sufficiently flexible that the provinces can launch recruitment missions abroad seeking to fill particular local labour market shortages.

The Philippines is the top source country for PNPs, with 80% of entrants contracted in Alberta. However, 10 provincial delegations were made to the Philippines in 2007 and a number of provinces have signed co-operation agreements with the Philippine government, suggesting wide regard for Filipino nominees.[55] Some of the demand is for nurses, but all provinces report labour market shortages across a wide variety of skill sets, if not all to the same degree as Alberta. For example, some smaller communities have recognised Filipino sociability as a form of 'capital' in the competition to retain immigrants who enter under the PNP. A scaled-down version of 'ethnic enclave' logic normally applicable to large metropolitan centres underlies the recruitment strategy. It is reasoned that since Filipinos seem to desire the company of compatriots, the presence of Filipinos is used to attract new immigrants. Apparently this strategy works, as evidenced by media reports in Canada about groups of Filipinos being imported to work in fast food service in remote regions of the country. Aside from common cultural values and practices, shared accommodation enables workers to maximise the economic benefits of low-skilled minimum wage jobs.[56]

Until very recently, Canada's TFW programme targeted caregivers and agricultural workers. However, there has been a significant increase in both the numbers of temporary entrants and a diversification of their occupations. The Philippines again provides an interesting lens into these recent changes. In 2004 the vast majority of TFWs entering Canada from the Philippines were caregivers. Only 390 TFW applicants presented with other skills. Here are some cumulative statistics obtained from the Canadian embassy in Manila.[57]

There were 2813 LCP visas processed in 2005 with an increase in 2007 to 4574. Total visas processed for other temporary workers went up from 586 in 2005 to 6786 in 2007. PNP visas showed a similar increase from 1380 in 2005 to 3728 in 2007. On the other hand, over the same period skilled worker visas declined from 6899 in 2005 to 4959 in 2007. While the types of visas applied for and issued changed, the total number of entrants to Canada across all visa categories remained relatively constant at 10 538 in 2005 and 10 324 in 2007. The embassy statistics record visas issued and applications received. Here again we see dramatic increases. By 2006, 3735 Filipino TFW applications had applied, a number which increased in 2007 to 10 179, in part because of a low-skilled worker pilot project arranged between HRSDC and Alberta. Initially TFW contracts were issued for 12 months but this has been extended to 24 months. Contracts are renewable but workers must leave for four months.[58] A further policy change in 2007 is that recruiters seeking to place TFWs in Canada are not legally allowed to charge migrant fees; instead employers must pay costs. Most interesting for the purposes of this paper is that there is new evidence that TFW recruits are successfully seeking to transfer from TFW contracts to PNPs (25 out of 100 low-skilled workers contacted in the past 12 months had converted to PNP immigration streams and it is anticipated more will do so). Each approval granted to a PNP immigrant is anticipated to multiply by a factor of three through family class immigration. It is also anticipated that as the TFW stream increases in size, the number of Filipinos in the programme will increase. Filipino social networks act as communication channels, aided by entrepreneurial immigration recruiters and consultants who recognise the potential of both the PNP and the TFW. Recruiters and consultants are also adept at knowing how to promote the relationship between these two programmes. These factors will ensure that Filipinos will remain dominant as a Canadian immigrant source country. The Philippine state also recognises this and is reported to be establishing consular offices in Vancouver with a satellite office planned for Calgary.

Looked at from a Philippine perspective, the PNPs and TFW appear to offer more opportunities to migrants destined for Canada. Clearly there are classed and gendered implications from this diversification in immigration streams. For the lower skilled migrants there remains the possibility that the economic boom driving the need for low-skilled migrants, for example in Alberta, might bust. This would throw TFWs out of work without recourse to unemployment insurance, or whatever union protection might be available to Canadian workers in equivalent jobs. There are also consequences from the gendering of jobs by skill, for example the more limited labour markets that women select from, or are constrained by, are typically skilled lower than many jobs geared towards men's skills.

Filipino labour markets and 'brain drain'

On a more serious note, the importation of Filipino skilled workers in PNPs begs transnational analysis. In the first instance, the Philippines is itself experiencing the kind of skilled labour shortages, but not for the same reasons, as Western labour import countries. In effect, there is a transnational mirror effect at play. A recent article in the *Philippine Star* (7 February 2008), citing Bureau of Labour and Employment (DOLE) statistics, describes a survey of over 5800 firms which reveals that 22.9% of companies experience difficulty in filling positions in skill-intensive positions in so called 'vital occupational categories': managers, supervisors, machine operators, accountants, auditors, civil engineers, electrical engineers, mechanics, sewers, linemen, food processors and welders. DOLE directly attributes this 'man-power shortage' to the exodus of skilled workers abroad.

Health-related industries constitute a particular subset of skilled occupations. The Philippines has been a major source country for the global export of healthcare workers, including many who downgrade their qualifications to work as caregivers in the absence of ready access to nursing employment. But the situation is more longstanding and complex than this. The Philippines is described in recent studies as the major exporter of nurses in the global economy,[59] with 70% of all Filipino nursing graduates working overseas.[60] There has long been a surplus of nurses produced for export and in accommodation to labour market demands. Canada's policy has fluctuated, sometimes allowing nurses to enter the country to work as nurses and sometimes restricting that form of work relative to demand and concerns raised by Canadian unionised nurses. The recorded rapid increase in nurses leaving the Philippines responds to increased demand in northern countries where it is tied to demographic trends. This is unparalleled in nurse migration history and is accompanied by a deterioration in the quality of nursing education.[61]

A further articulation is called for in what I am describing as Filipino flexibility relative to the trade in nurses. Ever attentive to labour markets, enterprising immigration industries in the Philippines are responding to the high demand for nurses in the USA, the UK and Ireland. Special educational institutions now offer streamlined nursing courses for Filipino doctors to retool—put differently to deskill themselves—in preparation for emigration as nurses.[62] This phenomenon surfaced in public debate over migration politics in 2004, when Dr Elmer Jacinto, the top scoring graduate of the Philippine medical board examinations declared his intention to emigrate to the USA to work as nurse.[63] He declared this was necessary because he was from a poor family and his earnings would be greater in the USA as a nurse than as an MD in the Philippines. The public debate, fuelled as always by media commentary, was seen by some observers to reflect generalised Filipino class ambivalence.[64] Elite voices spoke of Jacinto's betrayal of the nation, others defended the rights of migrants to seek economic improvement abroad. Diasporic Filipinos also weighed into the fray.

What appeared at the time to be a relatively isolated case has become a new trend and is looming as a major healthcare crisis. A recent report notes that since 2000 more than 3500 Filipino medical doctors have left as nurses and early in 2004 there were an estimated 4000 doctors enrolled in nursing schools across the country. As in Canada, more women than men attend the nation's 36 medical schools. Emigrant doctors are drawn from various specialities and range in age from 25 to 60 years old. Their years of practice as a physician range from zero, as in Jacinto's example, to 35.[65] Bilateral policy negotiations are called for given the looming health care crisis in the Philippines.[66] There are also implications for Philippine labour export policies inasmuch as the entrepreneurial theme to current policies appears to disregard the social and economic consequences of healthcare professional emigration.[67] Clearly capital is privileged over social agendas in terms of Filipinos who are not intending to emigrate either because they are unwilling or unable to. As Bauman so poignantly reminds us, global migration is cleaved along class lines.[68] Some are condemned to immobility because they lack the resources to attempt to migrate, while others are forced into it. Yet others profit extensively from their command over resources essential to the migration journeys of compatriots.

Skilled workers on the slow track

When it comes to qualitative research on migration decision making, skilled workers are perhaps the most overlooked and least researched category of immigrants to Canada. These workers, drawn from the Philippine middle-class, are deemed eligible to enter Canada because of their ranking under a points system which scores levels of education and employment experience, among other things. The delays are long, the immigrants seemingly patient. In recognition of the longstanding critique of the deskilling process that most skilled workers are forced into, despite the basis of their entry to Canada being skill-based, Canada is now taking steps to encourage a more realistic appraisal of Canada's occupational codes. A pilot project called the Canadian Immigration Integration Project has been launched in each of the three top source countries: India (reported in 2008 as the new lead country), China and the Philippines. All skilled workers are now invited to attend optional two day seminars, free of charge. The seminars review topics designed to induce better labour market outcomes for emigrants, covering such topics as preparing CVs for Canadian employers and the appraisal of Canadian occupational codes for matching skills to available jobs. This project is obviously helpful and participants seemed enthusiastic about the information garnered from the seminars.

Again the provision of the seminars suits neoliberal Canadian immigration policy, which prefers immigrants to 'land on their feet' and become economically productive as soon as possible. Immigrants must prove that they have su.cient resources to survive an adjustment period ($10 000 plus $2000 per dependent in 2008). This represents considerable capital given the relatively lower wages of skilled workers in the Philippines. Interviews revealed that varying degrees of hardship are involved, depending upon family resources and risk-taking. Most émigrés have relatives living abroad whom they turn to for help, and some have sold property in the Philippines. But most take years to arrange their finances. Those with the greatest amount of capital reported that they wished to retain some property in the Philippines, not wishing to completely rule out the idea of return at some stage. This was much less likely to be true for caregivers, who are not provided with Canadian government-sponsored seminars about their options as Canadian-landed immigrants. Here again, then, we see class and gender differences in migration streams plus a 'brain drain' effect combined with capital outflow from the Philippines, a process that has consistently defined immigration programmes valorising skilled and entrepreneurial migrants with more capital and presumably less potential claim on the streamlined neoliberal Canadian state.

A recent report from Statistics Canada indicates the Canadian government's commitment to Philippine immigrants, in various streams, is not without basis. The bulletin begins: 'Immigrants born in Southeast Asia, particularly those from the Philippines, had the strongest labour market performance of all immigrants to Canada in 2006, regardless of when they landed in the country'. This study compared very recent immigrants (landing between 2001 and 2006) and recent immigrants (landing from 1996 to 2001) with established immigrants, living in Canada for over 10 years. The study concluded: 'Among the very recent, only those born in Southeast Asia had unemployment rates, employment rates and participation rates that were more or less on par with the core working-age Canadian-born population'.[69] As I am arguing 'Brand Canada' and 'Brand Philippines' appear successfully matched in their respective labour export/immigration efforts. Immediately the Statistics Canada bulletin was posted, summaries of the report appeared in various Philippine websites sourcing data about the Philippine–Canada migration streams. The dance of flexibility and capital mobility continues.

Conclusion: the 'ideal' immigrant?

In many ways a picture emerges casting Filipinos as 'ideal immigrants' but there is surely more to the story. There are some constant themes across the board of all migrant/emigrant/immigrant decision-making. The idea of 'sacrifice' still pervades migration narratives but this is countered with ideas about what migration will contribute to familial well-being and to personal experience. Middle-class migrants are the most likely to claim despair at Philippine political corruption and economic instability as the motivation for their migration—in other words they desire class mobility and the status that goes with this, if not for themselves, certainly for their children. Contract workers, such as caregivers, have more basic concerns, typically about the greater economic security of family members remaining behind in the Philippines.

Although Canadian immigration policy, finely calibrated as it is to labour market and investment concerns, appears to offer varied paths of entry into Canada, there are deeper class cleavages being forged through mobility scenarios relative to who leaves and how, and who remains behind. TFWs span a range of skills and class positions but along this continuum vulnerabilities occur relative to skill sets and the deskilling of occupations essential to the migration strategies of caregivers, certain kinds of TFWs, and even those within the PNPs. There are also deeper inequalities developing within the pools of migrants-in-waiting, inequalities that disadvantage those without the social, economic or indeed cultural capital necessary to be nimble regarding the flexibilisation in immigration policy.

While Dobrowolsky's point about the securitisation, invisibilisation and marketisation of women in border and citizenship policy is well taken,[70] it would appear that the gendered consequences of this are varied in terms of class resources and for different immigration streams. Despite the new flexibility and the apparent strategic advantage accorded Filipinos as 'ideal immigrants', it remains the case that Filipino adaptability marries with the agendas of sending and receiving states more so than it does with the circumstances of the majority of migrants. Yet again, through attention to the structured agency of the migration process, it is possible to invoke the metaphor of Janus to reference the two faces of migration–immigration. One side favours elite players in migration industries in both contexts, the other entails the hardship, risk and hopes of Filipino women and men seeking a better more economically secure future for themselves and their children.

Notes

* This collaborative research project was funded by the Social Sciences and Humanities Research Council of Canada in 2006. Their assistance is gratefully acknowledged. My research partner, Belinda Leach of the University of Guelph, is conducting a comparative study of Trinidad-Canada migration pathways.

1 For example, S Castles & M Miller, *The Age of Migration*, New York: Guilford Press, 2003; R Cohen, *Migration and its Enemies: Global Capital, Migrant Labour and the Nation-State*, Aldershot: Ashgate Press, 2006; S Sassen, *Globalization and its Discontents: Essays on the New Mobility of People and Money*, New York: Free Press, 1998; and R Staring, 'Flows of people: globalization, migration , and transnational communities,' in D Kalb, M van der Land, R Staring, B van Steenbergen & N Wilterdink (eds), *The Ends of Globalization: Bringing Society Back In*, Lanham, MD: Rowman & Littlefield, 2000, pp 203–215.

2 D Harvey, *A Brief History of Neoliberalism*, Oxford: Oxford University Press, 2005.

3 See P Gardiner Barber & W Lem, 'Migrants, mobility, and mobilization', *Focaal: European Journal of Anthropology*, 51, 2008, pp 3–12.

4 L Basch, N Glick Schiller & C Szanton Blanc (eds), *Nations Unbound: Transnational Projects, Postcolonial Predicaments and Deterritorialized Nation States*, Langhorne, PA: Gordon & Breach, 1994; and Z Gille & S Ó Riain, 'Global ethnography', *Annual Review of Sociology*, 28, 2002, pp 271–295.

5 See A Wimmer & N Glick Schiller, 'Methodological nationalism the social sciences, and the study of migration: an essay in historical epistemology', *International Migration Review*, 37 (3), 2003, pp 576–610.

6 P Gardiner Barber, 'Contradictions of class and consumption when the commodity is labour', *Anthropologica*, 46, 2004, pp 203–218; Barber, 'Envisaging power in Philippine migration: the Janus effect', in J Parpart, S Rai & K Staudt (eds), *Rethinking Empowerment: Gender and Development in a Global/Local World*, London: Ashgate, 2002, pp 41–60.

7 International Organisation for Migration (IOM) Regional and Country Figures, 2005, at http://www.iom.int/jahia/Jahia/pid/255, accessed 27 April 2008.

8 See J Tyner, 'Global cities and circuits of global labor: the case of Manila, Philippines', in *Filipinos in Global Migrations: At Home in the World*, Quezon City: Philippine Migration Research Network and Philippine Social Science Council, 2002, pp 60–85.

9 The total was 1 062 567, up by 7.5% from 2005. Statistics are collected for land- and sea-based deployments; 26% of the 2006 total were sea-based. See http://www.poea.gov.ph/html/statistics.html, accessed 17 April 2008.

10 The deployment of women peaked at around 72% of documented land-based workers hired in 2004.

11 The countries were, in order of significance: Saudi Arabia, United Arab Emirates, Hong Kong, Kuwait, Qatar, Taiwan, Singapore, Italy, UK and South Korea. See http://www.poea.gov.ph/html/statistics.html, accessed 17 April 2008.

12 F Baggio, 'Migration and development in the Philippines', unpublished paper presented at the International Metropolis Conference, Melbourne, 2007.

13 J Gibson-Graham, S Resnick & R Wolff (eds), *Class and Its Others*, Minneapolis, MN: University of Minnesota Press, 2000; M Molyneux, 'Beyond the domestic labour debate', *New Left Review*, 116, 1979, pp 3–27; and K Young, C Wolkowitz & R McCullagh (eds), *Of Marriage and the Market*, London: Methuen, 1981.

14 N Constable, *Maid to Order in Hong Kong: Stories of Filipina Workers*, Ithaca, NY: Cornell University Press, 1997; and J Groves & K Chang, 'Romancing resistance and resisting romance: ethnography and the construction of power in the Filipina domestic workers community in Hong Kong', *Journal of Contemporary Ethnography*, 28 (3), 1999, pp 235–265.

15 A Agathangelou, *The Global Political Economy of Desire, Violence and Insecurity in Mediterranean Nation States*, New York: Palgrave Macmillan, 2004; B Anderson, *Doing the Dirty Work? The Global Politics of Domestic Labour*, London: Zed Books, 2000; C Chin, *In Service and Servitude: Foreign Female Domestic Workers and the Malaysian 'Modernity' Project*, New York: Columbia University Press, 1998; B Ehrenreich & A Hochschild (eds), *Global Woman: Nannies, Maids, and Sex Workers in the New Economy*, London: Granta, 2003; and R Parreñas, *Servants of Globalization: Women, Migration, and Domestic Work*, Stanford, CA: Stanford University Press, 2001.

16 C Katz, 'Vagabond capitalism and the necessity of social reproduction', *Antipode*, 33 (4), 2001, pp 709–728; P Pessar & S Mahler, 'Transnational migration: bringing gender in', *International Migration Review*, 37 (3), 2003, pp 812–846.

18 For an historical comparison, see R Cohen, *Migration and its Enemies: Global Capital, Migrant Labour and the Nation-State*, Aldershot, Ashgate, 2006. N De Genova, *Race, Space, and 'Illegality' in Mexican Chicago*, Durham, NC: Duke University Press, 2005, links the racialised subordination of migrant Mexicans to US 'nativism'.

19 This figure escalated from a preliminary figure of Can$76 million. http://www.cbc.ca/canada/story/2006/11/24/lebanon-cost.html, accessed 23 April 2008.

20 For example, E Gilbert, 'Leaky borders and solid citizens: governing security, prosperity and quality of life in a North American partnership', *Antipode*, 39 (1), 2007, pp 77–98; and A Pratt, *Securing Borders: Detention and Deportation in Canada*, Vancouver: University of British Columbia Press, 2005.

21 A Dobrowolsky, '(In)security and citizenship: security, im/migration and shrinking citizenship regimes', *Theoretical Inquiries in Law*, 8 (2), 2007, pp 628–661.

22 F Aguilar, *Filipinos in Global Migrations: At Home in the World?*, Quezon City: Philippine Migration Research Network and Philippine Social Science Council, 2002.

23 For example, J Gonzalez III, *Philippine Labour Migration: Critical Dimensions of Public Policy*, Manila: De La Salle University Press (ISEAS), 1998. The chronology here mostly follows Gonzalez.

24 Marcos held power from 1965 until his forced resignation in 1986 after a hastily called, rigged election. Corazon Aquino was president from 1986 to 1992, Fidel Ramos from 1992 to 1998, Joseph Estrada from 1998 to 2001, when he too was forced from office after a massive public demonstration. The current president, Gloria Macapagal Arroyo is embattled by accusations of corruption and voting irregularities. The next presidential election is in 2010.

25 Gonzalez, *Philippine Labour Migration*.

26 The Philippines was one of the first countries to undergo IMF structural adjustment, receiving nine loans between 1980 and 1999. IMF database at http://ifs.apdi.net/imf, accessed 10 April 2007. After nearly 20 years of these economic liberalisation policies, wealth disparities are as marked as ever. Rural areas have experienced further impoverishment resulting from stalled land reform, poor prices for agricultural products, and serious decline in natural resources, including fish stocks. Urban migration contributes to pressures for infrastructure, housing and services in major centres and continues to lay the foundation for overseas migration.

27 S Go, 'Remittances and international labour migration: impact on the Philippines', paper presented at the Metropolis Interconference Seminar on Immigrants and Homeland, Dubrovnik, 9–12 May 2002.

28 Gonzalez, *Philippine Labour Migration*, notes regional concentrations in the Middle East, Asia, Europe, the Americas and Africa through to the mid-1990s. See Note 23.

29 W Bello, *The Anti-Development State: The Political Economy of Permanent Crisis in the Philippines*, Quezon City: University of the Philippines Diliman/Focus on the Global South, 2004.

30 J Arnado, *Mistresses and Maids; Inequality among Third World Women Wage Earners*, Manila: De La Salle University Press, 2003.

31 Constable, *Maid to Order in Hong Kong*; Groves & Chang, 'Romancing resistance and resisting romance'; Agathangelou, *The Global Political Economy of Desire, Violence and Insecurity in Mediterranean Nation States*; Anderson, *Doing the Dirty Work?*; Chin, *In Service and Servitude*; Ehrenreich & Hochschild, *Global Woman*; and Parreñas, *Servants of Globalization*.

32 A Macklin, 'On the inside looking in: foreign domestic workers in Canada', in W Giles & S Arat-Koc, *Maid in the Market: Women's Paid Domestic Labour*, Halifax: Fernwood Publishing, 1994, pp 13–39;

and D Stasiulis & A Bakan, *Negotiating Citizenship: Migrant Women in Canda and the Global System*, Toronto: University of Toronto Press, 2005.

33 P Gardiner Barber, 'Cell phones, complicity, and class politics in the Philippine labor diaspora', *Focaal*, 51, 2008, pp 28–42; G Pratt, *Working Feminism*, Philadelphia, PA: Temple University Press, 2004; E Zontini, 'Resisting Fortress Europe: the everyday politics of female transnational migrants, *Focaal*, 51, 2008, pp 13–27.

34 For example, the Commission of Filipinos Overseas (CFO) has a mandate to promote the benefits of Filipino workers abroad. Dante Ang, CFO Chairman, visited Canada in April 200, sponsored by a Halifax-based recruitment agency. Halifax has a relatively small immigrant population. In the whole Atlantic region, *Citizenship and Immigration Canada: Atlantic Canada Facts and Figures*, 2006, shows the annual flow of foreign workers for 2006 to be 3094. The Philippines was the third top source country at 10.7% (330 people), after the UK (12%, or 317 persons) and the USA (22%, or 686 persons). The recruitment company sees potential in recruiting Filipino workers to regional labour markets. Since provincial employers complain about the shortage of local workers as a result of out-migration from the Atlantic provinces to Canada's booming energy-driven economy in Alberta, Filipinos will presumably replace local workers. The company sponsoring Ang's visit is staffed by new immigrants to Canada from the Philippines. Companies set up by diasporic nationals are able to mobilise social networks and policy translation more effectively than companies without such transnational experience.

35 I Bagasao, 'Migration and development: the Philippine experience', in S Mambo & D Ratha (eds), *Remittances: Development Impact and Future Prospects*, Washington, DC: World Bank, 2005, pp 133–142.

36 G Battistella & C Conaco, 'The impact of labour migration on the children left behind: a study of elementary school children in the Philippines', *Soujourn*, 13 (2), 1998, pp 220–241; *Hearts Apart: Migration in the Eyes of Filipino Children*, Joint Project of the Episcopal Commission for the Pastoral Care of Migrants and Itinerant People/Apostleship of the Sea-Manila, Scalabrini Migration Center, Overseas Workers Welfare Administration, Manila, 2004; K Laurie, 'Gender and Philippine transnational migration: tracing the impacts "home"', MA thesis, St. Mary's University, Halifax, 2008; and R Parreñas, 'Long distance intimacy: class, gender and intergeneration relations between mother and children in Filipino transnational families', *Global Networks*, 5 (4), 2005, pp 317–336.

37 Two cases shaped migration politics during the 1995 presidential elections. Flor Contemplacion was executed in Singapore for a crime many Filipinos believed she was not guilty of. In the United Arab Emirates, Sara Balabagan also received a death sentence, subsequently converted to lashings and a jail term, for killing her male employer whom she claimed was attempting to rape her. The Ramos administration hastily recrafted migration policy to address widespread protests about over-reliance on migration. He was re-elected for a second term.

38 J Tyner, *Made in the Philippines: Gendered Discourses and the Making of Migrants*, London: Routledge/Curzon, 2005.

39 J Bach & M Solomon, 'Labours of globalization: emergent state responses', *New Global Studies*, forthcoming, 2008; and Bello, *The Anti-development State*.

40 http://www.poea.gov.ph/, accessed 17 April 2008.

41 Barber, 'Cell phones, complicity, and class politics in the Philippine labor diaspora'; Pratt, *Working Feminism*; and Zontini, 'Resisting Fortress Europe'.

42 This line of reasoning is also taken up by Tyner, *Made in the Philippines*.

43 D Stasiulis & A Bakan, *Negotiating Citizenship: Migrant Women in Canada and the Global System*, Toronto: University of Toronto Press, 2005; and Pratt, *Working Feminism*.

44 Ibid.

45 SIKLAB is an abbreviation of *Sulong, Itaguyod ang Karapatan ng mga Manggagawa sa Labas ng Bansa* [Advance and Uphold the Rights and Welfare of Overseas Filipino Workers]. SIKLAB network members are active in several Canadian cities.

46 SIKLAB Canada, 'Advocacy groups critical of changes in Canada's migration policy', *Bulatlat*, VII (7), 18–24 March 2007.

47 G Pratt, 'From registered nurse to registered nanny: discursive geographies of Filipina domestic workers in Vancouver, BC', in T Barnes, J Peck, E Sheppard & A Tickell (eds), *Reading Economic Geography*, On-line Blackwell Publishing, pp 375–388, at http://www3.interscience,wiley.com/cgi-bin/bookhome/117881217/, accessed 14 January 2008.

48 Philippine women and men arriving in Canada under the LCP are considered 'professional' caregivers. Applicants must be functional in English or French and hold the equivalent of a Canadian high school education, plus six months of full-time training or 12 months (six months of which are continuous) of full-time paid employment in a related field. This experience must be within three years prior to application for the visa. Applicants must also secure a written employment contract, undergo medical tests and navigate Philippine exit visa requirements. Many migrants who target Canada submit to

specialised 'caregiver' training offered by an elite stratum of recruitment agencies (sometimes owned by diasporic Filipinos) that promises ease of placement and assistance with visa processing at home and abroad. The fees charged vary but are always burdensome for emigrants, who are typically deeply in debt—to relatives or money lending agents. Loan agents present in most migrant sending communities are called 5/6ers—meaning borrow 5000 pesos, pay back 6000. But the Philippine state now attempts more stringent regulation of the recruitment sector, mainly in response to political mobilisations from disgruntled migrants and their families. Despite regulation, placement fees remain problematically uneven. Even licensed agencies commit fee violations.

49 *The State of the Live-in Caregiver Program in Manila*, Citizenship and Immigration Canada, Manila, January 2005.
50 P Gardiner Barber, 'Cell phones, complicity, and class politics in the Philippine labor diaspora'.
51 See Constable, *Maid to Order in Hong Kong*; Groves & Chang, 'Romancing resistance and resisting romance'; Agathangelou, *The Global Political Economy of Desire, Violence and Insecurity in Mediterranean Nation States*; Anderson, *Doing the Dirty Work?*; Chin, *In Service and Servitude*; Ehrenreich & Hochschild, *Global Woman*; Parreñas, *Servants of Globalization*; Macklin, 'On the inside looking in'; and Stasiulis & Bakan, *Negotiating Citizenship*.
52 All these qualities have been critically subjected to analysis by research on how women workers are 'disciplined' for and in the global labour force. See the works cited above.
53 M Tobias, *Philippine Star*, 2 March 2008.
54 A Macklin, 'Public entrance/private member', in J Fudge & B Cossman (eds), *Privatisation, Feminism and Law*, Toronto: University of Toronto Press, 2002, pp 219–264.
55 The POEA website lists agreements with Manitoba, British Columbia and Saskatchewan. See http://www.poea.gov.ph/, accessed 17 April 2008. Agreements are under discussion with Alberta and New Brunswick (as of March 2008).
56 CBC Radio Documentary, 6 January 2008.
57 *Year-end Report, Cumulative Stats, 2005, 2007*, Manila: Citizenship and Immigration Canada, 2007.
58 In April 2008 extensions were proposed for workers in certain types of high-demand occupations, both skilled and unskilled.
59 L Aiken, J Buchan *et al*, 'Trends in international nurse migration,' *Health Affairs*, 23 (3), 2004, pp 69–77.
60 S Bach, 'International migration of health workers: labour and social issues', *Working Paper 209*, Geneva: International Labour Office, 2003.
61 J Tan, F Sanchez & V Balanon, 'The Philippine phenomenon of nursing medics: why Filipino doctors are becoming nurses', mimeo, 2004.
62 J Tan, 'The mass migration of Filipino health professionals: who pays? Who benefits? What can be done!', paper presented at the International Metropolis Conference, Melbourne, 2007.
63 P Abinales & D Amoroso, *State and Society in the Philippines*, Lanham, MD: Rowman and Littlefield, 2005.
64 *Ibid*, p 31.
65 Tan *et al*, 'The Philippine phenomenon of nursing medics'.
66 *Ibid*. The Canadian province of Saskatchewan holds an MOU with the Philippines and is concluding arrangements to import a second group of over 300 nurses later in 2008.
67 The situation has been described as a violation of human rights in US immigration policy, with a call for revised moral and ethical frameworks to guide US immigration policy. See D Drebdahl & K Dorcy, 'Exclusive inclusion: the violation of human rights and US immigration policy', *Advances in Nursing Science*, 30 (4), 2007, pp 290–302.
68 Z Bauman, *Globalization: The Human Consequences*, New York: Columbia University Press, 1998; and Bauman, *Wasted Lives: Modernity and its Outcasts*, Cambridge: Polity Press, 2004.
69 'Study: the 2006 Canadian immigrant labour market: analysis by region or country of birth', *The Daily*, Ottawa: Statistics Canada, February 13, 2008, at http://www.statca.ca/Daily/English/080213/d080213b.htm, accessed 16 February 2008.
70 Dobrowolsky, '(In)security and citizenship'.

Feminisation of Migration and the Social Dimensions of Development: the Asian case

NICOLA PIPER

Academic studies and reports from international organisations on contemporary flows of migration have increasingly acknowledged and highlighted a number of issues related to one of the key features of international migration today: its feminisation.[1] The notion of 'feminisation' is linked to the issue of gender and the differences between male and female migrants' experiences. An expanding literature on the subject of gendered migration has demonstrated that most, if not all, aspects of migration affect men and women differently, thus establishing gender as a crucial factor in our understanding of the causes and consequences of international migration.[2]

The phenomenon of 'feminisation of migration', however, is defined and understood in various ways by different people. It requires a comprehensive analysis in the context of the complexity of contemporary patterns of international migration. Recent studies have pointed to the increasing diversification (that is, differences *within* a specific nationality group as well as *across* nationality groups) and polarisation (that is, skilled versus less skilled) of the various migration streams, rendering 'migration' a highly stratified phenomenon. The notion of 'stratification' emphasises the combined effects of gender, ethnicity, legal status, skill level and mode of entry or exit, with the result of women's migration(s) emerging as highly 'stratified'.[3]

The gendered and stratified nature of migration has implications for labour market experience, entitlements and rights. In other words, a gender analysis emphasises the significance of broader social factors involved in influencing women's and men's roles and their access to resources, facilities and services. This has implications for the issue of development and the current revived debate on the 'migration–development nexus' which tends to be dominated by macroeconomic concerns, especially remittances, and is largely based on narrow empirical evidence mostly derived from South-to-North migration.[4] As a result, the social dimensions of the migration–development nexus, including its potential for higher levels of equality with regard to human relationships based on class, ethnicity and gender, are glossed over. Yet, when a gender dimension is incorporated into the analysis, it brings to the fore the very *social* dimensions of the issues under debate.

Despite being global in scope, significant flows of migration occur within regions rather than across them, generally from low-income to middle-income or high-income countries.[5] This can also be observed with regard to international migratory movements in Asia. This paper, therefore, begins with a discussion of the current debate on the 'migration and development nexus' with two objectives in mind: 1) to assess this debate's relevance to intra-regional migration in Asia; and 2) to redirect attention to the social dimension of feminised migrations and its relationship to development. In doing this, the focus is on the individual and family level to discuss the impact of migration on personal development as well as on interpersonal relations. What follows thereafter is a brief summary of the character and context of feminised migration in Asia, by approaching this issue from an intra-regional (that is migratory moves of Asians within Asia) perspective. The final section links the previous discussion to the issue of rights.

Linking migration and development—shifting from the economic to the social

The expansion of global markets and the concomitant socioeconomic transformations in recent decades have led to a quantitative increase in movements world-wide since the 1990s. With this, a renewed interest in the relationship between migration and development can be observed, triggered by origin governments' rising interest in remittances. The relationship between migration and development was already hotly debated in the 1970s and 1980s, mostly with a negative undertone in the assessment of the impact of migration on furthering development of origin countries.[6]

The recent revival of this debate has experienced a shift in emphasis towards the positive aspects of migration and development, together with a more explicit appreciation of the reciprocity of this relationship (in the sense that a certain level of development triggers migration and migration can contribute to development in both origin and destination countries). What has taken centre stage in the contemporary debate now more than ever is the individual migrant in her role as an 'agent of development'. This shift in attention toward migrants as potential 'agents of development' in the South has occurred especially in connection with the formation of 'diasporas' or 'transnational communities'.[7] Thus, the focus has been nearly exclusively on transnational or diaspora communities in economically advanced countries in the West. The classic examples these findings are based on are Indian Information Technology (IT) workers and Chinese businesspeople.[8] This is a heavily male-dominated category comprised of highly skilled migrants derived from the context of South-to-North migration. Other migrant groups, such as temporary labour migrants are seldom taken into consideration, even though this migration pattern is on the increase world-wide and is the predominant feature of intra-Asian migration, in addition to being heavily feminised.[9] The specific features of this migration stream, such as temporary return leaving families behind, may have significant and yet different developmental implications. Moreover, gender as a constituent element of migration has not yet entered mainstream debates on migration and development.[10]

Furthermore, on the issue of policy, most research has focused on emigration or immigration rules and regulations, largely ignoring the significance of other relevant policy areas. This reflects a conventional understanding of development and a narrowly defined economic paradigm, disregarding newer critiques of development thinking and newer concepts like human development. A gender lens allows us to redirect our attention to the individual and family or household level to assess the impact of migration on personal development as well as on relational changes, and thus on the social dimensions of the migration–development nexus.

Changing familial and gender relations

Because of the time limited nature of their contracts, many migrants in Asia re-migrate in order to remain in overseas employment. A considerable number of women working as domestic workers manage to obtain extensions on their contracts with the result that some spend many years, if not decades, abroad. In the absence of family reunification policies for this type of migrant, migrant families become what has been termed 'transnationally split households', either with one parent working abroad or both doing so but in different countries. Those women who have children left behind experience a phenomenon referred to as 'transnational motherhood'.[11]

With temporary migration involving highly feminised streams, this entails reversed gender roles by which a wife becomes the family's breadwinner while her husband is supposed to attend to the children and household. Studies have shown that marital conflict frequently results from this, at least in the initial stages, as such role reversal tends to challenge men's sense of masculinity, especially for those who experience long-term unemployment in a stagnant economy.[12]

On an individual level it has been noted that 'although all migrants can be agents of change, migrant women are more likely to have their personal development thwarted' (than men).[13] This is an overtly generalised statement which requires qualification. Research has shown that women tend to view out-migration more as part of their personal development (by breaking out of social conventions and gaining more personal space and freedoms, as well as higher economic/social status) than men.[14] In addition to having narrowly defined economic reasons (which are typically the main focus in the debate on the 'migration–development nexus', women also (and in some cases predominantly) use migration as an escape route from unwanted marriages or to get away from abusive relationships or husbands who do not manage to provide for the family.[15] This can also be an unintended consequence of the migration experience where the decision to migrate might have been initially driven purely by economic concerns. Sometimes women subsequently begin to appreciate life away from husbands and extended families. What has not been explored enough is the impact of women's out-migration on other women in the extended family and the additional burden placed on them (for instance sister-to-sister relations, or niece-to-aunt).

Research on Asian migrants has well demonstrated that migrants are socialised to treat out-migration as 'for the sake of the family'.[16] In this sense a focus on the family as unit of analysis for the investigation of the development outcome of migration is valid and important. Asis, for instance, maintains that the migration of individuals in the developing world is part and parcel of family strategies for securing livelihoods.[17] A focus on families allows us to establish a bridge between those who physically migrate and those who are left behind—and the gender dynamics and differences depending on who the migrants and non-migrants are. Studies on earlier waves of intra-Asian migration, which tended to involve predominantly men going to the Middle East, have mostly focused on the impact of male out-migration on women left behind, as in the case of studies on Kerala and the so-called 'Gulf wives'.[18] The findings were of a mixed nature: on the one hand women benefited from higher levels of independence and decision-making power; but the strain of the increased workload and responsibilities was in some cases found to have had negative implications.

More recent waves that involve greater levels of feminisation have triggered studies on the impact of women's out-migration on gender relations and families left behind. Research is particularly advanced in the case of the Philippines, where studies have been conducted on the reconstruction of men's sense of masculinity in the event of their wives' taking on the role of the main income earner by way of overseas employment. Pingol argues that there are basically two types of men: those who try to adapt and make the best of the situation and those who cannot cope and burden other (usually female) members of the family with responsibilities previously taken care of by their now absent wives.[19] Among the latter type are often those men who end up engaging in adulterous relationships, neglect work and their children.

Gamburd has shown that certain male 'vices' such as drinking and gambling are, however, often reasons why women opt for migration rather than the result thereof.[20]

Interestingly enough the focus of research on the impact of parental out-migration on children has been on the 'absentee' mothers and not on 'absentee' fathers. A case in point is the study conducted by Battistella and Conaco among elementary school children of Filipino migrants.[21] Comparing children from families where one parent is absent with those where both parents are working overseas, they found that most disruptive impacts occur when the mother is absent. Fathers were found to be unable to take on the mothering role effectively. Thus, the degree of involvement of other women in the extended family is an important determinant of the guidance that children can get. A newer study headed by the Scalabrini Migration Centre, however, shows a more complex and balanced picture of the so far purely negatively portrayed impact of absent mothers on their children. This study differentiates the category of 'child' into a number of age groups and shows by a number of indicators that 'not all is bad' when mothers migrate for work abroad.[22]

This issue area of changing family relations and the impact of migration on those left behind needs to be subject to more research, especially research that is based on data or surveys from different time periods to allow for an assessment of change over time. The topic of changes within family structures also represents an area which deserves more policy intervention by origin countries.

Feminisation of migration in Asia

According to the 2006 United Nations Population Fund (UNFPA) report on women and international migration, Asia as a whole is one of the two regions in this world (the other is Africa) where there were still slightly more male than female migrants by the year 2005. The number of women migrating from some countries in Asia, however, has clearly surpassed that of men.[23] Men, by contrast, are noted by the above UNFPA report as migrating from almost all developing countries in Asia without exception, whereas there are only three sources of countries from which the bulk of female migrants originate: the Philippines, Sri Lanka and Indonesia. These observations seem to contradict the view that a 'feminisation of migration' has occurred. It is argued here, however, that these observations need to be qualified.

Visibility and invisibility of migrant women

There is first of all the geographic dimension: UN reports typically make reference to 'Asia' by including West Asia, or the Gulf countries. It is also often not clear whether statements like those above relate to out-flowing or incoming migration. The numbers of women migrating *from* the Gulf countries in the search for work are negligible and the number of women migrating *to* Gulf countries is a little less than for men because of the huge demand for foreign workforce in both female and male dominated sectors. Likewise, with the exception of Sri Lanka, migration *from* South Asia is dominated by men (which is linked to the specific labour market demands by the destination countries this flow of migration is directed towards, as well as to social norms limiting women's physical mobility).[24] However, when shifting the lens to Southeast Asia, we find two countries which clearly represent the sources of the most feminised migration streams: the Philippines and Indonesia.

The second dimension is overall visibility of women in official statistics: conventionally women were long perceived as 'accompanying spouses' and not as independent labour migrants. Furthermore, statistics often capture only formalised jobs under temporary contract or any other legal schemes. Women are mainly represented in these temporary contract schemes as domestic workers although they also migrate in other, albeit often informal, streams which are not captured by official statistics. Hence, it often appears statistically as if fewer women migrated from certain countries or to certain countries although in reality this is not quite the case. Recent studies that include irregular migration have shown that women are well represented in such streams (eg Burmese migration to Thailand, which is to almost 50% male and female[25]).

Third, there is the labour market dimension which explains the increasing participation of women in migration as a result of growing demand for jobs in highly feminised sectors (health care, domestic work, entertainment, manufacturing/textile sector) in many destination countries in Asia, such as Hong Kong, Singapore and Malaysia. This is juxtaposed with the increasing inability of men to find full-time employment in origin as well as destination countries, pushing their wives or daughters into the role of main income provider.[26] In this sense, the 'feminisation of migration' can refer to a number of different issues, such as the absolute number of female migrants as out-going migrants or incoming migrants, the increasing participation rate of women (whereby the absolute number of male migrants might still be higher or the balance between the two sexes almost equal, such as in Cambodia and Vietnam), their dominance in certain sectors or specific migration streams, etc.

Hence changing labour market structures resulting in shortages or over-supply of specific types of workers at the origin and destination, as well as specific social norms allowing higher or lower degrees of women's physical mobility determine the gendered differences in migration. A rigid gendered division of labour determines that men are over-represented in the construction sector and security services, rubber plantations or the shipyard sector in Southeast Asia, and in the construction and manufacturing sector of small to medium-sized companies in East Asia, whereas women dominate in jobs connected to social reproduction (eg care and domestic work) or work which requires 'nimble fingers' (eg textile manufacturing).

Last but not least there is the policy dimension, which is to some extent linked to social norms and understanding of men's and women's appropriate roles. Out-migration of Vietnamese women as labour migrants, for instance, is numerically quite low because of the government's ban on allowing women to migrate to work as domestic and care workers. However, this partially explains the greater use of another channel for migration: international marriage (see below).

The feminisation of migration in Asia is most visible, and thus usually associated, with out-going flows from Indonesia, Sri Lanka and the Philippines, where women make up 62%–%75 per cent of workers who are deployed legally on an annual basis.[27] South Asia is mainly a labour exporting sub-region where women's (official) mobility is subject to serious restrictions (with the notable exception of Sri Lanka). Hence countries such as Bangladesh predominantly send male migrants. It has to be noted, however, that mobility is not limited *per se* but shaped by sector and skill level. In India and Bangladesh, for instance, skilled women's migration is not limited, but there are limits on domestic workers. In all these countries female internal migrants outnumber men because of marriage migration. In view of this, it is the specific nature of the mobility that is restricted and this is done through official controls (sex and domestic work) and unofficial controls (discursive limits on single female mobility because of the social construction of femininity, a gendered social order with an increased women's workload which is then not easily redistributed outside the family because of, among others, patrilocality.

If, however, irregular migrants were factored in, the feminisation of migration would involve more countries, such as women from Burma and Laos. This is backed up by figures on regularised migrants in Thailand: in the 2007 registration by the Ministry of Labour (MOL) in Thailand, the proportion of females among migrants was 46% in the case of Burma and 53% for those from Lao PDR.[28] Yet there are important gender variations even with regard to irregular migration. In the case of Indonesia most irregular migrants appear to be men going to neighbouring Malaysia to work on plantations and in the construction sector. As far as existing research is concerned, most Indonesian domestic workers enter under legal contracts. In the Philippines, by contrast, men and women are more or less equally represented in irregular migration streams.[29]

In addition, and of increasing significance, are the rising numbers of international marriages between Asians, with the typical scenario being a woman from a lower income country such as Vietnam or the Philippines marrying a man from a higher income country in East Asia (Japan, Korea, Taiwan) and also Singapore. If international marriage were included in official statistics, the gendered landscape of migration within Asia would take on a different dimension. It might appear odd to include foreign wives in the discussion of economic migration but, as argued by Piper and Roces, the two streams are interrelated: many women are originally economic migrants and, partly because of the temporary contract nature of their visa and work permits, they seek marriage to a local man as a strategy to enable them to remain in the destination country in a legally secure manner ('worker-turns-wife' scenario); or they migrate as a foreign spouse and subsequently seek to enter the labour market (often because they wish to remit money to their families back home) ('wife-turns-worker' scenario).[30] But international wives are absent from statistics on economic migration in Asia—with the result that issues such as 'integration', 'settlement' and 'citizenship' are largely absent from, or have only very recently begun to be addressed in, policy and academic debates.

Diversified landscape of gendered migration

Overall changes are gradually becoming evident not only with regard to the increased volume of female migrants, but also with regard to the diversified patterns of their migration, including source and destination countries, and the qualitative nature and experience of their migration (in terms of working conditions, range of entitlements, skill levels, etc). The largest proportion of these women, documented and undocumented, continues to work in job categories characteristically assigned to female migrants, such as live-in domestic workers, care givers, entertainers, sex workers and other service employees.[31] A smaller but substantial proportion of women work in the garment sector and as agricultural and fish farm hands.

Diversification and rising numbers of migrants are also related to changing politico-economic structures. Former socialist countries such as Mongolia and Vietnam, for instance, used to send migrants mostly to socialist countries in Eastern Europe. Since the change from centrally planned to market-driven systems in the 1990s, both countries have begun to actively 'export' increasing numbers of migrants by way of signing Memoranda of Under-standing (MOUs) with various destination countries in Asia and to a lesser extent elsewhere. Vietnam has as a result become a source country of male and female factory workers in Korea and Taiwan and more recently also of a small number of domestic workers in Taiwan after years of banning such migration. Mongolian labour migrants are mostly men but in Korea we find a great number of entire families, albeit mostly in an irregular situation because of a lack of family unification policies for lower skilled migrants.

From what is known about Cambodian out-migration it seems to be mainly destined for Thailand but more recently small numbers have also been found in Malaysia. In a study from 1999 their flows are divided into short-term/short-range border crossing (typically seasonal agricultural workers, the majority of whom are women) and longer-term/longer-range movements (mainly as construction workers, porters, factory and food processing workers, most of whom are men).[32] A recent mapping study for United Nations Development Fund for Women (UNIFEM), however, shows that, although overall numbers are still small, Cambodia women are increasingly migrating not only to Thailand but also to Malaysia as factory and domestic workers.[33] Migration of Laotian workers is equally mainly directed at Thailand, of whom more are female (59.4%) than male (40.6%).[34] Women from Burma, Cambodia and Laos are overtly represented in domestic employment in Thailand.

The policies of destination countries in East Asia also determine the gendered nature of migration flows. Neither Japan nor Korea allows the legal immigration of lower skilled migrants and each has in turn established so-called 'trainee systems' to allow the legal entry of this group of migrants. Partly because of pressure from civil society organisations backed up by some employers, Korea has begun to phase out its industrial training scheme and currently runs a parallel employment permit system for lower skilled migrants. These industrial trainees are mostly men and the number of women among them is negligible.[35]

Recently skilled and professional women have migrated in larger numbers in response to expanding employment opportunities in business, health, education and services.[36] Except for foreign doctors and nurses, of whom there are substantial numbers in the Gulf countries as well as Singapore and Hong Kong, however, the overall numbers of skilled women moving within Asia are small. This has partly to do with destination countries' policies. In Singapore, for instance, it was until recently impossible for a female professional migrant to bring her husband as 'accompanying spouse' (although this has always been possible for male professionals). Another reason might be that student migration of Asians within Asia is comparatively low,[37] with the exception of Singapore which is developing into a regional education hub. Yet studies have shown that student migration is often the first step towards economic migration for the skilled.[38] More destination countries in the North are in fact easing the shift from a student visa to employment visas in the wake of the global hunt for talent. This has not yet happened to any great degree in Asia.

Temporary contract migration

Although there are other types of migration—permanent migration, student migration, marriage migration, irregular migration—temporary contract migration has emerged as one of the predominant types of legal population movements in Asia.[39] Migration streams that are based on temporary contract work are both a characteristic of lower skilled sectors such as domestic work and of labouring jobs in the construction and shipyard sectors as well as for highly skilled workers in, for example, the health and education sectors. In this type of migration destination countries offer legal work permits for specific periods of time (ranging usually from one to three years) by tying migrants to a specific employer or sector. The result is a high level of flexibility in the event of labour market changes allowing the disposal of surplus workers in the event of economic downturns by avoiding long-term settlement. These contract labour schemes thus come with a bundle of restrictions, especially for the lower skilled, such as no permission for family or spousal unification; these do not apply to the highly skilled migrant worker. In general foreign worker policy in Asia can be broadly summarised as follows: limiting labour migration, limiting the duration of migration and limiting integration.[40] From the migrant worker perspective, although the strict regulations imposed on such workers have prevented their permanent settlement, the former have in other ways facilitated the regular employment of fairly large numbers of foreign labour.[41] For women the most easily accessible legal migration streams are domestic and care work.

In addition to domestic work a significant number of Southeast Asian (and other) women have also been entering East Asian countries, especially Japan and Korea, in response to a great demand for sexual labour. In order to allow these women legal entry (albeit limited to a period of six months, subject to renewal), the already existing visa category for artists or entertainers was broadened in the 1980s to include bar hostesses (who constitute potential sex workers). As a result, migrant women, mostly from the Philippines, Thailand and Korea, entered East Asian countries to work in the lucrative sex and entertainment industries via both legal and illegal channels. More recently, however, there has been a narrowing of these visa classes in part as a result of US pressure to counter trafficking, as for example in the case of Japan, which withdrew its hostess visas after pressure from the US State Department's Trafficking in Persons report in 2002. This resulted in tighter control of establishments and subsequently in decreasing numbers of (legal) foreign entertainers in Japan. To what extent this might have pushed more women into using illegal channels is unknown. But existing research has shown that this is typically what happens.

Changes in female migration

The above statistics and recent studies over the past few years point to at least two important changes in women's migration which are relevant to the discussion here.

First, and most evident, is the diversification of migrant women regarding origin countries in the search for overseas employment. As demands for migrant women's labour increased in the region and the sociopolitical situation changed in certain countries, opportunities opened up for women who originate from countries that had not previously been sources of migrant labour. These new faces include Vietnamese in Taiwan, Cambodians in Malaysia, and Mongolians and other Central Asians in Korea.[42] Needless to say this has increased the competition on the regional labour market and has led to undercutting in terms of wages in jobs such as domestic work. As touched upon above, this is also a result of the increasing number of MOUs and bilateral agreements signed between more and more countries.

The seeking of new sources of migrant labour is not related only to demand in terms of numbers, but also to demand for a different kind of worker: those less expensive, more docile (which is also a racialised position) and/or less 'rights' conscious. Successful campaigns for, and enforcement of, workers' protective mechanisms and/or rights in some countries have brought about unintended consequences in the nationality composition of their migrant work forces. An example is that of Filipino domestic workers in Hong Kong, who have been partially replaced by less organised, and thus less vocal and assertive, nationality groups,[43] such as Indonesians and Sri Lankans.[44] Partly because of the push by an expansive web of migrant associations, the Philippine government has been more proactive in negotiating on behalf of its citizens overseas than any other sending country in Asia.[45] Similarly, in Taiwan the proportion of Filipino women in the country's foreign domestic worker population is said to have plummeted significantly between 1998 and 2002 as they are being replaced by less 'expensive' Indonesian and Vietnamese women.[46] As a result, a new stratification is emerging, whereby women are ranked in the scale of demand and wages according to their nationality, ethnicity, class, educational level and available support networks.

Second, despite the absence of official settlement policies in Asia, changes are apparent in the prolonged duration of employment and residence among migrant women in destination countries. For example, since 2002 Taiwan has allowed migrant workers 'with good records' (in the sense of being compliant with employer demands and their migration status) to re-enter the country to work for up to six years.[47] There is evidence from Hong Kong that the number of Filipinas staying between five and 15 years is increasing as more of them choose to remain there (even if this entails an irregular status) rather than returning to the Philippines.[48] There has also been a considerable rise in the numbers and types of migrant women whose legal visa status grants them the right to reside and work indefinitely in the country to which they have migrated. This is evident from the rising numbers of women who arrive as wives of citizens in countries such as Japan, Korea,[49] Taiwan[50] and Singapore. Yet Asia, especially East and Southeast Asia, is conspicuous in terms of the absence of debates around issues such as integration, citizenship and rights to family unification. The predominant family life experienced by international migrants who are married and have children is currently that of transnationally split families. This has serious consequences for social relations and also social policy which remain largely unexplored.[51]

Many of the issues raised so far clearly point to the significance of broader *social* dimensions of development beyond narrowly economic aspects. But it is the latter which have to date dominated the debate on the migration–development nexus.

Last but not least: the issue of rights

Recent reports on migration and development have highlighted that this relationship should best work in two broad ways: 1) by enhancing the benefits of migration for all stakeholders (origin and destination societies as well as the individual migrants); and 2) by making migration more of a choice than a necessity. Both points essentially involve rights issues: the former in the form of transparent, legal migration policies which aim to protect basic rights for migrants (see below); the latter in terms of the 'right to not have to migrate in the first place', which would not only require the creation of more job opportunities locally, but also the realisation of broader social policy reforms.

Further on the individual level, not all migrants' personal development is enhanced by the migration experience, despite the recognition that migrants are not necessarily victims but also 'agents of change'.[52] Respecting migrant's rights, especially labour rights, as part of economic and social development is seen by some as the best long-term solution to reduce the pressures of out-migration.[53] Measures to improve the benefits of migration include providing migrants with a proper legal status, permission to change employer, and, for those accompanying their migrating spouses, permission to work when admitted for family reunification. For women migrants, these measures also include providing them with labour rights by acknowledging jobs such as domestic work as worthy of equal protection under labour laws to other sectors of work, or in the meantime providing standard contracts of employment which set out the agreed rights and minimum terms and conditions of employment between employer and migrant worker. In this regard important advancements have been made as the result of UNIFEM's (Bangkok regional office) migration programme in Jordan, with the adoption of standard contracts for all foreign domestic workers. This could serve as a good practice model for countries of destination elsewhere.

In the case where out-migration is chosen to secure livelihoods and for personal development, it has been argued that one of the important ways to ensure protection is via skills acquisition.[54] The higher the migrants' skills, the better their negotiating power and the more likely they get 'good deals' (level of wages, working hours, days off). In this sense there is a clear link to human and social capital building. The issue of 'skills' has received some attention in migration scholarship in a different context also: by pointing to the limitations to 'upward social mobility' for the lower skilled, especially in the case of female migrants (thanks to their positioning at the bottom end of gender and ethnically segregated job markets or in dead-end jobs such as domestic work). The issue of 'de-skilling' has also been raised by scholars pointing to the case of well educated female migrants taking on low-skilled work, such as a teacher turned into a domestic worker, because of the sheer demand and the relative inability to access other legal channels.[55]

One of the important ways of protecting female migrants and guaranteeing 'successful' migration, therefore, is via the acquisition of skills or the recognition of certain jobs as skilled (since the category of 'skilled' typically comes with better rights and entitlements than that of 'unskilled'). This relates to a broader understanding of 'rights' in the sense of 'right to self-development'.[56] This acquisition of new skills does not only refer to work-related skills (language, job training) but also to financial skills (budgeting, planning and strategising for the future) which would assist migrant women to reap financial rewards from their overseas employment. Too often in the past women have returned to find that their remittances were all spent and no savings made.[57] In this regard the training and skill programmes offered to foreign domestic workers by various non-profit organisations in Singapore, Malaysia and Hong Kong, partly based on a strategy developed by Filipino and Hong Kong based NGOs, called 'Migrant Savings for Alternative Investment' (MSAI), seem important developments to ameliorate this situation.[58]

The MSAI strategy was pioneered by the Asian Migrant Centre in Hong Kong and Unlad Kabayan, a migrant association in the Philippines to prepare migrants (mostly domestic workers) for their return. It encourages migrants' saving and, in co-operation with communities and organisations in the home countries, livelihood projects are designed and carried out with the migrants' savings. This strategy is, thus, an attempt to link the 'right to development' with the 'right not to have to migrate in the first place'.

Rights-based approach

What is still missing from the debate on the migration–development nexus are the broader connections between migration and development from a rights-based approach and a more fundamental understanding of the type of 'rights' at stake. Social rights (social security benefits, child care provisions, etc) are largely absent from this debate and hardly ever contextualised with migration policies. The broader right to family life has only recently become a topic on the agenda of migrant rights advocates in Asia. A systematic analysis of the linkages between migration, social development and social policy has not been undertaken, and as a result the long-term effects of migration on issues such as redistribution, social cohesion, equality (gender, caste, ethnic/racial) and rights are under-explored.[59]

As argued here, rights are one of the important ways in which to address the fundamental root causes of migration. This was highlighted by the Migrant Committee (the Treaty Body of the International Convention for the Rights of All Migrant Workers and their Families) in its statement contributing to the UN High-level Dialogue on Migration and Development of the General Assembly in September 2006. In this statement the Committee recalls 'that the human being is the central subject of development and should be the active participant and beneficiary of the right to development, as set forth in the Declaration on the Right to Development'.[60] As per Article 1 of this Declaration (from 1986), 'the right to development is an inalienable human right by virtue of which every human person and all peoples are entitled to participate in, contribute to, and enjoy economic, social, cultural and political development, in which all human rights and fundamental freedoms can be fully realized.' What deserves to be especially highlighted is the emphasis of rights-based approaches on being 'people-centred' and people's 'ability to claim rights or entitlements'.[61] Within the policy-making world at the global level this is especially recognised by the International Labour Organisation (ILO) in its activities surrounding the revival of its rights-based approach to economic migration, as well as by UNIFEM in Bangkok (in its *Empowering Women Migrant Workers in Asia—A Briefing Kit*).

This has specific relevance to women migrants from the South, who tend to face serious constraints on realising their labour and social rights based on the type of jobs they mostly perform and the rigidity of prescribed gender roles. A specific (and fairly well researched) example of migrant women demonstrating concrete action with regard to claiming their rights is the collective organising of foreign domestic workers in Hong Kong. The organising activities in Hong Kong occur 'trans-ethnically' (as domestic workers of various nationalities are involved) and 'trans-institutionally' (in the form of an NGO–trade union alliance).[62] One of the reasons why Hong Kong has emerged as a unique site for migrant rights activism is the political space given to trade unionism (the 'freedom of association' is a core labour standard championed by the ILO but its violation is widespread) and other civil society organisations, as well as the opportunity for migrants to set up their own organisations.[63]

Apart from the ILO framework for migrants' rights in their capacity as workers, an alternative human rights framework that can be invoked to address the specific concerns and needs of migrant women is the UN Convention for the Elimination of Discrimination Against Women (CEDAW).[64] This route could prove more successful given CEDAW's wide ratification rate.

Conclusion

This paper offers an initial and rudimentary discussion of the linkages between migration and development with reference to the feminisation of intra-regional migratory flows in Asia. Aiming to improve their livelihoods and that of their families in the face of rising male un- or under-employment, increasing numbers of women seek work in foreign countries in different types of occupations. Migration is not necessarily their first choice but at times a reflection of changing labour market structures 'at home' and 'abroad' that offer specific job opportunities abroad in highly gendered job categories. Restrictive migration policies and the prevalence of temporary contract schemes, in combination with many migrant women's economic and social contributions being undervalued and their work being often legally unrecognised, pose serious limitations to women migrants' chances for personal socioeconomic empowerment.

Notwithstanding the rich contributions migrants make, several reservations are therefore in order, particularly concerning a general tendency towards excessive (or at least premature) optimism with respect to the development potential of migration. On the positive side, scholars highlight a number of vehicles through which migrants affect development in their countries of origin via remittances, investment, skill development and other forms of 'learning' as well as through transnational communities and networks. This body of research highlighting these positive aspects, however, is largely based on quite specific case studies in the context of South–North migration which tend to be male dominated. The specific features of the temporary migration of lower skilled workers, many of whom are women, and of those who leave families behind, may have significant, but very different, development implications, about which we still know too little at the moment.[65]

What is clear, however, is that migration poses a new challenge in the subject area of women's rights, development and citizenship for research and policy makers alike.[66] Especially the conceptual and normative linkages between women's social and economic rights as they relate to migration need further exploration in specific geographic or cultural settings. At the policy level a deeper analysis of the linkages between various fields of policy (migration and public/social policy) is needed to inform relevant policy developments that target male and female migrants alike as well as their families left behind.

Notes

An earlier version of this paper is part of the *Regional Report on International Migration in East and Southeast Asia* which will be published later in 2008 by UNIFEM Bangkok.

1 United Nations, *World Survey on the Role of Women in Development—Women and International Migration*, New York: UN, 2004; UNFPA, *A Passage to Hope—Women and International Migration*, New York: UNFPA, 2006; Global Commission on International Migration (GCIM), *Migration in an Interconnected World: New Directions for Action*, Geneva: GCIM, 2005; and N Piper, 'Gender and migration', paper prepared for the Policy Analysis and Research Programme of the Global Commission on International Migration, Geneva, 2005.

2 N Piper (ed), *New Perspectives on Gender and Migration: Rights, Entitlements and Livelihoods*, London: Routledge, 2008; Piper, 'Gendering the politics of migration', *International Migration Review*, 40 (1), 2006, pp 133–164; and D Gabaccia, KM Donato, J Holdaway, M Manalansan IV & PR Pessar (eds), 'A glass half full? Gender in migration studies', *International Migration Review*, 40 (1), 2006, pp 3–26.

3 Piper, *New Perspectives on Gender and Migration*.

4 K Hujo & N Piper, 'South–South migration: challenges for development and social policy', *Development*, 50 (4), 2007, pp 1–7.

5 United Nations, *International Migration and Development—Report of the Secretary-General*, A/60/871, 18 May 2006, New York; and United Nations, *World Survey on the Role of Women in Development*.

6 H de Haas, 'Migration and development: a theoretical perspective', paper presented at the 'International Conference on Transnationalisation and Development(s): Towards a North–South Perspective', University of Bielefeld, 31 May–1 June 2007.

7 P Levitt, & N Nyberg Sørensen, 'The transnational turn in migration studies', *Global Migration Perspectives*, 6, Geneva: GCIM, 2004.

8 ET Gomez, 'Inter-ethnic relations, business and identity: the Chinese in Britain and Malaysia', in N Tarling & ET Gomez (eds), *The State, Development and Identity in Multi-Ethnic Societies: Ethnicity, Equity and the Nation*, London: Routledge, 2007, pp 19–40; and Gesellschaft für Technische Zusammenarbeit (GTZ), *Migration and Development*, Bonn: GTZ, 2006, at http://www2.gtz.de/migration-and-development/, accessed September 2006.

9 Piper, *New Perspectives on Gender and Migration*.

10 P Dannecker, 'Migration and the construction of development: a gendered approach', paper presented at the 'International Conference on Transnationalisation and Development(s): Towards a North–South Perspective', University of Beilefeld, 31 May–1 June 2007.

11 A Hochschild Russell, 'Love and gold', in B Ehrenreich & A Hochschild Russell (eds), *Global Woman: Nannies, Maids and Sex Workers in the New Economy*, New York: Metropolitan Books, 2002, pp 3–17; P Hondagneu-Sotelo, *Doméstica: Immigrant Workers Cleaning and Caring in the Shadows of Affluence*, Berkeley, CA: University of California Press, 2001; and P Hondagneu-Sotelo & E Avila, 'I'm here, but I'm not there': the meaning of Latina transnational motherhood', *Gender and Society*, 11 (5), 1997, pp 548–571.

12 R Gamburd, *The Kitchen Spoon's Handle: Transnationalism and Sri Lanka's Migrant Households*, Ithaca, NY: Cornell University Press, 2001; and RS Parreñas, *Children of Global Migration: Transnational Families and Gendered Woes*, Stanford, CA: Stanford University Press, 2005.

13 United Nations, *International Migration and Development*, p 15.

14 Dannecker, 'Migration and the construction of development'.

15 As found by Gamburd, *The Kitchen Spoon's Handle*, in the case of Sri Lankan domestic workers; by N Piper, 'International marriage in Japan: "race" & "gender" perspectives', *Gender, Place and Culture*, 4 (3), 1997, pp 321–338, in the case of Filipino entertainers; and by N Oishi, *Women in Motion—Globalization, State Policies, and Labor Migration in Asia*, Stanford, CA: Stanford University Press, 2005, in the case of various nationalities.

16 BSA Yeoh, E Graham & PJ Boyle (eds), 'Migrations and Family Relations in the Asia Pacific Region', *Asian and Pacific Migration Journal*, 11 (1), 2002, special issue.

17 MMB Asis, 'International migration and families in Asia', in R Iredale, C Hawksley & S Castles (eds), *Migration in the Asia Pacific: Population, Settlement and Citizenship Issues*, Cheltenham: Edward Elgar, pp 43–61.

18 KC Zachariah, ET Mathew & S Irudaya Rajan , 'Impact of migration on Kerala's economy and society', *Working Paper 297*, Trivandrum, Kerala: Centre for Development Studies, 1999.

19 A Pingol , 'Illocano masculinities', *Asian Studies*, 36 (1), 2000, pp 123–134.

20 Gamburd, *The Kitchen Spoon's Handle*.

21 G Battistella & MCG Conaco, 'The impact of labor migration on the children left behind: a study of elementary school children in the Philippines', *Sojourn: Journal of Social Issues in Southeast Asia*, 13 (2), 1998, pp 220–243.

22 Scalabrini Migration Center, Episcopal Commission for the Pastoral Care of Migrants and Itinerant People-CBCP/Apostleship of the Sea-Manila and Overseas Workers Welfare Administration, *Hearts Apart*, Quezon City: Scalabrini Migration Center, 2004.

23 *Ibid* (UNFPA), p 23.

24 For a more detailed discussion, see Oishi, *Women in Motion*.

25 I Phetsiriseng, 'Gender concerns in migration in Lao PDR—migration mapping study: a review of trends, policy and programme initiatives', study conducted for UNIFEM, Bangkok, 2007.

26 Piper, *New Perspectives on Gender and Migration*.

27 MMB Asis, 'Recent trends in international migration in Asia and the Pacific', *Asian and Pacific Population Journal*, 20 (3), 2005, pp 15–38.

28 I owe this point to Dr Jerrold W Huguet. Email communication, 10 September 2007.

29 Asis, 'Recent trends in international migration in Asia and the Pacific'.

30 N Piper, 'Wife or worker? Worker or wife? Marriage and cross-border migration in contemporary Japan', *International Journal for Population Geography*, 9 (6), 2005, pp 457–469; and N Piper & M Roces (eds), *Wife or Worker? Asian Women and Migration*, Lanham, MD: Rowman & Littlefield, 2003.

31 See 'Gender, migration and governance in Asia', *Asian and Pacific Migration Journal*, special issue, 12 (1–2), 2003.

32 C Sophal & S Sovannarith, 'Cambodian labour migration to Thailand: a preliminary assessment', *Working Paper 11*, Phnom Penh: Cambodia Development Resource Institute, 1999.

33 CC Lee, *Cambodian Women Migrant Workers: Findings from a Migration Mapping Study*, Phnom Penh: UNIFEM, 2006.

34 Phetsiriseng, 'Gender concerns in migration in Lao PDR', p 25.

35 Japan NGO Network on Indonesia (JANNI), *Technical Interns or Menial Labourers? The Reality of Indonesian Trainees and Technical Interns*, Tokyo: JANNI, 2001.

36 P Raghuram, 'Gendering skilled migratory streams: implications for conceptualisations of migration', *Asian and Pacific Migration Journal*, 9 (4), 2000, pp 429–457; LL Thang, E MacLachlan & M Goda, 'Expatriates on the margins: a study of Japanese women in Singapore', *Geoforum*, 33 (4), 2002, pp 539–551; and KD Willis & BSA Yeoh ,'Gender and transnational household strategies: Singaporean migration to China', *Regional Studies*, 34 (3), 2000, pp 253–264.

37 G Hugo, 'Migration and development in Asia', paper presented at the 'International Conference on Population and Development in Asia: Critical Issues for a Sustainable Future', Phuket, 20–22 March 2006.

38 FLN Li, AM Findlay, AJ Jowett & R Skeldon, 'Migrating to learn and learning to migrate: a study of the experiences and intentions of international student migrants', *International Journal of Population Geography*, 2, 1996, pp 51–67.

39 Piper, *New Perspectives on Gender and Migration*.

40 N Piper, 'Rights of foreign domestic workers—emergence of transnational and transregional solidarity?', *Asian and Pacific Migration Journal*, 14 (1–2), 2005, pp 97–120.

41 D Bell & N Piper, 'Justice for migrant workers? The case of foreign domestic workers in East Asia', in W Kymlicka & B Ye (eds), *Asian Minorities and Western Liberalism*, Oxford: Oxford University Press, 2005, pp 196–222.

42 K Yamanaka & N Piper, 'Feminised migration in East and Southeast Asia: policies, actions and empowerment', *UNRISD Occasional Paper 11*, Geneva: UNRISD, 2006.

43 The reasons for such variable 'national assertiveness' are themselves interesting.

44 C Ogaya, 'Feminization and empowerment: organisational activities of Filipino women workers in Hong Kong and Singapore', in M Tsuda (ed), *Filipino Diaspora: Demography, Social Networks, Empowerment and Culture*, Quezon City: Philippine Social Science Council/UNESCO, 2003, pp 25–46.

45 R Iredale, N Piper & A Ancog, 'Impact of ratifying the 1990 UN Convention on the Rights of All Migrant Workers and Members of Their Family: case studies of the Philippines and Sri Lanka', *APMRN Working Paper 15*, Canberra: Australian National University, Australia, 2005.

46 PC Lan, 'Political and social geography of marginal insiders: migrant domestic workers in Taiwan', *Asian and Pacific Migration Journal*, 12 (1–2), 2003, pp 99–125.

47 *Ibid*, p 105.

48 V Wee & A Sim, 'Hong Kong as a destination for migrant domestic workers', in S Huang, BSA Yeoh & N Abdul Rahman (eds), *Asian Women as Transnational Domestic Workers*, Singapore: Marshall Cavendish, 2005, pp 58–83.

49 HK Lee, 'Gender, migration and civil activism in South Korea', *Asian and Pacific Migration Journal*, 12 (1–2), 2003, pp 127–154; T Nakamatsu, 'International marriage through introduction agencies: social and legal realities of "Asian" wives of Japanese men', in Piper & Roces, *Wife or Worker?*, pp 181–202; and Piper, 'International marriage in Japan'.

50 UNFPA, *A Passage to Hope*.

51 Hujo & Piper, 'South–South migration'.

52 United Nations, *International Migration and Development*, p 15, with specific reference to migrant women.

53 United Nations, *World Survey on the Role of Women in Development*; UNFPA, *A Passage to Hope*; and GCIM, *Migration in an Interconnected World*.

54 N Piper & K Yamanaka, 'Feminised migration in East and Southeast Asia and the securing of livelihoods', in Piper, *New Perspectives on Gender and Migration*, pp 159–188.

55 Piper, *New Perspectives on Gender and Migration*.

56 This is also broader than the 'right to development' as per the 1986 UN Declaration on the Right to Development. See also next sub-section.

57 Personal communication from staff at the National Committee for UNIFEM, Singapore, March 2006.

58 L Macabuag & JM Dimaandal, 'Working together for migrants' empowerment', *Asian and Pacific Migration Journal*, 15 (3), 2006, pp 415–424; and K Gibson, L Law & D McKay, 'Beyond heroes and victims: Filipina contract migrants, economic activism and class transformation', *International Feminist Journal of Politics*, 3 (3), 2002, pp 365–386.

59 Hujo & Piper, 'South–South migration', pp 1–7.

60 Statement 2006, p 2. A hardcopy of this statement is in the author's possession but it is not available on-line.

61 J Grugel & N Piper, *Critical Perspectives on Global Governance: Rights and Regulation in Governing Regimes*, London: Routledge, 2007.

62 Piper, 'Rights of foreign domestic workers'.

63 N Piper, 'Political participation and empowerment of foreign workers—gendered advocacy and migrant labour organising in Southeast and East Asia', in Piper, *New Perspectives on Gender and Migration*, pp 247–274.

64 UNIFEM, *UNIFEM–CEDAW Panel on Addressing Women Migrant Workers' Concerns*, New York: UNIFEM, 2003.

65 Hujo & Piper, 'South–South migration'; and Dannecker, 'Migration and the construction of development'.

66 As also highlighted by the International Development Research Centre (IDRC), *Women's Rights and Citizenship—Program Initiative*, Ottawa: IDRC, 2006.

The Myth of Invasion:
the inconvenient realities of
African migration to Europe

HEIN DE HAAS

In recent years irregular migration from Africa to Europe has received extensive attention. Sensational media reportage and popular discourses give rise to an apocalyptic image of a wave or 'exodus' of 'desperate' Africans fleeing poverty at home in search of the European 'el Dorado' crammed in long-worn ships barely staying afloat.[1] Millions of sub-Saharan Africans are commonly believed to be waiting in North Africa to cross to Europe, which fuels the fear of an invasion.

The conventional wisdom underlying such argumentations is that war and poverty are the root causes of mass migration across and from Africa. Popular images of extreme poverty, starvation, tribal warfare and environmental degradation amalgamate into a stereotypical image of 'African misery' as the assumed causes of a swelling tide of northbound African migrants.

Politicians and the media on both sides of the Mediterranean commonly employ terms like 'massive invasion' and 'plague' to describe this phenomenon.[2] In July 2006 French President Jacques Chirac warned that

Africans 'will flood the world' unless more is done to develop the continent's economy. In North Africa, too, migration-related xenophobia towards sub-Saharan migrants is gaining ground. Not only media and politicians, but also scholars frequently resort to doomsdays scenarios to make their case. For instance, Norman Myers recently stated that the current flow of environmental refugees from Africa to Europe 'will surely come to be regarded as a trickle when compared with the floods that will ensue in decades ahead'.[3]

Irregular migration occurring from sub-Saharan Africa and the Maghreb to Europe has increasingly been defined as a security problem associated with international crime and, particularly since the attacks of 11 March 2004 in Madrid and 7 July 2005 in London, terrorism.[4] The migrants themselves are commonly depicted as 'desperate' and (supposedly passive) victims of 'merciless', 'ruthless' and 'unscrupulous' traffickers and criminal-run smuggling gangs. Or, as the United Nations Office on Drugs and Crime (UNODC) recently stated, 'The system of migrant smuggling ... has become nothing more than a mechanism for robbing and murdering some of the poorest people of the world'.[5]

Hence the perceived 'solutions' to this phenomenon—which invariably boil down to curbing migration—focus on 'fighting' and 'combating' illegal migration through a crackdown on trafficking and smuggling networks in combination with the intensification of border controls. In a perceived effort to 'externalise' border controls, EU states have exerted pressure on Maghreb states to clamp down on irregular migration occurring over their territory through increasing border controls, toughening migration law, readmitting irregular sub-Saharan migrants from Europe and deporting them from their own national territories.[6]

A second policy 'solution', advocated mainly by African states and humanitarian NGOs, is to spur development through aid and trade, which is believed to remove the need to migrate.[7] In the aftermath of the migration crises in the Spanish enclaves of Ceuta and Melilla in northern Morocco, Spain joined Morocco in calling for a 'Marshall Plan' for Africa in the hope that it will stem the flow of migrants to Europe.[8] A third 'solution' advocated by governments in Europe and Africa is the launch of information campaigns aiming to discourage migration by raising awareness among would-be migrants of the perils of the journey and the difficult life in Europe or to encourage migrants to return.[9]

This paper will argue that such views are based on fundamentally flawed assumptions about the actual magnitude, nature and causes of African migration to Europe, which is not so massive, new or so driven by 'African misery' as is commonly assumed. After describing how African migration to Europe has evolved over the past half-century, the paper will scrutinise policy approaches towards irregular migration, as well as their effects. Based on this analysis, the paper questions the idea that European states have (successfully) externalised border controls to the Maghreb and that European and African states, or the particular interest groups they comprise, are genuinely able and willing to stop migration.

Trends in African–European migration

Since the 1960s the overwhelming majority of African migrants moving to Europe has originated from Morocco, Algeria and Tunisia. At the turn of the 21st century, at least 2.6 million Moroccans, 1.2 million Algerians and 700 000 Tunisians (including second generation) were believed to be living in Europe.[10] Increasing immigration restrictions in Europe introduced since the 1973 oil crisis did not curb migration, but rather encouraged permanent settlement and family migration from the Maghreb to the traditional destination countries: France, The Netherlands, Belgium and Germany. Since the late 1980s Maghrebi migrants have increasingly moved to Italy and Spain in response to the growing demand for low-skilled labour in southern Europe.

Europe has long been familiar with irregular migration from the Maghreb. Since Spain and Italy introduced visa requirements for Maghrebi immigrants in the early 1990s, hundreds of thousands of Maghrebis have attempted to cross the Mediterranean illegally in *pateras* (small fishing boats chartered by smugglers), speedboats, hidden in vans and trucks, or carrying false papers. However, as the migration crises in Morocco's Spanish enclaves in 2005 and Spain's Canary Islands in 2006 exemplified, sub-Saharan Africans have increasingly joined Maghrebis in their attempts to cross the Mediterranean since 2000. This was preceded by a period of increasing trans-Saharan migration. While having ancient historical roots in the trans-Saharan trade, the foundations of contemporary trans-Saharan migration were laid in the 1970s and 1980s when (former) nomads and traders started migrating to work at construction sites and the oil fields of southern Algeria and Libya. Such immigration was often openly or tacitly welcomed, because migrants filled local labour shortages and fitted into policies to revitalise under-populated desert regions.

The air and arms embargo imposed on Libya by the UN Security Council between 1992 and 2000 played an unintended, but probably decisive, role in an unprecedented increase in trans-Saharan migration. Disappointed by the perceived lack of support from fellow Arab leaders during the embargo, Libyan leader Muammar al-Qadhafi embarked upon a radical reorientation of Libyan foreign policy towards a pan-African approach, in which he positioned himself as an African leader. In the spirit of pan-African solidarity, al-Qadhafi started to welcome sub-Saharan Africans to work in Libya. Traditionally a destination for migrants from North African countries, Libya rapidly evolved into a major destination for migrants from a wide array of countries in West Africa and the Horn of Africa.[11]

Attitudes towards immigrants hardened after Libya experienced a major anti-immigrant backlash after clashes between Libyans and African workers in 2000 led to the deaths of dozens or perhaps hundreds of sub-Saharan migrants. Consequently the Libyan authorities, responding to strong popular resentment against sub-Saharan immigrants, introduced more restrictive immigration regulations. This went along with lengthy and arbitrary detention of immigrants in poor conditions in prisons and camps, with physical abuse, and the forced repatriation of tens of thousands of sub-Saharan immigrants.[12]

Besides the increasingly irregular character of migration into Libya, this backlash resulted in a partial westward shift of trans-Saharan migration routes towards Algeria, Morocco and Tunisia. From there increasing numbers have joined Maghrebis in their attempts to cross the Mediterranean. In addition, sub-Saharan migrants in Libya have increasingly tried to cross to Europe from the Libyan coast. Trans-Saharan migrants have come from an increasingly diverse array of countries in West Africa, Central Africa and the Horn of Africa. Even migrants from China, India, Pakistan and Bangladesh have recently migrated to the Maghreb and Europe after having flown to West African capitals such as Accra or Bamako.[13]

Although commonly portrayed as destitute or desperate, migrants are often relatively well educated and from reasonably well-off backgrounds, not least because of the relatively high costs of the journey. Although migrants are commonly depicted as victims of unscrupulous traffickers and smugglers, empirical evidence has indicated that the vast majority migrate on their own initiative.[14] Migrants typically pay for one difficult leg of the journey, usually involving a border crossing, at a time.[15] Often smugglers are not part of international organised crime but tend to be former nomads and immigrants who operate relatively small networks.[16]

Between 65 000 and 120 000 sub-Saharan Africans are estimated to enter the Maghreb yearly, of whom 70% to 80% are believed to migrate through Libya and 20% to 30% through Algeria and Morocco.[17] Several tens of thousands try to cross the Mediterranean each year, not hundreds of thousands or millions, as media coverage might suggest. This counters common views that reduce North Africa to a transit zone, waiting room or springboard to Europe. The common term 'transit migrant' is potentially misleading because many migrants consider North Africa (particularly Libya) as their primary destination, and a considerable proportion of migrants failing or not venturing to enter Europe prefer to stay in North Africa as a second-best option rather than returning to their more unstable, unsafe and substantially poorer origin countries.[18]

At least 100 000 sub-Saharan migrants now live in both Mauritania and Algeria and at least one to 1.5 million in Libya. Tunisia and Morocco house smaller but growing sub-Saharan immigrant communities of several tens of thousands.[19] While mostly lacking legal status and vulnerable to exploitation, sub-Saharan migrants living in North Africa do find jobs in specific niches of the informal service sector (such as cleaning and domestic work), construction, agriculture, petty trade and fishery. Others try to pursue studies, sometimes also as a means to gain residency status.[20] Trans-Saharan migration has also caused trade to flourish and has helped revitalise desert towns.

Although the media focus on 'boat migrants', most sub-Saharan and, in particular, North African migrants use other, less risky, methods to enter Europe—tourist visas, false documents, hiding in (containers or vehicles on) vessels, scaling or swimming around the fences surrounding the Spanish enclaves of Ceuta and Melilla.[21] In fact, the majority of irregular African migrants *enter* Europe legally and subsequently overstay their visas.[22]

Policy approaches towards irregular migration

Since the 1990s European states have mainly responded to public fears about mass irregular immigration by further restricting immigration policies and intensifying border controls. This has involved the deployment of semi-military forces and hardware in the prevention of migration by sea.[23] The Spanish government erected fences at Ceuta and Melilla and has attempted to seal off its maritime borders by installing an early-warning radar system (Integrated System of External Vigilance— SIVE) at the Straits of Gibraltar and the Canary Islands.[24] EU countries have attempted to 'externalize' border controls towards the Maghreb countries by pressuring North African countries to clamp down on irregular migration and to readmit irregular migrants in exchange for development aid, financial support for border controls, military equipment, and limited numbers of temporary work permits for immigrants.[25]

Since 2003 Spain and Morocco, as well as Italy and Libya, have started to collaborate on joint naval patrols and readmission agreements in return for aid. In 2006 Spain received limited support from Frontex, the new EU external border control agency, to patrol the sea routes between West Africa and the Canary Islands. Frontex also intends to co-ordinate patrols involving Italy, Greece and Malta to monitor the area between Malta, the Italian island of Lampedusa, and the Tunisian and Libyan coast. Faced by recent changes in migration patterns, Italy and Spain have recently concluded agreements with sub-Saharan countries on readmission and border controls.

In 2003–04 Morocco and Tunisia passed new immigration laws that institute severe punishments for irregular immigration and human smuggling. According to critics, these new laws show that Morocco and Tunisia are bowing to pressure from the EU to play the role of Europe's 'policemen'.[26] Although the new Moroccan law makes reference to relevant international conventions, and seems to be a nominal improvement, migrants' and refugees' rights are often ignored in practice.[27] Both Morocco and Tunisia have regularly brought irregular migrants to their borders, where they are left to their fate.[28]

To reduce immigration, the EU is also seeking to boost co-operation on migration issues in the context of the European Mediterranean Association Agreements (EMAA). All North African countries except Libya have signed such agreements with the EU, which should lead to the establishment of free trade areas in the next decade. The EU support for the economic transition of North African countries is mainly implemented through the *Mesures d'Accompagnement* (MEDA) programme. Significant funds from the MEDA programme target the stated goal of immigration reduction through boosting (rural) development in origin countries.[29]

The EU has prioritised collaboration with Maghreb states on border control and readmission. In March 2004 following the communication issued by the European Commission in 2002 on 'Integrating Migration issues into the EU's External Relations', the EU adopted a regulation establishing a programme for financial and technical assistance to third countries in the area of migration and asylum (AENEAS). Its programme for 2004–08 has an overall expenditure of €250 million. Among its aims are 'to address the root causes of migratory movements', to forge 'a partnership on migration stemming', and 'specific and concrete initiatives to help these countries to increase their capacity in the area of migration management'.[30]

Although Libya has not signed an association agreement with the EU, it has collaborated more closely on migration issues with EU countries, and with Italy in particular.[31] This policy shift should be seen in the broader context of Al-Qadhafi's (rather successful) efforts to regain international respectability, to lift the embargo, and to attract foreign direct investments.

A co-operation treaty was signed in December 2000 between Libya and Italy related to combating drugs, terrorism, organised crime and undocumented migration. In 2004 Italian Prime Minister Silvio Berlusconi and the Libyan leader Al-Qadhafi made a pact to stop irregular migration to Italy, with Libya allegedly agreeing to deport unauthorised sub-Saharan migrants over Libyan territory to their origin countries and to seal off its southern frontiers. In October 2004, only a few days later, Libya for the first time accepted to readmit illegal migrants from Italy.[32] Two months after the Libyan–Italian agreement, the EU agreed to lift its 18-year arms embargo on Libya, which allowed Libya to import (semi-)military equipment officially destined for improving border controls. Italy financed training programmes for Libyan police officers and the construction of three detention camps for undocumented immigrants in Libya. Libya has also been collaborating closely with Italy in concerted expulsions of thousands of undocumented migrants from Italy via Libya to their alleged origin countries.[33]

The limited and perverse effects of border controls

The collaboration of some Maghreb countries in migration controls and internal policing has recently been described as 'effective'.[34] Although this might be true in a strictly technical or diplomatic sense—for instance through signing readmission agreements, joint declarations on combating illegal migration and collaboration in joint border patrolling—efforts to prevent migrants from entering Europe have not stopped most of them from doing so. In addition, they have had a series of unintended, often counterproductive, effects.

First, increasing border controls have led to a diversification of trans-Saharan migration routes and trans-Mediterranean crossing points since the late 1990s.[35] This has led to an unintended increase in the area that EU countries have to monitor to 'combat' irregular migration. In reaction to intensified border patrolling in the Straits of Gibraltar, Maghrebi and sub-Saharan migrants started to cross the sea from places further east on the Moroccan coast to mainland Spain; from the Tunisian coast to the Italian islands; from Libya to Italy and Malta; and from Algeria to Spain. Since

1999 migrants in Morocco have increasingly moved southwards to the Western Sahara in order to get to the Canary Islands, a Spanish territory in the Atlantic Ocean.

On the western edge of the continent since 2005 more and more West Africans have started to circumvent the central Saharan migration routes by sailing directly from Mauritania, Senegal and other West African countries to the Canary Islands. Migration to the Canary Islands surged to unprecedented levels of about 31 000 recorded (apprehended) arrivals in 2006. While recorded arrivals in the Canary Islands declined in 2007 and 2008, they went up in Sardinia (Italy) and Crete (Greece).

Second, increasing surveillance in the Straits of Gibraltar and elsewhere has led to the professionalisation of smuggling methods, with smugglers using larger and faster custom-made boats and zodiacs instead of fishing boats.[36] There has also been an increase in the number of minors and pregnant women attempting to cross, who are generally more difficult to expel. The capacity to prevent migrants travelling across the Sahara over the Mediterranean and the Atlantic is fundamentally limited. The huge length of land and maritime borders and widespread corruption among border guards and other officials make it virtually impossible to prevent people from crossing.

Although EU countries have signed readmission agreements with a growing number of African countries, expulsions are notoriously difficult and costly to enforce. Governments of sub-Saharan countries in particular are often reluctant to readmit large numbers of irregular migrants. Many migrants destroy their papers to avoid expulsion, while asylum seekers, minors and pregnant women often have the right to (at least temporary) residence on humanitarian grounds. Because of these practical difficulties, many apprehended migrants are eventually released, after the maximum detention period, with a formal expulsion order. This order is generally ignored, after which they either move to other EU countries or go underground in Spain and Italy, where migrants tend to find jobs in the informal agricultural, construction and service sectors.

Human rights issues and the refugee dimension

In response to increased domestic xenophobia and presumably also European pressure to clamp down on irregular migration, Maghreb states have also reinforced internal policing on irregular migrants. Consequently, after years of relative tolerance, there has been a notable increase in institutionalised racism and the violation of the rights of sub-Saharan immigrants.[37] North African states regularly conduct migrant raids in immigrant neighbourhoods, which are often followed by the immigrants' detention or deportation to land borders. Immigrants, including asylum applicants, risk being arbitrarily arrested, detained, deported or stripped of their assets. In Libya in particular, xenophobia is expressed in blanket accusations of criminality, verbal and physical attacks, harassment, extortion, arbitrary detention, forced return and possibly torture.[38]

When hundreds of Africans attempted to enter Ceuta and Melilla in October 2005, at least 13 sub-Saharan Africans died, some of them allegedly killed by border guards. After these events, the Moroccan authorities turned to nationwide raids and arrests of immigrants in cities and makeshift camps in the forests around Ceuta and Melilla. The Moroccan authorities subsequently attempted to remove perhaps as many as 2000 migrants to a remote desert border with Algeria.[39]

Each year significant numbers die or get seriously injured while trying to enter Europe. It has been claimed that at least 368 people died while crossing to Spain in 2005.[40] Human rights organisations estimate that 3285 dead bodies were found on the shores of the Straits of Gibraltar alone between 1997 and 2001.[41] The actual number of drownings is likely to be significantly higher because an unknown percentage of corpses are never found.

An unknown but significant proportion of sub-Saharan migrants has escaped persecution or life-threatening circumstances.[42] According to a recent empirical study by Collyer, the percentage of migrants in Morocco that would require humanitarian protection would vary between 10%–20% under the strict application of the 1951 refugee Convention definition and 70%–8% percent under more generous humanitarian measures—although this sample was not designed to be representative and may therefore be biased towards refugees and asylum seekers.[43]

Human rights organisations have argued that Spain and Italy risk seriously compromising the principle of non-*refoulement* by swiftly deporting African migrants and asylum seekers to Morocco and Libya, where their protection is not guaranteed.[44] The Libyan government has randomly deported migrants expelled from Italy to their alleged origin countries, which include Sudan and Eritrea, regardless of whether they fear torture or persecution.[45]

Until recently the United Nations High Commissioner for Refugees (UNHCR) kept a low profile in the Maghreb states;[46] currently, however, it is seeking to expand its operations there. Yet state authorities often do not co-operate, continue to deport asylum seekers and generally refuse to grant residency and other rights to refugees recognised by UNHCR.[47] Nonetheless in 2007 the Moroccan government signed an *accord de siège* with UNHCR, giving it fully fledged representation in Morocco.

Double agendas and conflicting interests

Irregular immigration from sub-Saharan Africa has created considerable tensions between the EU, North African countries and sub-Saharan states. On the surface North African leaders and governments seem to have largely conceded to European pressure and were also quick to adopt dominant European public discourses on 'combating illegal migration'. Yet North African states do tacitly or openly oppose several elements of these policies, partly because they are seen as reinforcing their position as destinations. For instance, with the exception of Libya, Maghreb states are reluctant to readmit large numbers of irregular migrants from third (sub-Saharan) countries. When such agreements exist on a bilateral level, sending and

84

transit states often obstruct or delay implementation in direct or indirect ways.[48]

African states have also tended to object against proposals by some EU member states to establish offshore 'processing centres' for immigrants and asylum claimants in North Africa, or to send naval ships to patrol African coasts. This is not only because they are seen as a possible breach of national sovereignty, but also because such centres (like UNHCR offices) are often seen as attraction points, which would encourage immigration and settlement on the territory of Maghreb states. At the same time, there remains a certain reluctance to deport large numbers of sub-Saharan immigrants. Apart from the high costs of such expulsions, they can potentially harm states' international reputation. Recent migrant raids and collective expulsions have caused major international embarrassment for Morocco. These events, which are at odds with Morocco's attempts to improve its own human rights record, have also faced vocal protests from Moroccan human rights organisations and migrants' organisations.

Another factor explaining a certain reluctance to fully comply with EU policies is the strategic geopolitical and economic interests of North African states to maintain good relations with sub-Saharan states. Not only 'pan-African' Libya but also other Maghreb states have pursued their African policies, aimed at extending their southern geopolitical sphere of influence in the continent through diplomacy, aid, investments and exchange of students.[49] For instance, over the past three decades Morocco and Algeria have been competing over the support of sub-Saharan states in their opposed positions on the issue of the Western Sahara. Both countries have invested heavily in their relations with sub-Saharan countries. Such relations can be severely harmed by mass expulsions, the maltreatment of immigrants, or the EU-pressured introduction of visa requirements for citizens of sub-Saharan states.

Recent pressure by EU states on West African countries like Senegal, the Gambia, and Guinea to crack down on (irregular) migration is also partly at odds with the freedom of movement enshrined in the 1971 protocol of the Economic Community of West African States (ECOWAS) on the Free Movement of Persons, the Right of Residence and Establishment. Citizens of ECOWAS states at least nominally have the right to settle, work and do business in other ECOWAS states. Although the implementation of the protocol on free movement leaves much to be desired,[50] West African states have few legal means to 'combat illegal migration' as long as migrants' presence on their territories is basically legal. Also, on a practical level, it seems virtually impossible to impede people from moving thanks to widespread corruption and the lack of enforcement capacity—if Europeans are unable to seal off their borders, African states can hardly be expected to do so either.

Considering the difficulty of reconciling conflicting interests and the practical inability to stop migrants from crossing borders, there is a clear sense of deadlock around the issue. Recent African–European migration summits, such as those held in July 2006 (Rabat) and November 2006 (Tripoli), have not moved beyond declarations of good intent and general agreements to increase Euro-African co-operation.

While there is a limited degree of collaboration on border controls, merely lip service is being paid to the second solution: 'addressing the root causes of migration ... through better targeted development policies'.[51] The whole concept of a Marshall plan for Africa suffers from a lack of credibility considering the lack of follow-up to such promises in the form of concrete support. However, apart from growing scepticism debate about the effectiveness of development aid, it is doubtful that development will actually decrease migration. Empirical and theoretical evidence strongly suggests that economic and human development increases people's capabilities and aspirations and therefore tends to coincide with an increase rather than a decrease in emigration, at least in the short to medium run. Any development take-off in sub-Sahara Africa is therefore likely to generate an emigration take-off.[52]

More generally the popular image of a misery-driven African migration is based on fundamentally flawed assumptions of the (complex) relation between development and migration.[53] For instance, there is evidence that most components of rural development either have no effect on migration or rather tend to encourage internal migration, casting fundamental doubt on the assumption that migrants can be kept 'down on the farm' by development projects. More generally development tends to be associated with increased levels of overall mobility.[54]

The issue of irregular immigration from African countries has also created considerable tensions within the European Union. In 2006 Spain, Italy, and Malta complained about the limited support for border patrolling from less directly concerned northern countries. Some northern European governments (such as France, Austria and The Netherlands) responded by blaming Spain and Italy for their recent mass regularisations, which they believe pull in even more irregular migrants.[55] Such tensions and a general unwillingness to give up national sovereignty in migration policies explain why most issues are still dealt with at the bilateral level.

In November 2006 EU Justice Commissioner Franco Frattini called for new job centres in Africa to help match supply with demand in an attempt to 'fight illegal immigration and trafficking'.[56] These centres would inform people about (temporary) job and education opportunities in Europe and about the risks of irregular migration. This echoes earlier (failed) proposals by Italy in 2002 to transpose the Italian system of legal immigration agreements in exchange for readmission agreements at the EU level.[57]

Again, the success of such proposals depends on the willingness of EU member states to give up part of their national sovereignty in migration issues by allocating immigration quotas to such centres, and on the willingness of African states to readmit irregular migrants. The latter is a condition for establishing job centres, which might fuel suspicions that these plans camouflage a hidden agenda of returning irregular immigrants. It is also entirely unclear how the intended temporariness of migration will be implemented, as return migration is notoriously difficult to enforce.

Vested interests in migration

What remains largely unspoken behind official discourses proclaiming they will 'combat illegal immigration' is that European and African states, or at least some powerful interest groups within them, have *little genuine interest* in stopping migration, because the economies of receiving and sending countries have become increasingly dependent on migrant labour and remittances, respectively.

First, there is a fundamental discrepancy between the official aim to curb immigration and the sustained demand for cheap (often irregular) migrant labour. The large informal and formal labour markets for agricultural labour, construction and other service jobs in (southern) Europe and Libya have become increasingly dependent on irregular migration labour.[58] In contrast to the usual, but one-sided, focus on 'human misery' allegedly pushing migrants out of Africa, irregular migration seems to be predominantly driven by labour market demand.[59]

Particularly in southern Europe, female migrants working as domestic or care workers gradually replace the low-paid or unpaid caretaking activities of native women. The informal economy feeds off both the strong demand for domestic and care services and a wealth of small businesses, where irregular migrants can easily find work.[60]

In a context of extraordinarily low fertility, labour market segmentation and high economic growth in sectors such as agriculture and construction, migration is a fundamental resource for economic development.[61] In Spain, for instance, there is a tacit alliance between trade unions and employers in favour of moderately open immigration policies.[62] Also in northern Europe there is a persistent and probably growing demand for irregular migrant labour.[63]

However, because of increasing migration controls and the institutional exclusion of irregular migrants, migrants have become more vulnerable to severe exploitation in the labour market in Europe and North Africa.[64] Libya faces the specific dilemma of maintaining the image of full compliance with policies to 'combat illegal migration' by regularly deporting sub-Saharan immigrants, while its economy is in fact heavily dependent on immigrant workers, whio represent at least 25% to 30% of its total population.[65] Therefore occasional expulsions seem primarily to serve to create the *impression* of compliance with policies to combat irregular migration.

The European and Libyan governments are under pressure from employers to allow more legal immigration or to tacitly allow irregular migration.[66] There is a discrepancy between a general public rhetoric hostile to (regular and irregular) immigration in attempted responses to public xenophobia, and public action, which has largely tolerated irregular immigration and has introduced mass regularisations.[67] Although new immigration and labour laws have increased penalties for employers who hire irregular workers, this is still often tolerated in practice.

Both Spain and Italy have quota systems that are formally based on labour-market needs. The fact that the yearly quotas never match real demand partly explains the persistence of large-scale irregular migration.[68] However, because many employers prefer migrants who already reside (illegally) in Europe or have migrated spontaneously,[69] it is unlikely that increased quotas will lead to a standstill of irregular migration.

To prevent the presence of large groups of irregular migrants, Spain, Italy and other southern European countries have regularly reverted to mass regularisations. Allasino *et al* have argued that the frequency of regularisations may contribute to the perception that unauthorised entry by the back door is more effective than via the front door of programmed flows and quotas.[70] Regularisations are generally sold to the public with the argument that they will stem further irregular migration, and are often accompanied by a concomitant tightening of immigration policies and a vow that no more regularisations will follow.[71] However, as long as demand for migrant labour persists, occasional regularisation programmes will not prevent further irregular arrivals.

In addition, Maghreb and sub-Saharan states have little genuine interest in curbing migration, because for them migration serves vital political and economic interests and constitutes a potential development resource. Emigration relieves pressure on internal labour markets and generates a substantial and rapidly growing flow of remittances. While having a fundamental interest in continuing emigration of their own nationals, governments of Maghreb countries also have little genuine interest in stopping migrants from transiting to Europe.

In this context many African states seem to adopt a strategy of paying lip service to Europe's 'fight against illegal immigration' to varying degrees, while using the migration issue as a bargaining chip in negotiating aid, economic relations, immigrant quotas or, in the case of Libya, the rehabilitation of its international reputation.[72]

For governments of African countries, the recent increase in sub-Saharan migration to the Maghreb and Europe is probably not as unwelcome as it seems at first sight. While shrewdly positioning themselves as 'victims' of illegal immigration, Maghreb states and, recently Mauritania, Senegal and the Gambia, have successfully capitalised on their new status as transit countries, which has increased their geopolitical leverage to negotiate migration agreements with European countries in exchange for financial aid and other forms of support.

As El Qadim has observed for Morocco, conditions are not unilaterally imposed by European countries and Morocco has not been 'forced' to comply with externalisation. In fact, Morocco has largely benefited from the increase in irregular migration over its territory. By consciously positioning itself as Europe's leading partner in the 'fight against illegal migration', Morocco has considerably strengthened its position in negotiations with the EU and its member states over support and collaboration.[73] At the same time, the focus on sub-Saharan migrants diverts attention away from the fact that Morocco is still the most important source country of (irregular and regular) African migrants in Europe.

Conclusion

Although there has been an incontestable increase in regular and irregular migration from sub-Sahara Africa and the Maghreb to Europe, apocalyptic representations of a massive exodus of desperate Africans pushed out of the continent by poverty, war and drought are fundamentally flawed. Concurrently the popular perception that irregular migration from Africa is growing at an alarming rate is deceptive. Since the introduction of visa requirements for Maghreb countries by Italy and Spain in the early 1990s, illegal crossings of the Mediterranean Sea have been a persistent phenomenon. Rather than an increase *per se*, the major change has been that, after 2000, sub-Saharan Africans started to join illegal Mediterranean crossings and have now overtaken North Africans as the largest category of irregular boat migrants.

However, the magnitude of African immigration remains limited. Of the estimated 65 000 to 120 000 sub-Saharan Africans entering the Maghreb yearly, several tens of thousands (not hundreds of thousands, as media coverage might suggest) try to cross the Mediterranean each year. Therefore, common views that reduce North Africa to a transit zone or springboard to Europe are inaccurate. Libya and, to a lesser extent, other Maghreb countries are destinations in their own right.

Several factors explain why it is likely that African Saharan migration to Europe will continue and why Maghreb countries may further consolidate their position as transit *and* immigration countries. First, there are substantial differentials in economic development and political stability not only between Maghreb and EU countries, but also between most sub-Saharan and Maghreb countries. Therefore migrants failing and unwilling to enter Europe often prefer to stay than to return.

Second, trans-Saharan migration is less unwanted than it might seem. Irregular migration has generally been beneficial for economies in transit and destination countries because of the cheap labour it generates and the migration-related trade and business activities of smugglers, entrepreneurs and state officials. The demand for cheap (unauthorised) immigrant labour in Europe, Libya and also other Maghreb countries is likely to persist. Segmentation of labour markets may increase the future scope for immigration. Migrants in Europe and the Maghreb tend to do work that natives shun, even if the latter are unemployed.

Third, it seems practically impossible to seal off the long Saharan borders and Mediterranean coastlines. The firm establishment of migration routes and migrant networks, as well as the improvements in communication infrastructure and trans-Saharan transportation infrastructure,[74] is likely to facilitate onward chain migration. In the same way, increasing trade between North African countries and Europe partly boosted by free trade agreements and the growth of the North African tourism industry are likely to further increase cross-border traffic. This is also likely to enhance opportunities for migrants to cross borders legally or illegally.

Dominant media and political discourses tend to identify extreme poverty, war and environmental degradation amalgamated into a stereotypical image of 'African misery' as the root causes of this migration. This typically accompanies the portrayal of African migrants as passive victims of poverty and war, as *desperate* people who are driven off their native lands into the hands of ruthless smugglers and merciless traffickers. However, such representations not only rule out migrants' own agency but are also fundamentally at odds with empirical evidence that the vast majority of migrants are not among the poorest, move on their own initiative and that trafficking plays a relatively unimportant role. While pleas for a 'Marshall Plan for Africa' lack any credibility, any development of sub-Saharan countries is likely to lead to increasing rather than decreasing emigration, because somewhat higher incomes and improved education and access to media and information will give more people the capabilities and aspirations to migrate.

For all these reasons it is unlikely that African–European migration can be significantly curbed. This leads us to a much more fundamental question: are governments genuinely willing to curb it? Probably not. Dominant policy discourses and media coverage systematically ignore—or obscure—the fact that African migration to Europe, Libya and, increasingly, other Maghreb countries is fuelled by a structural demand for cheap (irregular) migrant labour. However, the demand side of irregular migration is systematically obscured behind a series of discursive strategies that politicians and states use—for instance by portraying irregular migrants as victims of smugglers and traffickers—which seems to justify the *de facto* exclusion and marginalisation of irregular migrants through restrictive immigration laws and border controls.[75]

What remains largely unspoken behind discourses on 'combating illegal immigration' is that neither European nor African states have much genuine interest in stopping migration, because the economies of receiving and sending countries have become increasingly dependent on migrant labour and remittances, respectively. In order to understand this gap between rhetoric and practice, it is important to realise that states are no monolithic entities but harbour diverse, often conflicting political and economic interests—particularly between employers and more general economic interests favouring immigration and politicians keen on maintaining a tough public profile on immigration issues in order to get elected or to stay in power.

This corroborates the idea that 'elected leaders and bureaucrats increasingly have turned to *symbolic* policy instruments to create an *appearance* of control'.[76] Immigration is not always as 'unwanted' as politicians officially proclaim, since employers might benefit from cheap, undocumented workers lacking rights, and governments tacitly permit such movements.[77]

Thus a distinction should be made between political rhetoric and policy implementation. This also applies to international co-operation on the issue. Although collaboration between European and African states might be partly successful in a strictly technical sense—for instance through carrying out joint border patrols—it has failed to significantly curb migration. This is not only related to the inability to control all borders, and the high costs of expelling migrants, but also to the reluctance among leaders of sending states to take back large numbers of immigrants and the resistance and (international) protest such large-scale expulsions are likely to engender.

Despite lip service being paid to 'combating illegal migration' for electoral and diplomatic reasons, European and African states are neither able nor willing to stop migration. Yet 'harsh' political discourse on immigration accompanying such policies can be a catalyst for and might therefore reinforce the same xenophobia and the concomitant apocalyptic representations of a 'massive' influx of migrants to which they seem a political–electoral response. Policy making on this issue seems therefore to be caught in a vicious circle of more restrictions-more illegality-more restriction.[78]

There is a growing discrepancy between restrictive migration policies and the real demand for cheap migrant labour in Libya and Europe. This explains why restrictive immigration policies and border controls have invariably failed to stop migration, and have rather provoked a diversification of trans-Saharan migration routes and trans-Mediterranean crossing points. They have also increased the risks and costs of migration and the suffering and labour market exploitation of the migrants involved. There is a fundamental mismatch between labour needs and formal immigration policy. As long as no more legal channels for immigration are created to match the real demand for labour, and as long as large informal economies in the Maghreb and Europe continue to exist, it is likely that a substantial proportion of this migration will remain irregular. In brief, policies to 'fight illegal migration' are bound to fail because they are among the very causes of the phenomenon they claim to combat.

Notes

1 F Pastore, P Monzini & G Sciortino, '"Schengen's soft underbelly?" Irregular migration and human smuggling across land and sea borders to Italy', *International Migration*, 44 (4), 2006, pp 95–119.

2 See E Goldschmidt, 'Storming the fences: Morocco and Europe's anti-migration policy', *Middle East Report*, 239, 2006; and O Pliez, 'De l'immigration au transit? La Libye dans l'espace migratoire Euro-Africain', in Pliez (ed), *La Nouvelle Libye: Sociétés, Espaces et Géopolitique au Lendemain de l'Embargo*, Paris, Editions Karthala, 2004, p 145.

3 N Myers, *Environmental Refugees: An Emergent Security Issue*, Vienna: Organisation for Security and Cooperation in Europe, 2005, p 4.

4 See D Lutterbeck, 'Policing migration in the Mediterranean', *Mediterranean Politics*, 11 (1), 2006, pp 59–82; United Nations Office on Drugs and Crime (UNODC), *Organized Crime and Irregular Migration from Africa to Europe*, Vienna: UNODC, 2006; P Cuttitta, 'The changes in the fight against illegal immigration in the Euro-Mediterranean area and in Euro-Mediterranean relations', *Working paper*, Genoa: University of Genoa, 2007; Goldschmidt, 'Storming the fences'; and D Perrin, 'Le Maghreb sous influence, le nouveau cadre des juridique des migrations transsahariennes' [North Africa under control: the new legal frame of trans-Saharan migrations], *Maghreb-Machrek*, 185, 2005, pp 59–120.

5 UNODC, 'Organized crime and irregular migration from Africa to Europe', p 20.

6 M Collyer, 'States of insecurity: consequences of Saharan transit migration', *Working Paper 31*, Oxford: Centre on Migration, Policy and Society, University of Oxford, 2006; S Hamood, *African Transit Migration through Libya to Europe: The Human Cost*, Cairo: FMRS/AUC, 2006; O Pliez, 'Le Sahara libyen dans les nouvelles configurations migratoires', *Revue Européenne des Migrations Internationales*, 16 (3), 2005, pp 165–181; L Schuster, 'The realities of a new asylum paradigm', *Working Paper 20*, Oxford: Centre on Migration, Policy and Society, University of Oxford, 2005.

7 WR Böhning, 'Helping migrants to stay at home', *Annals of the American Academy of Political and Social Science*, 534, 1994, pp 165–177; M Schiff, *South–North Migration and Trade: A Survey*,

Washington, DC: World Bank, 1996; and P Stalker, 'Migration trends and migration policy in Europe', *International Migration*, 40 (5), 2002, pp 151–179.

8 *Der Spiegel*, 6 October 2005.

9 See for instance MA Diatta & M Mbow, 'Releasing the development potential of return migration: the case of Senegal', *International Migration*, 37 (1), 1999, pp 243–266.

10 H De Haas, 'Morocco's migration experience: a transitional perspective', *International Migration*, 45 (4), 2007, pp 39–70; P Fargues (ed), *Mediterranean Migration—2005 Report*, Cooperation project on the social integration of immigrants, migration, and the movement of persons, financed by the EC MEDA Programme, Florence: EUI–RSCAS, CARIM Consortium, 2005.

11 Hamood, *African Transit Migration through Libya to Europe*; and Pliez, 'De l'immigration au transit?'.

12 *Ibid*; and Schuster, 'The realities of a new asylum paradigm'.

13 H De Haas, 'Trans-Saharan migration to North Africa and the EU: historical roots and current trends', *Migration Information Source*, November 2006.

14 Collyer, 'States of insecurity'; C Escoffier, 'Communautés d'initérance et savoir-circuler des transmigrant-e-s au Maghreb', doctoral thesis, University of Toulouse II, 2006; and Pliez, 'Le Sahara libyen dans les nouvelles configurations migratoires'.

15 Collyer, 'States of insecurity'.

16 F Pastore *et al*, '"Schengen's soft underbelly?"'; and Pliez, 'De l'immigration au transit?'.

17 J Simon, 'Irregular transit migration in the Mediterranean: facts, figures and insights', in N Nyberg-Sorensen (ed), *Mediterranean Transit Migration*, Copenhagen: Danish Institute for International Studies, 2006.

18 See L Barros, M Lahlou, C Escoffier, P Pumares & P Ruspini, *L'Immigration Irrégulière Subsaharienne à Travers et vers le Maroc*, Geneva: ILO, 2002; and Escoffier, 'Communautés d'initérance et savoir-circuler des transmigrant-e-s au Maghreb'.

19 De Haas, 'Trans-Saharan migration to North Africa and the EU'.

20 J Berriane, 'Les étudiants subsahariens au Maroc: des migrants parmi d'autres?', paper presented at the workshop on African migration 'Comprendre les dynamiques des migrations sur le continent', Centre for Migration Studies and International Migration Institute, Accra, 18–21 September 2007; and H Boubakri, 'Transit migration between Tunisia, Libya and sub-Saharan Africa: study based on Greater Tunis', paper presented at the Council of Europe Regional Conference on 'Migrants in Transit Countries: Sharing Responsibility for Management and Protection', Istanbul, 30 September–1 October 2004.

21 De Haas, 'Trans-Saharan migration to North Africa and the EU'.

22 J Schoorl, L Heering, I Esveldt, G Groenewold, R van der Erf, A Bosch, H de Valk & B de Bruijn, *Push and Pull Factors of International Migration: A Comparative Report*, Luxembourg: Eurostat, European Communities, 2000.

23 Lutterbeck, 'Policing migration in the Mediterranean'.

24 Goldschmidt, 'Storming the fences'; and J Carling, 'Migration control and migrant fatalities at the Spanish–African borders', *International Migration Review*, 41 (2), 2007, pp 316–343.

25 J Chaloff, 'Italy', *Current Immigration Debates in Europe: A Publication of the European Migration Dialogue*, Brussels/Rome: Migration Policy Group, 2005; and P Cuttitta, 'Delocalisation of migration controls to Northern Africa', paper submitted to a workshop on 'The Europeanisation of National Immigration Policies', Berlin, 1–3 September 2005.

26 H Boubakri, 'Le Maghreb et les migrations de transit: le piège?', *Migrations Sociétés*, 18 (207), 2006, pp 85–104.

27 Collyer, 'States of insecurity'; and Schuster, 'The realities of a new asylum paradigm'.

28 Cuttitta, 'Delocalisation of migration controls to Northern Africa'; and Goldschmidt, 'Storming the fences'.

29 De Haas, 'Morocco's migration experience'.

30 European Commission, *Reference Document for Financial and Technical Assistance to Third Countries in the Area of Migration and Asylum, AENEAS Programme 2004–2006*, Brussels: EC, 2003.

31 R Andrijasevic, 'Lampedusa in focus: migrants caught between the Libyan desert and the deep sea', *Feminist Review*, 82, 2006, pp 120–125; Hamood, *African Transit Migration through Libya to Europe*; Human Rights Watch (HRW), *Libya—Stemming the Flow: Abuses against Migrants, Asylum Seekers and Refugees*, London: HRW, 2006; and Pliez, 'Le Sahara libyen dans les nouvelles configurations migratoires'.

32 Cuttitta, 'Delocalisation of migration controls to Northern Africa'.

33 Hamood, *African Transit Migration through Libya to Europe*; and HRW, *Libya—Stemming the Flow*.

34 UNODC, *Organized Crime and Irregular Migration from Africa to Europe*.

35 Barros *et al*, *L'Immigration Irrégulière Subsaharienne à Travers et vers le Maroc*; Boubakri, 'Transit migration between Tunisia, Libya and sub-Saharan Africa'; and De Haas, 'Morocco's migration experience'.

36 Carling, 'Migration control and migrant fatalities at the Spanish–African borders'.
37 Collyer, 'States of insecurity'; Hamood, *African Transit Migration through Libya to Europe*; and Schuster, 'The realities of a new asylum paradigm'.
38 Hamood, *African Transit Migration through Libya to Europe*.
39 Collyer, 'States of insecurity'.
40 Asociación Por Derechos Humanos de Andalucía (APDHA), 'Informe sobre la inmigración clandestina durante el año 2005', Seville: APDHA, 2006.
41 Schuster, 'The realities of a new asylum paradigm'.
42 Barros *et al*, *L'Immigration Irrégulière Subsaharienne à Travers et Vers le Maroc*; Collyer, 'States of insecurity'; Escoffier, 'Communautés d'initérance et savoir-circuler des transmigrant-e-s au Maghreb'; and Schuster, 'The realities of a new asylum paradigm'.
43 Collyer, 'States of insecurity'.
44 Hamood, *African Transit Migration through Libya to Europe*; and HRW, 'Libya: stemming the flow'.
45 *Ibid*.
46 Hamood, 'African transit migration through Libya to Europe'.
47 Collyer, 'States of insecurity'.
48 See N El Qadim, '"Gérer les migrations": renouveau d'un objet de négociations entre le Maroc et les pays Européens', PhD thesis, Institut Universitaire de Hautes Etudes Internationales, Geneva, 2007.
49 Berriane, 'Les étudiants subsahariens au Maroc'; Boubakri, 'Le Maghreb et les migrations de transit'; Goldschmidt, 'Storming the fences'; and Pliez, 'De l'immigratoin au transit?'.
50 A Adepoju, *Migration in West Africa*, Geneva: Global Commission on International Migration, 2005.
51 AU/EU, 'Joint Africa–EU declaration on migration and development', Tripoli, 22–23 November 2006.
52 H De Haas, 'Turning the tide? Why development will not stop migration', *Development and Change*, 38 (5), 2007, pp 819–841.
53 *Ibid*.
54 *Ibid*.
55 *Le Nouvel Observateur*, 21 September 2006.
56 BBC Online, 30 November 2006.
57 Cuttitta, 'Delocalisation of migration controls to Northern Africa'.
58 See Pliez, 'De l'immigratoin au transit?'; E Reyneri, 'Migrants' involvement in irregular employment in the Mediterranean countries of the European Union', *International Migration Papers 41*, Geneva: ILO, 2001; and R Sandell, 'Spain's immigration experience: lessons to be learned from looking at the statistics', *Working Paper (WP) 30/2006*, Real Institute Elcano, 2006.
59 Reyneri, 'Migrants' involvement in irregular employment in the Mediterranean countries of the European Union'.
60 E Allasino, E Reyneri *et al*, 'Labour market discrimination against migrant workers in Italy', *International Migration Papers 67*, Geneva: ILO, 2004.
61 G Dalla Zuanna, 'Population replacement, social mobility and development in Italy in the twentieth century', *Journal of Modern Italian Studies*, 11 (2), 2006, pp 188–208; and N Ortega Pérez, 'Spain: forging an immigration policy', *Migration Information Source*, February 2003.
62 Ortega Pérez, 'Spain'.
63 See B Anderson, *Doing the Dirty Work? The Global Politics of Domestic Labour*, London: Zed Books, 2000.
64 D Broeders & G Engbersen, 'The fight against illegal migration: identification policies and immigrants' counterstrategies', *American Behavioral Scientist*, 50, 2007, p 1592; and Pliez, 'De l'immigratoin au transit?'.
65 Pliez, 'De l'immigration au transit?'; and Boubakri, 'Transit migration between Tunisia, Libya and sub-Saharan Africa', p 2.
66 Chaloff, 'Italy'; and Pliez, 'De l'immigration au transit?'.
67 G Zincone, 'The making of policies: immigration and immigrants in Italy', *Journal of Ethnic and Migration Studies*, 32 (3), 2006, pp 347–375.
68 Chaloff, 'Italy'; Ortega Pérez, 'Spain: forging an immigration policy'; Sandell, 'Spain's immigration experience'; and A Serra, 'Spain', *Current Immigration Debates in Europe: A Publication of the European Migration Dialogue*, Brussels/Rome: Migration Policy Group, 2005.
69 See Cuttitta, 'The changes in the fight against illegal immigration in the Euro-Mediterranean area and in Euro-Mediterranean relations'.
70 Allasino *et al*, 'Labour market discrimination against migrant workers in Italy'. See also Serra, 'Spain'.
71 A Levinson, 'The regularisation of unauthorised migrants: literature survey and country case studies', Oxford: Centre on Migration, Policy and Society (COMPAS), University of Oxford, 2005.
72 Hamood, *African Transit Migration through Libya to Europe*; and Pliez, 'De l'immigration au transit?'.
73 El Qadim, '"Gérer les migrations"'.

93

74 C Oumar Ba & A Choplin, 'Tenter l'aventure par la Mauritanie: migrations transsahariennes et recompositions urbaines', *Autrepart*, 36 (4), 2005, pp 21–42; and A Pian, 'Aventuriers et commerçants Sénégalais à Casablanca: des parcours entrecroisés', *Autrepart*, 36 (4), 2005, pp 167–182.
75 See SA Fitzgerald, 'Putting trafficking on the map: the geography of feminist complicity', in V Munro & MD Giusta (eds), *Interrogating Supply/Demand Dynamics of Prostitution*, Aldershot: Ashgate Publishing, 2008.
76 DS Massey, J Arango, G Hugo, A Koudouci, A Pellegrino & J Edward Taylor, *Worlds in Motion: Understanding International Migration at the End of the Millennium*, Oxford: Clarendon Press, 1998, p 288, emphasis in the original.
77 S Castles & MJ Miller, *The Age of Migration*, Basingstoke: Macmillan, 2003.
78 I Van Liempt, *Navigating Borders: An Inside Perspective into the Process of Human Smuggling*, Amsterdam: Amsterdam University Press, 2007, p 283.

Globalisation and Migrant Labour in a 'Rainbow Nation': a fortress South Africa?

NICOS TRIMIKLINIOTIS, STEVEN GORDON &
BRIAN ZONDO

This paper attempts to locate the debates about the relation between global and regional processes (globalisation, regionalisation, integration) on the one hand, and the processes of migration and racialisation or xenophobia, on the other, as exemplified within the specific manifestations of these relations in the southern African context. The trends, debates and practices in the Southern African Development Community (SADC) region, particularly in South Africa, can be illuminating in informing the broader global debates on the subject, issues that are often not properly reflected upon at global level. Moreover, these issues may illustrate the relation in discourses, ideologies and state practices between postcolonial countries of the 'Global South' and the EU. The paper attempts to understand how and why it is possible for a post-apartheid state, committed to building a 'non-racial society', to 'racialise' a category of the population—migrant workers—particularly the undocumented ones. This is particularly important for understanding the socioeconomic and political processes that racialise migrants, as well the strategies for combating racial, ethnic, gender and class discrimination and exploitation of them at national, regional and potentially global levels. In this sense the historical antecedent of the treatment of migrant workers under apartheid and the struggles for its overthrow are crucial in shaping the current realities.

Globalisation/regionalisation and re-racialisation in southern Africa: who are the migrants in South Africa?

Migration: not new in South Africa

The historical background to migration to South Africa is indicative of how the dynamics of cross-border migration are closely interrelated with 'internal migration' and are very much the product of a historical relationship between the neighbouring countries to South Africa, the superpower of the region. The historical events in the 1990s, such as the 'negotiated transition' from apartheid, the collapse of 'actually existing socialism', the end of the war in Mozambique, and wars, disasters and famine elsewhere in Africa have been crucial factors in the rise of the numbers of migrants to South Africa. The 'traditional' migrant labour suppliers within SADC have been Mozambique, Zimbabwe, Lesotho and Malawi; however, migrants also came from the Democratic Republic of Congo (DRC), Nigeria and Kenya. The post-apartheid transition has brought about changes in internal migration: there has been massive urbanisation in search of jobs and a better life. The debate that surrounds the issue of illegal migration often present this phenomenon as a new and seemingly overwhelming problem for the post-apartheid state and its citizenry.[1]

Migration is no new subject for South Africa: what most persons would recall is the late 19th century migration when gold was discovered, whereby the combined effect of mining and industrialised centres attracted thousands of migrant workers from all over southern Africa. However, even before the discovery of diamonds and gold in 1860, there was an established system of labour migration: the colonists were using migrant labour from the entire region for multiple purposes; development and wealth were the product of various types of black labour, local and migrant labour from the region or imported indentured labour. Bepedi men from Sekhunland (what is today Limpopo and Mpumalanga province) had worked in the farms and public works of the Cape colony of the 1840s. Basotho migrant workers worked in the Orange Free State, while in the 1840s the Tsonga or Shangaan travelled all the way from Delagoa Bay area to Natal for wages. Mozambicans also worked as seasonal workers in the farms of the Western Cape.[2]

It was nevertheless the discovery of diamonds at Kimberley that created huge demand for unskilled labour: by 1874 there were 10 000 African mineworkers working for three to six months in the mines. The changes in mining methods from opencast to underground extraction in the 1880s, and the need for stable skilled labour, brought about changes: migrant labour was utilised as it was cheap and 'controllable'; housing was provided in closed compounds. Moreover, statutes and regulations prevented the establishment of an organised black working class: these anti-labour laws were to become a major instrument for the apartheid regime to divide the working class. When gold was discovered on Witwatersrand in 1886 more cheap labour was required as gold reefs were deep and ore quite low, a situation which required strong capital reserves. As a result there was a very expensive recruitment from neighbouring countries. By 1896 the South African Chamber of Mines Rand Labour Association (later known as WNLA[3]) was recruiting heavily, both locally and from the protectorates such as Botswana, Lesotho and Swaziland and from today's Mozambique, Malawi and Zambia. Between 1880 and 1899 there was a massive rise from 1400 to 97 000 migrant workers, 60% of whom were Mozambicans. It is noteworthy that 'during the period 1920–1990, virtually every country in the SADC region at one time or another sent migrants to the South African mines".[4]

'New' migration in 'new South Africa'

The ideology of Pan-Africanism could have served as the basis for a different regional migration regime after the collapse of apartheid in South Africa. However, the initiative to push for a free movement protocol in the development of a regionally harmonised approach to migration management in the SADC region was killed off by the new South Africa: the fear of being 'flooded' by migrants prevailed.[5] 'Free movement' has been replaced by tough migration control, which does little to deter migrants from entering the country in a desperate search for work and a better life; post-apartheid South Africa receives thousands of migrants, mostly undocumented, from neighbouring countries, as we analyse further down. However, the obsession with the numbers is itself 'racialising' migrant workers: 'race' is dreaded in South Africa.

The so-called 'numbers game' is being played, whereby the number of migrants is constructed and stigmatised as a 'problem' in the classical manner used by Moore, who was writing about Britain in the 1970s.[6] It seems that countries of new migration regenerate the same sort of game, even if these societies had traditionally been for years postcolonial net exporters of migrants: the pernicious 'numbers game' is being reproduced over and over.[7] Migrants thus become in the minds of the media and in the eyes of readers, the problem. The 'numbers game', though presented in the guise of ensuring 'good race relations', in fact accentuates racism and xenophobia. Having recognised this problem, we present some of the figures available so that we can get some picture of the kinds of issues debated. Figures are inaccurate, often out of date, while sometimes they are blown out of proportion.

A scholar working on citizenship and xenophobia in contemporary southern Africa, while recognising the large numbers of migrants from sub-Saharan countries, refers to the elusiveness of the migration statistics in these countries and their 'inflation for reasons of political expediency', as contributing to governments being worried about the numbers of migrants from neighbouring countries.[8] The end of apartheid saw the rise of migration to South Africa, 'especially by Africans north of Limpopo, long excluded or confined to migration to serve as labour zombies in the mines':[9] one estimation is that 'between 1994 and December 1996 at least 5 million illegal immigrants entered south Africa from African countries far and near'. However, this is thought to be a gross exaggeration for reasons of political expediency. In reality, the numbers of illegal immigrants are near impossible to calculate so we would hesitate to guess at figures. A recent article claimed that the illegal immigrant population was between three and 6.5 million.[10] There are reports that there are two million illegal Zimbabwean immigrants in South Africa alone. Migration has certainly risen, particularly in the mines in what was during apartheid called 'labour reserves'—some talk about a tenfold growth in this sector.[11]

A central issue in the debates refers to the scale of undocumented and irregular migrant workers or 'illegal migrants'; the main difficulty is the impossibility of accurately quantifying a clandestine population. In South Africa the numbers and the way undocumented migrant workers are categorised has divided academics and policy makers. As Gordon notes:

> The Human Sciences Research Council (HSRC) claims that South Africa's illegal immigrant population is somewhere between 2.5 and 4.5 million, and these estimated statistics have been often quoted by the Former Minister of Home Affairs, Dr Mangosuthu Buthelezi. However, the validity of these statistics were called into question, and in 2002 the HSRC figures were officially withdrawn. Notwithstanding, however, Dr Buthelezi himself has been known to quote a variety of estimates, some as high as 7 million.[12]

The official estimates vary from two to 3.5 million and those from the South African Police Service (SAPS) and South African National Defence Force are relatively more conservative than those of the HSRC. Carl Werth of the Freedom Front places the illegal immigrant population at almost eight million, or more than 19% of the current South African population,[13] while others have stated that the illegal immigrant population stands at almost 12 million, or one in four South Africans.[14] The media seem to quote a range of figures when discussing the issue, all of which go above the two million mark, as noted above. Scholars have strongly criticised these figures as being inflated, claiming them as largely imaginary and suggesting that the illegal migrant population in South Africa could be as low as 500 000.[15] These population estimates are in truth little more than guesses that are often labelled as guesstimates by the popular media. There is a dearth of reliable and accurate information available about illegal migrant workers in South Africa.

As Table 1 indicates, the majority of the illegal migrants deported since 1994 are citizens of countries within SADC. It is apparent the number of deportations from South Africa has grown significantly since the apartheid period as Department of Home Affairs (DHA) statistics indicate. From only 181 286 in 1988, deportation rates had reached the astonishingly high number of 151 653 by 2002. Since the advent of the economic crisis in Zimbabwe, the deportation rates have increasing dramatically, with roughly 155 000 deported in 2003 and more than 167 000 deported in 2004. Although no official data have made available, there is a wide consensus that these figures have risen substantially in recent years. According to unofficial sources the South African government deported nearly a quarter of a million people in 2006.

Zimbabwean migrants make up an increasing high percentage of those deported, increasing from some 47 697 (2001) to 74 765 (2004) and nearly 100 000 (2005). Although the Department of Home Affairs has not made the figures available, according to unofficial reports South Africa deports between 600 and 6000 Zimbabweans every week from a repatriation centre called Lindela. As the crisis in Zimbabwe deepens, the deportation rates continue to rise. In the first seven months of 2007 the Reception and Support Centre of the International Organisation for Migration (IOM) processed 117 737 people repatriated from South Africa at its Beitbridge centre on the Zimbabwean border.[16]

TABLE 1. Number of deportations per year and top three countries of origin

Country	1994	1995	1996	1997	1998	1999
Mozambique	71 279	131 689	157 425	146 285	141 506	123 961
Zimbabwe	12 931	17 549	14 651	21 673	28 548	42 769
Lesotho	40 723	4087	3344	4077	4900	6003
Other	2409	3759	5293	4 316	6 332	11 128
Total	90 692	157 084	180 713	176 351	181 286	183 861

Country	2000	2001	2002	2003	2004
Mozambique	84 738	94 404	83 695	82 067	81 619
Zimbabwe	45 922	47 697	38 118	55 753	72 112
Lesotho	5871	5977	5278	7447	7468
Other	9044	8045	8799	9541	5938
Total	145 575	156 123	135 870	154 808	167 137

Source: *Annual Reports*, Department of Home Affairs, 1994–2000; and Department of Home Affairs, Head Office, 2001–04, quoted in SL Gordon, 2005. 'The trade union response to alien workers within post-apartheid South Africa: an analysis of the nature of the response of the South African trade union movement to the issue of illegal migrant workers', unpublished Master's thesis, Albert-Ludwigs Universität, Freiburg and University of KwaZulu-Natal, 2005.

South Africa is currently in the midst of what has been described by the contemporary news media as the 'Mugabe Tsunami'—a 'wave' of more than 1000 illegal Zimbabwean migrants every day who are fleeing across the Limpopo to escape into South Africa.[17] Regional human rights groups have reported a surge in 'illegal' Zimbabwean migration into South Africa since the country's recent disputed election and the violent political crackdown that has followed. Media reports claim that as many as 49 000 illegal Zimbabwean immigrants now enter South Africa every month.[18] The United Nations High Commissioner for Refugees (UNHCR) estimates that there are more than three million displaced Zimbabweans in the SADCR region. A study by the state-sponsored Scientific and Industrial Research Centre (SIRDC), which came out in September 2005, showed that about half a million Zimbabweans, mainly professionals in the health and education sector, have emigrated.[19]

Another mechanism for gauging the Zimbabwean influx into South Africa is through refugee and asylum seeker registrations and applications. A temporary asylum permit is the only legal way for migrants to stay and work in South Africa, creating an incentive for persons to submit asylum applications despite their low probability of receiving accreditation or their substantial lack of documentation. In 2006 there were nearly 30 000 applications for asylum, Zimbabweans made up by far the largest percentage of this figure, accounting for some 24% of those requesting asylum in 2006.[20] The Department of Home Affairs claims, however, to have processed fewer than 2000 requests and granted asylum to little more than 100 applicants in 2006.[21] According to the World Refugee Survey, of the 171 400 registered refugees and asylum seekers in 2007 only 18 000 were Zimbabweans.[22]

Skilled migrants, who are the most 'preferred' category, were associated originally with the apartheid era (eg those from Zimbabwe between 1982 and 1988). In 2001 the number of documented immigrants to South Africa was 4832; about 11% were from neighbouring countries.[23] Legal migration into South Africa is low. Indeed, we can say that: 'This growing restrictionism has even penetrated the area of temporary migration for the purpose of work, and since 1990 there has been a decline in the issue and re-issue of temporary work permits'.[24] As a consequence, employers have found it increasingly problematic to hire personnel from abroad, even provisionally; those foreign workers who are recruited find themselves entangled in DHA red tape.[25] For all intents and purposes, it seems that South Africa is closing all legal roots of entry for foreigners who wish to work within her borders.

From the various figures alone it is difficult to draw any safe conclusions about the question of 'management' of migration, the migration regime and the situation on the ground:

> Although a tentative scrutiny of these deportation figures contributes to clarifying aspects concerning illegal migration in South Africa, it is immediately apparent that various extraneous variables tend to confound the drawing of conclusions. Apart from obvious factors such as priorities of policing strategy and prosecution procedures in a country in which crime rates are high, [13] there are other less conspicuous factors that confound attempts to use the

deportation statistics as a basis for conclusions. The so-called 'revolving door syndrome' whereby illegal immigrants have learnt to work the system by manipulating the deportation procedures so that deportation is no longer a deterrent to illegal migrants.[26]

Racialisation and xenophobia against migrants in South Africa: structural conditions

Anyone examining the position of migrant workers in South Africa as regards their exclusion and racialisation ought to examine the wider context of the transition of the country. Post-apartheid South Africa has enjoyed about a decade and a half of majority rule on the basis of a constitution which declares, as one of its fundamental principles and goals, the 'achievement of a non-racial society'. However, in spite of the efforts to create what Archbishop Desmond Tutu has called 'the rainbow nation', neither the question of 'race' nor the questions of class and gender oppression and exploitation have ceased to be central in contemporary South Africa. The defeat of apartheid, the bastion of state-organised racism, a regime based explicitly on racist institutionalisation, and its replacement by 'the new South Africa' is indicative of how 'race' and racism remain operational forces even after they have officially been declared dead. There is no consensus as to the current 'transitional' state of affairs: 14 years after the ANC took over from white nationalist/racist minority rule there is still considerable debate as to the direction, pace and nature of the post-apartheid regime.[27]

South Africans avoid using the term 'race' and its derivatives, such as 'racism' and 'racialisation', for anything other than the specific nature of the apartheid ideological and institutional frames; hence the use of the term to describe the position of migrant workers in South Africa is strongly objected to. This may be understandable at one level: 'the powerful are racist'; 'the subalterns are prejudiced, possibly xenophobic'. However, this may result in a licence to be racist, particularly when we are dealing with state-related processes.

It seems that 'race' remains a taboo subject in South Africa; yet there is considerable research that shows that 'race still matters in the new South Africa'.[28] Yasmin Sooka suggests that 'race remains an intrinsic factor in the debate on reconciliation in post-apartheid South Africa',[29] while Jeff Guy points out that, given the nature of South Africa's 'negotiated compromise' sacrifices were made 'of essential elements', which meant that 'elements of the old racial system were retained resulting in awkward continuities between the old racial system and the new unitary democratic one'.[30]

Recently, in an effort to rally support, African National Congress leaders have begun to make 'further racial emphasis', which is a dangerous practice. Moreover, new forms of racism and xenophobia are increasingly evident in 'non-racial' South Africa:

> The foregrounding of race can be extremely dangerous when it interacts with the predicament and the fears of the poor, the insecure, as well as ruthlessly ambitious. As an increasing number of Africans seek opportunities in South

Africa so xenophobia becomes more violent and intense, challenging what many see as the defining achievements of the transition from apartheid—the creation of a multi-racial nation out of racial tyranny.[31]

Alexander argues that the project of the ANC is essentially one of enlarging the black upper and middle class, and that the particular form of affirmative action taken, 'Black Economic Empowerment', has not led to the perpetuation of racial identities.[32] Similarly, MacDonald concludes not only that 'race still matters in South Africa' but argues that the transition to a liberal democracy is essentially a policy for 'stable democratic capitalism' whereby 'racial nationalism legitimizes a so-called non-racial democracy by building an African bourgeoisie along with black middle classes'.[33] His overall conclusion is that the acquisition of power by the ANC in the name of the black majority under the banner of achieving a 'non-racial society' has meant that 'the political economy was not de-racialised; it was multi-racialised.[34] Another scholar referred to 'a national schizophrenia about race', where race-based policies are assumed to be the means to achieve a 'non-racial society'.[35]

At the level of rhetoric Mandela's successors have always attempted to legitimise his politics by invoking his Africanness: this was the ideological starting point, the rallying point for his policies. One can see the attempt to give an ideological gloss on the policies he presided over and the direction of the ANC under Mbeki. He presided over the abandonment of the 'social' elements of the ANC programme with the abandonment of Reconstruction and Development Program (RDP) in favour of a neoliberal self-imposed structural adjustment programme known as 'GEAR'.[36] This, together with the liberalisation of trade, has resulted in the informalisation and irregularisation of labour, rising unemployment and an increase in inequality and poverty.[37] Seekings and Nattrass illustrate how the current social structure and distributional regime in South Africa has led to an increase in inequality.[38] Despite the policies of deracialisation, which were apparently put in place so that 'African workers secured benefits previously held by white workers', these failed to address mass inequality and poverty. In other words, deracialisation 'did not mean that the opportunities facing the unemployed and rural poor improved'.[39] However, there is a second dimension here that is often missed by cogent analyses such as that of Seeking and Natrass and others: migrant workers and the way in which restrictive migration has led to their marginalisation and exclusion. Mbeki has been a key figure in the international negotiations with neighbouring countries, including SADC and, more importantly, he has presided over both the continual use of the apartheid migration regime and the evolution to the 'new' regime. It remains to be seen whether Jacob Zuma, the new leader of the ANC, who will succeed Thabo Mbeki, will continue with the same migration regime.

Two of the most economically successful SADC countries, South Africa and Botswana, both of which colluded to kill off the Free Movement Protocol in SADC, exhibit serious xenophobic attitudes at a popular level. Yet popular xenophobia must not divert attention from the fundamental point of the 'global issue', where 'the tendency is for migrants, skilled and unskilled to be exploited.[40] This is the structural dimension that compels us to appreciate these socioeconomic relations as constituting processes of racialisation. The presence of migrants has already begun to change society; we can speak of social transformations of aspects of social life.

> In certain cases, whole parts of cities (eg Hillbrow in Johannesburg) have been appropriated by black African migrants—derogatorily referred to as Makwerekwere ... The new migrants largely come in as long-distance traders, asylum-seekers, students, professionals, entrepreneurs, traditional healers and pastors of mostly Pentecostal churches.[41]

Migrant workers are often preferred as cheap labour with limited, if any security and meagre pay. In other words, profits and other benefits for capital are the fruits of the exploitation of migrant workers.

At a state level the celebratory open citizenship for all South Africans is masking the second parallel process that is occurring: the 'rainbow nation' is being built on the exclusion of the black African 'other', the *Makwerekwere*. The fiction of the late Phaswane Mpe, *Wecome to Our Hillbrow*, records this duality: the *Makwerekwere* is depicted in unsubstantiated inflammatory statements by politicians as responsible for 'the current crime wave, rising unemployment, or even the spread of diseases.[42] Social surveys and studies indicate that the state apparatus often targets migrants for abuse: the police, the army, the DHA and the media alike.

What is most astonishing is that the old racist ideas are now targeting migrants, as skin-colour is once more an indication of the 'propensity' to commit crime as well as being used as a stereotypical profiling to capture the 'intruders': 'Dark skinned refugees and asylum-seekers with distinctive features are especially targeted for abuse'.[43] This has resulted in situations where South African citizens are mistakenly thought of as foreigners and are picked up, arrested and targeted by the police. Individuals are often assumed to be *Makwerekwere* on the basis that they 'look foreign' or are 'too dark' to be entitled to South Africa . 'Black South African citizens are sometimes mistaken for the dark, invading barbarians or stutterers who must be confined to the fringes'.[44]

In this sense we cannot but refer to the acts of the *post-apartheid* state against black migrants as 'racist'; there is no reason why one should refer to this policy, practice, and exclusionary ideology merely as 'xenophobic'; otherwise we may be making light of what is essentially a continuation of the policies of the apartheid regime and what appear to be state practices across many countries of the globe.

The contradictory responses of the South African trade union movement: pro-migrant but anti-immigration?

In line with the post-apartheid philosophy of democratic involvement, the creation of the current immigration legislation, the Immigration Act (No 13) of 2002 (hereafter the Immigration Act) was the product of a public participation process in which groups representing labour, civil society and business took part. This paper will now examine the role played by the trade union movement.[45]

During the apartheid period, immigration law was a product of the white minority's obsession with the construction of racial domination. For the black nationalistic discourse immigration was constructed as a form of labour control and an instrument of racial oppression. Immigration policy, and especially the migrant labour system, was a historically constructed mechanism for providing cheap, docile labour for white capital and expanding industrialisation. The main component was conceived as the impoverishment of the rural periphery (categorised as 'labour reserves') to privilege the urban centre. Such a system was perceived as a conspiracy by white employers and by the apartheid 'regime' more broadly, to divide and control the oppressed in general and the working class in particular. The migrant labour system was deemed a pure form of exploitation and social humiliation that perpetuated appalling conditions in single sex hostels, divided families and social dislocation. Thus systems of labour migration were seen as 'invented' from 'outside' and therefore 'artificial' and a means of 'foreign' control. This vision of the migrant labour system as an integral part of the apartheid apparatus and a causal factor in regional poverty creates such a negative historical view of the migration system that, in the new post-apartheid period, logic dictates that it must be discontinued.[46] In the post-apartheid period, labour immigration has been reconstructed as a mechanism for capital (referred to as employers within the documentation of organised labour) to undermine labour standards.

This logic allows the trade union movement to be anti-immigration while at the same moment pro-immigrant, declaring that the 'working people of Southern Africa are not the enemy of South African workers. The interests of South African workers are inextricably linked to the interests of our brother and sister workers in the surrounding region'.[47] Immigration policy is therefore conceived of as a potential threat not only to South African workers but to all the workers of Southern Africa. The enemy of the migrant labour system is, under this logic, the employers of 'illegal' migrants who become the causal factor behind the erosion of workers' rights. Rather than target the 'illegal' migrants themselves, the trade unions advocate heavy penalties and more extensive enforcement mechanisms to prevent the practice of employing 'illegals'.[48] In this manner the trade union movement demonstrates its commitment to greater worker solidarity throughout the region, while at the same time expressing support for a system in which foreigners are prevented from legally obtaining work in South Africa.

The pro-immigrant stance of the trade union movement can be revealed through its strong criticism of the government's position on illegal migrants during the drafting process of the Immigration Act. In a separate submission on the Draft White Paper on International Migration to the DHA, COSATU accused the former and its policy proposals of a xenophobic 'preoccupation with illegal migration [which] results in a failure to provide a coherent immigration policy and in certain respects the avoidance of issues'. It argued that such a preoccupation would 'further engender paranoia, which will then make it difficult to have a rational and humane approach to illegal migration'. This view is shared by the Department of Labour (DOL), which stated in a NEDLAC Report on the International Migration White Paper that the 'the notion of illegal immigrants posing a negative impact on provisions of service and society was replete with inappropriate assumptions'.[49]

However, despite these criticisms and statements, the contradiction between a pro-migrant and an anti-immigration stance become clear when the movement challenged many proposals in the drafting process that would create legalised means of entry into the labour market for foreign workers. Although the trade union movement shares its sympathies with migrants, it seems to believe that large-scale entry of foreigners into the labour market would disadvantage citizen workers,[50] and these citizen workers must have priority.[51] For example, the immigration legislation in South Africa is heavily focused on removing restrictions and obstacles in previous legislation that prevent skilled labour from working in South Africa. Organised labour criticise this openness, claiming that this focus is detrimental to local workers and local skill development.[52] The joint submission called on the government to strictly monitor and regulate skills permits;[53] according to the joint submission the goal is 'to ensure that national priorities are not undermined in respect of the development of the local skills base'.[54] However, it is the movement's opposition to temporary workers programmes (programmes that would allow South African employers to recruit workers from the SADC region) that is the most striking example of this contradiction. The White Paper (para. 4.4.7) and the Green Paper advanced the notion that the 'provision must be made to meet ... labour supply requirements when there is agreement to proceed'. This White Paper suggestion is basically that the labour demands of workers whose conditions of employment do not comply with the prevailing conditions should be satisfied through a legal and regulated system rather than ignored and fulfilled through illegal means. COSATU criticised the government for opening itself up to the possibility of a two-tier or multi-tier labour market. It also criticised the criteria of this logic, as 'it fails to take into cognisance one of the objectives of government policy, which is geared towards transforming the market through re-regulation'.[55] Although a duality in the labour market could weaken the position of labour within South Africa from the perspectives of both citizens and non-citizens, it can be argued that these temporary migrant workers could be unionised and receive rights within the South African labour system. But the movement envisions foreign recruitment as a possible threat rather than an opportunity to expand its membership base. COSATU perceives xenophobia as an 'irrational' and 'artificial' phobia created and spread by employers to divide workers; this logic feeds into the anti-immigration logic of the movement.

This conception of xenophobia serves to disguise the implicit contradiction that exists between the trade unions' pro-migrant character and their anti-immigration discourse. This 'artificial phobia' makes it possible for the trade union movement to promote and defend the interests of migrants while at the same moment offering support to policies that would restrict their access to forms of more open and regular migration. Therefore xenophobia, rather than this implicit contradiction, becomes the obstacle that blocks the realisation of trade union ideals of just and fair treatment for all those working in South Africa.

The public participation process was not a smooth one and a joint submission of the nation's major trade unions accused the DHA of blocking their influence and NEDLAC involvement.[56] Ultimately this demonstrates an inability on the part of the trade union movement to effectively contribute to policy creation. It also illustrates the divisive role played by the DHA in eroding the objective of replacing the Act with a more progressive legislative framework.[57] An examination of the numerous communications of the South African trade union movement to the DHA reveals that, while sympathetically acknowledging the economic imperatives driving migrants, both legal and illegal, to seek a better life in South Africa, the unions gave tacit and sometimes overt support to stringent influx regulation. In other words, while the trade union movement has criticised government migration policy, its criticisms have been empty and have failed to challenge government migration policy on a tangible note. In this regard the trade union response to this issue has resembled a hypocritical approach, acknowledging the seriousness of the situation in institutionalised forums (such as NEDLAC), while ensuring the advancement of 'legal' worker rights in the context of illegal migration and rising xenophobia through protective labour legislation.

A South African trade unionism of tomorrow: back to a future when we were all migrant workers?

Social sciences have approached migration from different angles given the complexity of the subject,[58] which inevitably calls for an interdisciplinary approach requiring a more unifying research sphere.[59] Hence the development of migration studies as a discipline in its own right.[60] Of course, there are different approaches to the various aspects of migration, which often create alternative or antagonistic perspectives, while in other contexts these perspectives are complementary. In any case it is apparent that only interdisciplinary approaches can capture the very complex nature of the plethora of migration-related phenomena. In this light comparisons are essential tools of the trade, if we are to understand these complex processes and the contradictions in migration regimes. Regional integration processes such as the EU and SADC lend themselves as useful, if not essential comparisons.[61] Whether one is seeking to understand the issues that derive from 'managing the divide'[62] in terms of the nature and types of 'soft or hard borders' for Europe,[63] or in order to locate the dynamics for cross-border migration in Southern Africa,[64] or to 'locate the leading issue',[65] the explanatory frames, the patterns, the practices and transformations illustrate the importance of adopting a comparative perspective.

The question of migration needs to be addressed in its regional context and therefore requires a regional approach based on the notion that in the modern world state and non-state actors must strive for free movement across borders. However, this needs to be done in a manner that does not reproduce inequality, discrimination, racism and xenophobia. This is the experience of 'the neoliberal management of mobility of migration at a regional level': drawing from the experience of the EU/eastern Europe and the relationship between North American countries with Central and Latin America, Pellerin and Overbeek illustrate the inherent 'connection between migration control frameworks and measures for labour restructuring, economic relocation and capital expansion'.[66] This creates conditions for new 'tensions between migrants and non-migrants, new kinds of contestations between labour and capital in the reconfiguration of the mobility–fixity nexus of neoliberal restructuring'.[67] It is apparent that similar kinds of issues and tensions emerge in the case of the relationship between South Africa and SADC. In this sense the search for an alternative model that enhances the position of workers across the borders and builds on existing trans-border trade union co-operation is a major challenge for the forces of labour.

We have traced the labour movement responses to the migration question and have pin-pointed changes in perceptions with regard to migration.[68] It can be argued that the proverbial synergy between political struggles, class consciousness and trade unionism have always been the lifeblood and tradition of the South African labour movement. It is no coincidence that Kim Moody includes South African trade unionism as an archetype of a new unionism that goes beyond 'labourism'. Moody refers to 'an international social-movement unionism', which is defined as 'an active strategic orientation that uses the strongest of society' s oppressed and exploited generally organised workers, to mobilize those who are less able to sustain self- mobilization: the poor; the unemployed, the casualized workers, the neighbourhood organizations.[69]

In fact, this specific 'recipe' has already been used with success to organise Mexican workers in the agricultural sector in Texas and New Mexico: the Union de Trabajadores Agricolas Franterizos or Union of Border Agricultural Workers (UTAF) consists of a majority of undocumented immigrant workers. Such practices have also been implemented with success among urban migrant workers.[70] Other examples of successful organisation include unemployed and precarious workers in Europe (eg France), Asia and Africa (eg COSATU in South Africa). However, in South Africa matters are now far more complicated than 10 years ago, when Moody was writing. Moreover, South African trade unions have failed to organise migrant workers, who are amongst the most vulnerable in society, illustrating the limits of trade unionism per se, even the more actistic type of trade unionism referred to by Moody.

It can be argued that the political ethos of South African trade unions has always differed from the norms and confines of what has produced trade unionism in other national contexts: the notion of 'internationalism', which is supposed to be the cornerstone of workers' solidarity in the tradition of 'workers of the world unite'. The tradition and identity of the labour movement in South Africa was defined by concrete factors, political and ideological, which cemented an alignment that articulated together 'race and class' in resistance. As Sitas shows, there is strong 'solidarity of "comradeship" since the 1980s", whereby the factors that have formatted 'the "elastic band" that held the movement together still hold despite class mobility, divergent socioeconomic needs and mounting challenges to its "elasticity"".[71] These traditions are perhaps more visible in the modern history of trade unions dating back to the 1970s untll today. They were born out of the labour struggles against political repression by the apartheid regime to African 'black' workers, they were marked by both a resistance to and defiance of apartheid racial/ethnic divisive logic in as much as they have paradoxically defined the legacy of the same apartheid they fought so vehemently against. This paradox contains the essence of the dilemmas of South African trade unionism, as COSATU, hailed as the leading national workers' force against apartheid, is now torn between, on the one hand, its struggling traditions of anti-racism as an essential strategy for the achievement of unity of all workers against capitalism and apartheid, and on the other, its sectional defence of a 'national working class' against (African) migrant labour. In this sense the South African labour 'exceptionalism' of a trade unionism beyond labourism threatens to be extinguished. This process can only be reversed if the trade union movement draws on its own traditions as well as on the experience of international trade unionism that has been transformed from a defensive and often xenophobic 'national' force that fell into the divisive trap, into champions of migrant workers' integration into the 'host' working class institutions.

The ideology of free movement and a 'borderless continent' remains wishful thinking: the postcolonial states perceived 'economic emancipation' as a national cause premised on ideas of 'developmentalism', and not as a whole continent-wide project. Thus we have created a multi-regionalisation[72] of Africa, while catastrophic nationalisms, ethnic conflicts and tensions between regions and nation-states are tearing the continent apart. Moreover, as a result of uneven [and combined] development, we have massive inequalities within and among African states, which inevitably cause mass migrations towards the richer regions in search of jobs. Economic development and relative political stability of some regions or countries have become a 'pull factor' for migrant labourers as free movement became a natural, viable and noble motive of Pan-Africanism. One must not loose sight of the historical fact that we are essentially dealing with artificial boundaries, colonial/postcolonial products and class-related processes. In the South African context the creation of the 'Bantustans' or 'native homelands' was precisely premised on the rigid racial separation and super-exploitation of migrant workers: even today workers from the 'independent' statelets of Lesotho and Swaziland are treated as 'external migrants', thousands of whom are 'deported' as illegal migrants, only to return in search for jobs, as they have always done. However, the traditions of struggle based on worker solidarity, together with the dream of African unity, are a powerful force within the trade union movement that can be a source of reflexivity and strategising for the future.

The answer to the migration question for South Africa requires regional responses. Trade unions, social movements and human rights organisations can be at the forefront of regularising and organising undocumented and irregular migrant workers. Moreover, the trade union movement can work towards a regional alternative for opening up the borders of SADC so as to improve labour standards, enhance inter-border co-operation over workers' rights and counter the neoliberal regionalisation taking place at the moment.

Notes

1 J Crush, 'Immigration, xenophobia and human rights in South Africa', *Migration Policy Series 22*, South African Migration Project (SAMP), Cape Town, 2001.
2 For a historical overview of migration see M Wentzel & K Tibela, 'Historical background to South African migration', in P Kok, D Gelderblom, T Oucho & J Van Zyl (eds), *Migration to South and Southern Africa: Dynamics and Determinants*, Pretoria: HSRC Press, 2006, p 72.
3 Witwatersrand Native Labour Association.
4 Wentzel & Tibela, 'Historical background to South African migration', p 73.
5 See J Oucho & J Crush, 'Contra free movement: South Africa and the SADC Migration Protocols', *Africa Today*, 48, 2001, pp 139–158.
6 R Moore, *Racism and Black Resistance in Britain*, London: Pluto Press, 1975.
7 See N Trimikliniotis, 'Racism and new migration to Cyprus: the racialisation of migrant workers', in F Anthias & G Lazarides (eds), *Into the Margins: Exclusion and Migration in Southern Europe*, Avebury: Ashgate, 1999, pp 139–178.
8 FB Nyamnjoh, *Insiders & Outsiders: Citizenship and Xenophobia in Contemporary Southern Africa*, London: Zed Books, 2006, p 30.
9 *Ibid*.
10 *Mail & Guardian*, 28 January 2007. See also SL Gordon, 'The trade union response to alien workers within post-apartheid South Africa: an analysis of the nature of the response of the South Africa trade union movement to the issue of illegal migrant workers', unpublished Master's thesis, Albert-Ludwigs Universität, Freiburg and University of KwaZulu-Natal, 2005.
11 J Crush & D McDonald, 'Introduction to the special issue: evaluating South African immigration policy after apartheid', *Africa Today*, 48, 2000, pp 1–14.
12 See J Crush & V Williams, 'Making up the numbers: measuring illegal immigration to South Africa', *Migration Policy Brief 3*, SAMP, Cape Town, 2001.
13 A Minaar & M Hough, *Who Goes There? Perspectives on Clandestine and Illegal Aliens in Southern Africa*, Pretoria: HRSC Publishers, 1996, p 127.
14 *Ibid*, p 128.
15 M Reitzes, 'Counting the uncountable? Undocumented migrants in South Africa', paper presented at Department of Labour seminar, Cape Town, 1998; and J Crush, 'Fortress South Africa and the deconstruction of apartheid's migration regime', *Geoforum*, 30, 1999, pp 1–11.
16 See http://www.zimbabwejournalists.com/print.php?art_id=3144.
17 See http://www.frontline.org.za/news/zimbabwe_mugabe.htm.
18 http://www.state.gov/g/drl/rls/hrrpt/2007/100505.htm.
19 Quoted in Gordon, 'The trade union response to alien workers within post-apartheid South Africa'.
20 United Nations High Commissioner for Refugees (UNHCR), *2006 Global Trends: Refugees, Asylum-seekers, Returnees, Internally Displaced and Stateless Persons*, Geneva: UNHCR, 2007.
21 The rise in the number of asylum seekers comes as the South African government is stepping up efforts to tackle a backlog of earlier applications from over 100 000 people—some years old. About 30 000 individuals have received official recognition in South Africa as refugees.
22 US Committee for Refugees and Immigrants (USCRI), *World Refugee Survey 2007*, at http://www.refugees.org/article.aspx?id=1941&subm=19&ssm=29&area=Investigate, accessed 23 April 2008.
23 Wentzel & Tibela, 'Historical background to South African migration'.
24 Crush & Williams, 'The new South African Immigration Bill: a legal analysis', *Migration Policy Brief 2*, SAMP, Cape Town, 2001.
25 CM Rogerson & J Rogerson, 'Dealing in scarce skills: employer responses to the brain drain in South Africa', in D McDonald & J Crush (eds), *Destinations Unknown: Perspectives on the Brain Drain in Southern Africa*, Pretoria: Africa Institute of South Africa, 2002, pp 73–98.
26 Gordon, 'The trade union response to alien workers within post-apartheid South Africa'.
27 See H Marais, *South Africa: Limits to Change—The Political Economy of Transition*, Cape Town, University of Cape Town Press,1998; and N Alexander, *An Ordinary Country: Issues in the Transition from Apartheid to Democracy*, Pietermaritzburg: University of Natal Press, 2002.

28 M Macdonald, *Why Race Matters in South Africa*, Kwazulu-Natal: University of Kwazulu-Natal Press, 2006.

29 Y Sooka, 'Race and reconciliation: *E Pluribus unum?*', in A Adebajo, A Adedeji & C Landsberg (eds), *South Africa in Africa: The Post-apartheid Era*, Kwazulu-Natal: University of Kwazulu-Natal Press, 2007, p 79.

30 J Guy, 'Somewhere over the rainbow: the nation-state, democracy and race in globalizing South Africa', *Transformations* (University of Kwazulu-Natal Press), 56, 2004, pp 70–71.

31 *Ibid*, p 85.

32 N Alexander, 'Affirmative action and the perpetuation of racial identities in post-apartheid South Africa', *Transformations*, 63, 2007, pp 92–108.

33 Macdonald, *Why Race Matters in South Africa*, p 4.

34 *Ibid*, p 177.

35 V Maphai, 'Race and the politics of transition: confusing political imperatives with moral goals', in C Mangani (ed), *On Becoming a Democracy: Transition and Transformation in South African Society*, Pretoria: University of South Africa Press, 2004, p 22.

36 See Marais *South Africa*; and Alexander, *An Ordinary Country*.

37 Mandela's shift of policy from RDP to GEAR is attributed to a large extent to Mbeki, according to his biographer. See M Gevisser, *Thabo Mbeki: The Dream Deferred*, Jeppestown: Jonathan Ball, 2007, p 674.

38 Seekings & Nattrass, *Class, Race and Inequality in South Africa*, Kwazulu-Natal: University of Kwazulu-Natal Press, 2006.

39 *Ibid*, p 375.

40 Nyamnjoh, *Insiders & Outsiders*, p 2.

41 *Ibid*, p 31.

42 *Ibid*, p 48.

43 Various studies are referred to in *ibid*. See p 48.

44 *Ibid*, p 49.

45 For more details on the subject of trade unions and migration in South Africa, see Gordon 2005.

46 For example, the National Union of Mineworkers (NUM) called for the dismantling of the migrant labour system in 1991, in favour of policies that focus on regional economic development.

47 Congress of South African Unions (COSATU), *Submission on the Draft Green Paper on International Migration*, presented to the Home Affairs Portfolio Committee, 5 September 1997, Section 2.4.

48 According to *ibid*, 'increased penalties should be imposed on employers who employ illegal migrants and effective enforcement mechanisms must be put into place' (Section 3.2. Migration Policy.7) and 'the detection and sanctioning of employers who employ illegal migrants should form a primary pillar in the enforcement of migration policy' (Section 3.3.3). According to the COSATU Statement on Xenophobia, 'Concrete steps should be taken by the authorities to halt this super-exploitation of migrants. The bosses who are employing illegal immigrants, clearly with the view of sidestepping fair labour market laws, must be severely punished'. Appendix B in Crush, 'Immigration, xenophobia and human rights in South Africa'.

49 NEDLAC, *Report on the International Migration White Paper*, submitted to the Department of Home Affairs, 31 January 2001.

50 According to COSATU, *Submission on the Draft Green Paper*, 'we agree with the general principle that "unregulated access" would lead to "unacceptable competition for jobs"' (Section 3.2).

51 According to the Joint Submission of COSATU, NACTU & FEDUSA, 2002, 'it is important to prioritise jobs for unskilled South Africans' (p 9). According to NEDLAC, *Report on the International Migration White Paper*, 2001, 'labour supported the licensing fee as a mechanism to prioritise South Africans' (Section 3.5).

52 According to the COSATU, *Submission on the Draft Green Paper*, 'Immigration policies aimed at attracting skilled workers must not jeopardise the priority of developing skills in the South African workforce and we should not compromise the Department of Labour's programme for improved skills training on the basis that attempts are being made to attract skilled labour from other countries' (Section 2.3.6); and 'COSATU has consistently argued that the implementation of legislation and policies to promote domestic skills development must be viewed as a primary economic priority. This priority should not be jeopardised or displaced by policies aimed at attracting foreign skills' (Section 3.2.1). According to NEDLAC, *Report on the International Migration White Paper*, 'Labour wanted … to devise a Human Resource Strategy regarding a long-term skills development strategy, in order to reduce dependence on skills of migrants' (Section 3.9).

53 Business leaders have accused the South African trade union movement of supporting the stringent—critics say draconian—bureaucratic requirements of current migration legislation intended to protect South African workers from alleged job insecurity feared from an influx of skilled immigrant workers. *Business Report*, 28 May 2002.

54 Joint Submission of COSATU, NACTU & FEDUSA, 2002, p 10.
55 COSATU, *Submission on the White Paper on International Migration*, presented to the Portfolio Committee, 19 May 2000, p 7.
56 Described in the joint submission as a 'source of considerable frustration for the labour constituency'. Joint Submission of COSATU, NACTU & FEDUSA, p 3.
57 NEDLAC, in its own submission to the DHA on the Draft Immigration Regulations, claimed that the enactment of the Bill took place through a process that has undermined the principle of public participation, the role of NEDLAC as an institution and even parliament itself. This submission called the process of public consultation a 'sham'. *Labour Submission on the Draft Immigration Amendment Bill*, submitted to the NEDLAC Labour Market Chamber, 6 July 2004, p 1.
58 C Brettel & JF Hollifield, 'Migration theory: talking across the disciplines', in Brettel & Hollifield (eds), *Migration Theory: Talking across the Disciplines*, London: Routledge, 2000, p 1.
59 *Ibid*, p VII.
60 S Castles, 'Migrations and minorities in Europe: perspectives for the 1990s—twelve hypotheses', in J Wrench & J Solomos (eds), Oxford: Berg, 1993, p 30.
61 For such a comparison, see N Trimikliniotis, SL Gordon & B Zondo, 'Migration, globalization, regionalization and re-racialization: challenges for the Labour Movement', forthcoming 2008.
62 J De Bardeleben (ed), *Soft or Hard Borders? Managing the Divide in an Enlarged Europe*, Adershot: Ashgate, 2005, pp 1–2.
63 N Neuwah, 'What borders for which Europe?', in *ibid*, pp 23–43.
64 See P Kok, D Gelderbloom, T Oucho and J van Zyl, 'Introduction', in Kok *et al*, *Migration to South and Southern Africa*.
65 A Adepoju, 'Leading issues in international migration in sub-Saharan Africa', in C Cross, D Gelderblom, N Roux & J Mafukidze (eds), *Views on Migration in Sub-Saharan Africa: Proceedings of an African Migration Alliance Workshop*, Pretoria: HRSC Press, 2006, p 25.
66 H Pellerin & H Overbeek, 'Neo-liberal regionalism and the management of people mobility', in A Bieler & AD Morton (eds), *Social Forces in the Making of the New Europe: The Restructuring of European Social Relations in the Global Political Economy*, Basingstoke: Macmillan, 2001, pp 137–157.
67 *Ibid*, pp 154–155.
68 We expand on these ideas in another paper. See Trimikliniotis *et al*, 'Migration, globalization, regionalization and re-racialization'.
69 K Moody, *Workers in a Lean World: Unions in the International Economy*, London: Verso, 1997, p 276.
70 See *ibid*, pp 175–178.
71 A Sitas, 'Thirty years since the Durban strikes: black working-class leadership and the South African transition', *Current Sociology*, 52 (5), 2004, p 830.
72 Free movement campaigns were driven by regional organisations and only concentrated on cross-border migration.

'Keeping Them in Their Place': the ambivalent relationship between development and migration in Africa

OLIVER BAKEWELL

In the past decade migration has risen to the top of the development agenda after being of marginal interest to development studies and development policy and practice for many years. Today the potential contribution of migration to development is being trumpeted by states—especially industrialised states—multilateral organisations, non-governmental organisations (NGOs), wider civil society and academics. The old rhetoric of migrants' remittances being used for 'conspicuous consumption' is being supplanted by an analysis which highlights both the scale and the economic multiplier effects of the money sent home. Migrants who, having left their country, were once seen as embodying the problem of the 'brain drain' are now being courted as agents of development.

The ongoing search for approaches to migration that simultaneously maximise its benefits for areas of origin and destination and for the migrants themselves has generated a huge volume of new research, policy initiatives and interventions, in which the relationship between migration and development is often portrayed as operating in a virtuous circle. This envisages the process of migration generating remittances and increases in human capital, which flow back to the countries of origin through financial transfers, transnational linkages and return migration. This increases the level of development in sending regions, which in due course reduces the rate of emigration.

What is missing from this analysis is any critique of the concept of development under consideration; questions are posed about how migration affects the process of development, without asking what development means. In this article, I argue that this is a critical flaw, as there is a persistent sedentary bias in much of the theory and practice of development, which makes it impossible to incorporate migration into the development agenda without fundamentally reassessing the concept. In particular, I suggest that migration raises challenging questions about the nature of the good life, the focus on the nation-state and the inherent paternalism found in the current notions of development.

The article focuses on the particular context of 'interventionist' development approaches as they are commonly applied across the African continent. It starts by reflecting on the roots of the 'development project' in Africa and shows how it has long been associated with the colonial concern about the control of mobility. This has been continued by development actors, who have consistently framed both internal and international migration as a problem to be addressed, with the widespread expectation that development progress will reduce migration pressures. The recent enthusiasm for exploring the links between migration and development has not been accompanied by a significant change in development actors' ambivalent views of migration; there remains an underlying assumption that development is about enabling people to stay at 'home'. It argues that these concepts of development fail to take account of people's different development goals, struggle to cope with transnationalism, which takes development beyond the borders of nation-states, and maintain echoes of colonial paternalism. In conclusion, it calls for development to be reconceptualised for a mobile world.

While the arguments of this article may have broader application, its scope is limited in three ways. First, the discussion is restricted to the concepts of development arising from the 'modernist ideology' shared by the modernisation, dependency and world-systems schools of thought in development studies. These hold to a fundamental belief in the concept of progress. Such development ideas have been fundamentally questioned by 'post-development' authors, such as Escobar, but, while such literature has stimulated important and ongoing debates, it has had limited impact on the practice of development.[1]

This is the second limitation of this article; it is coming from the perspective of interventionist development studies, which is concerned both with development as a vision for progressive change or idea of a desirable future state, and with how to bring about such change. It focuses on the ideas and world of development aid as a distinct area of practice, conducted by development organisations staffed by development professionals, and often informed by academics engaged in development studies. This includes line ministries in developing countries, development departments in donor governments, multilateral organisations (such as World Bank, United Nations Development Programme, African Development Bank) and civil society organisations, in particular national and international development NGOs.

The significance of such development aid as a driver of change within developing countries may often be overstated, especially by development actors. In many cases it may be of marginal importance compared with many other factors like political reform, new private sector investments and technological advances. However, it still constitutes a significant portion of the national economy in many countries in the poorest regions of the world. In particular, in Africa official development aid represents over a quarter of GDP in 11 of the 53 countries across the continent.[2] Sub-Saharan Africa is the only region of the world where official development assistance still outweighs remittances and foreign direct investment. Hence, the third limitation of this paper is that it focuses primarily on interventionist development ideas as they are put into practice in Africa.

Colonial roots of development in Africa

The origins of the notion of development as a distinct arena of social practice are commonly traced back to the middle of the 20th century with the establishment of the Bretton Woods institutions and a concern to ensure that newly independent states moved firmly into the capitalist global order. However, while this period may represent the beginning of the institutionalisation of development practice, and of the field of development studies, the concept has much deeper roots.[3] Cowen and Shenton argue that the notion of 'development' emerged as an attempt to address the perceived chaos caused by the rapid technological, social and economic change of the industrial revolution in the 18th century. More 'advanced' societies were seen as having a responsibility to introduce ideas of tolerance and rationality to replace primitive custom in order to create the conditions for development. Such arguments directly underpinned the colonial doctrine of 'trusteeship', which aimed 'to create conditions under which education, choice, individuality—in a word development—might occur'.[4]

Although these roots in colonial administration are seldom acknowledged by those engaged in development today, they were clearly carried across into postcolonial ideas of development as a 'professional' practice. Many of the early development practitioners had transferred from colonial service and there were close parallels between ideas of trusteeship and the theories of modernisation which dominated development studies in the 1960s.[5] While the theories and practice of development appear to have moved away from such blatant hangovers from the colonial past, many of these roots remain in place; in particular, the ongoing ambivalence, or at times hostility, towards human mobility that is outside the control of states.

From the earliest days of widespread European incursions into Africa a major concern was to gain control over the movement of people in order to direct it towards the aims of the invaders. This took its most brutal form in the transatlantic slave trade as the export of the people's labour power was the primary interest. As the Europeans established their colonies and directed their attention to the massive exploitation of the mineral wealth and natural resources that lay within the continent, they faced the challenge of how to engage the labour of Africans in the colonial endeavour. This was achieved by various means, including the use of forced labour, the introduction of hut and poll taxes, the expropriation of the best land for settler agriculture, and the provision of services for wage labourers. Such policies served to ensure Africans had to provide their labour for the mines, plantations and colonial administrations across the continent.

Thus the functioning (and profitability) of the colonial state relied on the migration of labour. It needed large concentrations of populations to come together to provide the labour for mines, plantations and the colonial administration. At the same time, with this mass movement of people there was great concern to ensure that such people did not settle permanently in these new centres.[6] Labourers were welcome but they should retain their link with their homelands and ideally, when they finished their contract or came to retirement, they would return 'home' to make way for new labourers.

While the colonial authorities established a labour system based on the continuous (circular) migration of Africans, they were also keen to encourage them to maintain their 'traditional' way of life in the villages; to preserve the 'homes' to which labour migrants could return. In many areas this was assumed to be a largely sedentary existence based around stable villages in fixed locations populated by particular (static) 'tribes'. The colonial systems for the collection of taxes, the imposition of colonial law, and the provision of government services all relied on a good understanding of who was where. Mobility confused the picture:

> Colonial rulers were dismayed at the high mobility exhibited by villagers in Northern Province [of Zambia] and could not understand why people did not stay put in 'proper villages'. They were sure that such behaviour was not 'traditional' but the result of recent pathology brought on by industrial development and the 'migrant labour system'. Small temporary villages, with people moving about in an undisciplined manner between them, they felt sure, were a sign of the 'breakdown' of traditional institutions, a breakdown that government policy would have to check if 'detribalization' was to be avoided.[7]

As African states gained their independence in the second half of the 20th century, the control of urban growth remained an urgent policy concern. In South Africa the apartheid state implemented its racist pass laws in order to control permanent urban settlement and try to ensure the black African population remained in their 'homelands'. In other parts of the continent, while many of the newly independent states showed an urban bias in policies of industrialisation and modernisation in the cities, many aid programmes focused on the development of rural areas, which was seen as essential to enable people to stay in their villages rather than try their luck in the ever growing cities.[8]

There were massive government investments in rural development programmes, agricultural extension, and rural infrastructure (such as roads, water supply, health facilities and schools). The generations of rural development initiatives supported by donors left a legacy of office compounds, broken down vehicles and reports in district centres across Africa, but did not bring the desired change in the rural economies or a reduction in rural emigration.[9]

This is not to suggest that the control of rural–urban migration was the only reason for such rural development policies. Conditions in many rural areas were appalling and increasing agricultural production, both to ensure the food supply to the growing cities and for export crops, was a critical issue. However, throughout these development initiatives, whether they arise from states or NGOs, there has been an underlying sedentary bias and desire to control mobility.[10] A common belief is that improved conditions in rural areas will reduce rural–urban migration and consequently reduce the growth of urban poverty. Based on this belief, many rural development interventions have been justified partially on the grounds that they will reduce urban migration.[11]

What is remarkable about these attempts to control rural–urban migration through rural development and controls in urban areas is that they have been largely futile. Development in areas of origin has usually been accompanied by increased migration.[12] Far from being an indicator of successful development, reverses in rural–urban migration have been associated with economic decline and the collapse of employment opportunities in urban areas.[13]

Migration moving to centre stage

Therefore, from its earliest roots, development practice in Africa has commonly seen a reduction in migration as either an (implicit or explicit) aim of intervention or an indicator of a programme's success. While many early anthropological studies explored the complex relationship between migration and change in rural and urban societies, the emerging field of development studies focused on the negative impact of out-migration on rural production, growing inequality, the use of remittances for consumption rather than investment and growing pressure on embryonic urban structures. In general, within the development literature migration has been framed as a problem: a response to crisis rather a 'normal' part of people's lives.[14]

The longstanding concerns about rural–urban migration are clearly mirrored in current debates about international migration from developing countries to industrialised states. International migration is widely seen to be driven by relative poverty and the lack of opportunity in developing countries (push factors) and by a growing demand for labour in industrialised states (pull factors). In the same way that migration was seen as reducing productivity in rural areas, the disproportionate presence of highly educated and skilled people among migrants from Africa has provoked widespread concern about the impact of this 'brain drain' on their countries of origin. While migrants' remittances provide large flows of income to some developing countries, it has often been argued that their contribution to development is limited because they are used for consumption and exacerbate inequality as they do not benefit the poorest households, who are not connected to migrant networks.[15] Thus, analogous debates about the costs and benefits of migration have been rehearsed for movements from developing countries (the new 'villages') to industrialised states (the new 'cities').

Such truths about migration and development have held sway in much of the literature over many years, despite the weakness of the theoretical and empirical base of many of them. In 1998 Massey *et al* concluded in their review of migration theories:

> Because neither theory nor data have been up to the task of evaluating migration's effects on economic development, and have largely asked and answered the wrong questions, we believe the prevailing view is unduly pessimistic and harsh.[16]

However, the picture has changed dramatically in the past decade as the relationship between migration and development has moved to the centre stage of academic interest, policy and practice. This shift is all the more striking when one recalls that until very recently the subject of migration was often absent from mainstream development discourses. For example, neither migration nor migrants are mentioned in the Millennium Development Goals—except with respect to the spread of disease.

A number of factors explain this renewed interest in migration and development. First, since the late 1990s international migration, in particular the increases in migration from the developing regions to the Western world, has frequently been portrayed as a global crisis demanding urgent attention. However, the scale of migration in proportion to the world's population is not unprecedented; there have been historical antecedents for much large movements of people in the last quarter of the 19th century.[17] What has increased dramatically is the diversity of migrants and migrants' destinations. Migrants are now concentrated in industrialised states (63%), a reverse from the 1960s, and since the 1990s net migration from Africa to wealthier regions of the globe has grown.[18] The very visible forms of undocumented migration from Africa into Europe through people smuggling, trafficking and other illegal routes have helped to make immigration a major political priority in the EU. The pictures of young African men arriving on boats in the tourist destinations of the Mediterranean and Canary Islands give a popular impression of migration out of control, even though the numbers of people involved are relatively small. Such movements are seen to be driven by desperation and poverty, in other words by the failure of development, and they create a huge pressure to find solutions that stop such desperate measures.[19] The other side of the story is the need for labour within the EU, which cannot be met from its own population. While ever more stringent measures to stop illegal movement are devised, there is every incentive for people to come and for businesses to employ them.[20]

Second, the issue of migration was thrust into the foreground in mainstream development circles when the World Bank *Global Development*

Finance 2003 report drew attention to the massive growth in migrants' remittances, which were dwarfing levels of official aid and foreign direct investment in many developing countries. According to the World Bank, migrants' remittances sent to developing countries rose from US$85 billion in 2000 to an estimated $199 billion in 2006.[21] In 2002 Africa received $12 billion in remittances, 15% of the global total. Two-thirds of this was sent to North Africa, in particular to Egypt and Morocco. In sub-Saharan Africa recorded remittances are rising more slowly than in other regions and are still considerably less than official development aid, but they still make a vital contribution to the balance of payments and, of course, to recipient households and communities. The development potential of these funds has therefore become a subject of extreme interest.[22]

Striking a more sceptical note, Kapur observed that the 'new development mantra' of remittances is not simply the result of new research findings but also a reflection of changing ideologies and the failure of other development approaches. After half a century of development interventions there is still very limited progress. This is especially the case in Africa, which is frequently discussed in apocalyptic terms of worsening crisis, disaster and decline. Development as practised over the past 60 years has not delivered the hoped-for results. In other regions there is significant progress towards the Millennium Development Goals, but across Africa the prospects of achieving many of them remain very slim to vanishing. Remittances 'strike the right cognitive chords' as they resonate with participatory approaches of self-help and because, as private flows, they do not need expensive (and corrupt) government bureaucracies to direct aid. 'Immigrants, rather than governments, then become the biggest provider of "foreign aid"'.[23]

Third, alongside this interest in remittances, there is also a growing recognition of the importance of transnational practices in shaping the relationship between migration and development. Migrants maintain links with the country of origin through a complex network of cultural, economic, social and political relations, which can now be sustained through new technologies (internet, mobile telephony) and cheaper travel.[24] This recognition of the ongoing transnational linkages between migrants (and their descendants) and their countries of origin has spurred a growing interest in the role of these diasporas in development. Until recently the concept of 'diaspora' was seen as the preserve of cultural studies and appeared rarely in development studies (or African studies) literature, which maintained an 'ostrich-like detachment from issues of race and diasporan concerns'.[25] Today it is firmly established in the development lexicon and there is a rapidly expanding literature on the potential engagement of the diaspora in development processes.[26]

Development actors and migration

As a result of such factors, the links between migration and development have become a topic of immense importance across the world and generated a huge range of initiatives, for example those of UN High Level Dialogue on International Migration and Development in 2006 and the Global Forum on

Migration and Development in 2007. Despite these shifts in recent academic and policy debates, many actors engaged in development practice, such as African governments, international development NGOs and donors, have maintained at best an ambivalent, or more commonly a negative view of migration, if they consider the subject at all. Development practice still clings to its sedentary roots within many African governments, NGOs and many donors.

The attitudes of African governments towards migration can be seen in the way in which they incorporate it into their development planning. In 2003 the Sussex Centre for Migration Research conducted a review of the Poverty Reduction Strategy Papers (PRSPs), which are developed in collaboration with states, donors, the World Bank and civil society to lay out the framework for national development plans. It found that most PRSPs which mentioned migration did so in pejorative terms. Of the 22 African PRSPs included in the survey, only six had anything positive to say about migration: Cape Verde, Ethiopia, Mali, Niger, Rwanda and Senegal. In Nigeria migration has hardly figured as a policy concern and until recently no connection was made between international migration and development. There has been much more focus on internal rural–urban migration, which was considered to cause social dislocation and create urban unemployment. In Nigeria's PRSP there is the warning that, if internal migration continues, 'the rate of urban unemployment could become unmanageable. The implications for poverty—and crime, conflict, and the maintenance of democracy—are grave'. In Ethiopia, the PRSP suggests, perhaps unsurprisingly, that controlled migration, which occurs as part of the state policy of planned resettlement from lowlands to highlands can be beneficial; in contrast, spontaneous migration causes natural resource degradation.[27]

The negative rhetoric of 'mainstream' international development NGOs is equally striking. For example, sifting through the websites of Oxfam International, ActionAid, Save the Children UK, Christian Aid and Concern Worldwide, the references to migration almost invariably cast it as the cause or symptom of multiple problems in developing regions, especially Africa. It is portrayed as:

- increasing labour demands on those left behind;
- making a negative impact on the crisis in agricultural production—alongside the production of illicit crops;
- a desperate measure to avoid poverty;
- causing the spread of HIV/AIDS;
- undermining traditional institutions;
- undermining health services.[28]

Of course this is by no means representative of all development NGOs working across Africa but it illustrates the perspectives of some of the larger international organisations that have greater access to current research and policy debates than most African NGOs. Moreover, the former are often acting as conduits for donor funds through partnership agreements with national NGOs. As a result, they play a major role in shaping development practice. It is hard to find any evidence of African development NGOs that depart significantly from this negative view of the relationship between migration and development.

Many development donors appear to hold to the view that migration is a result of poverty, and that investment in development can serve the purpose of reducing the levels of out-migration from rural areas to cities or from developing regions to industrialised states. For example, in Ethiopia the African Development Bank has given loans and grants to a total of $86 million to the Ethiopian government to 'control what it sees as a massive explosion in rural to urban migration'.[29]

In its review, *The Global Approach to Migration One Year On: Towards a Comprehensive European Migration Policy*, the European Commission makes its view of the link between migration and development quite explicit:

> Turning to the migration and development agenda, the prime challenge is to tackle the main push factors for migration: poverty and the lack of job opportunities. The EU must recognise that creating jobs in developing countries could significantly reduce migratory pressure from Africa. Migrants should be supported in contributing to the development of their countries of origin ... Promoting investments in labour intensive sectors in regions with high outward migration will be an important priority.[30]

In contrast to such attitudes, the UK Department for International Development (DFID) has taken a lead in bringing migration as a positive factor into its development agenda. In March 2007 it published a policy paper, *Moving out of Poverty—Making Migration Work Better for Poor People—* which sets out its strategy for future work on migration and development. It appears to place migration in the centre of development processes, stating that 'DFID believes that actions to allow the movement of people deserve as much attention as the movement of capital, goods and services, to enable the benefits of globalisation to be sustained and shared equitably'.

It highlights a range of policy priorities for DFID, incorporating migration issues into its work to 'maximise the benefits and minimise the risk of migration for poor people and developing countries'. These include 'managing migration' at national regional and international levels, creating opportunities for legal migration, improving migrants' access to their human rights, facilitating the flow of remittances, and supporting positive diaspora activity and circular migration. The DFID document illustrates the growing concern among donors to bring about the win-win-win scenario, where migration is good for the country of origin, the country of destination and the migrants themselves.[31]

Rethinking development in a mobile world

Throughout this reappraisal of the links between migration and development the underlying model of sedentary development remains largely intact.

A win-win-win situation can be achieved by a virtuous circle, in which migration contributes to development through mechanisms such as remittances and increases in migrants' skills. As the economic conditions in the country or region of origin improve, this reduces inequality between countries and provides new opportunities for people at 'home'. As a result, there is less incentive for people to leave their country and the flow of migrants will slow down. Indeed, as the conditions improve further, the flow of migration may be reversed as old migrants return to their country of origin. This rests on the assumption that migrants will be able and keen to maintain links with their country of origin and *at some stage return to it*.[32]

While it may be realistic to expect that improved economic conditions will change the pattern of migration and may even reduce the net outflow of people in the long term (for instance, drawing on the experience of Ireland, Italy and Portugal), many of the policy statements about migration suggest that investing in development is a *means* to reduce migration. They are phrased in terms that suggest sympathy for those who are forced to leave their homes on account of poverty to search for opportunity elsewhere. They use the technical language of migration management to ensure the legal movement of people under the control of states.

The trouble with this virtuous circle is that it assumes that all the actors involved have a common view of the 'good' ends to which the process leads them. It operates on the assumption that the normal and desirable state for human beings is to be sedentary. However, all the evidence suggests that, as people get more opportunities to move, they take them up in ever larger numbers. It is not the poorest of the poor who migrate—they cannot afford it—but it is those with lower-middle incomes. Mobility is a privilege of the relatively wealthy.[33] This is not to suggest that everyone would become a migrant given the chance—far from it. However, it is very likely that more people would move given the chance and, once they have moved, is it safe to assume they will want to return?

Moreover, too often the programmes that aim to increase the contribution of migration to development are still focused on initiatives to improve the livelihoods of people at home, with the expectation that they will then stay in their place. For example, it is hard to see the difference between the International Organisation for Migration's (IOM) Migration for Development in Africa (MIDA) Guinea Women's Project, which supports women's micro-enterprise development with training provided by members of the Guinean diaspora, and many other similar projects using training from other sources.[34] Mobility is still excluded from the underlying model of development.

In order to make sense of the complex interaction between migration and development, it is necessary to go further than analysing how far migration affects development as it is currently conceived. The contribution of migrants to existing development practices may be valuable (to the extent that existing development practice is valuable), but it is based on the ideal that everyone should be able to stay at 'home' or go 'home'. It is impossible simply to bring migration into development[35] without raising fundamental questions about the nature of development and how it is put into practice. These include

121

asking about the conception of the good life in development goals; about the appropriateness of models of development based on the nation-state; and about the inherent paternalism of development practice.

Different conceptions of good life

The goals and objectives of development organisations can be characterised as being concerned with improving the quality of life of those who are living in appalling poverty. This necessarily entails having a conception of what constitutes an improved quality of life; how do we know this good life when we see it? The work of development organisations is framed by a (usually implicit) conception of the good life to which people will (or should) aspire. Over the past 50 years development goals have evolved from an early focus on improvements in income, to a broader analysis of poverty, livelihoods and more recently notions of 'well-being'. This has been accompanied by a growing concern within development organisations to understand the perspectives of the people with whom they work; to move away from 'blueprint' planning and undertake 'bottom-up' development, embracing notions of 'participation', 'empowerment' and 'ownership' of the development process.

Most development initiatives are focused on geographical areas and aim to have an impact on the lives of people within the programme area—the nation, the region, the district, the city or the village. A 'successful' development programme will help to create the conditions in that area in which people are able and willing to live and flourish. They will improve the quality of life to such an extent that people do not feel the desire to move away. Therefore, in general, a reduction in out-migration is taken to be an indicator of development success. A development programme operating in a particular area will be seen as a failure if there is a continued exodus of population from the area.[36]

When it comes to migration there still appears to be a gulf between development organisations' conception of the good life and that of many people with whom they work. While the former look to a future where people can achieve a better quality of life at 'home', the latter may see improved quality of life related to new opportunities, which may include moving and establishing a new 'home' elsewhere. Such autonomy is an essential part of the notion of development-as-freedom put forward by Sen but it is not clear how it can be incorporated into the mainstream of development practice.[37]

Part of the problem may be the longstanding concern of development initiatives to preserve people's ways of life as far as possible. This echoes the colonial interests in maintaining 'tradition' and reflects static, essentialised notions of culture, at least with respect to place of residence.[38] For example, it is easy to assume that subsistence farmers want to make their way in agriculture rather than have aspirations to become traders in the cities. Of course, many farmers may want to maintain their rural livelihoods, but is it reasonable to assume that they (and future generations) will always hope for the same rural existence, especially as their horizons expand with improved education, communication and transport links, which expose them to (and prepare them for) the possibilities of life in the city or overseas?[39] The life of a subsistence farmer is tough and may offer few chances for improvement over the generations. If anything the prospects are shrinking across Africa as it engages in the global economy and more people are likely to move off the land—and see it in their best interests to do so.[40] Similarly, life in Asmara, for instance, may be hard and if you can take a chance to get to Italy to pick tomatoes, it will be difficult but you may see more chance of fulfilling your aspirations. Thus, such sedentary development initiatives may be aiming to maintain a way of life which a significant portion of their 'target groups' may wish to abandon, given the chance.

National models of development

Apart from the sedentary assumptions underlying development goals and practices, the concept of development is spatially bound by its focus on 'developing' or 'underdeveloped' states.[41] Throughout the development industry the nation-state is the primary unit of analysis for the assessment of levels of development. The broad concern of most development actors is to see the situation of people living in particular territories improve. If those people move outside the development sphere, say to Europe, to a large extent they are no longer interesting to development actors, except in as far as they maintain their links with people who remain in place.

The fact that the individuals who migrate may increase their income many times over, be able to send their children to school, have access to good healthcare and the other benefits of Western life (alongside the many costs), counts for little in development terms. As Rimmer has put it:

> No matter how remunerative migration might be, it is likely to be thought an unsatisfactory answer to the question of how Africa is to be developed. Individuals and their kin become better-off, but their places of origin remain backward or under-developed. But this perception signifies only in the context of a world we divide into nations or states. In this context Sudan counts for more than the Sudanese, Nigeria for more than the Nigerians, Ethiopia for more than the Ethiopians.[42]

It is obvious why both donors and developing states must be drawn into models of development bound by national borders. It is unsurprising that national NGOs in developing countries focus on their own country. It is less clear why international development NGOs, which purport to care about global inequality and injustice, uniformly follow the same path.

If we look at development within nation-states, assuming people have the resources and the freedom to move, we expect to find changing patterns of residence in response to changes in the economy, technology, the environment, culture and many other factors. As economies have developed, there has been a general shift from rural areas to the cities and the proportion of the population engaged in agricultural production has gone down dramatically. Looking at the USA, the overall population has doubled since the 1930s, but huge areas have seen high levels of out-migration and population decline in that period. The population of a contiguous area of Kansas and South Dakota larger than Ghana fell by 28% between 1930 and 1990. If such large areas in the USA cannot hold their populations, despite the wealth available in the nation to support the rural infrastructure and rural livelihoods, it raises the question of whether there are similar areas across Africa which might be destined for such decline into 'ghost countries'. It is important to emphasise that this is not to suggest that the people are in decline but, given the option in the long term, they may vote for the country and a lifestyle with their feet to find 'better' lives elsewhere. Development action to sustain some rural areas or even whole countries may be attempting to create artificial incentives to keep people in their place. In some cases it could perhaps be asked if investing such aid is wasteful when migration may be a more attractive and sustainable option for those people who have the opportunity to take it.[43]

Pritchett suggests that, while the focus of development policy is on nation-states and national development, in some cases the easiest way of improving the living standards of people may be to allow them to move out of their country:

> to insist on the interests of nation-states to control their borders over all other considerations—including the well-being of human beings, who through no action or fault of their own are trapped in economically non-viable regions—is not a normatively attractive view.[44]

This view is echoed by Rimmer, who argues that the extent to which migration is allowed into advanced economies from Africa and other poor regions is 'an exacting test of how serious we are about reducing inequality in the world'. He suggests that most advocates of international aid fail this test.[45] Such ideas raise profound challenges for the development industry and its relationship with international migration.

Paternalist paradigms

The prevailing paternalism of development discourse is another major obstacle to development actors accepting the possibility that migration may be an important strategy for many people in poor countries to improve their quality of life. Not only does this mean that development organisations often assume sedentary goals which may fail to match the interests of their 'target groups' as noted above. It also means that they fail to understand the rationale for people's mobility and tend to assume away the agency of migrants, especially poor migrants, casting them as victims who need assistance.

It is easy to portray the migrants caught up in this global labour market as powerless in the face of a vicious system. Indeed, many of them may be. Amin, writing from a structuralist position, argues that the migrant 'rationalises the objective needs of his situation' so the necessity to migrate becomes an ideal, always underpinned by an economic rationale. He is then able to write off individual motivations as 'nothing but rationalisations of behaviour within the system'.[46] However, this does not explain why some move while others remain at home; nor does it make sense of why people still migrate in the face of large obstacles and reasonable opportunities that would enable them to stay at home.

This is not to deny that many of those who migrate across borders start their journeys as reluctant migrants, who would prefer to stay at home. Many are exploited, cheated and abused along the way. However, having suffered such hardships on the road, many look forward to a new life in a new country. Migration can be a rite of passage for the young. It may not be a comfortable process, it may be dangerous but it will remain a very important option for people who are looking to improve their lives and move out of poverty. Development agencies are quite rightly concerned to fight against the abuse of rights and exploitation, but they struggle to understand and respect people's decisions to take such risks. They tend to focus on international migration as the problem rather than looking at the abusive institutional framework within which it has to occur. People want to move, but for many often the only means to do so is through irregular channels which are often exploitative.[47]

The discourse can become very moralistic. There is an underlying sense that African migrants must be desperate to abandon their families and take the dangerous journey to reach Europe as a last resort. Any idea that they may have other options yet choose this route is unacceptable. The world of migrants becomes divided into the morally acceptable victims, who have no choices and need protection, and the morally irresponsible, who choose to take risks, or worse make money from organising people's journeys, and can therefore be criminalised.

The language of both development studies and migration studies has been replete with examples of emotive and moralising terms about migrants over a long period. It is still commonplace to hear complaints of their remittances being used for *conspicuous* or *ostentatious* consumption in the home areas, such as purchasing televisions or cars.[48] Apart from the large volume of research over many years challenging the 'myth' of conspicuous consumption,[49] the term comes loaded with moral connotations of extravagance and recklessness which seem to be easier to apply to migrants from developing countries than Europeans loaded up with electronic goods on their return from Japan. Terms such as 'brain drain' and 'brain waste' both suggest some failure of people either to contribute as they should to their country of origin or to make the best of themselves. The current interest in migrant's engagement in development is overlaid with an expectation that migrants *should* want to maintain their links with the country of origin and, moreover, want to contribute to its development. Of course, as much recent work has shown, migration is often part of a household strategy and many, if not most, migrants retain multiple obligations to their families and wider community. The point here is not to deny this reality, which has been empirically verified, but to object to the moralistic overtones of the assumption that migrant Africans should provide support not only to their kin but to the broader 'nation' for development. The idea of a migrant from Africa moving to a European state, changing citizenship and cutting links with his/her place of origin, without any particular interest in supporting its development, remains an uncomfortable one.

The discourse of migration and development in Africa is in danger of operating with an essentialised notion of 'belonging' to a particular place that even carries over generations through the diaspora. Of course, today it is becoming easier to sustain and develop transnational identities and networks that constitute important elements of many people's livelihoods and also make a vital contribution to development. The point here is to ask whether it is reasonable to assume that all people share such an interest and to imbue it with a sense of moral superiority.

Conclusion

In this paper I have suggested that the rediscovery of the relationship between migration and development raises major questions for the nature of the concept of development found within the 'interventionist' development industry, especially within Africa. The negative view of migration is changing and the hunt is on for the win-win-win scenario where migration is good for countries of origin, countries of destination and migrants themselves. The challenge which is being widely presented is how to identify the conditions under which this triple win can be achieved. However, the deeper challenge, which is often neglected, is to agree on the nature of the 'good' for the different actors involved.

While migration and development have risen up the agenda, mainstream development agencies remain ambivalent about how they should bring migration into their work, or if they should do so at all. This article has argued that this is a reflection of the sedentary nature of their concept of 'development' in Africa, which can be traced back to its roots in colonial practice. Although in many areas of development practice it may be possible to ignore the colonial inheritance—at least enough to provide a cloak of respectability to allow the industry to function—the current emphasis on migration and development makes such subterfuge unsustainable. The internal contradictions in a concept of development that says that migration can support development, but it is better if people stay at home, become too blatant.

For international development organisations, mostly based in industrialised states, casting migration as a problem conveniently fits with a model of development that keeps poor people 'out there'. This remains acceptable in the wealthy constituencies of international development organisations. However, as Skeldon observed a decade ago, 'policies that accept the wider mobility of the population are likely to accord with policies that will enhance the well-being of greater numbers of people'.[50] It will be a brave chief executive of a European development NGO who suggests that facilitating higher levels of migration from developing countries into Europe may be a more effective way of reducing poverty than the launching of another development programme in Africa.

If there is to be a move away from paternalistic notions of development that assume that people want to stay in their place, it may be better to consider the broader processes of social transformations which are not bound to particular 'developing' regions of the world. If migration is analysed as a global phenomenon, shared by all humanity, the task for scholars is then to understand the complex relationship between migration and social transformations. This then raises questions of how mobility affects changes for better and worse in any society, rather than discussing it as an exceptional problem for Africa.[51] This might make it easier to avoid the assumption that mobility is normal for the wealthy, international elite, but a symptom of failure among the poor.

Notes

1 See A Escobar, *Encountering Development: The Making and Unmaking of the Third World*, Princeton, NJ: Princeton University Press, 1995; and D Simon, 'Separated by common ground? Bringing (post)development and (post)colonialism together', *Geographical Journal*, 172, 2006, p 11.
2 Based on 2004 figures from World Bank data, at http://devdata.worldbank.org/data-query/.
3 J Harriss, 'Great promise, hubris and recovery: a participant's history of development studies', in U Kothari (ed), *A Radical History of Development Studies: Individuals, Institutions and Ideologies*, London: Zed Books, 2005, pp 17–46; and M Watts, '"A new deal in emotions": theory and practice and the crisis of development', in J Crush (ed), *Power of Development*, London: Routledge, 1995, pp 44–62.
4 M Cowen & R Shenton, 'The invention of development', in Crush, *Power of Development*, p 41.
5 U Kothari, 'From colonial administration to development studies: a post-colonial critique of the history of development studies', in Kothari, *A Radical History of Development Studies*, pp 47–66.
6 C Rakodi, 'Global forces, urban change, and urban management in Africa', in Radoki (ed), *The Urban Challenge in Africa: Growth and Management of its Large Cities*, Tokyo: United Nations University Press, 1997, pp 17–73.
7 J Ferguson, *Expectations of Modernity: Myths and Meaning of Urban Life on the Zambian Copperbelt*, Berkeley, CA: University of California Press, 1999, p 39.
8 C Rakodi, 'Conclusion', in Rakodi, *The Urban Challenge in Africa*.
9 Such as Area Development Programmes and Integrated Rural Development Programmes. See JM Cohen, *Integrated Rural Development: The Ethiopian Experience and the Dbate*, Uppsala: Nordiska Afrikainstitutet, 1987.
10 P Deshingkar & S Grimm, 'Internal migration and development: a global perspective', *IOM Migration Research Series*, Geneva: International Organisation for Migration, 2005, p 46.
11 R Rhoda, 'Rural development and urban migration: can we keep them down on the farm?', *International Migration Review*, 17 (1), 1983, p 35.
12 A de Haan, 'Livelihoods and poverty: the role of migration—a critical review of the migration literature', *Journal of Development Studies*, 36 (2), 1999, p 20; and Rakodi, *The Urban Challenge in Africa*.
13 Ferguson, *Expectations of Modernity*; D Potts, 'Urban lives: adopting new strategies and adapting rural links', in Rakodi, *The Urban Challenge in Africa*; D Simon, 'Urbanization, globalization, and economic crisis in Africa', in Rakodi, *The Urban Challenge in Africa*; and R Skeldon, *Migration and Development: A Global Perspective*, London: Longman, 1997.
14 de Haan, 'Livelihoods and poverty', p 2. For examples of anthropological studies from Zambia alone, see E Colson, *The Social Consequences of Resettlement: The Impact of the Kariba Resettlement upon the Gwembe Tonga*, Manchester: Manchester University Press, 1971; AI Richards, *Land, Labour and Diet in Northern Rhodesia: An Economic Sudy of the Bemba Tribe*, London: Oxford University Press for the International Institute of African Languages and Cultures, 1939; J Van Velsen, 'Labour migration as positive factor in the continuity of Tonga tribal society', *Economic Development and Cultural Change*, 8 (2), 1960, pp 265–278; and W Watson, *Tribal Cohesion in a Money Economy: A Study of the Mambwe People of Zambia*, Manchester: Manchester University Press, 1958. For examples of development studies perspectives on migration, see CB Keely & BN Tran, 'Remittances from labor migration: evaluations, performance and implications', *International Migration Review*, 23 (3), 1989, p 502; M Lipton, 'Migration from rural areas of poor countries: the impact on rural productivity and income distribution', *World Development*, 8, 1980, pp 1–24; and C Rakodi, 'Global forces, urban change, and urban management in Africa', in Rakodi, *The Urban Challenge in Africa*, pp 17–73.
15 See H de Haas, 'International migration, remittances and development: myths and facts', *Third World Quarterly*, 26 (8), 2005, p 1274; and EJ Taylor, 'The new economics of labour migration and the role of remittances in the migration process', 37 (1), 1999, p 72.

16 DS Massey, J Arango, G Hugo, A Kouaouci, A Pellegrino & JE Taylor, *Worlds in Motion: Understanding International Migration at the End of the Millennium*, Oxford: Clarendon Press, 1998, p 272.

17 A Mckeown, 'Global migration 1846–1940', *Journal of World History*, 15 (2), 2004, pp 155–189; and N Nyberg-Sørensen, N Van Hear & P Engberg-Pedersen, 'The migration–development nexus: evidence and policy options state of the art review', *International Migration*, 40 (5), 2002, p 6.

18 All figures from UN, *Trends in Total Migrant Stock: The 2005 Revision*, New York: United Nations Department of Economic and Social Affairs, 2005. This still represents a small proportion of the overall level of international migration originating in Africa; the vast majority of African migration remains within the continent. D Ratha & W Shaw, 'South–South migration and remittances', *World Bank Working Paper*, Washington, DC: Development Prospects Group, World Bank, 2007, p 6; and C Sander & SM Maimbo, *Migrant Labor Remittances in Africa: Reducing Obstacles to Developmental Contributions*, Washington, DC: World Bank, November 2003.

19 M Baldwin-Edwards, 'Between a rock & a hard place': North Africa as a region of emigration, immigration & transit migration', *Review of African Political Economy*, 33 (108), 2006, pp 311–324. This pressure is only increased by the association with organised crime and the security threat arising from undocumented strangers. International Institute for Strategic Studies (IISS), cited in D Lutterbeck, 'Policing migration in the Mediterranean', *Mediterranean Politics*, 11 (1), 2006, pp 59–82.

20 S Castles, 'Back to the future? Can Europe meet its labour needs through temporary migration?', *IMI Working Paper Series*, Oxford: International Migration Institute, 2006.

21 The International Fund for Agricultural Development (IFAD) estimates that migrants' remittances to developing countries exceeded $300 billion in 2006. IFAD, *Sending Money Home: Worldwide Remittance Flows to Developing and Transition Countries*, Rome: IFAD, 2007.

22 D Ratha, 'Workers' remittances: an important and stable source of external development finance', *Global Development Finance 2003*, Washington, DC: World Bank, 2003, at http://siteresources.world bank.org/INTRGDF/Resources/GDF2003-Chapter7.pdf; and Sander & Maimbo, 'Migrant labor remittances in Africa'. It is important to note that these recorded remittances grossly underestimate the total remittance flows to Africa as migrants use many informal channels to transfer money. World Bank, 'Remittance trends 2006', *Migration and Development Brief 2*, Washington, DC: Development Prospects Group, Migration and Remittances Team, World Bank, 2006.

23 D Kapur, 'Remittances: the new development mantra?', *G-24 Discussion Paper Series*, New York: United Nations Conference on Trade and Development, 2004, p 7.

24 V Mazzucato, 'Ghanaian migrants' double engagement: a transnational view of development and integration policies', *Global Migration Perspectives*, Geneva: Policy Analysis and Research Programme of the Global Commission on International Migration, 2005; Nyberg-Sørensen *et al*, 'The migration–development nexus'; and S Vertovec & R Cohen, *Migration, Diasporas, and Transnationalism*, Cheltenham: Edward Elgar, 1999, p 9.

25 A Zack-Williams, 'Development and diaspora: separate concerns?', *Review of African Political Economy*, 22 (65), 1995, p 351. See also G Mohan & AB Zack-Williams, 'Globalisation from below: conceptualising the role of the African diasporas in Africa's development', *Review of African Political Economy*, 29 (92), 2002, pp 211–236.

26 H de Haas, *Engaging Diasporas: How Governments and Development Agencies Can Support Diaspora Involvement in the Development of Origin Countries*, The Hague: Oxfam Novib, June 2006; L Henry & G Mohan, 'Making homes: the Ghanaian diaspora, institutions and development', *Journal of International Development*, 15 (5), 2003, pp 611–622; D Ionescu, 'Engaging diasporas as development partners for home and destination countries: challenges for policymakers', *Migration Research Series*, Geneva: International Organisation for Migration, 2006; Mohan & Zack-Williams, 'Globalisation from below'; and Nyberg-Sørensen *et al*, 'The migration–development nexus'.

27 R Black, 'Migration and pro-poor policy in Africa', Development Research Centre on Migration, Globalisation and Poverty, University of Sussex, 2004, pp 9, 24–26; F Ellis & N Harris, 'New thinking about urban and rural development', DFID Sustainable Development Retreat, University of Surrey, Guildford, 13 July 2004, p 9; and Nigerian PRSP, cited in H de Haas, 'International migration and national development: viewpoints and policy initiatives in countries of origin—the case of Nigeria', *Working Papers Migration and Development Series*, Nijmegen and The Hague: Radboud University and Directorate General for International Cooperation, Ministry of Foreign Affairs, 2006, p 14.

28 http://oxfam.intelli-direct.com/e/d.dll?m=235&url=http://www.oxfam.org/en/files/pp030827_corn_dumping.pdf; http://www.christianaid.org.uk/wafrica/harvest.htm; http://www.oxfam.org/en/policy/briefingnotes/bn0604_coffee_groundsforchange; http://www.actionaid.org/main.aspx?PageID=187; http://www.concern.net/news-and-features/features/a767/Committed-to-change-Nothing-to-be-ashamed-of.html; http://www.oxfam.org.uk/what_we_do/issues/livelihoods/landrights/downloads/hivsynth.rtf; and http://www.savethechildren.org.uk/scuk/jsp/resources/details.jsp?id=3977&group=resources&section=news&subsection=details, all accessed 9 May 2007.

29 R Black, LM Hilker & C Pooley, 'Migration and pro-poor policy in East Africa', Development Research Centre on Migration, Globalisation and Poverty, University of Sussex, 2004, p 15.

30 Commission of the European Community (CEC), *The Global Approach to Migration One Year On: Towards a Comprehensive European Migration Policy*, Brussels: CEC, 2006, p 5.

31 DFID, *Moving out of Poverty—Making Migration Work Better for Poor People*, London: DFID, March 2007, p 3, also pp 37–40.

32 See African Union, 'Draft African Common Position on Migration and Development', African Union, Addis Ababa, 2006, p 4; and H Olesen, 'Migration, return, and development: an institutional perspective', *International Migration*, 40 (5), 2002, pp 125–150.

33 Skeldon, *Migration and Development*, p 2.

34 International Organisation for Migration (IOM), *World Migration Report 2005: Costs and Benefits of Migration*, Geneva: IOM, pp 46–47.

35 For example, by 'inserting' migration into the Millennium Development Goals as IOM suggests in its World Migration Report 2005. *Ibid*, p 266.

36 See DFID, *Moving out of Poverty*, p 33.

37 AK Sen, *Development as Freedom*, Oxford: Oxford University Press, 1999.

38 There seems to be less concern about preserving other fundamental aspects of tradition, such as family size.

39 M Peil & PO Sada, *African Urban Society*, Chichester: John Wiley, 1984; and Simon, 'Urbanization, globalization, and economic crisis in Africa'.

40 F Ellis, *A Livelihoods Approach to Migration and Poverty Reduction*, London: DFID, 2003.

41 Zack-Williams, 'Development and diaspora'.

42 D Rimmer, 'Learning about economic development from Africa', *African Affairs*, 102 (408), 2003, p 488.

43 See L Pritchett, 'Boom towns and ghost countries: geography, agglomeration, and population mobility', *Working Paper 36*, Washington, DC: Center for Global Development, 2004, p 36; and Pritchett, *Let their People Come: Breaking the Gridlock on International Labor Mobility*, Washington, DC: Center for Global Development, 2006, for details of this argument.

44 Pritchett, 'Boom towns and ghost countries', p 50.

45 Rimmer, 'Learning about economic development from Africa'.

46 S Amin, 'Migrations in contemporary Africa: a retrospective view', in J Baker & TA Aina (ed), *The Migration Experience in Africa*, Uppsala: Nordiska Afrikainstitutet, 1995, pp 92–99.

47 See B Anderson, 'Motherhood, apple pie and slavery: reflections on trafficking debates', *COMPAS Working Paper 48*, Oxford: Centre on Migration, Policy and Society, 2007.

48 C Thouez, 'The impact of remittances on development', in United Nations Population Fund (UNFPA) (ed), *International Migration and the Millennium Development Goals: Selected Papers of the UNFPA Expert Group Meeting, Marrakech, Morocco 11–12 May 2005*, New York: UNFPA, 2005, p 43.

49 For example, see RH Adams, 'International remittances and the household: analysis and review of global evidence', *Journal of African Economies*, 15, 2006, pp 396–425; and RT Appleyard, 'Migration and development: myths and reality', *International Migration Review*, 23 (3), 1989, pp 486–499.

50 R Skeldon, 'Rural-to-urban migration and its implications for poverty alleviation', *Asia-Pacific Population Journal*, 12 (1), 1997, pp 3–16.

51 EM Roe, 'Except-Africa: postscript to a special section on development narratives', *World Development*, 23 (6), 1995, pp 1065–1069.

Capitalist Restructuring, Development and Labour Migration: the Mexico–US case

RAÚL DELGADO WISE &
HUMBERTO MÁRQUEZ COVARRUBIAS

Since the 1970s developed countries have been led by the USA into a wide and complex process of capitalist restructuring. Its pertinent implementation strategies include innovations in the field of information and communication technologies (ICTs) and financial internationalisation, along with two fundamental processes: the internationalisation of production and the transnationalisation, differentiation and precarisation in the labour market. Contemporary capitalism has organised a new world order within the framework of neoliberal globalisation, and this has replicated the socioeconomic asymmetries between developed and underdeveloped countries on an unprecedented scale. It has also deepened social inequalities, poverty and marginalisation within migrant-exporting, underdeveloped nations. The welfare state is being dismantled in both sending and receiving countries, while the flexibilisation and precarisation of the labour market become extreme and the environment irreversibly deteriorates. In this context the vision of development present in the discourse of international organisations and the US political agenda serves to mask the implementation of neoliberal structural adjustment policies that have deepened the substandard conditions in so-called Third World nations. The implantation of development as a tool for social transformation is, in fact, one of the greatest challenges currently facing humankind.

The significant increase in migration flows, especially those from South to North, is one of the many current expressions of the growing asymmetries that characterise contemporary capitalism. In 1980 international migration involved almost 100 million people: 47.7 million were from developed countries while 52.1 million came from underdeveloped ones.[1] By 2006 the rate had grown to nearly 190 million migrants: 61 million had moved from South to South, 53 million from North to North, 14 million from North to South, and 62 million had relocated from South to North.[2] A substantial component of these flows is labour-related. Indeed, the flow of family remittances sent from North to South has increased even more, from US$48 000 million in 1995 to $199 000 million in 2006. If we include informal, non-registered sending channels, this number increases by 50% or more, at which point remittance flows exceed foreign direct investment (FDI) and more than double the official aid packages provided to underdeveloped nations.[3]

The accelerated growth of North to South remittances flows and an increase in poverty, marginalisation and social inequality have led the main international promoters of neoliberal structural adjustment to focus on migration and development and suggest that migration can become a development tool for countries with high emigration rates. Some authors have referred to this theory as the 'new development mantra',[4] a belief that remittances can be channelled into productive investments that can propel development. 'Or to put it less positively, the idea is that some of the most exploited workers in the world can make up for the failure of mainstream development policies.'[5] This optimistic vision is based on the idea that 1) remittances can be used as a tool for development on several levels; 2) the diaspora is an agent of development; 3) return migration results in the incorporation of new abilities and attitudes; 4) the circulation of talent is a source of human capital; and 5) temporary worker programmes can benefit both sending and receiving countries.

The paradigmatic case of Mexican migration to the USA serves to explore the relationship between migration and development in the context of ongoing capitalist restructuring and, in particular, in relation to the implementation of structural adjustment policies. The USA, the architect behind the concept of 'globalisation', is also the world's largest immigrant receiver and remittance sender. Mexico, on the other hand, is one of the world's largest migrant exporters and remittance receivers, along with India. The USA and Mexico participate in a scheme of regional integration which, strengthened by the North American Free Trade Agreement (NAFTA), regulates current migration dynamics. Migration can be seen as a historical tradition conditioned by vicinity (the 3000-km long border is one of the most transited on the planet), a unidirectional character (98% of Mexican emigrants go to the USA) and massive flow (the Mexican exodus is the world's largest);[6] it is also mostly labour-based. Specifically its present dynamics are a response to the productive internationalisation strategy employed by the large USA corporations,[7] which is linked to the transnationalisation and precarisation of labour markets brought about by neoliberal policies of structural adjustment. Far from creating a 'free trade' pattern that benefits both nations, regional integration has resulted in new relations of production that involve a novel, unequal system of exchange in which Mexico becomes a specialised provider of cheap labour force and, to an extent, also natural resources.

The purpose of this article is to examine the current dynamics of Mexican migration and its links to US restructuring processes. This poses a number of theoretical and conceptual challenges involving a critical assessment of the relationship between capitalist restructuring, regional integration and labour migration, as this analysis must supersede the prevailing views of the relationship between migration and development. Regardless of the singularities of the Mexico–USA case, such an analysis can help us illustrate the regressive consequences of structural adjustment policies in Southern countries and contest the idea that migration can be employed as a motor of development.

The perspective of a political economy of development

Our subject cannot be approached from the limited perspective of current migration theories or the extant, embryonic theories involving migration and development. We suggest that the best way to do this is to place the phenomenon within the framework of *critical development studies*. Here we use the field of the political economy of development to construct a new theoretical perspective that will allow us to examine the nature of contemporary capitalism and its relationship with migration dynamics.

An offshoot of political economy and Latin American structuralist and dependency theories, the political economy of development provides an unparalleled set of analytical tools employing the following factors:

1. The ample range of interactions inscribed within the North–South (or development–underdevelopment) dynamic without losing sight of the levels of differentiation present in each pole of the relationship.
2. The interactions between several spatial levels (local, national, regional and global) and social dimensions (economic, sociological, political, cultural, environmental).
3. A transdisciplinary vision that, contrary to the 'economicist' and 'structuralist' stereotypes sometimes applied to this area, makes theoretical use of several fields of study.
4. A concept of development that surpasses limited, normative and decontextualised concepts by acknowledging the need for social

transformation, based in the structural, strategic and institutional changes required to advance the living standards of the underlying population. This process must comprise a variety of actors, movements, agents and social institutions operating on several planes and levels.

According, then, to the political economy of development, international migration is tied to the problems of development and its deep causes and effects cannot be found if we study it on its own. In order to approach migration's cause-and-effect relationship with development and examine specific moments in the dialectical interaction between development and migration, two issues must be addressed.

First, strategic practices. This refers to the confrontation between different projects that espouse diverging interests, which in turn underlie the structures of contemporary capitalism and its inherent development problems. There are currently two major projects. The hegemonic one is promoted by the large transnational corporations, the governments of developed countries led by the USA, and allied elites in underdeveloped nations, all under the umbrella of international organisations. The project's loss of legitimacy under the aegis of neoliberal globalisation means that, nowadays, rather than speak of hegemony we can use the term 'domination': the implementation of this project is not the result of consensus but, rather, military action and the financial imposition of the Washington and Post-Washington Consensuses. The second, alternative project consists of the sociopolitical actions of a range of social classes and movements as well as collective subjects and agents who endorse a political project designed to transform the structural dynamics and political and institutional environments which bar the implementation of alternative development strategies at the global, regional, national and local levels.

The second issue that requires addressing is structural dynamics. This refers to the asymmetric articulation of contemporary capitalism on several planes and levels. These include the financial, commercial, productive, and labour market spheres, as well as technological innovation (a strategic form of control) and the use and allotment of natural resources and environmental impacts. These factors condition the ways in which developed, developed and underdeveloped, and underdeveloped countries relate to each other. They also determine the fields in which interactions between sectors, groups, movements, and social classes take place. All of this is expressed differently at the global, regional, national and local levels.

Regional integration and labour migration

During the 1970s the USA began promoting neoliberal structural adjustment policies in Mexico and other underdeveloped countries. The policies were based on privatisation, deregularisation and liberalisation strategies and were imposed by the IMF and the World Bank in alliance with the dominant elites and national governments. They promised to reduce the asymmetries between nations and open a new path towards economic development.

Instead, the Mexican economy was forced to focus on exports in response to a new mode of regional integration based on the depreciation of the labour force and characterised by the following three factors: 1) the dismantling and rearticulation of the production apparatus; 2) the generation of vast amounts of surplus population, well beyond the conventional formulation of the reserve army of the unemployed; and 3) the acceleration of migration flows.

The dismantling and rearticulation of the production apparatus

Mexico has been subjected to a progressive dismantling of the production apparatus created during its import substitution period (which, in a way, is reminiscent of new forms of primitive capital accumulation[8] and creative destruction[9]) and forced to reorient its economy toward a peculiar form of exportation based on cheap labour force. This and the particular mode of regional integration determined by NAFTA are the result of strategic policies implemented by agents of large transnational corporations and the US government under the umbrella of certain international organisations. NAFTA itself was created and implemented by a sector of the US political class allied to the large transnational corporations and their counterparts in Mexico and Canada.[10] In the case of Mexico a sector of the Mexican business elite led by the Consejo Coordinador Empresarial (Enterpreneurial Council), which is linked to the Comisión de Organismos Empresariales de Comercio Exterior (Commission of Entrepreneurial External Commerce Organisations) participated actively in this process, as did the government.[11] Mexico soon became Latin America's major exporter and the world's 13th, supposedly because of the successful implementation of the economic reforms. At first glance, 90% of its export platform was comprised of manufactured products, 39.4% of which was classified as 'technical progress-diffusing goods'.[12]

However, in order to understand the Mexican economy's regional integration process we must reveal what it is that the nation really exports and demystify the idea that it possesses a buoyant manufacturing exports sector. We contend that the Mexican economy follows a *labour force export-led model*, an externally oriented restructuring process that responds to US capital's need for cheap labour that can undertake productive restructuring on a bi-national level. We employ this definition to characterise a complex export strategy that involves a generally poorly qualified, precarised and flexibilised labour force and is based on three strongly interrelated mechanisms: 1) the assembly and manufacturing sector or *maquila*; 2) disguised *maquila*,[13] and 3) labour migration.

In order to conceptualise the assembly and manufacturing sector better known as *maquila*, we must first take into account its role in the international production system. Assembly plants located in foreign countries supplement manufacturing industries in developed countries via the integration of production chains that globalise design, production and commercialisation while remaining under the control of the matrix. The displacement of operations to plants located in countries like Mexico is stimulated by powerful fiscal incentives, governmental support and, essentially, an abundance of cheap and docile labour. In other words, what distinguishes the *maquila* industry from the traditional export process is that, from its very beginning, it has constituted a response to strategies employed by US firms, such as General Electric, RAC, Zenith and General Motors, seeking to diminish production costs by employing cheap labour in assembly plants that are usually located in northern Mexico. These operate by relocating the machinery, infrastructure, technology, design and organisational schemes used in the US-based corporations, which they combine with untaxed inputs to operate foreign factories.

An analysis of Mexico's new export profile illustrates the importance of *maquiladoras* and their exports, which increased 28 times between 1982 and 2005 and, during this last year, amounted to over half ($96.756 million) of manufactured exports ($174.521 million). On the other hand, the added value of the *maquila* represents an ever decreasing contribution to the sector's total production: in 1990 it amounted to 20% and, by 2003, it had fallen to 8%.

The Mexican manufactured exports industry has another sector that operates similarly to the *maquila* but is not officially classified as such. It encompasses 30% of manufactured exports and is known as *disguised maquila* for the following reasons.[14] First, like the *maquila*, it benefits from the subsidies and fiscal exemptions offered by the Mexican government's temporary imports programme (which, in turn, explains the 84.6% rate attained by Mexican exports in 2004. Second, unlike the *maquila*, its productive system is characterised by greater intensity and technological complexity (the automotive and electronics industries, which are usually under the direction of large transnational US firms, are two prototypical cases). Third, operationally speaking, the *maquila* and *disguised maquila* are linked by intra-firm commerce and outsourcing practices; the resulting commercial relationships comprise between 65% and 75% of imported inputs.[15] Fourth, the *disguised maquila* employs at least 500 000 labourers[16] who, unlike those in the *maquila* sector, are more qualified and specialised, have more consolidated unions and earn at least 50% more money. The *maquila* and *disguised maquila* sectors comprise around 1.5 million jobs (some 30% of total manufacturing employment) with income differences of one to 11 in the case of the *maquila* and one to seven for the *disguised maquila*.[17]

Having taken all this into account, we must now focus on Mexico's real exports through the *maquila* and *disguised maquila* sectors. Given the high import content of both industries (between 80% and 90% of the value of exports), Mexico's gains are limited to wage flows; that is, the value of the labour force participating in the exports sector. This constitutes indirect or disembodied labour force export, a crucial concept that demystifies the supposedly manufacture-based nature of Mexican exports and points to a regression in the export platform. If to this we add direct labour force export via labour migration, the real content of Mexican exports becomes quite clear. This is why we characterise the current export growth model as a cheap labour force export-led model.

We must also point out that the *maquila* production scheme linked to the export of the disembodied labour force does not imply that any portion of the profit received from these activities remains in Mexico. In the *maquila* transactions prices are artificially fixed by the firms themselves, thereby avoiding the necessity of declaring profits in Mexico. This is how the *maquila* firms transfer net profits outside of Mexico while the jobs are subsidised by the Mexican economy. In fact, the Mexican export model contravenes the notion of the interplay of free market forces and constitutes a pillaging of surpluses that would otherwise invigorate the Mexican economy.

The generation of vast amounts of surplus population

The labour force export-led model is sustained by a neoliberal macroeconomic policy that dogmatically pursues economic stability by fighting inflation and public deficit reduction—that is, pro-cyclical macroeconomic instruments which, in a recessive international environment, restrict the possibilities of economic growth.[18] If we take into account that this anti-inflationary policy has been surreptitiously used to contain and diminish the value of the labour force, we will see that the improvement in the working and living conditions of the majority of the population amounts to little in the neoliberal agenda. The resultant production apparatus is characterised by:

- an externally oriented production sector which, despite being at the centre of official policy, does not fulfil its role as a motor of national development and takes advantage of the cheapness of the labour force to decrease its production costs, as in the case of indirect labour force export;
- a declining and disconnected segment of the economy that is focused on the internal market but does not have the capacity to invigorate national economic growth, lacks governmental support and continues to generate employment in increasingly limited and precarious conditions;
- a subsistence sector that responds to the self-generated need to create a labour space in the face of precarious and insufficient formal employment, as is the case of the informal sector;
- a transnationalised labour sector that comprises labour migration and, in the past decade, has been the most dynamic.

Mexican neoliberal policy has effectively cancelled the possibilities for economic growth. During the period that preceded neoliberalism (1941–82), the nation's gross domestic product (GDP) grew at an annual rate of 6.3%; this rate has fallen to 2.4% with the implementation of neoliberal policies (1983–2005). This low growth rate is the result of the economy's structural inability to generate enough formal, high quality employment. According to data from the Instituto Mexicano del Seguro Social (Mexican Institute of Social Security—IMSS), formal employment grew at an annual rate of 489 000 jobs between 1991 and 2004. This amounts to 30.19% of the overall increase in Mexico's economically active population (EAP). Unemployment, under-employment and emigration plague Mexican society: lacking unemployment insurance, an estimated 69.2% of the EAP has been forced to approach the informal sector or the US economy.[19]

The dynamics involving the generation of formal employment are quite erratic. Between 1990 and 1994 (the period preceding the formal implementation of NAFTA) employment generation rose slightly. This trend increased in 1995 and kept on doing so until 2000, when IMSS registered 10.9 million permanent jobs. This period corresponds to the peak of the indirect or disembodied labour force export process, which resulted from occupational growth in the *maquiladora* sector and other exporting industries based in the country. 2000 represents the breaking point, as the amount of jobs in the *maquiladora* sector decreased and labour migration took precedence as a direct form of labour export.

The acceleration of migration flows

Under the labour force export-led model, Mexico–US migration has grown exponentially over the past two decades. This growth has been heightened by the implementation of NAFTA, turning Mexico into the world's major migrant exporter to the USA. The sheer dimension of this phenomenon speaks for itself: in 2007, the US population of Mexican origin—including Mexican-born documented and undocumented migrants, as well as US citizens of Mexican ascendancy—was estimated at 30 million people. It is the world's largest diaspora to be established in a single country. According to UN estimates, during the 1990–95 period Mexico was the country with largest annual number of emigrants (a total of 400 000 people *vis-à-vis* 390 000 from China and 280 000 from India).[20] Between 2000 and 2005 the Mexican annual exodus rose to 560 000. The country has consequently experienced an exponential growth in received remittances and, along with India, is the world's major receiver.[21] In 2006 Mexico received remittances amounted to $23.7 million.[22]

Practically all of Mexico's territory shows incidence of international migration. In 2000 96.2% of national municipalities experienced some type of migration-related activity. At the same time, even though the Mexican immigrant population in the USA is still concentrated in a handful of states, in the past few years it has expanded throughout most of the national territory. Migration circuits have stretched to the eastern and central-northern areas,[23] which is were some of the most dynamic centres of industrial restructuring are located.[24]

In educational terms 38.9% of the Mexican-born, US-residing population aged 15 and older has a higher education. This number increases to 52.4% when we take into account all the US population of Mexican origin. In contrast, the Mexican average is 27.8%, which means that the country is losing qualified workforce and there is a clear selective trend. Yet, when compared with other immigrant groups in the USA, Mexicans have the lowest overall educational level, which demonstrates Mexico's serious educational lag.[25] In 2006 1.6 million Mexicans residing in the USA had technical or postgraduate education.[26]

There has also been a change in migration patterns, which have moved from circular to established migration and show increased participation on the part of women and complete families.[27] Even though the evolution of migration flows often leads to established migration, in this case the tendency has been accompanied by a unilateral closing of the border that, in contravention of its goals, has not contained the exodus; rather, given the risks and difficulties of return, it has encouraged new migrants to prolong their stay indefinitely. These changes, and Mexico's decreasing birth rate, have resulted in a growing tendency towards depopulation: between 2000 and 2005, 832 of the nation's 2435 municipalities, or one in every three, had a negative growth rate.[28]

Because of the hemispheric extension of the economic political integration promoted by the US government, Mexico has also become a transit country and must address the concomitant problems. In 2004, nearly 400 000 people moved through the Mexican Southern border; most of them Central American undocumented migrants.[29]

Labour insertion of Mexican immigrants

As has been pointed out previously, Mexico experienced an unprecedented migration flow toward the USA with the implementation of NAFTA, to the point that it became the world's major migrant sender. What matters is that this dynamic and the qualitative changes that accompany it are linked to the role played by Mexican workers, who act as a reserve and source of cheap labour to be employed in the US economy. This function is complemented by a Mexican policy of labour depreciation and precarisation. The productive restructuring led by the US economy has propitiated the reassignment, or spatial and sectorial redistribution, of the labour force on a bi-national level. This process is supported by the transnational precarisation of the labour force, as indicated by factors such as the growing wage gap, longer working days, the dismantling of unions, lack of employment security, and restricted access to social benefits. The transnational labour market has, in fact, affected both the Mexican and US working classes. But it is the Mexican labourers who find themselves in some of the most flexibilised and precarious areas, including outsourcing and day labour. The labour insertion of Mexican immigrants is mostly channelled either towards sectors that operated before the productive restructuring and are characterised by substantial precariousness and social exclusion (eg agriculture, domestic and cleaning services), or towards equally precarised occupational areas that are linked to productive restructuring through a number of branches that feed main sectors, the production of income-goods, and mature industries in the process of being rescued.

Migrants have a growing presence in the construction, manufacturing, services and commerce industries, as well as in tainted sectors that serve as the industry's 'backyards': sweatshops, subcontracting, domestic work, day labour, etc. Despite the relatively minor importance of the sector, the participation of Mexican workers in the agricultural sector is substantial: three out of every four agricultural labourers were born in Mexico. Most of them are undocumented (53%) and there is a strong indigenous and female presence, which reveals a certain hierarchy and labour diversification. Immigrants' social insertion also differs depending on their migration circuits. It spans transnational exclusion and vulnerability (especially among indigenous immigrants) and an ascending pattern of assimilation for those who belong to the oldest migration circuit, which covers Mexico's central-western region.

Most of the manufacturing activities are centred on basic metal products, machinery and equipment (502 000 Mexican-born workers) sectors on the one hand, and on the food and clothing industries on the other. The first case comprises mature industries that use labour migration as part of a rescue strategy. The second involves income-goods which directly contribute to the general depreciation of the labour force. In 2004, 1.2 million Mexicans worked in the manufacturing sector. Between 1995 and 2005 US manufacturing jobs decreased by 17%, from 17.1 to 14.2 million. Two things are happening: the overall decrease in manufacturing jobs, and the replacement of some sectors by Mexican labourers, which has created a significant labour niche for Mexican workers.[30] If we add the number of workers in the US manufacturing sector (14.2 million) to those who work in the *maquila* (1.2 million) and *disguised maquila* (0.5 million) industries in Mexico, the total is 15.9 million labourers. This means that those Mexican workers who, in a general sense, participate in the US manufacturing industry amount to 2.9 million (18% of the total labour force). That is one in every five workers.

By replacing better paid, more experienced and unionised workers (usually US citizens), the Mexican labour force diminishes labour costs and increases global competitiveness. Mexican workers receive the lowest wages when compared with the native population and all other immigrants. On the other hand, the wage disparities in the manufacturing industry illustrate the asymmetries between the Mexican and US economies: in Mexico the hourly wage for a manufacturing job is $2.57, while in the USA the formal employment rate is $16.45. In the case of undocumented immigrants (a substantial number of Mexican workers), hourly wages drop to $5. Even though this amount double the average Mexican wage, it still constitutes a form of extreme precarisation. Most jobs involve low qualifications, low wages, limited or inexistent benefits, instability, unilateral and informal (or authoritarian) work relations, risks, and illegal abuse on the part of employers (eg wages below the legal minimum, unjustified layoffs, lack of disbursement for additional hours). In addition to the segmentation and precarisation of labour markets, the differentiated insertion and degrees of assimilation among the immigrant population can lead to instances of translational exclusion and vulnerability that affect both the second and third generations. This process is tied to the dominant trend in the US labour market, which seeks to replace permanent workers with temporary ones.

Two macrostructural elements at the base of labour transnationalisation help propel massive migration: productive internationalisation both disintegrates and complements the intra- and inter-industrial productive chain while affecting the bi-national labour market; additional demographic factors such as an ageing US population and a younger Mexican populace encourage

139

Mexican flow to the USA. The productive restructuring, in short, is supplemented by changing demographic patterns.

By losing its labour force to this massive exodus Mexico is also losing one of its most valuable resources in the accumulation process. The direct exportation of workers represents a drain on human resources that, in turn, leads to the abandonment of productive activities, represents a waste of resources spent on the formation of the emigrating labour force and, to an extent, causes the displacement of relatively qualified labour and the consequent weakening of labour sovereignty. Overall this drain represents a loss of potential wealth. According to Ruiz Durán, migrant Mexican workers contribute 8.1% of the USA's GDP; at the same time, they cease to contribute 27.4% to Mexico's own GDP, a significant loss in the Mexican accumulation process.[31]

As the income distribution gap increases in the USA, Mexican immigrants are often subject to labour precarisation and social exclusion:

- Most Mexican immigrants live in substandard conditions, confined to dilapidated and segregated neighbourhoods while their children face discrimination in public schools.[32]
- Most Mexican immigrants receive the lowest wages and have the highest poverty rate among the immigrant and native population.
- Despite their contributions to the US economy, Mexican immigrants have the most limited access to health services in the nation. In 2006 54.1% of them lacked health insurance.[33]

The persistent socioeconomic deterioration of first, second and subsequent generations of Mexican immigrants has shut the door on social mobility. Mexicans have relatively high levels of lumpenisation and incarceration, which affect US society in general. In addition, their political and electoral participation is the lowest among all immigrant groups.

The implications and paradoxes of regional integration

It is evident that the promises made by the promoters of regional integration have only benefited a small segment of the Mexican and US elites, particularly the latter. This reveals the policy's true purpose and explains why its supporters continue to brag about the success of the restructuring strategy and the regional integration scheme.

The following is a brief summary of the effects this process has had on the Mexican economy and society, which have been the most affected.

First, disaccumulation processes have been generated in the Mexican economy. The indirect export of labour via the *maquila* and *disguised maquila* industries implies a transfer of net profits to the US economy. This constitutes a new mode of dependency that is even more acute that those examined in the structuralist and dependency theories previously endorsed by the Economic Commission for Latin America and the Caribbean (ECLAC).

Second, there has been a loss of a labour force whose formation costs fall on the national economy. Mexican labour migration represents a drain of valuable human resources which, in turn, leads to the neglect of productive activities, constitutes a waste of resources spent on the formation of the emigrating labour force, and, to an extent, the displacement of relatively qualified workforce.

Third, a substantial part of the Mexican production apparatus has been dismantled. Economic regional integration and the implementation of the current export model have contributed to the progressive dismantling of the internally focused production apparatus, which plays an irrelevant role in the neoliberal agenda. There is evidence that at least 40 production chains in the in the small and medium-sized business sector have been destroyed after the implacable reorientation of the economy towards the external market.[34]

Fourth, there has been a reduction and precarisation of high-quality formal employment. Neoliberal policies have failed to create high-quality formal employment; rather, they have destroyed employment sources and increased precarisation and flexibilisation in the current formal job market. In the absence of benefits such as unemployment insurance, the informal sector is a source of precarious subsistence for large sectors of the population who have been excluded from the formal job market. The informal employment sector comprises a large population which lives at subsistence level and serves as a labour reserve that further depreciates labour costs both in Mexico and the USA. Paradoxically the informal sector (a sort of safety net for the Mexican labour market) and migrants' remittances have breathed artificial life into a development model that exacerbates social inequalities and damages the country's productive activities.

In order to bring this section to a close, we wish to point out that the labour force export-led model on which the Mexico–USA migration process is based involves two paradoxes that point to the unsustainable nature of the present scheme of economic integration.

First, economic integration under NAFTA does not promote equal degrees of development between Mexico and the USA; rather, it has contributed to the deepening of asymmetries between the two nations. While, in 1994, the US per capita GDP was 2.6 times higher than the Mexican, in 2004 the gap had grown to 2.9. In 1994, US manufacturing wages were 5.7 times higher than in Mexico; in 2004 the difference was 6.8. Paradoxically this growing income gap does not mirror productivity levels, which have declined. In fact, Mexico has shown more productivity in certain sectors, particularly those related to the labour force export-led model.

Second, economic integration has not encouraged the creation of job opportunities in Mexico; rather, it has become a motor for the direct export of the labour force and increased socioeconomic dependence on remittances. According to official data, remittance reception in Mexico has increased thirty-fold. On a macroeconomic level remittances are the second source of foreign currency and the one with the most consistent growth rate, given the relative loss of importance of other sources of external financing (eg FDI and manufactured exports). At a microeconomic level, remittances support family consumption and ensure the subsistence of 1.6 million homes.[35] To a lesser extent they serve to fund public works and productive investments through programs such as *Tres por Uno* (Three for One).

Having taken all this into account, it is possible to assert that migration unintentionally operates as a crucial cog in the neoliberal machinery, providing it with an appearance of 'stability' and, paradoxically, a 'human face'. At a macroeconomic level remittances serve to extend the life of a development model that is already showing signs of unsustainability. At a microeconomic level they help ease poverty and marginalisation inasmuch as they involve a transfer of resources that lack any solid ties to savings strategies but improve productive capacity and economic growth.

Lessons on capitalist restructuring, labour migration and social transformation

Capitalist restructuring results in forced migration toward developed nations. In the current neoliberal system developed countries have deployed a restructuring strategy that, besides internationalising production, commercial and financial processes, appropriates the natural resources, economic surpluses and cheap labour force of underdeveloped nations. This type of relationship between central and peripheral and postcolonial nations deepens the latter's conditions of underdevelopment. Underdeveloped countries produce redundant population reserves that are unable to find labour conditions that allow for personal and family development in their own nations. This is a result of diminished accumulation processes brought about by the asymmetrical relationships established between developed and underdeveloped countries, which evolve into different forms of surplus transference. These unsustainable social conditions lead to forced migration, which we understand as a population flow derived from the lack of adequate living and working conditions or political or social conflicts that threaten the population's life. In some cases the exacerbation of forced migration can result in relative or sometimes absolute depopulation in places of origin. The loss of qualified and unqualified labour force also leads to the abandonment of productive activities and the loss of potential wealth.

Further, migrants contribute to the process of capitalist restructuring in the receiving country. Developed countries require large amounts of cheap, qualified and unqualified labour force; in fact, lack of proper documentation increases the vulnerability and further reduces the value of this human merchandise. This demand responds to 1) an increased accumulation capacity brought about the transfer of resources and surpluses from underdeveloped countries; and 2) processes of demographic transition and an ageing population. Immigrants contribute to the general depreciation of the labour force: they participate in sectors that are work-intensive, generate income-goods, or are in the process of being rescued; they also supplant workers who receive higher rates and receive better benefits. Although qualified immigrant workers are part of a 'labour elite', they are still relatively cheaper than equally qualified nationals. Both qualified and unqualified migrants greatly benefit the receiving country, which has not spent any resources on their training or education. Migration, then, is a transfer of cheap labour as well as of formation expenses. This gives receiving nations a static comparative advantage derived from the reduction of production costs at the same time that it provides dynamic comparative advantages derived from immigrants' participation in the acceleration of innovation processes. Overall immigrant workers and their families contribute to the strengthening of the receiving nation's internal market through consumption. Even the so-called nostalgia market represents a growing consumer sector that fortifies internal economic activity. Immigrants pay taxes but do not receive the same benefits or have access to the same public services, which denotes a criterion of social exclusion. In addition to all this, immigrant contributions are helping settle the acute pension problem caused by the massive retirement of the baby boomer generation. Even if these contributions compensate for some of the consequences that the dismantling of the welfare state has had on developed economies, they clearly do not constitute a permanent solution.

Migrants also help sustain precarious socioeconomic stability in countries of origin. A fraction of migrants' wages is allocated towards monthly remittances that ensure the subsistence of family members in countries of origin.[36] To a lesser extent remittances help finance small establishments in a subsistence economy. Migrant organisations collect resources that are channelled towards public works and social projects in communities of origin. In Mexico this practice has been institutionalised through the Three for One (*Tres por Uno*) programme, which has been replicated in other countries. A small amount of migrants who have accumulated savings or are entrepreneurs use their resources to finance microprojects in their communities of origin. However, wage-based remittances meant for family consumption are the most important type, which demonstrates that the resources sent by migrants are not part of a development processes geared toward social transformation. On a macroeconomic level, remittances benefit neoliberal governments that use them as a source of foreign currency to sustain their frail 'macroeconomic stability' instead of promoting real development alternatives. Remittances have even been used as guarantees when soliciting foreign aid. In the absence of a real development project, migrants have been lauded as the 'heroes of development', which means they are held accountable for promoting progress in a situation where the state, claiming minimal interference, declines to take responsibility. In the absence of a development project that involves migrants and other social sectors and propels actual processes of social transformation, neoliberal fundamentalism kowtows to market forces. Ultimately underdeveloped countries continue to function as labour reserves. Real possibilities of development are deliberately obstructed in order to benefit increasingly small national elites, which in turn associate with the even more exclusive elites in developed countries, led by US capital.

If used as a tool of social transformation, development could curtail forced migration. Even though neoliberal and pro-globalisation discourses maintain their economic system's inevitability, we must theoretically and pragmatically assert the viability of alternative processes of development on a variety of levels. We must begin by redefining the terms under which developed countries subject underdeveloped ones to an asymmetric set of relationships based on a series of principles that have been turned into fetishes and include democracy, freedom and free trade. This involves examining imperialist practices that increase inequality, marginalisation, poverty, social exclusion and unfettered migration. Neoliberal governments assume that migration is an inevitable process and are content to make use of remittances until they reach a breaking point. A project of real social transformation must include the participation of migrants and non-migrants alike, and do more than curtail forced migration: it must also reverse the processes of social degradation that characterise underdevelopment and go so far as to endanger human existence.[37]

Notes

1 United Nations Department of Economic and Social Affairs (UNDESA), *World Economic and Social Survey 2004: International Migration*, New York: UNDESA, 2004.
2 UNDESA, *International Migration and Development*, New York: UNDESA, 2006.
3 World Bank, *Remittances Trends 2006*, Washington, DC: Migration and Remittances Team, Development Prospects Group, World Bank, 2007.
4 D Kapur, 'Remittances: the new development mantra?', *Discussion Paper*, Washington, DC: World Bank, 2004.
5 S Castles & R Delgado-Wise, 'Introducción', in Castles & Wise (eds), *Migración y Desarrollo: Perspectivas desde el Sur*, Mexico City: Miguel Ángel Porrúa, 2007, p 12.
6 J Durand & D Massey, *Clandestinos: Migración México–Estados Unidos*, Mexico City: Miguel Ángel Porrúa, 2003.
7 G Gereffi, 'Las cadenas productivas como marco analítico para la globalización', *Problemas de desarrollo*, 32 (125), 2001, pp 9–37.
8 W Bello, 'The capitalist conjuncture: over-accumulation, financial crises, and the retreat from globalisation', *Third World Quarterly*, 27 (8), 2006, p 1345.
9 D Harvey, 'Neoliberalism as creative destruction', *Annals of the American Academy of Political and Social Science*, 610, 2007, p 33.
10 J Cypher, 'The ideology of economic science in the selling of NAFTA: the political economy of elite decision-making', *Review of Radical Political Economics*, 25 (4), 1993, pp 146–163; and J Faux, *The Global Class War*, Hoboken, NJ: John Wiley, 2006.
11 C Puga, *Los empresarios organizados y el Tratado de Libre Comercio de América del Norte*, Mexico City: Miguel Ángel Porrúa, 2004; and J Cypher & R Delgado Wise, 'Restructuring Mexico, realigning dependency: harnessing Mexican labour power in the NAFTA era', working paper, Doctoral Programme in Development Studies, University of Zacatecas, 2007.
12 Comisión Económica para América Latina (CEPAL), *Globalización y desarrollo*, Santiago: CEPAL/ILPES/UN, 2002.
13 R Delgado Wise & H Márquez, 'Migración, políticas públicas y desarrollo: reflexiones en torno al caso de México', paper presented at the Seminar on 'Problemas y Desafíos de la Migración y el Desarrollo en América', Red Internacional de Migración y Desarrollo, Cuernavaca, 7–9 April 2005; and R Delgado Wise & J Cypher, 'The strategic role of labour in Mexico's subordinated integration into the US production system under NAFTA', working document 12/11/2005, Doctoral Programme in Development Studies, University of Zacatecas, 2005.
14 *Ibid.*
15 J Durán & BSV Ventura-Dias, *Comercio intrafirma: concepto, alcance y magnitud*, Santiago: CEPAL, 2003.
16 M Capdevielle, 'Procesos de producción global: ¿alternativa para el desarrollo mexicano?', *Comercio exterior*, 55 (7), 2005, pp 561–573.
17 R Delgado Wise & J Cypher, 'The strategic role of Mexican labour under NAFTA: critical perspectives on current economic integration', *Annals of the American Academy of Political and Social Science*, 615, 2007, pp 120–142.
18 J Calva, 'México: la estrategia macroeconómica 2001–2006—promesas, resultados y perspectivas', *Problemas del desarrollo*, 36 (143), 2005, pp 59–87.
19 R Delgado Wise & H Márquez, 'Para entender la migración a Estados Unidos: el papel de la fuerza de trabajo barata mexicana en el mercado laboural transnacional', *Problemas del desarrollo*, 38 (149), 2007, pp 11–24.

20 United Nations, 'Seguimiento de la población mundial, con especial referencia a la migración internacional y el desarrollo', Report of the Secretary General, E/CN.9/2006/3, 25 January 2006.
21 International Fund for Agricultural Development (IFAD), *Sending Money Home: Worwide Remittance Flows to Underdeveloped Countries*, Rome: IFAD, 2007.
22 Banxico, 2006, Remesas familiares, at www.banxico.org.mx, accessed September 2007.
23 V Zúñiga & R Hernández-León (eds), *New Destinations: Mexican Immigration in the United States*, New York: Russell Sage Foundation, 2005.
24 D Champlin & E Hake, 'Immigration as industrial strategy in American meatpacking', *Review of Political Economy*, 18 (1), 2006, pp 49–70.
25 Organisation for Economic Co-operation and Development (OECD), 2005, at http://www.oecd.org.
26 Conapo, *Series sobre migración internacional*, Mexico City: Conapo, 2007.
27 R Delgado Wise, H Márquez & H Rodríguez, 'Organizaciones transnacionales de migrantes y desarrollo regional en Zacatecas', *Migraciones internacionales*, 2 (4), 2004, pp 159–181.
28 Instituto Nacional de Estadística, Geografía e Informática (INEGI), *Conteo de población y vivienda*, Mexico: INEGI, 2006.
29 Instituto Nacional De Migración (INM), *Propuesta de política migratoria integral en la frontera sur de México*, Mexico City: INM, 2005.
30 R Delgado Wise & J Cypher, 'The strategic role of Labour in Mexico's subordinated integration into the US production system under NAFTA'.
31 C Ruiz-Durán, 'Integración de los mercados labourales en América del Norte', research report, 2004, at http://www.ietrabajo.org.mx.
32 E Levine, 'El proceso de incorporación de inmigrantes mexicanos a la vida y el trabajo en Los Ángeles, California', *Migraciones internacionales*, 3 (2), 2005, pp 108–136.
33 Conapo, *Series sobre migración internacional*.
34 G Cadena, 'Manufactura, en la ruta de la "desindustrialización"', *El Financiero*, 16 August 2005.
35 Conapo, *Migración internacional*, 2005, at http://www.conapo.gob.mx.
36 H Márquez Covarrubias, 'El desarrollo participativo transnacional basado en las organizaciones de migrantes', *Problemas del desarrollo*, 37 (144), 2006, pp 121–144.
37 W Bello, 'The capitalist conjuncture', p 1345; and Harvey, 'Neoliberalism as creative destruction', p 33.

The Violence of Development and the Migration/Insecurities Nexus: labour migration in a North American context

MARIANNE H MARCHAND

'Crossing borders': an activity that in certain academic circles is heralded as something positive, reflecting a modern, if not postmodern, attitude towards life and a high degree of mobility. As such, the act of crossing borders is often seen in conceptual terms between genres of music or art, between 'cultures', creating new hybridities, or the travelling of ideas and theories. Against this background the crossing of physical borders through migration is one more expression of mobility and (post)modernity. However, such characterisation of migration depends very much on who is engaging in it and under what circumstances. The experience of a Mexican undocumented migrant trying to cross the Arizonan desert in 50°C. weather conditions and facing gun-toting vigilantes is quite distinct from that of the American CEO who is flying into Mexico City for a meeting with his local executives in a posh boardroom overlooking the Mexican capital's skyline. Granted, both face danger in their act of crossing, but the possibility of dying from dehydration, being bitten by a snake or facing abandonment and/or robbery by a 'pollero'[1] is much more imminent than the risks involved in frequenting and facing the trials of Mexico City.

Over the past couple of years, and particularly since the events of 11 September 2001, much has been written about the increased risks (and violence) involved in crossing the border between the USA and Mexico. While this article is not directly challenging such narratives, it intends to present a slightly different take and to engage in a reflection about the nexus between migration and the violence of development. The primary argument is that migration is a multidimensional process which is imbedded in violence, and extends beyond the aspect of border crossing. In particular since 9/11 migrants are constructed as a security threat to the state—that is at least the dominant view in many migrant receiving states. In contrast with this dominant view, the present article will introduce a different view on the relationship(s) between migration and security, from a migrant's perspective: the migration–insecurities nexus.

Examples to support the argument will be drawn from migrants' experiences in the region of 'North America', that is Mexico, the USA and Canada. As is well known, most migration flows go north from Central America and Mexico to the USA and, increasingly Canada. However, it should be noted that significant flows of people also go in a southerly direction, including so-called snow birds who want to spend the winter months in Mexico, Americans and Canadians who have decided to spend their retirement in Mexico (often in retirement communities), students, and business people. It is to be expected that experiences from the latter group of migrants do not necessarily match those of the former.

The emerging practices around migration and the involvement of what Castles and Miller have dubbed the 'migration industry' provide some degree of security for migrants,[2] especially the activities by pro-migrant groups and human rights organizations. At the same time, however, actors such as 'polleros' are also the cause of increasing insecurities for migrants.

The two tales of Mexican migration experience

Much has been written about Mexican migration to its northern neighbour (see also the article by Raúl Delgado Wise and Humberto Márquez Covarrubias in this issue). Without going into a detailed analysis, a few issues about these flows need to be highlighted. Mexican migration to the USA has a long tradition, dating back to the late 19th century. With limited restrictions in terms of border crossings, Mexicans in search of (temporary) work in agriculture would just walk across the border and find their way to such states as California, Texas and Florida to harvest crops. It is not until the 1920s that the US government actually starts to systematically check and control its southern border, with the establishment of the border patrol.[3]

For most of the 20th century Mexican migration flows to the north have been characterised by three main features. First, the majority of Mexican migrants has traditionally worked in agriculture, providing cheap labour for harvesting fruit and vegetables. Another feature is that these flows have tended to be dependent on economic cycles. In periods of severe economic downturn border controls have increased, as have deportations of Mexican migrants, either legally or illegally residing in the USA. Third, for most of the period these flows have been characterised by their circular and seasonal nature: after the harvests migrants would return home to be with their families, celebrate the local town's patron saint and attend their own plots of land. However, this pattern in migration has changed drastically since the late 1980s.

For one thing, migration flows have diversified in their destination: many Mexican migrants are now working in services, construction, and the meatpacking industry, as well as in the 'care sector' and landscaping. This has resulted in Mexicans migrating to urban areas and regions such as the Mid-west and the South.

In addition, US border policy took on a new direction in the early 1990s with the implementation of 'Operation Gatekeeper' in the San Diego area and 'Hold the Line' on the border between El Paso and Ciudad Juarez, resulting in a 'securitisation' of the border.[4] While both initiatives were established with the objective of stemming the perceived tidal flood of Mexican migrants crossing the border, it has been argued that the effect has been counter-productive because these measures haven't really stopped the flow of migrants. To the contrary, they have created a situation in which undocumented migrants are staying for extended periods of time, because of the increased risks in crossing the border.[5]

Both initiatives form part of an important turn in US migration policies since the mid-to-late 1980s, reflecting an attempt to gain greater control over migration into the country. The policies consist of two parts. On the one hand, the Immigration Regulation and Control Act of 1986 (IRCA, aka the Simpson-Rodino Act) intended to regularise the migratory status of many undocumented migrants who had been staying in the country for a long time. On the other hand, both initiatives mentioned above, and which were first introduced locally instead of at the federal level, reflected an attempt to increase border controls. Together these policies constituted an important element of the state's attempt to regain control and sovereignty over its territory, through exerting control over its population.

The above account mostly reflects a receiving country's perspective, in this particular case that of the USA. If we approach migration, and the migration experience, from the perspective of sending communities and of migrants themselves a very different story emerges.

South–North labour migration is clearly connected to development, or rather 'mal-development' or underdevelopment, in sending countries. In Mexico this is also the case. During its long experience with migration it has mostly been *campesinos* or small farmers from impoverished regions who have migrated. This also explains the regionally organised pattern of Mexican migration. For instance, the central-western part of Mexico, encompassing such states as Michoacan, Jalisco, Zacatecas and Nayarit, has a longstanding migratory tradition, mostly from the countryside. As small farmers (and their sons) were unable to provide for their family the decision to migrate, either in the context of the *Bracero* programme or as undocumented workers, was made in order to increase household income. The relative neglect of the countryside was an inherent feature of Mexico's economic development model of Import Substitution Industrialisation (ISI). When this model started to run into problems and the country as a whole was facing severe problems with the debt crisis of 1982 and later the peso crisis of 1995, migration not only increased but also expanded to include other sending regions in the center-south of the country. States like Oaxaca, Puebla, Veracruz and Hidalgo are reflective of this trend. And, in particular since 1995, migrants not only included farmers, but also increasingly people from urban areas, such as Mexico City and Puebla, who tended to be skilled or semi-skilled.[6]

Between push and pull factors it is impossible to establish which contributed to a larger degree towards the changing composition of Mexican migration. On the Mexican side the 1995 peso crisis made a profound impact on the urban middle and working classes, while trade liberalisation, reinforced by the North American Free Trade agreement (NAFTA), deepened the crisis in the countryside. On the US side the economy has been transformed into a post-industrial, service economy in need of a different kind of precarious or casualised labour force, in addition to the continuing need for agricultural workers.[7]

The violence of development

The general picture above provides an overview of the complex, interrelated structural causes of migration. However, migration is a complex, multi-dimensional phenomenon which encompasses economic, social, cultural and political dimensions and which cannot be captured entirely by a structural explanation. Instead, one needs a transversal approach, linking the local to the global, to tease out migration's multidimensionality and the nexus between migration and the violence of development, which in turn is creating a situation of multiple insecurities for migrants and their families.

The term violence of development was used in a special issue of the journal *Development*. According to the issue's editors:

> Violence, then, in its manifold manifestations is inherent in the current patterns of development. It cannot be dealt with by safety nets and superficial solutions, or by palliatives such as micro-credit schemes, capacity building workshops, etc. These development programmes and projects, however well designed, fail to address the causes of the violence, the destruction of nature and culture and of plural ways of knowing, being and doing, the inadequacies of the dominant democratic process, the inequality of access to resources and spaces for expression.[8]

In the same piece the two editors argue that their perspective on violence-related development may not be the usual one. They argue that it is important to develop a perspective on the violence of development which takes as vantage point that of the people who have been affected by it:

> In illuminating the contentious link between development and violence, we are deliberately posing the question of whose vantage point counts. Is it possible to give primacy to the perspective of those excluded and victimized by development? How do forest dwellers, traditional fisher people, women and men eking out a living in urban slums, tribal and indigenous communities, contract workers, domestic workers far from home, displaced and migrant people, sex workers, orphans and refugees understand development given the violence of their everyday exclusion, exploitation, discrimination and marginalization?[9]

This notion of the multiple, complex levels of violence is further elaborated by Arturo Escobar in his contribution to the special issue. According to him development and modernity are two processes that engender displacement: 'Both modernity and development are spatial–cultural projects that require the continuous conquest of territories and peoples and their ecological and cultural transformation along the lines of an allegedly rational order'. Development, in Escobar's eyes, is the final product of those processes which find their culmination in the 'consolidation of modern capitalism'.[10]

As I have argued elsewhere, in the case of Mexico its neoliberal modernisation project involves a 'violent restructuring of state–society relations', including various forms of disciplining as well as outright violence.[11] Migrants can in part be seen as the victims of this restructuring and displacement producing process, resulting in their exit. However, this does not mean that they have entirely escaped the disciplining of the state's modernity project. In a highly globalised world, where migrants increasingly form transnational communities in order to stay in touch with their families and communities of origin, the state and international institutions such as the World Bank are now designing projects and policies to capture and channel (collective) remittances of migrant organisations 'abroad' to support local development projects.

The nexus between migration and the violence of development can be traced through the various dimensions of the migration experience:

- the reasons why people migrate;
- the insecurities to which migrants are exposed in their journey towards the North;
- the issues migrants are facing once arrived at their destination, including finding a job, having to share cramped housing, facing discrimination and abuse;
- the implications for family members which stayed behind and communities of origin;
- the increasing risks of being deported after having been the victim of a raid by immigration officers at workplaces and other locations frequented by migrants.

In addition, as mentioned above, there is the dimension of the state trying to discipline migrants to send collective remittances to support local development projects, which ironically are being used to buttress its neoliberal development project.

Marginalization and migration

In the case of Mexican migration, the nexus with the violence of development is quite evident. Most (potential) migrants come from poor backgrounds and face a future and vicious circle of relative marginalisation and poverty which they wish to break through. With our research project in the state of Tlaxcala, situated in the central part of Mexico, we were interested in exploring the links between migration and development: on the one hand, how has a situation of underdevelopment stimulated migration and, on the other, how is current migration affecting development of sending regions, both negatively through the out-migration of young people in their most productive years and potentially positively, through the sending of (collective) remittances?[12] The state of Tlaxcala is one of the new migrant sending states. Although there was a tradition of internal migration to major cities such as Mexico and Puebla, people from Tlaxcala had not really joined the stream of Mexicans to the USA. This situation changed in the 1990s as a result of repeated economic crises and, in particular, after the peso crisis of 1995.

Based on surveys and interviews we executed in two municipalities with a medium level of out-migration, improving one's standard of living and taking care of the family are the most cited reasons for migrating. Migrant men, in particular, suggest that they wish to migrate in order to earn money and support their families. The remittances are used to support wife or partner and children in their day-to-day basic needs. In other words, migration has clearly become a family survival strategy.

Although Mexican women have always migrated, in particular for family reunification reasons (in combination with work), they are now increasingly migrating independently. Interestingly in Tlaxcala, a state which recently joined the ranks of sending states, female migration is still low. Among the reasons for this are changed US immigration policies, making family reunification more complicated, and the fact that migrant networks for people from Tlaxcala are still relatively young. Women are more inclined to migrate when they have access to well established migrant networks, giving them a higher degree of security and predictability. The relative absence of such predictability and security has prevented Tlaxcaltecan women from migrating in large numbers. Of the adolescents we interviewed 39% of the men and 30% of the women indicated that they would be interested in migrating, which means that between 60% and 66%, respectively do not have any intentions to migrate at this point.[13]

As part of our investigation we also looked for differences between men and women in terms of their reasons for migrating. The findings reveal certain differences for both adults and adolescents. In the case of the adults, the men responded that they wanted to earn money and in the second place to work, while women told us that they would migrate to work and earn money as a second option. These different responses may reflect distinct conceptions of the relationship between work and money—while men indicate that they want to earn money, women assume that a job, assumedly any kind of job, will assure them a monetary income. Another surprising finding is that women gave as a third reason for migrating the wish either to better their (family's) quality of life or to get to know the USA. In other words, migration is being associated with travel (see Figure 1).

As part of our research we also surveyed adolescents to find out whether a 'culture of migration' is developing irrespective of economic needs.[14] Among Tlaxcaltecan adolescents there doesn't appear to be such a 'culture of migration' yet. Interestingly many of the attitudes we found among adults were mirrored by the adolescents aged between 12 and 16 whom we surveyed at two different middle schools. They indicated that their reasons for wanting to migrate where to work in order to earn money, to support their family and to 'set up house' (see Figure 2).

This last response was only given by boys, clearly reflecting society's expectations about their role as future breadwinner and provider for the family. In contrast, many girls responded that they wanted to migrate to get to know different places and experience different cultures. Both boys and girls were also interested in migrating in order to study abroad. In other words, for these adolescents there is a conflation of the reasons usually mentioned for migrating with those for travel (as if travel is not a different or separate endeavour), but the reasons for migrating are still predominantly traditional: improving one's economic situation and that of the family.

The violent journey

For migrants the journey toward their destination begins at home. Within the family migration is pursued as a household survival strategy and most

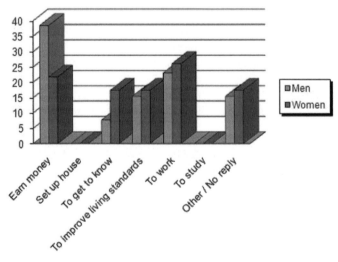

FIGURE 1. Adults: Why do you want to migrate?

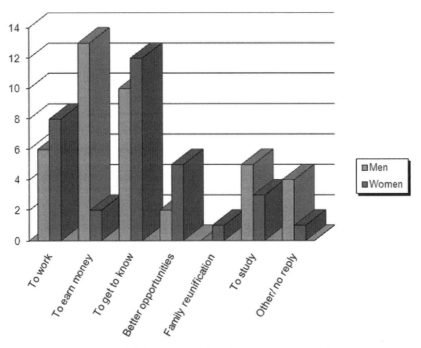

FIGURE 2. Adolescents: Why do you want to migrate?

migrants rely on family members' support to undertake the journey north. This support is often monetary in nature, when family members who are already living in the USA send money to pay the '*pollero*' or smuggler. With the so-called securitisation of the border, crossing the border and getting to one's destination have become much more difficult and dangerous. The risks not only involve being caught by the border patrol but also being exposed to extreme weather conditions, in, for instance, the Arizona desert, or having to swim through the treacherous currents of the Rio Grande while not being a very good swimmer. This is why the amount one has to pay to the *pollero* has increased significantly. At the moment the sum one needs to pay is around $2500, a small fortune for many migrants.

Given the risks involved in crossing, as well as the amount one has to pay, it is extremely important to engage a reliable *pollero*. This means a smuggler who will not leave people behind in the desert (or locked up in the back of a truck or container), nor will rob or do physical harm to those in his charge, and who is 'well connected'. In other words, someone who has access to information about activities and movements of the border patrol in order to avoid detection, so that the chances of crossing successfully are relatively good. The practice which has evolved in about the last 15 years is that reliable smugglers will 'deliver' migrants to relatives on the US side of the border. Also, they will extend a guarantee—up to three attempts to cross the border for the same fee. This implies that those migrants who can afford a higher fee have access to more reliable smuggler services. Those who do not have family

153

members or friends in the USA and cannot pay the high-end fees for the *pollero* tend to run more risks.

As academics as well as NGOs have argued, this situation has led to an increase in border crossing-related deaths.[15] For instance, many migrants, in their attempt to find a location where they can get to the other side of the border without being detected, now try to cross the Sonora and Arizona desert, often with disastrous consequences. In the period from 1 October 2004 to 3 September 2005 a total of 279 people were found dead in the Arizona desert (and three more in the Sonora desert). Of these 279 people 22% were women, 8% children aged 16 and below and 73% men.[16] The breakdown in terms of causes of death are as follows: motor vehicle accident (4.7%); hypothermia/dehydration/exposure to the elements (61%); gunshot wound/blunt force trauma/hanging/asphyxia (7.2%); health related causes (1.1%); and other/unknown (26%).[17] These cold facts do not really reveal the personal and familial traumatic stories behind them, including being left behind by the *pollero* in the desert without water, being attacked/raped/murdered by the *pollero*, or by a rancher or vigilante, or succumbing to injuries sustained from a car accident because the *pollero* tried to evade the border patrol.

Facing new realities at their destination

Related to the violence experienced during the journey is the situation migrants face once they arrive at their destination. As they have to pay back the money they received from family members for their journey and are supposed to start supporting the family back home with remittances, migrants need to find a job immediately. This is where the migrant networks fulfil an invaluable role. They help migrants to find a place to stay (often shared with other migrants—sometimes 20 per small apartment, taking turns sleeping) and a job.[18] However, being undocumented makes migrants vulnerable to various forms of exploitation. Often their labour rights are ignored, they have to work under dangerous conditions, and their pay tends to be below the minimum wage level.[19] Migrants also run the risk of being denounced to the authorities from the Immigration and Naturalization Service (INS—now part of the Department of Homeland Security) by, for example, their employers or other employees. In sum, migrants are exposed on a daily basis to multiple forms of violence in terms of their living arrangements and their work environment, making migration a very insecure enterprise.

Impact on family members and community

The violence described has a severe impact on family members who stay behind. In our conversations with people being interviewed quite a few spouses and children told us of their fears and worries when husbands, fathers, brothers and cousins leave for their journey north. These anxieties may translate into some form of depression or, for instance, cause children to act up and not perform well at school. In other words, crossing the border not only exposes migrants themselves to serious risks but also has secondary effects of violence on family members. One form of such violence is the recent phenomenon of blackmailing. The usual pattern is that family members in Mexico (or the USA) will receive a phone call explaining that the migrant in question is being held hostage and that a considerable sum of ransom money needs to be paid for his (or her) safe delivery at the previously agreed upon destination. Often the person in question is not in fact being held hostage, but because family members have no way of knowing his or her whereabouts or of being able to get in touch, the ransom money is quite often paid to the criminal organisation. Under the circumstances the family is usually too afraid to go to the police and report the blackmail.

In addition to the effects on migrants' families it is also important to consider the impact on communities with a relatively high incidence of migration. In the literature there exists quite some evidence about the social transformations in sending communities.[20] In addition to remittances being used as a household survival strategy, primarily for sustenance, health and education, many migrants are also sending money home in order to construct a house or improve current living conditions. The result is that in the communities of origin a new inequality is being created between those who have family members abroad and those who do not. Migrant families tend to have larger homes, built with durable materials such as concrete, blocks or bricks, while non-migrant families often live in laminated houses (see Figure 3).

The emergence of a so-called migrant elite in small rural towns results in many tensions at the community level. For instance, migrants and their families feel that they have made many sacrifices in order to improve their situation. For them migration is often a survival strategy at the level of the

Inequality

Photo's: Marianne H Marchand

FIGURE 3. Rising inequality in migrant sending communities.

household. Therefore, they may resent the demands that are placed on them to provide not only for their immediate family members but for the community-at-large. In conversations with family members they would often mention the sacrifices they are making to improve the family's socioeconomic situation. Such sacrifices include being separated for extensive periods of time from the migrant, having to make ends meet with the money they receive (thus creating an economic dependency with which many women are not very comfortable), having to run the household and raise the children mostly by themselves.[21]

This view contrasts significantly with that of neighbours who do not have migrants as family members. The opinions they expressed in conversations focused primarily on the increased and sometimes ostentatious wealth (as displayed in the houses being constructed) of families with migrants. Many people resented this, especially if the houses remained unoccupied for long periods of time as a result of most members of the immediate family living in the USA. Sometimes this resentment was in part fed because the prices of land and construction have increased thanks to the migrant 'construction boom'.[22]

On the more positive side migrants are also the providers of collective remittances (although the overall amount is no more than 2%–4% of total remittances) which are being used for projects in communities of origin, ranging from embellishing the local church to paving roads, electrification and other productive projects.[23] In addition, migrants are the bearers of 'modernity' and transmitters of new ideas, consumption patterns, cultural trends—the so-called social remittances. In going back and forth between two communities and societies they introduce hip hop music, 'New York pizza by the slice' and other icons of American popular culture into Mexico's rural communities.[24] Obviously, not all these developments are negative— they are part of profound transformations in the country's countryside. Other social transformations include changing gender relations as women gain more independence because they have been exposed to a migratory experience themselves or through female relatives or because they are now the *de facto* heads of households as their partners have migrated north.[25]

Being 'raided' at work and facing deportation

As an undocumented worker, or '*sans papiers*', one is taking many risks. Not only is the journey to the receiving country fraught with obstacles and problems, but the everyday living experiences of undocumented migrants are dominated by the need to avoid detection by immigration services. While in the past receiving states did not really put much emphasis on detecting undocumented workers—the reigning climate was one of condoning, or 'let live'—since the mid-1990s states' efforts to control migration flows have increasingly focused on detection and deportation. In the USA the adoption of the Illegal Immigration Reform and Immigrant Responsibility Act (IIRIRA) in1996 signified increased attention to controlling 'illegal' or undocumented migration and provided additional grounds for deportation of legal migrants who had been found guilty of criminal activities, including minor non-violent felonies.[26] However, it was not until after 9/11 that the law was really implemented to its fullest extent.

In general terms the creation of the Department of Homeland Security implied that efforts to control undocumented migration and the surveillance of legal non-citizen residents were now part of the state's national security and anti-terrorism activities. It is in this context that in 2003 the Immigration and Customs Enforcement unit (ICE) is being created. According to its website the *raison d'être* and objectives of ICE are as follows:

> [The] Immigration and Customs Enforcement (ICE) is the largest investigative branch of the Department of Homeland Security (DHS). The agency was created after 9/11, by combining the law enforcement arms of the former Immigration and Naturalization Service (INS) and the former US Customs Service, to more effectively enforce our immigration and customs laws and to protect the United States against terrorist attacks. ICE does this by targeting illegal immigrants: the people, money and materials that support terrorism and other criminal activities. ICE is a key component of the DHS 'layered defense' approach to protecting the nation.[27]

The results of ICE's creation and the stepped-up surveillance of the US–Mexico border, including the introduction of a smart border initiative and the construction of a wall along parts of the border are not only that it has become more difficult to cross the border illegally, but also that the amount of raids on workplaces and deportations have increased exponentially. As of January 2008 it is now reported that an average of 2000 Mexicans per day are being deported. In addition, the raids on workplaces known to employ undocumented migrants have sky-rocketed.

Although many of the migrants who have been deported will try to return as soon as possible to the USA and join their family members or friends, quite a few of them are now looking for other alternatives—either in their communities of origin or in other destinations, such as Canada. Much of this is still going unreported, but incidental evidence from the field indicates a possible change in migratory trends. So far Mexican authorities have not yet anticipated or planned for increased return migration or reduced amounts of monetary remittances, which have also been affected by the economic downturn in the USA. The extent to which such changes will affect communities of origin and, in particular, poverty in rural Mexico, needs to be addressed.

Conclusion

This paper set out to reconceptualise the migration/violence nexus. Much attention these days is being paid to the dangers involved in migrating, in particular in crossing borders in an 'irregular' way. As is argued here, we need to broaden our notion of violence and consider that the development process itself is inherently violent, involving displacement and margin-alisation of certain groups of people. Another important element in the reconceptualisation of the migration–violence nexus is that not only migrants but their family members also have to cope with insecurities, ranging from not knowing where their loved ones are to being unsure whether they have been able to cross the border safely. In addition, those staying behind are facing further insecurities: in particular when and whether they will receive the now so much awaited and expected remittances. Such remittances are creating new dependencies and anxieties among those staying behind. The now much vaunted social remittances may also not always be positive.[28] In the case of the Mexican countryside there are now increasing reports of gang-related violence among young (mostly male) migrants who have returned or been deported. Finally, migrants and their families are also exposed to diseases and labour-related accidents. Although not much research exists about the presence of HIV/AIDS in migrant sending communities, there are indications that it is on the rise.

It goes without saying that the migration–violence nexus is gendered. Men and women are affected in different ways and the violence to which they are exposed is related to their position with respect to the migration–violence nexus. Ironically the increase in workplace raids to apprehend undocumented workers may affect men disproportionably. As men tend to frequent public places such as construction sites, etc they may be easier targets for ICE. Women, however, are often employed as maids or nannies and, thus, located in the private sphere of homes—which makes it more difficult to locate them.

Although much of what has been argued in this article is well known to migration experts, the importance of the argument lies in the presentation of a different vantage point on the migration–security nexus. Looking at the nexus from a migrant's perspective the central question becomes: whose security? By understanding migration as a social process, it is clear that the security of many is involved, from family members, in particular children, to migrants themselves and those who are aiding them in finding work in the new society. As such the narrowly defined national security agenda of receiving states creates many perverse consequences, including insecurities for migrants and their communities as well as for those of sending states.

Notes

1 A 'pollero' is the Spanish (Mexican) term for migrant smuggler. It should be noted that a *pollero* can be part of a large, criminal network or can be someone of the migrant's hometown and working relatively independently. In the latter case the *pollero* is someone embedded in the community's social network.
2 S Castles & M Miller, *The Age of Migration*, Basingstoke: Palgrave Macmillan, 2003.
3 J Nevins, *Operation Gatekeeper: The Rise of the 'Illegal Alien' and the Making of the US–Mexico Boundary*, New York: Routledge, 2002.
4 *Ibid.*
5 *Ibid*; and P Andreas, *Border Games: Policing the US–Mexico Divide*, Ithaca, NY: Cornell University Press, 2000.
6 J Durand, DS Massey & René Zenteno, 'Mexican immigration to the United States: continuities and changes', *Latin American Research Review*, 36 (1), 2001, pp 107–127; and J Durand & DS Massey, *Clandestinos: Migración México–Estados Unidos en los albores del siglo XXI*, Mexico City: Universidad Autónoma de Zacatecas/Miguel Ángel Porrúa, 2003.
7 A Canales, 'International migration and labour flexibility in the context of NAFTA', *International Social Science Journal*, 165, 2000, pp 409–419; and Durand & Massey, *Clandestinos*.

8 S Kothari & W Harcourt, 'Introduction: the violence of development', *Development* (special issue), 47 (1), 2004, p 6.

9 *Ibid*, p 3.

10 A Escobar, 'Development, violence and the new imperial order', *Development*, 47 (1), 2004, p 16.

11 MH Marchand, 'Neo-liberal disciplining, violence and transnational organizing: the struggle for women's rights in Ciudad Juárez', *Development*, 47 (1), 2004, pp 88–89.

12 The information for this section comes from the project 'Apizaco y Huamantla. Estudio comparativo de comunidades expulsoras de migrantes: Modelo de análisis de las causas e implicaciones de los flujos migratorios para solucionar la falta del desarrollo sustentable social de la región (clave Fomix-Tlax-2003-02-12453), 2004–2006', for which the author received funding from the Mexican Council for Science and Technology. See also MH Marchand (ed), *Tlaxcala: ¿Migración o Desarrollo Local?* Puebla: Consejo Nacional de Ciencia y Tecnología/Universidad de las Américas, Puebla, 2006; and http://www.ceres.org.mx/migraciontlaxcala/general.htm.

13 Marchand, *Tlaxcala*.

14 W Kandel & D Massey, 'The culture of Mexican migration: a theoretical and empirical analysis', *Social Forces*, 80 (3), pp 981–1004.

15 Andreas, *Border Games*; Nevins, *Operation Gatekeeper*; Humane Borders, *Humane Borders Water Station Maps and Warning Posters*, 2006, at http://www.humaneborders.org/news/news4.html, accessed 20 June 2008; and Coalición de Derechos Humanos, *Final Count for Recovered Bodies on the Arizona–Sonora Border 237 as Border Patrol Continues to Report Decreases in Crossings*, 2007, at http://www.derechoshumanosaz.net/images/pdfs/10-11-07%20press%20release.pdf, accessed 20 June 2008.

16 Of 1.9% of the bodies found the sex could not be determined.

17 The figures provided here come from my own calculations based on the information in Coalición de Derechos Humanos/Alianza Indígena sin Fronteras, *Migrant Deaths*, 2006, at http://www. derechoshumanosaz.net/deaths.php4, accessed 13 February 2006. This information is now available at http://www.derechoshumanosaz.net/index.php?option=com_content&task=view&id=20&Itemid=34, accessed 20 June 2008.

18 A Portes, L Guarnizo & P Landolt, 'El estudio del transnacionalismo: peligros latentes y promesas de un campo de investigación emergente', in Portes *et al* (eds), *La Globalización desde Abajo: Transnacionalismo Inmigrante y Desarrollo—la Experiencia de Estados Unidos y América Latina*, Mexico City: Flacso, 2003, pp 15–44; and RC Smith, *Mexican New York: Transnational Lives of New Immigrants*, Berkeley, CA: University of California Press, 2005.

19 WA Cornelius, 'The US demand for Mexican labor', in WA Cornelius & JA Bustamante (eds), *Mexican Migration to the United States: Origins, Consequences, and Policy Options*, La Jolla, CA: Bilateral Commission on the Future of US–Mexican Relations, 1989, pp 25–47; and Human Rights Watch, *Blood Sweat and Fear: Workers' Rights in US Meat and Poultry Plants*, New York: Human Rights Watch, 2006, at http://www.hrw.org/reports/2005/usa0105/, accessed 20 June 2008.

20 N Glick Schiller & L Basch, 'From immigrant to transmigrant: theorizing transnational migration', *Anthropological Quarterly*, 68 (1), 1995, pp 48–63; T Faist, 2000, 'Transnationalization in international migration: implications for the study of citizenship and culture', *Ethnic and Racial Studies*, 23 (2), 2000, pp 189–222; Portes *et al*, 'El estudio del transnacionalismo'; Smith, *Mexican New York*; and LF Herrera Lima, 'Hacia una agenda de investigación del trabajo en el espacio laboral transnacional de Norteamérica', *Trabajo*, 2 (3), 2006, pp 89–121.

21 Marchand, *Tlaxcala*.

22 *Ibid*.

23 R García Zamora, *Migración, remesas y desarrollo local*, Zacatecas, MX: Programa de Doctorado en Estudios de Desarrollo, University of Zacatecas, 2003.

24 Smith, *Mexican New York*.

25 L Goldring, 'Gender, status, and the state in transnational spaces: the gendering of political participation and Mexican hometown associations', in P Hondagneu-Sotelo (ed), *Gender and US Immigration: Contemporary Trends*, Berkeley, CA: University of California Press, 2003; and P Hondagneu-Sotelo, *Doméstica: Immigrant Workers Cleaning and Caring in the Shadows of Affluence*, Berkeley, CA: University of California Press, 2007.

26 Human Rights Watch, *Forced Apart: Families Separated and Immigrants Harmed by United States Deportation Policy*, New York: Human Rights Watch, 2007, at http://hrw.org/reports/2007/us0707/index.htm, accessed 28 June 2008.

27 Immigration and Customs Enforcement, 2008, at http://www.ice.gov/about/, accessed 27 June 2008.

28 Smith, *Mexican New York*.

'Remittances are Beautiful'?[1] Gender implications of the new global remittances trend

RAHEL KUNZ

> We are gathered here today because of the shared belief that there is a huge potential for scaling up the impact of remittances on poverty reduction efforts in developing countries.[2]

Migration and remittances are not new phenomena. Migration has existed since the beginning of humankind and migrants have sent home and invested their money for a long time and in a number of ways. Over the past few years, however, a new trend has emerged within the international community, which I call the new global remittance trend (GRT). In brief, this trend refers to the process whereby government institutions, international (financial) organisations, non-governmental organisations and private sector actors have become interested in migration and remittances and in their potential for poverty reduction and development, and have started to devise institutions and policies to harness this potential.[3] The emergence of the

GRT can be situated against the backdrop of a number of ongoing global transformations, such as the increase in international migration and remittances over the past decade or so, and the crisis in development financing to achieve the Millennium Development Goals (MDGs).

Increasing international migration has lead to a growing awareness of migratory processes. The UN estimates that about 190 million people lived and worked outside the country of their birth in 2005, up from around 150 million in 1990, and 75 million in 1960.[4] This global increase in international migration has been accompanied by a growing sum of remittances. According to World Bank statistics, remittance flows to developing countries are estimated to have reached US\$161 billion in 2004 and \$239 billion in 2007.[5]

Given the current crisis in development finance, vast sums like these have warmed the hearts of members of the international community. Although the international community has agreed on a common framework for development—the MDGs—there is a constant lack of resources to finance the achievement of these goals. Multilateral development aid has decreased during the past decade, while world-wide remittance flows exceed total development aid and have become the second-largest—and for some countries even the largest—financial flow to developing countries after foreign direct investment. This has spawned interest among the international community to harness remittances for development.

Over the past few years a mainstream way of framing the links between migration, remittances and development has emerged within the GRT. References to women or gender issues are scarce within this framing. Thus, at first sight, the GRT seems to be gender-neutral, ie without gender-specific dimensions and implications. However, as feminist scholars have been demonstrating for some time, many discourses that seem, or claim, to be gender-neutral are in actual fact based upon gendered assumptions and representations.[6] Similarly, this article suggests that the GRT is not gender-neutral but gender-blind, ie the projected gender-neutral stance obscures the gendered assumptions and realities within which the GRT is embedded.

An overview of the literature reveals that there is a number of critical voices,[7] but gender analyses of the GRT are still scarce. In order to start filling this gap, the objective of this article is twofold: first, to trace the emergence of the GRT and the way the link between migration, remittances and development is framed within it; and, second, to subject the GRT to a critical gender perspective to explore its gendered foundations and its gender-specific implications.

The article uses two analytical tools: the concept of framing and gender analysis. The concept of framing can be defined in terms of a two-part process: 'one, drawing attention to a specific issue (such as the environment or urban unemployment); two, determining how such an issue is viewed'.[8] The aim of framing is to get 'an issue to be seen by those that matter, and ensure that they see it in a specific way', whereby framing can 'limit the power of potentially radical ideas to achieve change'.[9] Thus, specific discourses, representing the interests of certain actors, acquire the status of common sense while counter-discourses are de-legitimised. Framing practices include both conceptual and institutional components, and are embedded in power constellations. The concept of framing serves to examine how the links between migration, remittances and development came to be put on the agenda of the international community, which institutions were involved, how the issue was presented and what the implications are.

Generally, the term 'gender' can refer both to a dynamic that structures social life, and to a tool for analysis. In the former meaning it is used as referring to a historically and culturally specific social construction which operates through various mechanisms—such as representations, social structures and institutions, etc—and which has concrete implications in determining how women and men think, act and live. As defined by Peterson and Runyan, a gender-sensitive lens enables us 'to "see" how the world is shaped by gendered concepts, practices, and institutions'.[10] This article uses gender as an analytical tool, in order to examine the GRT through a gender-sensitive lens.

Background to the new GRT

The GRT refers to the heightened interest of different actors—governments, international organisations, non-governmental organisations and private sector actors—in the development potential of international migration and remittances, and the strategies they have designed to harness this potential. What is new about the GRT is the way in which migration and development have become linked in theoretical and practical ways; the number and variety of institutions that have become involved in numerous activities; the ways in which new institutions and policies have been set up at the international, national and local levels; and the extent to which migration and remittances have gained popularity as an instrument to finance development and poverty reduction.

At the heart of the GRT lies a major shift in thinking about migration and development. Traditionally, there was a tendency to perceive migration as either a completely distinct area of concern from development, or as the outcome of lacking or failed development. Within this view poverty is seen as the root cause of migration and it is believed that through aid and development migration can be prevented or at least mitigated. For a long time this conventional view was the mainstream approach within the international community, adopted by states and international institutions alike. The Council of the European Union, for example, declared in its conclusions of the Conference in Seville in 2002:

> The European Council considers that combating illegal immigration requires a greater effort on the part of the European Union and a targeted approach to the problem, with the use of all appropriate instruments in the context of the European Union's external relations. To that end, in accordance with the Tampere European Council conclusions, an integrated, comprehensive and balanced approach to tackling the root causes of illegal immigration must

remain the European Union's constant long-term objective. With this in mind, the European Council points out that closer economic cooperation, trade expansion, development assistance and conflict prevention are all means of promoting economic prosperity in the countries concerned and thereby reducing the underlying causes of migration flows.[11]

In the 1990s a new paradigm emerges, whereby the two areas of migration and development become linked in the so-called 'migration–development nexus'.[12] Migration is no longer seen as a *problem*, but as a *tool* for development. Within this approach migration is taken as a fact and the aim is to manage migration and harness remittances in such a way as to increase their impact on development in the countries of origin. Thus, the linkages between migration and development are perceived in a positive way and there is a tendency to instrumentalise migration and remittances for development. This shift was emphasised by the International Conference on Migrant Remittances in 2003:

> [Migration] is no longer simply seen as a failure of development but increasingly as an integral part of the whole process of development with a potentially important role to play in the alleviation of poverty.[13]

It is important to note that the emergence of the migration–development nexus has not meant a complete paradigm shift, as some have it, or the eradication of the conventional paradigm. Rather, different institutions adopt the two paradigms to different extents and in different ways, as we shall see below. In some cases there is a combination of the two approaches, which may result in the coexistence of inconsistent policies.[14]

This shift in thinking about the links between migration and development resulted in efforts by the international community to find out more about the nature of these links, and how they could be influenced in order to increase the positive impacts of migration and remittances on development. In this way remittances have become the centre of attention, which led to the emergence of the GRT. The GRT consists of a number of conceptual and institutional components and its emergence can be traced in documents, conference and other activities by the international community. In what follows, a few milestones will be used to trace the emergence of this trend. This is by no means an exhaustive list, but merely an account of some of the most significant events.

The main actors involved in the GRT are international organisations (eg the International Labour Organisation (ILO) and the International Organisation for Migration (IOM)); international financial institutions (eg the World Bank, IMF and Inter-American Development Bank (IDB)); national development agencies of migrant-receiving countries (eg the UK Department for International Development (DFID) and the US Agency for International Development (USAID)); NGOs (eg Inter-American Dialogue, Women's World Banking); and government institutions of major migrant-sending countries like Mexico and the Philippines. The GRT consists of a wide range of activities: research, conferences, setting up of taskforces and encouraging norm-setting, for example in the transfer of remittances, facilitating the transfer and investment of remittances, and setting up migration-linked development projects. Over time more and more members of the international community have become involved in the GRT in one form or another.

The ILO was among the first international institutions to point to the importance of migrant remittances. As early as 1949 the International Labour Organisation Convention on Migration for Employment (No 97) refers to the 'earning and savings of the migrant' and urges countries to allow migrants to transfer remittances.[15] However, at this stage, the ILO did not make an explicit link between migration, remittances and development.

The IOM is something of a pioneer of the new migration–development paradigm. According to its Mission Statement, the IOM is 'committed to the principle that humane and orderly migration benefits migrants and society' and acts to 'encourage social and economic development through migration'.[16] Thus, linking migration and development and focusing on its positive linkages have been part of IOM's mission right from the start. In 1964, well before the broad emergence of the new paradigm, the IOM (then called ICEM) launched the 'Migration for Development' programmes 'aimed at recruitment and placement of highly qualified migrants to developing countries in Latin America', and in 1974, the 'Return of Talent' programme for Latin Americans residing abroad.[17] Within the broader international community these were rather isolated efforts to link migration to development and are certainly to be understood as the *raison d'être* of the institution itself. In addition, the GRT focus was not explicitly on the development potential of migrant remittances.

One of the first milestones in the emergence of the GRT was the Cairo Programme of Action, which noted in 1994 that migration has potential benefits for both the country of origin, which receives remittances, and for the country of destination, which obtains needed human resources.[18] The programme also urged source countries to implement policies to facilitate the transfer of remittances and to channel them towards productive investment.

In November 2000 the ILO organised a conference on 'Making the Best of Globalisation: Migrant Worker Remittances and Micro-Finance' in order to 'assess possibilities and constraints for channelling remittances through micro-finance institutions towards productive investments'.[19]

The issue of remittances was also addressed in the Monterrey Consensus. This Consensus is part of the report adopted at the International Conference on Financing for Development (FFD summit) which was held in 2002 in Monterrey (Mexico). The aim of the conference was to consider new sources to finance development and efforts to achieve the MDGs. It was the first United Nations-hosted conference to address financial and development issues and provides 'the new global approach to financing development'.[20] The issue of remittances is addressed within the area of domestic financial resources. The Consensus states: 'It is also important to reduce the transfer costs of migrant workers' remittances and create opportunities for development-oriented investments, including housing'.[21]

In response to growing awareness of the implications of international migration the Global Commission on International Migration (GCIM) was established in 2003, with the encouragement of the UN Secretary-General.[22] Its main mandate was to 'anayls[e] gaps in current policy approaches to migration and examin[e] inter-linkages with other issue-areas', such as development, trade, security and human rights.[23]

Before 2003 the World Bank was a relatively minor player in the GRT. This changed rapidly with the publication of the Global Development Finance Annual Report in 2003, entitled *Worker's Remittances: An Important and Stable Source of External Development Finance*. In this report the World Bank for the first time took formal notice of remittances as a source of development finance, raising global awareness of the development potential of migration and remittances. Chapter 7 suggests that remittances have become an important source of development financing, and discusses measures to increase remittances and thereby their positive impact on development.[24] Remittances are referred to as 'an increasingly prominent source of external funding for many developing countries'.[25]

This publication illustrates the approach of the World Bank to the issue, ie taking as its main focus the financial aspects of the issue and the transfer of remittances. It also led to a number of World Bank empirical studies within its Research Program on International Migration. What is interesting to note is that the World Bank does not explicitly mention earlier efforts by other institutions, such as the ILO for example, to address the issue of remittances.

Later in 2003 the first international meeting focusing entirely on migrant remittances, the 'International Conference on Migrant Remittances: Development Impact, Opportunities for the Financial Sector and Future Prospects', took place in London. The conference was organised jointly by DFID and the World Bank in collaboration with the International Migration Policy Programme (IMP). It attracted over 100 participants from 42 countries: representatives of banks, and non-bank financial institutions, government officials, multilateral and bilateral donors, UN and other international institutions, NGOs, academics and consultants.[26] The conference report makes reference to the Monterrey Consensus and aimed to 'identify and establish collaborative strategies between interested stakeholders to strengthen the development impact of remittances'.[27]

At the Sea Island Summit in 2004 the G8 adopted the Action Plan 'Applying the Power of Entrepreneurship to the Eradication of Poverty'. This Action Plan recognises the key role remittances can play in private-sector development efforts, and commits to reducing the transfer costs for remittances and increasing financial options for the recipients of remittances in order to maximise their developmental impacts.[28]

In 2005 the first International Forum on Remittances took place at the IDB headquarters in Washington, DC, organised by the Multilateral Investment Fund (MIF).[29] Prompted by the increase in remittances in Latin America and the Caribbean region, the MIF started to get involved in the GRT at the beginning of the new millennium and has become one of the major players in the field of remittances, focusing on activities such as research, the organisation of conferences, and concrete remittance-linked development projects. In May 2001 the IDB/MIF organised the first ever Latin American conference on remittances entitled 'Remittances as a Development Tool: A Regional Conference'.[30] Also in 2005 the International Forum on Remittances included a session on gender and remittances for the first time, which was co-organised by United Nations International Research Training Institute for the Advancement of Women (UN-INSTRAW) and brought together experts from academia and the international community.[31]

In March 2006 the Conference on Migration and Development took place in Brussels, jointly organised by the Belgian government, the IOM, the World Bank and the European Commission. The purpose of the conference was to discuss 'how migration and related policies can contribute to economic development in countries of origin or transit, and how development policies in turn can address root causes of migration such as poverty and lack of socio-economic prospects, and ease the pressures on people to emigrate unwillingly'.[32]

The Brussels conference also aimed at preparing an input for the United Nations High-Level Dialogue Meeting on International Migration and Development. Launched in December 2003 through General Assembly Resolution 58/208, the first High-Level Dialogue took place in New York in September 2006 and brought together a broad range of actors. The Dialogue aims:

> to discuss the multidimensional aspects of international migration and development in order to identify appropriate ways and means to maximize its development benefits and minimize its negative impacts. Additionally, the high-level dialogue should have a strong focus on policy issues, including the challenge of achieving the internationally agreed development goals, including the Millennium Development Goals (MDGs).[33]

As a result of the High-Level Dialogue, many states expressed their interest in continuing the dialogue by means of an informal, voluntary and state-led forum, which led to the establishment of the Global Forum on Migration and Development (GFMD). The first meeting of the GFMD took place in Brussels in July 2007, to mark the start of a new global process designed to enhance the positive impact of migration on development (and vice versa) by adopting a more consistent policy approach, identifying new instruments and best practices, exchanging experience about innovative tactics and methods, and establishing cooperation between the various actors involved.[34]

Later in 2007 the second International Forum on Remittances took place in Washington, DC, organised by the MIF in co-operation with the International Fund for Agricultural Development (IFAD). The aim of this conference was 'to shed light on the rural dimension of [remittance] flows, estimated at 40 per cent of total flows, [to] explore the links between remittances and banking, technology and microfinance, and discuss ways to integrate development agencies' agendas on remittances'.[35] The conference emphasised the potential of remittances to empower women:

> Women represent almost half of the estimated 200 million economic migrants in the world, and they are also often the heads of households that receive

remittances. Remittances can enhance the economic status of women and change traditional gender roles and ideologies. However, very little research has been conducted on the gender dimension of remittances. The development potential of remittances can be increased by looking at remittances from a gender perspective.[36]

The aforementioned milestones in the emergence of the GRT illustrate the broad variety of institutions involved in it, creating a dense network of activities in the field. These different institutions focus on different aspects of the GRT and adopt different ways of framing the links between migration, remittances and development. Despite this variety, there are several key assumptions that are shared by most institutions involved in the GRT and have become the basis of a mainstream framing within it. The next section outlines the different framings of the GRT and how they have shifted over time.

Framing the GRT

In general it can be observed how over the years the framing of the issue of migration, remittances and development has shifted with the changing constellation of institutional involvement in the GRT, as shown in the last section. For a long time, it was mainly the ILO and the IOM that dealt with issues linked to migration and development. Their focus was on protecting migrant's rights in terms of decent working conditions and the right to remit, and on harnessing the potential development impact of their return to the country of origin. This approach adopts a rather cautious view when it comes to the consequences of migration, taking into account the potentially negative effects of migration and remittances. It also warns that evidence on the positive correlation between remittances and the economic performance of the migrant-sending country is still rather shaky.[37]

When the issue was taken up by international financial institutions, such as the World Bank, the IMF and the regional development banks, it was reframed in more narrowly, such that the focus moved towards the financial aspects of migration—remittances—and their potential to reduce poverty and to finance development. According to this framing, remittances are the most visible feature of international migration and they are seen as being endowed with many positive characteristics and the potential to contribute to development and poverty reduction in the sending countries. Thus, for example, World Bank documents present remittances as 'beautiful', 'vital to the economy', or 'a powerful tool to reduce poverty'.[38] Using such positively connoted adjectives creates an image of remittances as a 'good' and powerful force that will help to solve the problems of development and poverty. Within this framing, a note of caution is raised pointing to the fact that remittances are private money, and there is some awareness that remittances might have problematic impacts that need to be addressed.[39] However, optimism about the development potential of remittances predominates, and the challenges of migration and remittances are seen to be outweighed by their positive impacts.

Thus the emergence of the GRT has been accompanied by framing conflicts. Broadly speaking, we can distinguish between two competing ways of framing within the GRT: the rights-based, people-centred approach based on a broad understanding of the linkages between migration and development (adopted by the ILO and the IOM for example), versus the more narrow economic, money-based approach (adopted by the international financial institutions). This frame competition occurs not only *between* different institutions, but also between different departments *within* institutions.[40]

Over the past few years the money-based framing has become the mainstream within the international community. However, this shift does not mean that the rights-based framing no longer exists, or that institutions such as the ILO and the IOM are no longer active in the field. There is a continued debate over the framing of the issue taking place in different platforms, such as the UN High-level Dialogue on International Migration and Development and the Global Forum on Migration and Development. It remains to be seen whether this dialogue will contribute to reinforcing the mainstream framing, or to a reframing of the issue, which could broaden the agenda and place more importance on non-financial aspects of the nexus between migration and development.

The mainstream framing within the GRT consists of a number of key assumptions that most institutions involved in the GRT have come to share. First, migration is generally perceived as a positive process or as a given, and its development potential is emphasised. The objective is to manage migration in order to maximise its positive impacts on development and poverty reduction. Second, remittances are typically defined in financial terms as 'money sent home by immigrant workers abroad'.[41] Third, the focus is generally on the positive characteristics of remittances: Compared with other sources of external finance (such as foreign direct investment (FDI) and aid) remittances are said to be relatively stable; counter-cyclical (ie they increase in times of economic downturn); evenly distributed among development countries; and received mainly by low-income countries and even by so-called 'failed states'. Thanks to these characteristics remittances are alleged to have positive impacts for developing countries in terms of poverty alleviation and an increase in well-being; economic growth; private sector reconstruction; micro-finance; debt repayment; and creditworthiness. The following two quotes illustrate this:

> Remittances help to lift recipients out of poverty, increase and diversify household incomes, provide an insurance against risk, enable family members to benefit from educational and training opportunities and provide a source of capital for the establishment of small businesses.[42]

> Remittances augment the recipients' incomes and increase their country's foreign exchange reserves. If remittances are invested, they contribute to output growth; if they are consumed, they generate positive multiplier effects.[43]

Thus, within the GRT there is a general attitude of optimism towards the benefits of migration and remittances for development, and a belief that the challenges posed by migration and remittances can be addressed successfully to create 'win-win-win' solutions for developing and developed countries and for migrants.[44] Subjecting the framing of the GRT to a gender perspective means to critically examine these assumptions and their implications.

Gendering the GRT

Picking up a few core aspects of the mainstream GRT framing, this section outlines some key entry points for unpacking the gender implications of the GRT. The analysis proceeds in three main steps: first, it focuses on the gender-blindspots of the mainstream framing within the GRT, revealing what is 'left out' and how existing analyses have tried to 'bring it back in'. The second step critically examines what is already there, analysing gendered representations and stereotypes. In a third step, the gender-specific implications of such representations are explored.

Revealing gender-blindness

Within the mainstream framing of the GRT, most documents do not include references to women or gender issues. Thus, at first sight, it seems to be gender-neutral.[45] However, I argue that the GRT is not gender-neutral but gender-blind: this appearance of gender neutrality is a result of the narrow definition of remittances and the level of abstraction within which the issue of remittances is framed. Uncovering the underlying realities and contextualising remittances reveals the gendered assumptions and implications of the GRT framing.

As outlined above, one of the key assumptions within the GRT is that remittances are a sum of money with mainly positive characteristics and a strong potential for alleviating poverty. This definition is based upon a narrow, financial notion of remittances as a source for development funding, and an abstract and macroeconomic perspective, focusing mainly on the (positive) implications of remittances at the international level.

This understanding of remittances is problematic because it evades delving into the complex and varied human, social, political and economic realities, within which remittances are embedded, and which are an integral part of the phenomenon and make them possible in the first place. Moreover, portraying remittances as a powerful force to solve the problems of poverty and development in migrant sending countries draws our attention away from the negative impacts of remittances, obscuring the problematic realities which underlie the remittance issue, such as the human and social costs of migration for the migrants themselves and for their non-migrant relatives and home communities. Thus, there is a need to broaden the perception of the issue of remittances and situate remittances within their underlying contexts. This goes hand in hand with breaking through the levels of abstraction and directing attention beyond the macro aspects of the issue, without losing sight of the bigger picture. In this way the social dynamics within which remittances are embedded—such as gender, class and ethnicity—become visible.

Critical gender analyses of the link between migration, remittances and development are still scarce. However, there is a number of contributions which have started to challenge the narrow notion of remittances and to reframe the issue in broader terms. Some of these contributions do not explicitly mention gender issues, but they open up theoretical space to move beyond seeing remittances as a mere sum of money, and broadening the focus beyond the macro level, which holds the promise for a gender analysis. A short overview of the literature reveals four types of contributions that can lay the groundwork for such an analysis.

The first type of contribution consists of different typologies of remittances. Establishing such typologies contributes to countering the image of remittances as a 'unitary package' and to stretching the definition of remittances.[46] Among the most influential contributions is Durand's typology that distinguishes between different types of 'migradolares' according to their use or function: remittances as wages or salary (sent to support relatives); remittances as investment (directed at buying land or building a house); and remittances as capital (money to be spent on productive investments).[47] Based on Durand, Goldring established an elaborate typology of remittances, distinguishing between family/individual, collective and investment remittances.[48] This disaggregating of remittances has opened up space for stretching the definition of remittances.

The second type of contribution has broadened the term of remittances to include non-economic remittances. Levitt has introduced the concept of 'social remittances', as distinct from 'economic remittances', in order to complement the picture of transnational flows.[49] Social remittances are defined as 'the ideas, behaviours, identities, and social capital that flow from receiving to sending-country communities'.[50] Nichols has used the term of 'technical remittances' to refer to the flows of knowledge, skills and technology associated with migration.[51] Others have focused on 'political remittances', ie the transformation in political identities, discourses and practices associated with migration.[52] These contributions hold potential entry point for a gender analysis to explore the gender implications of social remittances, for example.

Third, the literature on transnationalism has also made a contribution. In their pioneering work Basch et al define transnationalism as 'the processes by which immigrants forge and sustain multi-stranded social relations that link together their societies of origin and settlement'.[53] This literature situates remittances within transnationalism more broadly and refers to remittances as a transnational activity. Such a transnational framework portrays remittances not in isolation, but as part of a larger whole, rendering visible the underlying realities within which remittances are embedded. These realities include, among others, the context within which the decision to migrate is taken; the human, social, political and economic consequences for migrants and non-migrants; the networks which enable migration and remittances; the legal status of migrants who send remittances; the power structures which permeate processes of migration and remittances; and the socioeconomic status of migrants. All these realities are part of the issue of remittances and are essential for producing this sum of money in the first place, as Ramirez *et al* observe:

> Remittances are more than just periodic financial transfers; they are the result of complex processes of negotiation within households that are immersed in an intricate network of relations between the Diaspora and the countries of origin.[54]

Reframing remittances as a transnational activity renders visible how the muted realities, silenced by the mainstream framing, are influenced by a variety of social dynamics—such as gender, ethnicity and class. This serves to reveal the complexity and variety of remittances as transnational processes and to uncover the underlying social relations. Realising the potential that a transnational framework holds for including a gender analysis, some authors have started to reveal the gendered realities underlying remittances. They emphasise the ways in which gender influences the migration experience and vice versa: the gendered character of migration; the gendered characteristics of the international division of labour; the ways in which gender aspects influence who sends and who receives remittances, how they are being used, who decides what they are being used for; and the gendered power relations linked to the remittance process.[55]

Ethnographic research into the implications of remittances for the lives of migrant and non-migrant people constitutes a fourth type of contribution. This research shows how in concrete contexts migration and remittance processes play out in many different ways. It also documents the many negative 'side-effects' of migration and remittances, affecting women and women migrants in particular ways. These negative effects include the trafficking and forced migration of women; the often traumatic experiences for women migrants and non-migrant women staying behind while their husbands migrate; the exploitative situations that women migrants face, for example in the domestic sector or the sex industry; and the social transformations that non-migrant women have to deal with.[56] In my own fieldwork with Mexican rural communities I have observed these gendered ways in which migration and remittances play out at the level of families and communities in complex and somewhat contradictory ways.[57] Raising awareness about the negative aspects of migration and remittances is essential to challenge the mainstream perception of remittances as a neutral sum of money or a largely positive force.

These four types of literature have made important contributions to the development of a gender analysis of remittances by challenging the gender-blindness of the seemingly neutral way of framing remittances, broadening the narrow perception of remittances and revealing the gendered social realities within which remittances are embedded. However, I want to suggest that there are two main shortcomings in the literature that need to be addressed. First, existing studies tend to focus mainly on what is missing, and then add the missing aspects. Thus, for example, they criticise the lack of attention paid to migrant women, and consequently focus on migrant women and their remitting behaviour, emphasising the need for sex-disaggregated data taking into account the sex of the senders and receivers of remittances. This is a necessary and important step, but I would argue that we also need to critically examine what is already there, ie *what* is actually being said about women and gender in the GRT, *how* it is said, *who* gets to say it, and *why* it is said in this specific way. This means directing our attention to gendered forms of representation and stereotypes.

Second, existing studies tend to be rather descriptive. They often limit themselves to describing how women behave differently from men in remittance activities. This is an important first step, as it entails disaggregating gender-blind statements within the GRT. However, I would argue that we need to move beyond, in order to explain why women behave differently from men in a specific context, ie we need to look at the gendered representations, norms and institutions that influence the behaviour of women and men in remittance activities, and how remittance activities in return influence gender relations.

Exploring gendered representations and stereotypes

As shown above, the GRT framing is largely gender-blind and there is scant reference to women or gender issues. Thus, for example, World Bank publications within the contain almost no references to women and gender whatsoever. Similarly, IDB/MIF documents also rarely mention gender and women, apart from generating sex-disaggregated profiles of remittance senders and receivers.[58] Examining one of the key publications within the GRT, the *Report of the Global Commission on International Migration*, we find two references to gender and women in connection with remittances:

> It is also noteworthy that migrant women and lower-paid migrants at times transfer a higher proportion of their income than others.[59]

> Households and communities in countries of origin should be assisted to make effective use of remittance receipts through the provision of appropriate training and access to microcredit facilities. Some studies indicate that women make the most effective use of remittances, therefore special efforts should be made to target women in such initiatives.[60]

These two quotes illustrate how women's specific roles in the remittance activity are represented through gender stereotypes. The GCIM report does not indicate where the evidence for these statements about women's specific behaviour in remittance activities comes from, and what 'some studies' (cf the quote above) refers to. When I asked a member of the Commission at the UK launch of the report (December 2005) where the information for these types of statements had come from, the answer was that the GCIM had not done studies or case studies on the gender aspects of remittances that would support these statements. Instead, they were based on information from the World Bank and World Bank informants. Given that the World Bank has little to say about the gender dimensions of migration and remittances and uses a largely gender-blind discourse, it seems crucial to critically evaluate such statements.

Another key publication in the field, the BRIDGE *Cutting Edge Pack* on 'Gender and migration' (2005), asserts that 'It is generally believed that women send home a greater share of their earnings in remittances'.[61] This statement is based on a quote from an article by Ninna Nyberg-Sørensen which reads:

> Despite female migrants' lower incomes, it is generally assumed that women by and large send back home a greater share of their earnings in remittances than men and also tend to be better savers. In addition to being the largest receivers of remittances, women—when in control of remittances—are also believed to channel overseas financial transfers into better health, nutrition and education for their entire family, hereby supporting the development of stronger and more productive communities.[62]

At the presentation of this *Cutting Edge Pack* at a DFID workshop on 'Migration and Gender' in London, the only reference to gender and remittances was that women tend to send more remittances than men and that therefore, more opportunities for women to migrate could be good for the sending country, although this could present an additional burden for women migrants.

Finally, in the 2006 issue of *id21 insights* an article by Sarah Mahler on the gender dimensions of remittances asks:

> Do financial institutions, or indeed the women themselves, know that migrant women dedicate a higher percentage of remittances than men to capital and asset-building? This finding could empower women to demand more access to finance—such as loans and insurance—and shows that incorporating gender is one of the most promising routes to improving policy.[63]

These examples show how gender-related statements within the GRT are mostly limited to focusing on women's behaviour in the remittance process, reducing gender to women. Such statements about women's behaviour are largely based upon secondary data sources, assumptions or stereotypes that often emerge through generalisations from one concrete case study. Alternatively they are based upon gendered assumptions or expectations about the social roles of women and men, such as the 'women = mothers' bias. Within the GRT the most commonly used stereotypes include the following:[64]

- Men are mainly remittance senders and women are mainly (passive) remittance receivers.
- When women are remittance senders, they tend to send more remittances than men.
- Women make better use of remittances than men

There are two ways to deal with such gender stereotypes: to examine whether they can be empirically verified, and to explore their implications. Empirical research into the gender dimensions of remittances provides contradictory and complex findings.

The first stereotype, ie that women are mainly (passive) remittance receivers, has been somewhat overhauled by the evidence that women now represent almost half of the migrants world-wide and the majority in certain countries, such as the Philippines.[65] However, in the Mexican context, the representation of migrant men as active breadwinners and women as passive remittance receivers is still very present. In my fieldwork in rural Mexico I have observed that in many cases women are neither passive nor remittance receivers. With the migration of their male family members many women are left in charge of child care, household work, administering resources, livestock and agricultural work and in addition take on some income-generating activity to make ends meet. Often there is a considerable time lag before remittances arrive and sometimes they never do or dry out after a while. In addition, the out-migration of a family member is usually linked to considerable expenses which have to be reimbursed. And, on top of it all, women also often face social pressure when they live without their husband. In rural Mexican areas, for example, it is considered inappropriate for women to leave their houses without male company. Thus women have to develop ways of performing their additional tasks under difficult circumstances.[66]

The second stereotype, ie that women remit more than men, has been challenged by a variety of ethnographic studies. Evidence from a recent study on Filipina and Filipino migrant workers by Semyonov and Gorodzeisky reveals that men send more money than women, and that therefore households with male migrants have a higher income level than households with female migrants.[67] Another study by Zontini on Filippina and Moroccan migrants in Barcelona shows how 'for Moroccan women the obligation to send remittances is not as strong as for Filipinas', revealing the cultural specificity of remittance practices.[68] She also notes that Moroccan women migrants often do not send remittances at all, as they migrate in order to escape rigid gender roles within their society of origin.[69] These studies challenge the stereotype that women *a priori* send more remittances than men and illustrate the importance of context.

Empirical evidence into the gendered use of remittances reveals the variety of ways in which gender influences remittance behaviour. Some studies do indicate that women spend money differently from men in certain circumstances. However, a number of issues need to be considered: what is the context within which remittances are spent and which are the options? What does 'better' or more effective use of remittances mean? Who determines the criteria for a more or less effective use of remittances? My own fieldwork shows that the spending of remittances involves complex processes of decision making and negotiating among the members of a household, based on gendered power relations. In many cases women are advised how to spend remittances by the migrant or some male family member.

Thus, empirical studies can contribute to unsettling and challenging gendered representations and stereotypes. They suggest that generalisations about the gender dimensions of remittances are problematic and context specificities need to be taken into account. While it is important to subject representations and stereotypes to a 'reality check', it is also important to explore their implications, as they can have very real effects even if their empirical foundation is shaky.

Analysing gender implications

Broadly speaking, we can identify two main types of implications of gendered representations and stereotypes. On the one hand, they portray a certain type of behaviour as 'normal' and thereby naturalise and reproduce existing gender norms and gendered forms of behaviour. Thus, for example, the above quoted statements contribute to the reproduction of social expectations of women's roles and behaviour in the remittance process, and the social pressure that goes with it. They also homogenise the experiences of different groups of women and men. In this way they may hamper efforts to transform gender roles and empower women, and may even impede development.

On the other hand, gendered representations and stereotypes contribute to shaping policy-making and development initiatives. Thus, for example, the way women's roles in the remittance process are portrayed influences the types of interventions that are designed to harness the development potential of migration and remittances. This link between the discursive use of representations and stereotypes and their implications for policy making is emphasised in the GCIM report: 'Some studies indicate that women make the most effective use of remittances, therefore special efforts should be made to target women in such initiatives.'[70]

Depending on the context, gendered representations and stereotypes can have positive or negative policy implications. In some cases they have proven useful from an advocacy point of view. Thus, for example, the stereotype of women being the 'poorest of the poor' has been very effective in getting donor money for projects aimed at women.[71] However, stereotypes can also have detrimental effects, or negative long-term implications. This has been demonstrated in the case of micro-credit strategies targeting women, which have become the most prominent poverty reduction tool in the international development community. While some women might experience micro-credit projects as empowering and enhancing their well-being, it has been documented that such strategies can have negative impacts for women, ranging from increased violence against women to increased child labour to debt cycles.[72]

To examine the implications of gendered representations and stereotypes within the GRT we need to look at specific contexts. This can be illustrated with an example from my fieldwork in Mexico. When asked about the role of women and gender in the remittance process, a Mexican government official answered:

> I think women's role is very important because now they are doing productive work, it's not the same ... imagine, if you lived in Mexico and your husband

175

went to the US and sent you remittances, let's say $500 a month, but you wouldn't do anything, you just receive the money and that's it, no? Well, ok, you eat, you dress and you bring the kids to school, but you don't do anything productive, you just receive the money, yes? So, I think that these productive projects are women's contribution as a counterpart to remittances, so that apart from receiving remittances from their husbands, they also produce.[73]

Thus, women are portrayed as passive remittance receivers who are not doing anything 'productive'. This reflects the general discourse prevalent in Mexico, which portrays migrant men as heroes and non-migrant women as passively waiting at home for remittances to arrive.[74] Confronting this statement with the lived realities in rural Mexican communities reveals a striking discrepancy: as described above, rural women don't just 'eat and dress and bring the kids to school', but take on the totality of biological and social reproduction tasks while also engaging in income-generating activities.

Their shaky empirical foundation notwithstanding, these gendered representations have very real implications for policy making and lead to a complex and somewhat contradictory situation. On the one hand, women portrayed as passive remittance receivers are often not deemed in charge of the decision making on the use of remittances and are therefore excluded from participation in remittance-linked activities. In terms of policy making the implication is that women are often ignored when it comes to the design and implementation of remittance-linked development projects. Thus, for example, the major migration-linked development initiative in Mexico, the 'Iniciativa 3x1', targets migrants, based on the representation of the active migrant in control of financial decisions.[75] Furthermore, projects implemented within the Iniciativa 3x1 often do not take into account gender dimensions and women's specific needs and preferences. On the other hand, women have become the target of initiatives to set up productive projects in order to generate income, based on the 'unproductive remittance receiver' stereotype. As shown above, this is based on the assumption that women have been 'unproductive' and should be included in the 'productive' sector. This reopens the debate about the definition of 'being productive', and the gender distribution of social reproduction chores. Fieldwork in rural Mexico reveals how such initiatives have led to an increase in women's workload and an intensification in the social pressure they face.[76]

This example illustrates how gendered representations and stereotypes have concrete context-specific policy implications and lead to complex and seemingly contradictory processes of gender exclusion and inclusion within the GRT, which can be made visible through a gender analysis.

Conclusion

Moving beyond existing gender analyses, this article focuses on gendered representations and stereotypes to reveal the powerful gender implications of the GRT. To further develop such a gender analysis a number of key areas must be explored. First, there is a need to monitor closely the struggle over the framing of the GRT, in order to seize the windows of opportunity opening up spaces for gendering the GRT. The ongoing UN High-level Dialogue on International Migration and Development and the Global Forum on Migration and Development might present such an opportunity to broaden the rather narrow mainstream GRT framing and to include the wider realities within which remittances are embedded.

Second, we need more context-specific analyses of the gender implications of the GRT on the ground. This means moving beyond generalising about women's and men's remittance behaviour to examine why people behave in certain ways in specific contexts, and how their behaviour is linked to gendered representations and social norms. Such context-specific analyses could feed into context-specific gender-sensitive policy making.

Third, collective remittance processes constitute another important entry point for gender analysis. So far, the focus has largely been on gender-specific forms of behaviour in the individual remittance process. There is a general lack of research examining the different dimensions of collective remittance processes, such as in the organisation of migrant money collection in the country of destination, in decision-making processes regarding the ways in which the money will be spent, in the communication and co-operation between the migrants and the communities of origin, and in the design and implementation of specific migration-linked development projects. Such research could contribute to pushing for the inclusion of a gender assessment of migration-linked development initiatives, such as projects implemented within the Iniciativa 3x1 in Mexico, which tend to ignore gender dimensions.

It is only at the cost of ignoring the underlying gendered social realities that remittances can be presented as beautiful. Given the potentially adverse gendered realities and implications, remittances may not be so beautiful after all—at least not for everybody.

Notes

The research for this article was carried out during a Visiting Fellowship at the International Gender Studies Centre of the University of Oxford, which was made possible by the generous financial assistance of the International Federation of University Women (IFUW), the Fondation Boninchi (Geneva) and the Société Académique de Genève. I would like to thank Ronaldo Munck, the anonymous reviewers, Marianne Marchand, Bernd Balkenhol (ILO) and Rhiannon Lambert for their helpful comments on earlier versions of this article.

1 Quote from a World Bank interview with Samuel Munzele Maimbo, Senior Financial Sector Specialist in the World Bank's Africa Finance and Private Sector Unit.

2 Opening Statement by Cesare Calari, Vice President of the Financial Sector, World Bank, at the International Conference on Migrant Remittances in London, 2003. See http://www.livelihoods.org/hot_topics/docs/RemitConfFinal.doc.

3 Remittances are commonly defined as the money that migrants send back to their families or communities of origin. We can distinguish between individual remittances (sent to the family) and collective remittances (sent to the community of origin).

4 Population Division of the Department of Economic and Social Affairs of the United Nations Secretariat, *Trends in Total Migrant Stock: The 2005 Revision*, 2005, at http://esa.un.org/migration.

5 World Bank, *Migration and Remittances Factbook 2008*, 2008, at http://econ.worldbank.org/WBSITE/EXTERNAL/EXTDEC/EXTDECPROSPECTS/0,,contentMDK:21352016~pagePK:64165401~piPK:64165026~theSitePK:476883,00.html. The official numbers do not include informal remittances, which are thought to be substantial. A note of caution is necessary: the increase in official remittances figures could be influenced by the increased capacity for registering such flows.

6 For example, International Relations has been, and often still is, assumed to be a gender-neutral discipline and field of enquiry, despite years of feminist IR scholarship.

7 See, for example, L Binford, 'Para salvar la economía mexicana: la trampa de las remesas', *Working Paper*, 2004, at http://meme.phpwebhosting.com/~migracion/modules/seminarioe/binfordleight.pdf#search=%22binford%20leigh%20trampa%20de%20las%20remesas%22; and H De Haas, 'International migration, remittances and development: myths and facts', *Third World Quarterly*, 26 (8), 2005, pp 1269–1284.

8 M Boas & D McNeill, 'Introduction: power and ideas in multilateral institutions—towards an interpretative framework', in Boas & McNeill (eds), *Global Institutions and Development: Framing the World?*, London: Routledge, 2004, p 1.

9 *Ibid.*

10 SV Peterson & AS Runyan, *Global Gender Issues: Dilemmas in World Politics*, Boulder, CO: Westview Press, 1993, p 1.

11 Council of the European Union, *Seville European Council 21–22 June 2002: Presidency Conclusions*, EU Doc 13463/02, 24 October 2002.

12 NN Sørensen, N Van Hear & P Engberg-Pedersen, 'The migration–development nexus: evidence and policy options', *International Migration*, 40 (5), 2002, pp 49–71.

13 Department for International Development (DFID) & World Bank, *International Conference on Migrant Remittances: Report and Conclusions*, London, 2003, p 11, at http://www.livelihoods.org/hot_topics/migration/remittances.html.

14 Thus, for example, there is typically a disagreement between internal affairs departments and development departments of receiving countries. Internal affairs departments have to deal with the implications of migration for the receiving country and the often negative attitudes of the population towards immigrants, which tends to produce more restrictive approaches to migration, whereas development departments, given their field of concern, are often in favour of relative openness towards migration. The UK Home Office, for example, tends to adopt a more conventional approach aimed at preventing migration, whereas the Department for International Development (DFID) is among the frontrunners of the GRT. Within the EU there is also a certain policy incoherence and a number of obstacles to achieving a certain policy co-ordination. For an analysis of the EU context, see S Lavenex & R Kunz, 'The migration–development nexus in EU external relations', *Journal of European Integration*, 30 (3), 2008, pp 439–457.

15 International Labour Organisation (ILO), Migration for Employment Convention, C97, Geneva, 1949, Article 9, at http://www.ilo.org/ilolex/english/convdisp1.htm.

16 See http://www.old.iom.int/en/who/main_mission.shtml.

17 See http://www.old.iom.int/en/who/main_history.shtml.

18 Cairo Programme of Action, 1994, Section X, at http://www.iisd.ca/Cairo/program/p00000.html.

19 ILO, *Making the Best of Globalization: Migrant Worker Remittances and Micro-Finance*, Geneva: ILO, 2000, p 2.

20 FfD website at http://www.un.org/esa/ffd/ffdconf/.

21 United Nations, Monterrey Consensus, Monterrey, 2003, p 8, at http://www.un.org/esa/ffd/Monterrey-Consensus-excepts-aconf198_11.pdf.

22 See http://www.gcim.org.

23 See http://www.gcim.org/en/a_mandate.html.

24 D Ratha, 'Workers' remittances: an important and stable source of external development finance', in *Global Development Finance 2003*, Washington, DC: World Bank, 2003, p 157.

25 *Ibid.*

26 For further information about this conference, see http://www.livelihoods.org/hot_topics/migration/remittances.html.

27 DFID & World Bank, *International Conference on Migrant Remittances*, p 3.

28 Sea Island Summit, G8 Action Plan, 2004, at http://www.g7.utoronto.ca/summit/2004seaisland/poverty.html.

29 Within the Inter-American Development Bank (IDB) it is mainly the Multilateral Investment Fund (MIF) that has been involved in issues linked to remittances and development. See http://www.iadb.org/mif/v2/index.html.

30 For more information about the conference, see http://www.iadb.org/mif/events.cfm?language=English&parid=9.

31 For further information about the session on gender and remittances co-organised by INSTRAW, see: http://www.un-instraw.org/en/index.php?option=content&task=view&id=1003&Itemid=121.

32 See the Conclusions of the conference at http://www.migrationdevelopment.org/index.php?id=11.

33 See http://www.un.org/esa/population/hldmigration/.

34 For more information about the GFMD, see http://www.gfmd-fmmd.org/en/public/global-forum-migration-and-development-0.

35 See http://www.iadb.org/mif/events.cfm?language=English&parid=9&topic=&subtopic=REMS.
36 See http://www.ifad.org/events/remittances/index.htm.
37 ILO, *Towards a Fair Deal for Migrant Workers in the Global Economy*, report presented at the International Labour Conference, 92nd Session, Geneva: ILO, 2004, p 25, at http://www.ilo.org/wcmsp5/groups/public/—dgreports/—dcomm/documents/meetingdocument/kd00096.pdf.
38 World Bank, 'Remittances a powerful tool to reduce poverty if effectively harnessed, analysts say', *News*, 30 June 2005; and World Bank, 'When money really matters: remittances vital to South Asia', *News*, 19 July 2005.
39 SM Maimbo & D Ratha (eds), *Remittances: Development Impact and Future Prospects*, Washington, DC: World Bank, 2005; and Ç Özden & M Schiff, *International Migration, Remittances and the Brain Drain*, Washington, DC: World Bank, 2006.
40 Thus, for example, within the ILO the two sections involved in the GRT—MIGRANT and the Social Finance Unit—adopt a slightly different framing. The MIGRANT department focuses on migrants' rights and social justice and tends to adopt a more rights-based approach. The Social Finance Unit deals with the financial aspects of migration, ie remittances and their investment, but also with the costs and risks related to migration, and in general tends to be more optimistic about the beneficial impacts of migration and remittances on development.
41 Ratha, 'Workers' remittances'.
42 Global Commission on International Migration (GCIM), *Migration in an Interconnected World: New Directions for Action*, Geneva: GCIM, 2005, p 26.
43 Maimbo & Ratha, *Remittances*, p 32.
44 World Bank, *Knowledge for Change Charter*, no date, at http://siteresources.worldbank.org/INTKNOWLEDGEFORCHANGE/Resources/491519-1128696349273/2005-3R-KFC_CharterFINAL_eBook.pdf. The notion of 'win-win-win' strategies was initially brought up by the World Bank and later adopted by the ILO, for example in its contributions to the High-Level Dialogue. ILO, *International Labour Migration and Development: The ILO Perspective*, report presented at the 61st Session of the General Assembly High-Level Dialogue on International Migration and Development, Geneva: ILO, September 2006, pp 73–81, at http://www.solidarnosc.org.pl/migracje/dokumenty/ilo/dokumenty/ILO%20Intern%20Migr%20Persopectives%202006.pdf.
45 This idea that remittances and the link between migration and development is gender-neutral was also reflected in my interviews with Mexican government officials and development personnel, who often told me that remittances had nothing to do with gender.
46 L Goldring, 'Family and collective remittances to Mexico: a multi-dimensional typology', *Development and Change*, 35 (4), 2004, p 804.
47 J Durand, 'Los migradólares: cien años de inversión en el medio rural', *Argumentos: Estudios Críticos de la Sociedad*, 5, 1988, pp 7–21; and Durand, *Más allá de la línea: Patrones migratorios entre México y Estados Unidos*, Mexico City: Consejo Nacional para la Cultura y las Artes, 1994.
48 Goldring, 'Family and collective remittances to Mexico'; and Goldring, 'The gender and geography of citizenship in Mexico–US transnational spaces', *Identities*, 7 (4), 2001, pp 501–537.
49 P Levitt, 'Social remittances: a conceptual tool for understanding migration and development', *Working Paper 96.04*, Cambridge, MA: Harvard, 1996; and Levitt, *The Transnational Villagers*, Berkeley, CA: University of California Press, 2001.
50 Levitt, 'Social remittances', p 2ff.
51 S Nichols, 'Another kind of remittances: transfer of agricultural innovations by migrants to their communities of origin', paper presented at the 'Second Colloquium on International Migration: Mexico–California', University of California, Berkeley, 29 March 2002.
52 L Goldring, 'La migracion México–EUA y la transnacionalización del espacio político y social: perspectivas desde el México rural', *Estudios Sociológicos*, X (29), 1992, pp 315–340; and M Moctezuma, 'La organización de los migrantes zacatecanos en Estados Unidos', *Cuadernos Agrarios*, 19–20, 2000, pp 81–104.
53 L Basch, N Glick Schiller & C Szanton Blanc, *Nations Unbound: Transnational Projects, Postcolonial Predicaments, and Deterritorialized Nation-states*, Amsterdam: Gordon and Breach, 1994, p 7.
54 C Ramirez, M Garcia Dominguez & J Miguez Morais, *Crossing Borders: Remittances, Gender and Development*, Santo Domingo, DR: INSTRAW, 2005, p 21.
55 Levitt, 'Social remittances'; Levitt, *The Transnational Villagers*; NN Sørensen, 'Migrant remittances, development and gender', *DIIS Brief*, 2005; Ramirez *et al*, *Crossing Borders*; and PR Pessar & SJ Mahler, 'Transnational migration: bringing gender in', *International Migration Review*, 37 (3), 2003, pp 812–846.
56 See, for example, D Barrera Bassols & C Oehmichen Bazán (eds), *Migración y Relaciones de Género en México*, Mexico City: GIMTRAP, UNAM/IIA, 2000, pp 119–134; J Carling, 'Gender dimensions of international migration', *Global Migration Perspectives*, 35, 2005; B Ehrenreich & A Hochschild (eds), *Global Women: Nannies, Maids, and Sex Workers in the New Economy*, New York: Metropolitan

Books, 2003; G Mummert, 'Dilemas familiares en un Michoacán de migrantes', in G Lopez Castro (ed), *Diáspora Michoacana*, Zamora: El Colegio de Michoacán, Gobierno del Estado de Michoacán, 2003, pp 113–145; and B Suárez & E Zapata (eds), *Remesas: Milagros y Mucho Más Realizan las Mujeres Indígenas y Campesinas*, Vols I–II, Mexico City: GIMTRAP, 2004.

57 R Kunz, 'The "social cost" of migration and remittances: recovering the silenced voices of the global remittance trend', paper presented at the Second International Colloquium, 'Migracion y Desarrollo', 2006, at http://www.migracionydesarrollo.org.

58 See http://www.iadb.org/mif/remesas_map.cfm?language=EN&parid=4&item1id=2.

59 GCIM, *Migration in an Interconnected World*, p 26.

60 *Ibid*, p 28.

61 BRIDGE, 'Gender and migration', *Cutting Edge Pack*, Brighton: IDS, 2005, p 26, at http://www.bridge.ids.ac.uk/reports/CEP-Mig-OR.pdf.

62 Sørensen, 'Migrant remittances, development and gender', p 3.

63 SJ Mahler, 'Gender matters', *id21 insights*, 60, 2006, p 8.

64 These stereotypes are not all that new. The stereotype that women make 'better' use of money than men and spend money in ways which benefit the family rather than just themselves has been used since the emergence of Women in Development (WID) discourses and has served to legitimise specific development practice, for instance in the case of poverty reduction programmes based on handing out sums of money to women in poor households (such as the Mexican poverty programme Oportunidades).

65 United Nations Population Fund (UNFPA), *The State of the World Population in 2006: A Passage to Hope—Women and Migration*, 2006, p 1, at http://www.unfpa.org/swp/2006/english/introduction.html.

66 For more details, see R Kunz, 'The "social cost" of migration and remittances', p 18ff; M Marchand, R Kunz, M Mejía, E Meza, A Nieto Aguilar, R Osorno Velázquez, D Pardo Sánchez, U Revilla López, M Ricciardi & A Vences Estudillo, *Tlaxcala: ¿Migración o Desarrollo Local?*, Puebla: CONACYT, 2006.

67 M Semyonov & A Gorodzeisky, 'Labor migration, remittances and household income: a comparison between Filipino and Filipina overseas workers', *International Migration Review*, 34 (1), 2005, pp 45–68.

68 E Zontini, 'Immigrant women in Barcelona: coping with the consequences of transnational lives', *Journal of Ethnic and Migration Studies*, 30 (6), 2004, p 1128.

69 *Ibid*, p 1123.

70 GCIM, *Migration in an Interconnected World*, p 28.

71 For an analysis of the 'feminisation of poverty' discourse and its implications, see R Kunz, 'Frauen als die Ärmsten der Ärmsten? Eine kritische Gender Analyse der sozialen Deutung der Feminisierung der Armut', in D Grisard, J Häberlein, A Kaiser & S Saxer (eds), *Gender in Motion: Die Konstruktion von Geschlecht in Raum und Erzählung*, Frankfurt: Campus Verlag, 2007, pp 316–340.

72 For research on the consequences of microcredit programmes, see, J Lairap, 'The disciplinary power of microcredit: some preliminary evidence from Cameroon', unpublished doctoral thesis, University of Amsterdam, 2004; R Mallick, 'Implementing and evaluating microcredit in Bangladesh', *Development in Practice*, 12 (2), 2002, pp 153–163; A Rahman, 'Micro-credit initiatives for equitable and sustainable development: who pays?', *World Development*, 27 (1), 1999, pp 67–82; and H Weber, 'Global governance and poverty reduction: the case of microcredit', in R Wilkinson & S Hughes (eds), *Global Governance: Critical Perspectives*, London: Routledge, 2002, pp 132–151.

73 Translated from Spanish by the author: 'yo creo que el rol de la mujer es muy importante, porque, está dentro del sector productivo, no, o sea, no es lo mismo que tu, si vivieras aqui en Mexico y tuvieras un esposo que se fuera a EEUU, te esta mandando dinero, digamos 500 dollares al mes, pero tu no hagas nada, no, ossea, nada mas recibes el dinero, y ya, no? ... bueno si comes y te vistes y llevas a los ninos a la escuela, pero no estas haciendo nada de productivo, nada mas estas recibiendo el dinero, no, entonces yo creo que esto [estos proyectos productivos] es el complemento que ellas realizan, que a parte que reciben el dinero de sus esposos como remesas, tu tambien estas produciendo ... hay una complemetaridad entre mujeres y hombres'. Mexican Government Official, April 2005.

74 The representation of Mexican migrants as heroes became prominent during the presidency of Vicente Fox. See, for example, http://www.elporvenir.com.mx/notas.asp?nota_id=160764.

75 The Iniciativa 3x1 works as a matching-funds system, whereby migrant organisations in the USA can donate money and apply for additional funding from the three levels of the Mexican government to finance a development project in their community of origin. Thus, the migrants put in one part and the project receives another three parts of funding from the three levels of the Mexican government (municipal, state and federal).

76 Kunz, 'The "social cost" of migration and remittances', p 18ff; and Suárez & Zapata, *Remesas*.

Development and Return Migration: from policy panacea to migrant perspective sustainability

MARIEKE VAN HOUTE & TINE DAVIDS

Increasingly restrictive asylum policies in Europe, as well as a growing emphasis on the return of rejected asylum seekers, refugees and irregular migrants, have increased the attention of governments and international organisations to the processes of return migration.[1] Return is increasingly seen as the natural thing to do for migrants, while at the same time positive influences for the country of return are attributed to it. Return is seen as an indicator of the maturing of a state and a way of contributing towards peace processes of post-conflict countries or, in the case of former Yugoslavia, as a means of reversing ethnic cleansing. The most recent buzzword in emphasising the bright side of return is that it could be linked to the development of the home country.[2]

European policy makers have been quick to embrace this view and to incorporate it into their migration policies. In 2003, for instance, the Dutch minister for Integration and Alien Affairs, Rita Verdonk, suggested that development co-operation should be used as a strategy to contain the influx of migrants.[3] The minister for Development Co-operation, Agnes van

Ardenne, wrote in a policy memorandum that, although containment of migration and development co-operation are not the same, they are indeed linked together, suggesting that an effective return could be possible through development co-operation.[4] In addition, sustainable return could contribute to development. However, while the policy of returning migrants is applied on a large scale throughout Western Europe, little is known about how these returnees manage to build up their lives again after return, let alone contribute to development.

Non-governmental organisations (NGOs) that are involved in development and migration are divided in their attitude towards these policies. While some NGOs working with migrants, refugees and development are very reluctant to become part of these return policies, others see it as their duty to help migrants who face the increasingly restrictive asylum policies that are focused on return.[5] In an attempt to support these migrants, NGOs work together with partner organisations in societies of return, assisting migrants to return independently and safely to their country of origin, aiming to contribute to sustainable return.

This article explores the question of whether return can be sustainable and what the role of NGOs can be in making return sustainable. This is done through applying a transnational approach that analyses migration as a cycle in relation to processes of mixed embeddedness of returnees in their home countries. This approach is transnational in connecting the motives and experiences of migrants in the host country, as well as the migration policies of those countries, to the everyday epistemologies of returnees upon return. The article is based on a pilot study conducted in 2006 among a total of 131 voluntary and involuntary returning migrants from Western Europe and relocated migrants mainly from Angola, Guinea, Bosnia–Herzegovina and Somalia, and on a standardised monitoring study from 2007–2008 on assistance to 178 involuntarily returning irregular rejected asylum seekers and ex-refugees in six different countries in three different continents: Sierra Leone, Togo, Armenia, Bosnia–Herzegovina, Afghanistan and Vietnam.[6] In these studies quantitative methods such as standardised surveys and regression analysis were used in combination with qualitative methods such as in-depth interviews and assembling and analysing life histories.[7]

Return migration

In recent years criticism of the perceived positive link between return migration, sustainability and development has increased. In particular, the referral by policy makers to migrants going 'home' has been problematised. As Ghanem states: 'How can it be assumed that refugees are returning "home" when the very reasons they left were that they did not feel "at home" anymore?'.[8] The reality is much more complex, and is often related to the changed identity of the migrant and the changed context in the home country.[9] Returning to a changed country, where social relations, political structures and economic conditions are not what they used to be may be equivalent to arriving in a new place.

Furthermore, De Haas warns that the development potential of return is strongly dependent on the possibilities provided by the contextual factors at the political, economic and social level.[10] Already poor and unstable societies could slide further into crisis because of the extra pressure of returnees on an already weak economy and fragile social system. Additionally potential conflicts between returnees and those who stayed behind can result in further displacement.[11] While return is held to contribute to development, in such a situation it risks causing the opposite effect.

This is particularly true for involuntarily returning migrants who did not have the intention to return in the first place and therefore cannot be expected to remain or to invest in a society where they do not want to be.[12] Nevertheless, forced migrants who have not been recognised as refugees, or whose temporary refugee status has been revoked, have the obligation to leave the territory of the state in which they applied for asylum. Where a forced migrant is obliged to return to his or her country of origin, and does so without being forcefully expelled, this is generally referred to by policy makers and NGOs as 'voluntary return'.

However, it can be argued that return can never be voluntary when there is no plausible (legal) alternative. Even where no sanctions have been imposed or force has been used, it is even more questionable whether return under the threat of these sanctions can still be called voluntary.[13] A return is only voluntary when, 'after reviewing all available information about the conditions in their country of origin, refugees decide freely to return home. Thus, the decision to repatriate is based on a free and informed choice.'[14] This is important to bear in mind, as it puts the intentions to return in a completely different perspective. Thus, in contrast to what NGOs and policy makers refer to as 'voluntary return', in this article those migrants who did not manage to obtain a permanent permit to stay and/or return outside of their own personal desire to do so are referred to as involuntary.

Even when return could be sustainable for the individual returnee, the question is whether such return can contribute to development. Previous research has shown that the extent to which the stay-behind majority will accept the supposedly innovative practices of the returnee minority is often limited, while returnees' efforts to induce change are not always successful.[15] De Haas, furthermore, emphasises that the discrepancy between restrictive immigration policies and the stimulation of return migration of migrant-receiving countries seems to alienate returnees and 'decrease their inclination to return, circulate, invest and participate in public debate'.

What follows from the above is that, in order to have the potential for development, return migration must be sustainable for the individual returnee. According to Black *et al*, there are three elements of sustainability: the subjective perspective of the returnee, the objective conditions of the returnee, and the aggregate conditions of the home country.[16] Building on the concept of embeddedness, which we will elaborate further below, this means that not only measurable socioeconomic indicators are taken into account, but also the importance a returnee attributes to the different elements of the process of returning have to be considered. Despite the fact that most returnees suffer harsh realities, they are considered to be actors who posses the agency to shape their own lives.

The construction of livelihoods needs to be investigated in relation to factors beyond the control of the individual. These are, as one would expect, highly contextual and dependent on the way in which identity markers and categories like gender, age, class and ethnicity are ascribed to the returnees within a certain context and the way people deal with and rework these categories in their every day life. To explore the relation between remigration and development, however, two factors are singled out in this article. Next to assistance, which was investigated as a dependent variable from the start, it turned out that the migration cycle is an important factor that influences the livelihoods of returnees. Furthermore the article assumes that individual sustainability is needed to prevent harm being done to the stability of the home society. To be able to get an idea of this, a bottom-up and holistic perspective on this theme is needed.

Return as a process of re-embeddedness

In both studies on which this article is based return was conceived as a process, and in order not to be normative about the way a returnee should behave upon return, sustainable re(turn) migration was relabelled as a process of mixed embeddedness.[17] Embeddedness is a concept used mainly within the context of institutional economics, as developed in 1985 by Granovetter to measure trust as part and parcel of social networks that are crucial for successful company transactions.[18] Mixed embeddedness has also been used by Aldrich, Waldinger and Kloosterman to explore immigrant entrepreneurship.[19] The basic idea of this concept as the process, in which a person, organisation or company is able to participate in a given society socially as well as economically, was complemented with an identity dimension. Translated to remigration research, (re-)embeddedness entails a multidimensional concept that refers to an individual finding his or her own position in society and feeling a sense of belonging to and participating in that society.[20] It consists of an economic dimension, a social networks and a psychosocial dimension that are interrelated and reinforce each other.[21]

Economic embeddedness

The economic dimension of embeddeness includes the question of whether a returnee can rebuild a sustainable livelihood. In practice a livelihood comprises the extent to which an individual owns, or has access to resources and assets, such as income, housing, land, stock, transportation, education and healthcare. Moreover, it is about individuals' livelihood capabilities to maintain and expand on these assets. Following on from Chambers and Conway, a livelihood is sustainable when it can avoid or respond to stress and shocks, or recover from them quickly.[22]

Involuntarily returning migrants often return to a society that is still suffering from the legacy of a conflict and/or from a severe economic crisis,

184

where the population still struggles to make a living. In this environment returnees have a difficult time rebuilding their lives, and have additional problems related to their position as a returnee.

Although most returnees who participated in the research projects managed to meet their basic daily needs, such as accommodation and obtaining a certain amount of income, their situation is often unstable. Access to housing is for all returnees the most indispensable asset immediately after return. However, house ownership among these returnees turned out to be very low. Returnees who had owned a house before migration were often forced to sell their belongings to pay for the costly journey abroad, or it was destroyed or taken in the conflict. As a consequence returnees who do not possess a home in the country of origin anymore often come to live with relatives.

While in some instances this leads to overcrowded homes and tensions within the family, living together with the extended family is in some countries like Vietnam and Afghanistan considered as the natural and even preferred thing to do. Nevertheless, not all returnees are in a position to go and live with their families. Death or displacement of relatives or disturbed relationships can prevent returnees from finding accommodation within the family. The other option is to rent a house, which is often an unfavourable solution, because it is costly and incomes and savings are small. Furthermore, renting a house or flat often takes place under informal conditions, rising prices and the possibility of being forced to leave again at short notice, creating unstable living conditions for the returnee.

Next to the immediate needs of shelter, according to Chambers and Conway, a sustainable livelihood requires an income that is sufficient, stable and independent. Independence and stability of income will contribute to the maintenance or enhancement of one's capabilities and assets. Nevertheless, also in terms of income, most returnees remain in an unstable and dependent position. Of the sample in the 2007 return migration study, 50% fully depended on sources of income other than their own income-generating capacities, such as allowance from relatives, remittances, loans, public relief or humanitarian assistance. Not having control over their own income, while continuity and the conditions under which these dependent sources of income were provided could be changed or ended at any time, put these returnees in a very vulnerable position.

The respondents who managed to generate a predominantly independent income, generated through salary, wage labour or revenue from trade (50%), were not necessarily in a sustainable income position either. A division can be made based on the stability and perceived continuity of the income generated. Stable employment is held to guarantee a certain continuity of income, which is considered to be the case with permanent wage labour and formal entrepreneurship. Semi-stable employment causes constant insecurity about whether one will have an income in the coming months, weeks or days, which is the case with temporary, seasonal or daily wage labour, or when working as an informal entrepreneur.

However, it becomes clear that having access to stable employment is still no guarantee of a sustainable livelihood, as only 30% of those in stable employment indicated that their income is sufficient to support themselves and their dependants. Thus, although several gradations of independence and stability of income can be recognised, only a small number of returnees are able to build up a sustainable income with this.

The two last aspects of a sustainable livelihood are being resistant to shocks and maintaining livelihood capabilities into the next generation. Institutional access such as education and healthcare can ensure this latter aspect, although formal access to healthcare (and education) was often more determined by the situation in the country of return than by the personal capabilities of the returnee or their migration experience. Furthermore, the capability to respond to the unexpected event of an accident or sickness can give an insight into the ability to deal with shocks. The results of this were much diversified. In most of the countries investigated, the most basic health care is free but medicines and hospital treatment have to be paid for privately. Mainly as a result of financial restrictions, 39% of the respondents therefore reported not having access to health services at all. When asked what they would do if they were to become sick, many returnees stated that they would have to try to borrow money from relatives or friends, while the most vulnerable people said they could not see any option but to pray to stay healthy.

Where economic embeddedness is concerned, for most returnees it cannot be said that they are able to build up a sustainable livelihood. Furthermore, compared with the pre-migration situation, a general trend exists of a reduction in access to housing and employment. Thus, contrary to the above-described optimistic view that migration and return migration may lead to development, the opposite is true: instead of individual returnees benefiting from their migration experience, they are economically worse off, and instead of returnees enhancing the situation of the family household, they form a burden to them.

Psychosocial embeddedness

Next to material well-being, psychosocial well-being is equally essential to finding one's place in society, and to get a sense of belonging to that society. An important aspect of belonging is being able to construct and express one's identity.[23] It provides an individual with a place in society, and at the same time establishes the connection between the self and that society. Being free to construct one's identity and having this identity accepted in the wider society leads to a feeling of belonging and attachment to certain localities.[24]

A majority of the returnees participating in the research claimed not to have problems with expressing their identity according to their personal characteristics and interests. Seventy percent did claim, however, that they had changed during their time abroad and that they sometimes faced difficulties in the country of return because of this. As many returnees have often stayed abroad for years, they have adopted some of the norms and values of the host country. This has influenced how returnees perceive, and behave towards, the home country.

The way returnees are perceived by the society in the country of return strongly depends on the extent to which a returnee has had a 'successful' migration experience. When a returnee was forced to leave the host country or did not manage to bring back money or assets, return was seen as a failure. As a result, these returnees were often stigmatised, excluded and discriminated against. Any differences in attitude or behaviour from the dominant patterns are moreover not accepted as positive. This makes it difficult for returnees to construct a feeling of belonging. As a result, almost 40% of the respondents claimed that they had trouble expressing their identity as a returnee, and some of them preferred to conceal their 'returnee' status by trying to adjust to the dominant culture again. Behaviour that deviates from the norm is generally not well received and frowned upon.

In contrast, those returnees with a positive and successful migration experience were happy to be back and gained status from their newly acquired skills. As the changes in them also led to something meaningful for them and their family members, their behaviour was generally better tolerated. This shows how different dimensions of embeddedness are interrelated and reinforce each other.

It also illustrates that identity is always dynamic, multidimensional and contextual.[25] Identity is not a fixed and given character of a person. Rather it is a dynamic process, a changing view of the self and the other. It is constantly influenced by different processes.[26] The process of migration and remigration is one of these processes.[27] A change in geographical and cultural settings can lead to dramatic identity changes. Additionally, returnees may construct a transnational identity, which is a set of new hybrid cultural forms, combined out of different cultures.[28] Upon return a complex situation emerges. The returnee's new hybrid identities do not necessarily fit into the home society, which has probably also undergone significant changes. In the ideal situation, the migrants will combine the best of both worlds and benefit from this.[29] However, this situation can also create a feeling of in-betweenness for the returnee; of not belonging anywhere anymore.[30]

The experience of migrating and returning has affected each returnee, and in some cases particularly affected their psychosocial well-being. Experiences before migration, especially for returnees from countries with a conflict history, can have long-term traumatizing effects. This was particularly the case in Sierra Leone and Bosnia–Herzegovina, where the civil wars resulted in brutal practises. Furthermore, living conditions in the host country also severely affect the returnees' psychological well-being. Restrictive and patronising living conditions resulted in returnees adopting a passive and dependent attitude and in a loss of self-esteem. This psychological instability from previous migration phases makes it very difficult to cope with the economic hardships faced upon return. This is compounded by the denigrating and disappointed way that returnees are looked upon by their relatives, which results in feelings of uselessness and failure. It became clear from the research project that psychological problems keep adding up as the situation of insecurity and hardship continues. It can thus be seen that, also at the psychological level, the different stages of migration, as Boyd and Grieco describe, all have an impact on the next stage.[31]

Two other aspects of the psychosocial dimension of embeddedness are psychological condition and the feeling of safety. In the predominantly post-conflict societies whence migrants migrated this is a big issue in itself. Furthermore, the migration experience can cause a feeling of cultural bereavement, which may include the loss of social structures, cultural values and self-identity. This can cause serious psychological disorders such as depression, phobias and schizophrenia.[32]

An element of psychosocial embeddedness that is specific to (post-)conflict countries is the feeling of safety. Physical lack of safety was often still felt in post-conflict countries because of lasting disputes, and social or political tensions. This affects the mobility and place of residence for the returnees and, particularly in (post-)conflict countries, returnees felt restricted in returning to, or visiting, their pre-war homes or communities. Furthermore, in almost all the countries surveyed, a lack of safety was identified with unstable economic conditions and an unsustainable livelihood.

The majority of all returnees are in vulnerable psychosocial positions. Psychological problems and a rejection by the home society of certain elements of their identity, and therefore the tendency to adjust to the dominant norms and values, affect their psychosocial embeddedness. However, these hardships did not prevent 64% of the respondents feeling at home in the community of return. The presence of family and friends, home ownership and personal identification with the country were indicated as the most important reasons for this.

Social embeddedness

Social networks are the third dimension of embeddedness. Boekestijn noted that social relations provide migrants with the feeling of being accepted, and that social acceptance is a crucial factor for migration success. Social networks are important for acquiring information as well as sharing personal and intimate relations. In a more practical vein social networks add to social capital.[33]

The extent to which a returnee can benefit from social capital depends on the type of social networks he or she has. Not only the quantity and frequency of individual social contacts are important. Social contacts become valuable when there is some sort of closeness, the feeling that one can really rely on the other. According to Cassarino, social networks are crucial to understanding the ways in which returnees mobilise their resources while at the same time being involved in the dynamic and maintenance of cross-border social and economic networks. These networks are responsive to specific pre- and post-return conditions.[34]

The crucial role that meaningful social networks can play has become clear in the previous sections on economic and psychosocial embeddedness. Therefore the role of social networks can be seen as a crucial dimension that can provide access to the other dimensions of embeddedness. It is not so much the size as it is the meaningfulness of returnees' social networks that count. Both in terms of emotional and material support, the possibility of relying on social relations is crucial for returnees to become embedded.

A majority of returnees can rely on their social contacts for emotional support. This includes being able to confide in their social contacts, feeling trust towards and comfort with their contacts, sharing experiences and spending time together. Married respondents are highly dependent on their spouse to find emotional support and to share their problems with.

Where fulfilling material needs is concerned, it is much more difficult to find meaningful social contacts. Forty-two percent of the respondents said they could rely on their social contacts for material support. In the first place such support included mainly accommodation. Living with family members not only meant having access to shelter, but also sharing in the household's other assets and income. Furthermore, having access to meaningful networks could also bring returnees into contact with their relations, who could provide them with employment or help them rebuild their livelihoods in other ways. However, only returnees from privileged socioeconomic backgrounds seemed to have access to these kinds of social relations.

In less wealthy families, as returnees stretch the already limited budget of the household, they cause a major burden to them. This explains part of the frustration relatives sometimes have towards their returnee relatives. It may be no surprise that relatives in an already unstable economic position cannot be a source of material assistance to returnees, since, so many returnees state: 'they do not have anything themselves'.

For a number of reasons most returnees only have a small network of people on whom they can really rely. These are mostly members of the nuclear family. This again puts returnees in a vulnerable position. Returnees who lose these relations or, for any other reason, do not have enough contacts on whom they can rely for their emotional and material needs, run the risk of becoming isolated.

Membership of a religious, political or other association sometimes substituted for the lack of meaningful social contacts. It contributed mainly to a feeling of being involved in a group and thus a feeling of belonging. In general, however, membership of such organisations was particularly low.

A clear illustration of the overall image of embeddedness is the large percentage of respondents (76%) who stated they would leave their country again if they had the possibility to do so, although the percentage of people really making plans to do so is relatively small. Only 35% of the population wanted to try and become embedded again in their country of origin. What remains is a group of people who do not have the means to re-emigrate but are unwilling to accept the fact that they have to stay in their country of return. Such returnees are not likely to invest in their existence in the country of return as they do not see future prospects for themselves. This is reinforced by the dependent economic and psychosocial situation that people are in. This is a very unstable situation, which indicates the overall lack of embeddedness on all dimensions.

Factors influencing embeddedness

Return always takes place within the context of the country. The economic, political social and cultural circumstances form the conditions that shape the possibilities to re-embed in the society of return. Juggling different discourses on gender roles, the position within the household and socioeconomic class plays a role in the experience of embeddedness and the construction of identities as re-migrants. For women, for example, this experience can be given a meaning while articulating their identity as mothers. The meaning of motherhood, however, turned out to be ambiguous because, while it could work on women's behalf, enhancing the acceptance of being unemployed and at home taking care of their children and husband, at the same time staying at home could cause feelings of being isolated, thereby hampering the process of social embeddedness. While men are usually in a more independent position, especially as the main breadwinner, this can also cause them to feel more pressured into taking care of their dependants. Moreover, if they fail to live up to this ideal of masculinity, it causes frustration and insecurity, interfering with their process of identity construction and feelings of belonging.

Class interferes also in stimulating or hampering return. Being part of a more wealthy family can help returnees, as they can conveniently make use of this family wealth to make a start in rebuilding their own lives. Also, being part of a privileged socioeconomic class can provide access to higher education and more easily opens doors to influential networks that can help find employment, housing or other assets.

Age additionally plays a role in embeddedness. While younger returnees (18 to 30) often face a gap in their education or vocational training and have less attachment to their country of return, older returnees (47 and above) are, with high unemployment rates, often considered too old to be hired.

Ethnic or religious differences can also play a role. In particular in Bosnia favouritism towards some groups over others had a decisive influence on access to employment. The differences in opportunities according to different contexts and individual characteristics show that returnees are not a homogeneous group: each has different characteristics that provide challenges or opportunities to become re-embedded.

The scope of this article is too short to address all the different contextual factors investigated. From both research projects it turned out that, despite the very different contexts—next to assistance which was investigated as a dependent variable from the start—the migration cycle itself was the most important factor that influenced the process of (re-)embedding and the way it coloured their experiences of it.

Migration cycle

Experiences in the returnee's migration cycle play a crucial role in his or her opportunities upon return. In particular, the circumstances under which one came to and left the host country, and the living conditions abroad, had an essential impact on psychosocial embeddedness, thereby strongly influencing social networks and economic embeddedness upon return.

All respondents from the post-conflict countries in the case studies stated that insecurity and a lack of safety were important reasons for their flight. But next to these macro-structures there are always other often personal reasons at the micro-level that are the direct motivation for leaving the country. The caseload proved that motivations to flee or move were never one-dimensional but always a complex combination of different factors and motivations.

A migrant from Angola interviewed in The Netherlands stated that he had wanted to migrate for a long time for economic reasons. After the conflict broke out and was internationally recognised he was supplied with legitimate grounds for migration and a refugee status.[35] A female migrant from Somalia fled to another part of the country and eventually left it because she did not belong to any clan there, which affected her identity and safety in the new pro-clan policy; at the same time she fled from her husband, whom she did not want to see anymore.[36] Here a combination of ethnicity, safety and gender-related reasons formed the basis for flight. These are examples of situations where the conflict was an important reason to leave the country, but seldom the only one.

Qualitative research and life histories can unravel the way in which macro- and micro-factors work together in a complex connectivity to stimulate a person to become a migrant or refugee.[37] These motivations and stimuli can easily appear in large-scale surveys as only or mainly economic or political, while in reality they are far more complex. The reasons and events that cause people to migrate are related to the expectations they had of their stay in the host country. It appears that, if migrants and returnees go with the intention of eventually returning or are informed of what they can expect during their stay in the host country (ie temporary protection until return once the conflict had ended), this contributes to returnees being psychologically better prepared to accepting their return and to rebuild their lives once returned. Furthermore, it appears that migrants who expected they would have to return eventually invest more in their transnational social networks. The extent to which these reasons and events still play a role after return also have an effect on the way returnees can accept being back.

The living conditions in the host country also play a crucial role. Migrants often spend a significant period of their lives in the host country. Currently the majority of forced migrants become (more) depressed because of the insecurity and the problems they face during their stay in the host country. This applies especially to those migrants who have no chance to make themselves useful with work or study in the host country. A forced migrant interviewed in the host country said: 'I don't like thinking too much, because I almost get sick ... Too much pressure what will happen tomorrow. I am exhausted.'[38]

Returnees who managed to maintain independent living circumstances abroad through work, having access to independent housing and by having the freedom to develop social contacts are on all dimensions significantly better embedded than those who did not have these opportunities. Although migrants who do not yet have a permanent permit to stay often engage in low-skilled jobs below their qualifications, and the skills or knowledge necessary for the jobs were often not very relevant to employment upon return, they can benefit greatly from the opportunity to work in a number of ways. First of all, it gives them the chance to save some money, which they send back to their country of origin, thus strengthening their social networks, or take back after return. Both savings and remittances contributed to the returnees' economic and social embeddedness. Moreover, being incorporated in a working environment abroad and generating one's own income gives migrants the possibility to retain their self esteem and survival skills.

Social contacts, independent living circumstances and the possibility of working allowed migrants to take control over their own situation and lead an active life without having it provided for them in the asylum centres and through social benefits. In contrast, those respondents who did not have these possibilities, but were held in dependent positions in asylum centres and dependent on social welfare, often did not manage to take control over their lives upon return and thus faced a disadvantage in their chances of becoming embedded. It cannot be said that independent conditions abroad cause a large improvement in people's life compared with the life they had before migration; rather particular conditions may prevent the degradation of self-esteem and survival skills, and thus provide significant help to people to become embedded upon return.

A final influencing factor of the migration cycle are the conditions under which return takes place. The legal status of migrants at the point of return influences the agency they have in the decision to return. Those who returned as a result of pressure or force from the authorities expressed their frustration at not being ready yet, both mentally and practically. Furthermore, this had an impact on the way returnees were perceived by the people in their home society. For example, in Sierra Leone, word spread quickly when a forcibly deported returnee arrived handcuffed and under the supervision of policemen, and these people were often severely stigmatised. This chiefly affected their psychosocial embeddedness. The different individual characteristics of returnees, combined with their experiences in the migration cycle, form a returnee's complex background that should be taken into account when considering providing assistance to this returnee.

Assistance

What emerges from what has been described above is that the biggest challenges for migrants upon return are building up an independent and sustainable livelihood, gaining trust and respect from social networks, and developing a feeling of belonging. Considering the obstacles that many returnees face, it is of interest to see to what extent assistance can help to overcome these obstacles.

Pre-return preparation assistance, with the aim of facilitating a free and well informed choice to return, contributes to all dimensions of embeddedness when offered by friends or family. When migrants are able to make use of accurate information from people they trust on the situation in their country of origin, it gives them the feeling of having a say in the decision to return. This relation could not be found, however, when offered by institutions conceived of by migrants as the actors that were pushing them out of the host country. In addition, while returnees initially did have confidence in the sincere intentions of NGOs, many of them stated that they were disappointed in them after return, as the expectations that were raised about the possibilities in the home country, did not come true.

This is not necessarily the result of purposefully being given false information, but rather of unclear and under-defined communication about assistance possibilities. For example, this is the case when NGOs communicate with their clients through third parties, who may not share the same vision on return. In the return migration monitoring study of 2007, the communication between the NGO and the returnee took place through a governmental organisation that had more interest in the return of migrants and therefore may have given a brighter image of the available assistance to encourage agreement to return.

Giving incorrect or sometimes misleading information that is meant to convince migrants to return causes returnees to feel tricked into agreeing to do so. Frustration, disappointment and the feeling that their return is a result of an unfair procedure prevent returnees from accepting being back. Therefore pre-return preparation and information assistance can only have a positive impact when it contributes to the return in the first place being based on a well informed choice and in the second place being followed up by post-return assistance. NGOs have to date not been able to make use of this potential when trying to assist returnees.

Post-return assistance is the most direct way to try to respond to returnees' needs. A majority (67%) of the interviewed returnees in the 2007 return migration monitoring study had access to assistance from an institution after return, at least to some extent. While a large variety of assistance facilities is available after return, the focus is usually on financial assistance, which can take the form of unconditional sums of money, monetary assistance for starting a business, or provision of money for (temporary) housing or for medication for a certain period of time. Less tangible forms of assistance, such as information and psychosocial counselling, are less frequently provided.

From the perspective of the assistance agency, giving financial assistance is often the easiest, quickest and most measurable method of helping, especially in situations where a lot of people are returning to their country of origin at the same time and need assistance. From the perspective of the returnee, too, the primary needs after return are material. Monetary assistance given to the returnees is rarely monitored and therefore often spent on other purposes than those aimed for. This unmonitored and incidental financial assistance provided in cash or in kind does not lead to a sustainable livelihood.

In contrast, assistance in setting up a business does significantly and positively influence embeddedness. An explanation for this lies in the fact that it is a more conscious process aimed at generating an independent income. It is often given in guided steps, in which planning and some non-material guidance is included to help the returnee decide in what area he or she would like to set up a business and take active steps towards doing so.

It can be concluded that, while financial assistance is important, it is the combination with human guidance aimed towards an independent sustainable livelihood with the possibility of incorporating this into social networks which makes business assistance a success.

As an alternative to business assistance, recent initiatives are providing assistance in finding employment through subsidised programmes where a returnee is hired for six months by an employer. These programmes were still running at the time of study and it is questionable whether, in a country of high unemployment, participants can keep their job after the subsidy has expired. However, the strength of the initiative is that it recognises the fact that not every individual returnee has entrepreneurial skills and can be expected to run a business. It is important to follow the development of these projects to see whether the concept can work.

In addition to material assistance, practical information is also essential after return. At the moment returnees often get lost in bureaucratic requirements that they do not know of. In none of the countries studied, however, could an information package for returnees be found that guided them through practical procedures. This is something that partner organisations could prepare for returnees. In certain contexts psychosocial assistance is also crucial, particularly in conflict and post-conflict societies. The absence of these types of assistance can have a negative influence on embeddedness.

The most important actors in return assistance, especially after return, are host-government programmes implemented mainly by the International Organisation for Migration (IOM) and local organisations funded by Western NGOs. There exists a clear difference in scale and approach among these two different actors.

Government-funded institutions such as IOM have an advantage in their scale and budget. For returnees from host countries which have a programme with IOM and which qualify for assistance, there is a substantial amount of money available. However, local organisations that are funded by NGOs have the potential to contribute to embeddedness through their small-scale, more personal and flexible approach; there is more room for them to incorporate the specific needs of individual returnees in the assistance they offer. Nevertheless, this potential was not fully realised in the countries studied in this research. This is largely related to budget and scale limitations, but also related to the characteristics of the partner organisations, which are often not specialised in issues of return migration. Therefore, NGOs that work in this way do not optimally use the added value that local organisations could offer. The flexible and informal character of the assistance may also become a weakness when there are no clearly defined boundaries about what returnees can expect and what an NGO has to offer.

Compared with the contextual factors and the migration cycle, assistance plays a much smaller role in the embeddedness of returnees. Moreover, the potentially positive influence that assistance can have is not always fully taken advantage of. While the challenges of building a sustainable livelihood are only sometimes addressed, other equally important dimensions of embeddedness, such as building on social networks and gaining a feeling of belonging, are often left aside. What is needed is a complementary approach, where both material and human assistance are provided, and which can be incorporated into the social networks structure of the returnee. A careful implementation is needed to make assistance work.

Final considerations

Western policy makers have taken up the assumed link between migration and development in order to add a developmental touch to their policies of returning irregular migrants, rejected asylum seekers and ex-refugees. This article has explored the question of whether return migration of involuntary returning ex-refugees, rejected asylum seekers and irregular migrants can be sustainable, and whether the assumed link between return migration and development is justified.

It appeared from both research projects that, in order to fully understand the complex reality of the opportunities and obstacles to sustainable return, a holistic approach is needed. The obstacles and opportunities faced by returnees are directly related to and cannot be understood without knowing previous migration phases. Furthermore, the fact that sustainability has several dimensions, which are interrelated and reinforce each other should be taken into account. And in order to include the meaning migrants give to their migration experience as part of building up a sense of belonging to their society of return, return migration also needs to be studied from a bottom-up perspective, which provides a better understanding of return and migration patterns. The concept of mixed embeddedness used in these studies applies to this type of research.

The meaning returnees attribute to their experiences of return are interwoven with the experience of leaving their countries of origin, their stay in host countries and the way in which they had to return. Instead of being considered simply as 'going home', return migration should not simply be studied within the limits of the national borders of the country of origin, since it is linked to all the aspects of the migration cycle and is therefore an intrinsically transnational phenomenon.

In both studies on return migration, it appeared to be extremely difficult for an involuntary returnee to become re-embedded in the country of origin at the economic, psychosocial and social networks level. Returnees were often worse off in terms of access to independent housing and income compared to their pre-migration situation. While achieving sustainable return for the individual returnee is thus already an enormous challenge, returnees cannot be expected to contribute to development. Rather, the opposite is true; returnees often form a burden on the household budget and put higher pressure on already limited employment, health care and education facilities in the country of return. In contrast to what is the common thinking on migration and development, in this sample the migration experience led to deprivation and underdevelopment for the individual, the household and ultimately the country of return, rather than to development.

The opportunities upon return always take place within the context of the country of return and are also always dependent on individual characteristics. However, the most important factors that influences the re-embeddedness of returnees are their experiences in the migration cycle, and more specifically their living conditions in the host country. As emerged clearly from both research projects, there is a direct and transnational interconnectedness between restrictive living conditions in the host society and their often negative effect on the possibilities to re-embed after return to the country of origin.

These findings reveal a great inconsistency in Western European migration policies. While the intention is expressed, and budget assigned, to make return migration contribute to development, this intention is undermined by extremely restrictive migration policies and limited rights of migrants during their stay in the host country. These patronising, restrictive and sometimes even inhumane living conditions cause migrants to become passive and dependent on social welfare and entail a loss of survival skills and self-esteem. Irregular migrants and refugees are constructed as citizens in between states, left with no substantial ways of contributing to or earning a position in the host society, in a sense they are seen as 'superfluous'.

Such migration policies could be understood as part of what Agamben has defined as 'biopolitics', the technological approach to and regulation of the body: 'life management' through public health, drug prohibition, and immigration policies etc, which have contributed to regarding human life as 'superfluous'.[39] The multiplication of the displaced and the stateless, the political and economic 'superfluousness' of huge masses of human beings, are cases in point of such biopolitics.

After spending years in these circumstances, too much damage is done to a returnee than can be fixed with assistance programmes, which are furthermore too limited to be able to make a difference. To encourage migration to contribute to development, can not be accomplished by means of these assistance programmes. This results in the strange paradox of expecting return migrants, at a certain stage of their migration process defined as superfluous, to transform into actors who rebuild their societies at another stage of their migration process. However, rather than arguing that returnees can not help rebuild their countries of origin, our point is that the recent emphasis on return as possible impetus for development veils the neglect of the relation between restrictive migration policies and the conditions for that possible development.

If Western European governments are sincere in their ideas to make return migration contribute to development, it is absolutely necessary to give migrants more rights to live an independent life while in the host country. An important element of this is to allow migrants to work in the host country while they are undergoing their asylum procedure, as has happened in Germany for instance. This is of tremendous value for migrants, who maintain their most basic survival skills, namely providing for their own income. In doing so, they can save money in order to secure their economic and social network embeddedness upon return.

As our research found, 64% felt at home in their countries of origin. Questions could be raised therefore as to whether these migrants are likely to return on a permanent basis to Western Europe. However, extremely restrictive migration policies cause people to try to stay by all means possible, as it is their only chance. Giving migrants more space in their decision to come and go, will release some pressure and could change the tenacious attitude of migrants.

This would imply loosening the restrictive migration policies for temporary labour migration. Pleas in that direction can be heard within Western Europe. In France a report has come out from a special committee headed by Jacques Attali, former advisor to President Mitterand, suggesting that France is in need of more immigrants to keep up its economic growth. In The Netherlands it is noted that immigrants form Poland can not fill the need for low- and medium-skilled labour anymore, employers are urged increasingly to seek employees outside the borders of the European Union.[40] Therefore a debate has to be stimulated about migration and remigration from a transnational perspective, connecting development issues in sending countries to the building of 'fortress Europe', while Eastern Europe seems to be evolving as its semi-periphery.[41]

For NGOs working in the field of migration and development, it is important to acknowledge the limited impact of their assistance programmes and therefore to be modest about their role in the process of re-embeddedness. At the same time they should be aware of the role that governments attribute to them. Based on the trust and backing they have in society, they are seen as the actors that can contribute to a more effective return.[42] Claims that their assistance can lead to sustainability and even development not only creates expectations among potential returnees but also among policy makers. The danger is that these claims of NGOs are being used by governments as a further legitimisation of their return policies.

Alternatively, as the success of return assistance is very much dependent on these internal migration policies, a new role for NGOs working with the issue of involuntarily returning migrants should be to start a strong lobby of host governments to remove the inconsistencies in migration policies by applying more humane and less restrictive policies, in order to not affect the rest of migrants' lives in such a negative way.

In general it can be said that, when looking at the social reality of returnees, the link between return migration and development is too ambitious. In some cases the two are even negatively linked. With current policies it is therefore unjustified and misleading to suggest that return migration may promote development.

Notes

1 R Black & S Gent, 'Sustainable return in post-conflict contexts', *International Migration,* 44 (3), 2006, pp 15–38.
2 M Eastmond, 'Transnational returns and reconstruction in post-war Bosnia and Herzegovina', *International Migration*, 44 (3), 2006, pp 141–166; R Black & S Gent, *Defining, Measuring and*

Influencing Sustainable Return: The case of the Balkans, Brighton: Sussex Centre for Migration Research, 2004, p 5; and R Black, 'Return and reconstruction in Bosnia and Herzegovina: missing link, or mistaken priority?', *School of Advanced International Studies Review*, XXI, 2001, pp 177–199.

3 MCF Verdonk, *Terugkeernota, maatregelen voor een effectievere uitvoering van het terugkeerbeleid*, 's-Gravenhage: Sdu Uitgevers, 2003, p 5.

4 A Van Ardenne, 'Kamerbrief aan Eerste en Tweede Kamer over de notitie "Aan elkaar verplicht"', 2003, at http://www.eerstekamer.nl/9324000/d/292/w29234b1.pdf, accessed 15 April 2007.

5 PON – Instituut voor advies, onderzoek en ontwikkeling in Noord-Brabant, *Kansrijk Terugkeren of Doormigreren?*, Noord-Brabant: PON, 2004.

6 See also M Van Houte & M de Koning, 'Towards a better embeddedness? Monitoring assistance to involuntary returning migrants from Western countries', research report, Nijmegen: CIDIN, Cordaid and AMIDSt, 2008.

7 The authors would like to acknowledge the researchers whose work this article is based on: master students engaged in the 2006 pilot study—Adriaan Kauffmann, Lieke van der Putten, Suzanne van Hattum, Marieke van Houte, Maaike Derksen, Maaike van Kruijsdijk, Femke Knoben, Judith Stegemen, Bas Kleinhout, Laura Huls & Femianne Bredewold; and the researchers involved in the 2007 research project—Maaike Derksen, Moira Galloway, Alice Johansson, Mireille de Koning, June de Bree and Machteld Kuyper.

8 T Ghanem, *When Forced Migrants return 'Home': The Psychological Difficulties Returnees encounter in the Reintegration Process*, Oxford: Refugee Studies Centre, 2003, p 21.

9 L Hammond, 'Examining the discourse of repatriation: towards a more proactive theory of return migration', in R Black & K Koser (eds), *The End of the Refugee Cycle? Refugee Repatriation and Reconstruction*, New York: Berghahn, 1999, pp 227–244; K Koser & R Black, 'The end of the refugee cycle?', in Black & Koser, *The End of the Refugee Cycle?*, pp 2–17; G Gmelch, 'Return migration', *Annual Review of Anthropology*, 9, 1980, p 135–159; and JP Cassarino, 'Theorising return migration: the conceptual approach to return migrants revisited', *International Journal on Multicultural Societies*, 6 (2), 2004, pp 253–279.

10 H De Haas, *International Migration, Remittances and Development: Myths and Facts—Global Migration Perspectives*, Geneva: Global Commission on International Migration, 2005.

11 Black & Gent, *Defining, Measuring and Influencing Sustainable Return*, p 13.

12 De Haas, *International Migration, Remittances and Development*.

13 G Noll, 'Rejected asylum seekers: the problem of return—new issues in refugee research', *Working Paper 4*, UNHCR, 1999.

14 M Dimitrijevic, Z Todorovic & N Grkovic, *The Experience of Decision-making and Repatriation Process: Return of Serbian Refugees to Croatia*, Belgrade: Danish Refugee Council, 2004.

15 FP Cerase, 'Expectations and reality: a study of return migration from the United States to southern Italy', *Journal of International Migration Review*, 28 (1), 1974, pp 245–262; and S Ammassari, 'From nation-building to entrepreneurship: the impact of elite return migrants in Cote d'Ivoire and Ghana', *Population, Place and Space*, 10 (2), 2004, pp 133–154.

16 Black & Gent, 'Sustainable return in post-conflict contexts'.

17 See also T Davids & M Van Houte, 'Remigration, development and mixed embeddeness: an agenda for qualitative research?', in JP Cassarino (ed), *Contemporary Challenges in Return: In Theory and in Practice*, Florence: Robert Shuman Centre for Advanced Studies, forthcoming 2008.

18 M Granovetter, 'Economic action and social structure: the problem of embeddedness', *American Journal of Sociology*, 91 (3), 1985, pp 481–510.

19 R Kloosterman, 'Mixed embeddedness as a conceptual framework for exploring immigrant entrepreneurship', Eurex Lecture 8, Amsterdam Institute of Metropolitan and International Development Studies, 2006; H Aldrich & R Waldinger, 'Ethnicity and entrepreneurship', *Annual Review of Sociology*, 16, 1990, pp 111–135; and R Waldinger, 'The other side of embeddedness: a case study of the interplay of economics and ethnicity', *Ethnic and Racial Studies*, 18 (3), 1995, pp 555–580.

20 Davids & Van Houte, 'Remigration, development and mixed embeddeness'.

21 Typically a multidimensional approach would also include a political dimension. However, as embeddedness is a concept which refers to the individual, it is here only taken into account insofar as it influences one's identity, and is therefore incorporated into the psychosocial dimension.

22 R Chambers & G Conway, *Sustainable Rural Livelihoods: Practical Concepts for the 21st Century*, IDS Discussion paper 296, Brighton: Institute of Development Studies, 1991. See also L De Haan, M Kaag & M De Bruijn, *Ways Forward in Livelihood Research*, Dordrecht: Kluwer, 2004; and L De Haan & A Zoomers, 'Development geography at the crossroads of livelihood and globalisation', *Tijdschrift voor Economische en Sociale Geografie*, 94 (3), 2003, pp 350–362.

23 I Ter Maat, *I am a Tree with Roots in Chile, and Branches and Fruit in The Netherlands*, Nijmegen: Vrouwen Alliantie Media Producties, 2002.

24 A Appadurai, *Modernity at Large: Cultural Dimensions of Globalization*, Minneapolis, MN: University of Minnesota Press, 1996.

25 A Giddens, *Modernity and Self-Identity: Self and Society in the Late Modern Age*, Cambridge: Polity Press, 1991; and S Hall, 'Ethnicity: identity and difference', *Radical America*, 203 (4), 1991, pp 9–20.

26 H Ghorashi, *Ways to Survive, Battles to Win: Iranian Women Exiles in The Netherlands and the US*, Nijmegen: Katholieke Universiteit Nijmegen, 2001.

27 CR Nagel & LA Staeheli, 'Citizenship, identity and transnational migration: Arab immigrants to the United States', *Space and Polity*, 8 (1), 2004, pp 3–23.

28 D Bryceson & U Vuorela, 'Transnational families in the twenty-first century', in Bryceson & Vuorela (eds), *The Transnational Family*, Oxford: Berg, 2002, pp 3–30; A Brah, *Cartographies of Diaspora*, London: Routledge, 1996; and C Dwyer, 'Negotiating diasporic identities: young British South Asian muslim women', *Women's Studies International Forum*, 23 (4), 2002, pp 475–486.

29 H Ghorashi, 'Iraanse vrouwen, transnationaal of nationaal? Een (de)territoriale benadering van "thuis" in Nederland en de Verenigde Staten', *Migrantenstudies*, 3, 2003, pp 140–156.

30 Ghorashi, *Ways to Survive, Battles to Win*, p 119.

31 M Boyd & E Grieco, *Women and Migration: Incorporating Gender into International Migration Theory*, Washington: Migration Policy Institute, 2003.

32 D Bhugra & MA Becker, 'Migration, cultural bereavement and cultural identity', *World Psychiatry*, 4 (1), 2005, pp 18–24.

33 C Boekestijn, 'Intercultural migration and the development of personal identity: the dilemma between identity maintenance and cultural adaptation', *International Journal of Intercultural Relations*, 12 (2), 1998, pp 83–105.

34 Cassarino, 'Theorising return migration', p 275.

35 F Knoben, *Een 'nieuw' bestaan in het land van herkomst? Een onderzoek onder uitgeprocedeerde asielzoekers in Nederland*, Nijmegen: Centre for International Development Issues, 2006.

36 M Van Kruijsdijk, *I am in Between: I am not Belonging to There, I am not Belonging to Here—Identity Reconstruction of Dutch Somalis living in Leicester, United Kingdom*, Nijmegen: Centre for International Development Issues, 2006.

37 S Ruba, 'Moroccan migrant women: transnationalism, nation-states and gender', *Journal of Ethnic and Migration Studies*, 27 (4) 2001, pp 655–671.

38 Knoben, *Een 'nieuw' bestaan in het land van herkomst?*

39 G Agamben, *Homo Sacer: Sovereign Power and Bare Life*, trans Daniel Heller-Roazen, Stanford, CA: Stanford University Press, 1998. See also A Duarte, 'Biopolitics and the dissemination of violence: the Arendtian critique of the present', *HannahArendt.net*, 2005, at http://hannaharendt.net/research/biopolitics.html, accessed 13 February 2007.

40 HD Hekking & M Visser, 'De Polen bieden geen soelaas meer, werkgevers kijken buiten Europese Unie voor oplossen van groeiend aantal onvervulbare vacatures', *Financieel Dagblad*, 21 February 2008, p 3; and 'Parijs: Frans Rapport: meer immigranten nodig', *Financieel Dagblad*, 11 January 2008, p 3.

41 M Blagojević, 'Migrating gender scholar: epistemic and other consequences', unpublished paper presented at the 'Migrating Feminisms Conference', Budapest, 2006; and Blagojević, 'Creators, transmitters, and users: women's scientific excellence at the periphery of Europe', in *Gender and Excellence in the Making*, Brussels: European Commission Research Publications, 2003.

42 ACVZ, *Terugkeer, de nationale aspecten: beleid, uitvoering en draagvlak*, The Hague: ACVZ, 2005.

Migrant Workers in the ILO's *Global Alliance Against Forced Labour* Report: a critical appraisal

BEN ROGALY

Just as official events were being held in 2007 to mark the bicentenary of the abolition of British involvement in the transatlantic slave trade, several organisations made reference to the continuity of unfree labour relations, including slavery-like conditions, in present times. In this context it would thus seem appropriate to appreciate the continuing global-level work of the International Labour Office (ILO) on employment rights, decent work, and in particular on forced labour. However, in this paper I use a geographical perspective on migrant labour to raise questions about how migrant workers have been represented in the ILO Director General's most recent report on the subject: *A Global Alliance Against Forced Labour* (GAAFL).

While acknowledging the well intentioned work that has gone into producing the ILO report, the importance of highlighting situations where unfree labour continues to exist, and the negotiation and compromise required for the production of a document of this kind,[1] I present a critique of the report's conceptual apparatus and the possible effect of this on policy and practice at various sites and scales. In particular I draw attention to the danger that such an approach can residualise lack of freedom in employment relations, obscuring in turn the connections between such lack and the workings of capitalism with all its variety and contingency.[2] As has been noted in the case of 'globalisation', a discourse can develop a power of its own, reproducing the notion of its own inevitability.[3]

I focus on the agriculture sector, drawing on collaborative work I have undertaken with colleagues in India and in the UK to argue, first, that the report's analysis, by prioritising the regional and national scales and obscuring the scales of individual and household, denies migrant workers' agency. Thus, for example, paid work carried out by migrant workers is not analysed in relation to the unpaid reproductive work on which it relies,[4] nor does the report seek to understand recruitment or workplace bargaining, co-operation or conflict from the perspective of individual workers.[5] As a result, policy prescriptions emerge which do not reflect or give space to the interests migrant workers may have in keeping hold of a short-term tie to a particular employer, nor to the apparently small but often meaningful ways in which workplace arrangements may be subject to continual (re)negotiation by workers. Rather than being represented as knowing agents, migrant workers employed in conditions defined by the authors of the report as forced labour, are portrayed as victims. Indeed, the report uses the word 'victim' 180 times in its 87 pages.

The second major issue I take up with the report, and illustrate through the Indian and UK case studies, is the omission of an analysis of capitalism and, in particular, of the connections between specific forms of capitalism and unfree labour relations. There are no mentions of 'capitalism' and only six of capital, three of which refer to 'social capital'. Scalar analysis is vital here too, as it can bring out the differences between the interests of individual capitals and capital-in-general,[6] as well as the conflicts between large-scale monopoly capital and small-scale capital, and relations between capital and the state. Lerche has suggested that the ILO could not be expected to direct analytical attention towards capitalism because of its tripartite structure, made up of representatives of governments, employers and workers. In fact, he goes on, this is strategic on the part of the ILO, as it seeks to isolate the 'worst forms of "un-decent" labour so that these incidents can be dealt with in isolation, without challenging the overall system that created the conditions for their occurrence in the first place.'[7]

I will argue that, by constructing scalar representations of state action which implicitly deny the interrelation of government, intergovernmental and private corporate actions, a perspective on policy towards migrant workers emerges which misses the opportunity of advocating regulation of those economic relations between fragments of capital that produce unfree labour relations. Reports such as GAAFL and the discourses they adopt are thus political interventions, not only through the explicit claims that are made and the call for wider campaigns urging states to legislate against forced labour, but also through what they leave out.

The paper proceeds as follows. In the next section I argue that scale provides an important and critical conceptual frame for the analysis of labour–capital relations. I then go on to summarise the aims of GAAFL, its key concepts, and the connections it makes between forced labour, migrant workers and agriculture. I refer in particular to two examples of the social construction of scale in the report: first, the aggregation of forced labour into categories of global North and South and, second, characterisation of migration in the state of Bihar in India. In the fourth section I discuss two case studies of migrant working in agriculture, based on empirical work I have carried out in India and the UK. These illustrate the importance both of migrant workers' agency in employment situations that might have been subsumed within the category 'forced labour' in GAAFL, and of states' accommodations with large-scale capital in producing degrees of unfreedom and exploitation, including worsening employment conditions. In conclusion, it is argued that a focus on the 'perpetrators' of 'forced labour' may be in the interests of states that would like to see the continued expansion of the power of capital in relation to labour, because it shifts attention away both from the ironic combination of unfreedom and insecurity associated with actually existing labour–capital relations and from ways of challenging them.

Why scale matters here

Geographers once saw scalar boundaries such as nation, region, locality or household as given and immutable. However, in recent decades they have become understood as both socially constructed and, potentially at least, made use of politically.[8] It has been argued, for example, that the discursive use of the global scale can be disabling or disempowering, when a particular normative version of how to embrace global change is portrayed as the only way forward for national economic policy.[9] In direct relation to the employment of migrant workers in agriculture, Don Mitchell showed how, during industrial conflict in 1930s California, large-scale agrarian capital used the *idea* of the local roots of agricultural businesses to portray migrant workers as outsiders, and indeed dangerous subversives, thus appealing to law enforcement agencies to arrest them.[10]

Geographers' analyses of the social construction and political use of scale thus provide specific kinds of insights into power relations. Yet Marston, Jones and Woodward have argued for an end to the use of scalar analysis altogether.[11] Their argument is that such analysis is inherently hierarchical, privileging higher, larger, scales (eg the global) over lower, smaller ones (eg local, home). Marston *et al* call for scale to be dumped and for it to be replaced by a 'flat ontology'. Part of their argument relates to the disempowering effect of 'globalisation' already referred to. They argue that 'the current intellectual preoccupation with globalisation blinds us— researchers, policy makers and laypeople—to the ways 'global' discourses produce identities that disempower us as agents'.[12] Encouraged to accept that capitalist economic globalisation has a hegemonic hold, we are less likely to contest or resist it.

This is a fair point. However, as critics such as Leitner and Miller retort, surely Marston *et al* are wrong to suggest that scale is *necessarily* used in a hierarchical way. Moreover 'power asymmetries between different scales are always contested and subject to struggle',[13] and national and global discourses can themselves be challenged, as has been shown in a number of arenas, including in recent scholarship in labour geography.[14] For example, Leitner and Miller point out, 'in the aftermath of the Immigrant Workers' Freedom Ride' in the USA in 2006, 'sponsors of the ride formed the New American Opportunity Campaign ... which mobilizes, coordinates and organizes grass-roots lobbying on immigrants' rights at the national scale'.[15]

As feminist geographers such as Rachel Silvey have argued in relation to the scales of nation and household, the social deconstruction of scalar categories remains an intellectually valid and politically important mode of scholarly engagement.[16] Research at multiple scales also importantly reveals the disjunctures and apparent contradictions found at different scales, albeit that they are socially constructed. For example, drawing on Gibson-Graham, Andrew Herod argues that 'when considering processes of economic restructuring, what is seen from a "global" perspective (perhaps a worldwide economic slowdown) may appear different from what is seen from a "local perspective" in particular places (some places may actually be experiencing economic expansion during such a global economic slowdown)'.[17]

A similar point can be made with respect to agricultural production relations. To understand employers' logic, including the recruitment of particular kinds of workers, it is necessary to analyse relationships between workers, labour contractors, growers, their marketplace and the state. The social construction of scale as a means to political and economic ends may well be part of this.[18] Yet, if this logic is characterised at a particular imagined scale, difference can be expected at other scales. So while we can note current tendencies towards, say, the use of seasonal student workers from outside the European Union to pick strawberries in Herefordshire, England, and that this is likely to involve working in polytunnels and digital recording of work performance, a consideration of the practices of individual strawberry growing businesses in the same county will reveal significant diversity between them. Some small-scale growers may still be using just locally resident workers, while others harvest the strawberries themselves alongside small groups of migrant workers.[19]

Scale in the *Global Alliance Against Forced Labour* report

A reading of GAAFL with a scalar lens raises questions about the particular constructions of scale used in the report. In this section I will set out the main concepts used in GAAFL, and some key findings, before going on to present a critique of the construction of a clear line of difference in forced labour between North and South, and the way conclusions were reached in the analysis of forced labour involving migrant workers from the state of Bihar in India.

The report's stated aims are to build momentum for laws, policies and practical action to eradicate forced labour. It defines forced labour in the same way as the first ILO convention on the subject in 1930. Forced labour refers to 'all work or service which is exacted from any person under the menace of any penalty and for which the said person has not offered themself [sic] voluntarily'.[20] Slavery is seen as one form of forced labour, one which involved the 'absolute control of one person over another'.[21]

The connection between forced labour and *migrant labour* at the global scale is made explicit: 'In all countries and regions, migrant workers, particularly irregular migrants, are at particular risk of coercive recruitment and employment practices' (p 18). This is symptomatic of a wider discourse portraying migrants as victims. For example, a recent report published by the UK's Joseph Rowntree Foundation on contemporary slavery in Britain suggests that: 'Migrant workers ... are most at risk of *slavery or slavery-like working conditions'*.[22]

Importantly, according to GAAFL, while the contemporary imaginary of forced labour relates to exploitation for commercial sex, and to forced labour imposed by the state, the ILO's own surveys found that 64% of forced labour was exacted by 'private agents' for 'economic exploitation' (p 12). Agriculture is highlighted as a major user of forced labour worldwide. 'Almost two-thirds of total forced labour in Asia and Pacific is private-imposed for economic exploitation, mostly debt bondage in agriculture and other economic activities' (p 13). An ILO 'study on returned migrants in four eastern and south-eastern European countries found that, out of a sample of 300 forced labour victims, 13 per cent [had been trafficked] into agriculture' (p 46).

This portrayal of a split between the manifestations of forced labour as debt bondage (in the global South) and as trafficking (in the global North) is widened elsewhere in the report. According to GAAFL, migrant workers tend to be involved in forced labour differently according to the continents from which, or within which, they migrate. So international migrants to 'industrial, Middle Eastern and transition countries' from the global South, are subject to 'modern' forms of forced labour (p 9), 'linked to globalization, migration and *human trafficking*' (pp 12–13, emphasis added), whereas migrant workers moving both across and within the borders of nation states in Asia, Africa and Latin America experience 'traditional' forms of forced labour, characterised by 'servitude' and 'bonded labour' (p 12). Although the report concedes that these categories of older and newer kinds of forced labour are 'not watertight' (p 9), tricontinental representations, such as the global South, may hide more differences than they reveal when contrasted with the global North. Multiscalar analysis is required and GAAFL makes an attempt at this when discussing the cases of India, Nepal and Pakistan separately.

Bihar's migrant agricultural workers

Information in GAAFL about the recruitment and employment of migrant agricultural workers from the eastern Indian state of Bihar by or on behalf of farmers in the western Indian state of Punjab is used to argue that this migration stream is characterised by bonded labour, itself considered a form of forced labour by the report's authors.[23] Lerche draws on conversations with ILO staff to explain that the report's estimate of close to six million workers in unfree labour relations in the Asia and Pacific region as a whole is much lower than the estimates made by non-governmental bodies because the report does not classify as unfree 'short-term relations' which do not involve 'threats, means of coercion or other violent acts' (p 437). But this is exactly what the report *does* do, implicitly at least, by building up its portrayal of bonded labour through selectively drawing on studies of seasonally migrant workers in a particular migration stream.

Indeed, the report rightly points out that indebtedness is often a key characteristic of unfree labour relations. It states that 'cases of coercive recruitment and debt bondage have affected migrants moving from poorer Indian states such as Bihar to commercial agriculture in the wealthier Punjab' (p 30). Although this passage does not claim that this is the case for all migrant agricultural workers moving between Bihar and Punjab, there is no consideration of the alternative picture. Yet one does not have to look further than the pages of the widely-read *Economic and Political Weekly* (EPW) to find such an analysis of the same migration stream which is quite contradictory to that alluded to in the report.

Alakh Sharma has carried out detailed and extensive research over decades in Bihar. In an article published in GAAFL in 2005 he narrates the impact on the agrarian economy of the permanent settlement under which *zamindars* were appointed as intermediary rent collectors. The article considers the lack of effective implementation of land-ceiling laws when the *zamindars*, following independence, were confined to their homesteads and private lands, and reflects on the connection between continuing inequality in the distribution of land and the emergence of peasant political mobilisation from the 1960s. This mobilisation lead to a degree of protection of workers from *begar*, a form of unpaid, forced, labour; and to effective resistance to payment of the very lowest wages. Alongside this politicisation of the poor peasantry, migration also had a major positive effect on wages by tightening the labour market. Real wages rose by between 50% and 100% across the state between 1981–82, when Sharma first surveyed agrarian relations there, and 1999–2000, when he carried out a resurvey.[24] Sharma concluded that: 'These two developments—mobilisation of the poor peasants and increased migration—appear to be the most important agents of change in rural Bihar during the last three decades or so'.[25]

A separate study by Gerry and Janine Rodgers, published five years before Sharma's, showed that migration to Punjab, Haryana, Uttar Pradesh and Delhi 'had radically changed the balance of labour supply and demand in the villages and [was] clearly the primary factor behind the rise in wages'. Like Sharma for Bihar as a whole, they found most of the migration from Purnia—the district their study was limited to—was by men. Migrants were able to save between Rs500 and Rs1000 per month per worker. Both studies found that migration had turned from a survival strategy into a source of cash savings. There had been substantial changes in living conditions as a result, for example in the proportion of households with access to handpumps and the presence of TVs in the villages.[26]

How debt-bondedness and forced labour are conceptualised clearly matters, as it influences the kinds of conclusions that are drawn about the meaning, experience and effects of temporary periods spent working away from home as a migrant.[27] Variations in scale of analysis also affect conclusions about temporary migration. Interactions between migration, different kinds of inequality and social and economic change at various scales have a mix of outcomes over time. Rodgers and Rodgers report, for example, that with the migration they were studying being mainly done by men, the gap between male and female wages for local wage work had widened. Inequality between *classes* may have declined, yet *gender* inequality increased.[28] So it is important not to condemn migration without looking at its diverse effects across time for individual men, women and children of different classes, castes and religion-based communities. In a situation of lack of choice, migration even for hard manual work can be, for some people, an escape from, or challenge to, established relations of dominance, as Lenin found in 19th century Russia.[29]

Nevertheless GAAFL uses limited evidence on out-migration from Bihar to imply that debt bondage, and by extension forced labour, characterise labour relations in which migrant agricultural workers are involved, not only for India but, in combination with studies from other countries, for Asia as a whole.[30] This not only plays down spatial variations. It also implies that temporary migrant workers in Asia have no power at all, not just in agriculture, but in all sectors. However, as Andrew Herod put it 'although capital may have the upper hand, the production of scale and landscapes is never unproblematic'.[31] The idea that workers have a degree of power within capitalist labour relations is accentuated in agriculture because so many agricultural processes are seasonal, and reliant on nature.[32] Growers of crops who rely on manual workers at harvest often require a larger workforce for the harvest season than they do for the rest of the year. Workers may be able to play on this in seasons of peak labour demand, in that they may be able to negotiate terms that would not be available in lean seasons. Growers' anxieties can be heightened for outdoor crop harvests by the unreliability of nature, for example a rainstorm between the cutting and storing away of the crop. Thus, in agriculture, as in other industries, there is mutual dependency, albeit unequal, between workers and their employers.

Workers' agency and capitalist accumulation in agriculture

A more nuanced picture of labour–capital relations in agriculture would highlight not only workers' agency but how workers' interests change over the life-course. For example, involvement in hard manual work away from home may be undertaken for adventure at one stage of life, and out of extreme poverty and a need or desire for greater earnings at another. Later in life physical, bodily limitations may necessitate seeking lower paid but secure work nearer home, perhaps involving a long-term commitment to a particular employer.[33] Brass, wrongly in my view, includes such voluntary ties in his definition of bonded labour.[34] There is also a cultural logic to work-seeking.[35] The meaning of work changes according to who sees one doing it, so that doing work considered degrading near home may be more problematic than doing the same work away from home. Moreover, the wage labour relation itself, involving having to acquiesce to the requirements of a manager/employer is considered by many workers to be demeaning compared with working on one's own account.[36] Individually as well as collectively, workers as knowing actors may seek ways to further such interests.

Lerche rightly concludes that discussions of unfreedom in labour relations 'need to move away from unhelpful dichotomies and acknowledge the fluidity of actually occurring levels of unfreedom'.[37] As we have seen, this fluidity arises in part from two important interrelated areas which GAAFL does not explore: the agency of workers and the contingency of power relations in the employment of migrant workers in agriculture. However, looked at from a more macro-scale, the report also misses the opportunity to analyse the role of relations between fractions of capital, and their respective relations to the state, in producing unfree labour relations.

Just because capitalism is relatively slow to develop in agricultural *production*, because of the links of that production to nature, the relatively slower turnover time of capital in agriculture, and the mismatch of production time and labour,[38] this does not mean that there is no scope of capital accumulation in and through agriculture. In fact, as has been shown in the case of Californian agriculture, the obstacles to capitalist accumulation in production can force capital to innovate. For example, large profits may be made by banks through loans for production. Retailers and others involved in marketing may appropriate profits from farmers.[39] Value may be added through processing and/or packaging to create a niche product with little additional return to growers. In their struggles over the surplus, fractions of capital seeking to accumulate through agriculture may have opposing interests. There may be conflicts of interests, for example between larger- and smaller-scale growers, with the former better disposed towards quality standards imposed by processors, wholesalers or retailers.

The discursive directing of attention away from actually existing labour–capital relations and their connections with particular modes of capital accumulation towards a safer (for the tripartite ILO), residualised, 'forced labour' is a *de facto* intervention in what are often fraught political contests.

Rural capitalisms and temporary migrant workers

In what follows I will draw on two such contests, in West Bengal (India) and in the UK. In both cases temporary migrant workers (including seasonal migrants) are vital to capitalist accumulation through agriculture. To understand these accumulation processes, it is necessary to take account of the regulatory role of the state, its relations with different fractions of capital, and relations between those fractions. In each case, when considered at the scale of the individual seasonally migrant worker, capital does not have absolute power. There are spaces of negotiability.

The two cases taken together also illustrate the importance of understanding the contingency of capital–labour relations in broader sets of power relations involving the state, which is 'omnipresent in the countryside'.[40] State regulation, together with the workings of markets for agricultural outputs, underpins production relations in agricultural workplaces. As we shall see, this includes state regulation of land-ownership, of the relation between traders and producers, of migration, and through tie-ups with companies that lend some credence to Harvey's contention that the increased returns to capital relative to labour in the last quarter of the 20th century emerged out of class action by elites (including the use of a discourse of the inevitability of globalisation) to gain power and influence over state executives.[41] In both examples the governments concerned were, nominally at least, governments of the left.

West Bengal

Collaborative research with five colleagues in West Bengal in 1999 and 2000 revealed the specificity of agrarian capitalism within a particular region, in this case imagined as the intensively cultivated 'rice bowl' of the central southern part of the state centered on Barddhaman District. Here relatively small-scale 'peasant' capitalists competed with each other for seasonal harvest workers, making for a relatively high degree of negotiability of labour arrangements.[42] This can be contrasted with the imposition of conditions of work by colluding sugar producers in Gujarat in Western India, who tied workers in through labour contractors and their use of dependency and debt.[43] In both cases there was a reliance on migrant workers. However, the contrast between them again gives the lie to any standard 'model' of bonded migrant labour in Indian agriculture, such as that evoked in the ILO report.

Spaces of negotiability were expressed by workers in West Bengal, where, together with colleagues, I studied the way workers viewed the deals they made with prospective employers at bus stands and roadside labour market places. One worker interviewed more recently in Murshidabad District made plain the ways in which certain kinds of work arrangements were sought out, and others avoided. The power to shape the arrangement into which one entered varied according to the acuteness of need for a job, and urgency with which the prospective employer needed to harvest, both of which were related to seasonality.

> Sometimes I thought from the next time, before I migrate I would settle the wage, but in vain. When we are in dire need we lose our bargaining power ... [However we refuse to] include threshing in our [harvesting] contract. Suppose after cutting and binding, paddy is left in the field. Suppose it started raining. Then it would not be possible to bring the paddy to the yard and thresh it. So if we include threshing in the contract we cannot go elsewhere ... After cutting and binding, if we see that the weather is favourable for threshing then again we go for a separate contract for threshing. (young migrant man, 12 October 2005)[44]

The Communist Party of India (Marxist) (CPI(M)) came to power in 1977 at the head of a coalition Left Front Government and is still in power at the time of writing 31 years later. The CPI(M)-led regime oversaw a boom period in rice production in the 1980s, with a dramatic shift from stagnation to rapid growth, the causes of which have long been disputed.[45] However, there was no doubting the commitment of the CPI(M) to putting vigour into the ongoing programme of redistributing land to landless people, enforcing the tenancy rights of sharecroppers, and implementing local democratisation through the *panchayats*. Each of these measures risked causing conflict between different rural classes and, in order to work against this, the rhetoric of the CPI(M) and its peasant organisation the Krishak Sabha, stressed the need for 'peasant unity'. Peasant unity was a scalar construction, indeed an important one, in trying to forge a cross-class alliance between peasant capitalist bosses and wage workers in the countryside against the former large-scale landowners. The invocation of the scale of the rural within the state worked well electorally for the CPI(M), helping it to channel discontent away from the state government towards the government at the centre and international forces.[46]

Scalar representations and the acquisition of agricultural land by large-scale industry.

However, there has been a change in emphasis in recent times, with a move in party statements away from peasant unity (at the scale of the West Bengal countryside) towards the importance of large-scale industrialisation at the scale of West Bengal as a whole. It is the view of CPI(M) leaders that this should include the location of large-scale industries in rural areas. In 2007 the Chief Minister of West Bengal, Buddhadeb Bhattacharya, released a statement justifying the state government's policy of acquiring farmland for use as industrial sites by large corporations. 'It is incumbent on us to move ahead, otherwise there would be the end of history. The process of economic development evolves from agriculture to industry. The journey is from villages to cities . . . For setting up new industries West Bengal needs more land.'[47] This change of scale, emphasising the interests of West Bengal as a whole over those of the peasantry, has been used to justify the compulsory purchase of agricultural land at Singur in Hugli District to make it available to large-scale industrial capital in the form of a new factory to produce Tata Nano cars. According to one commentator, 'it is strange to .nd the government reversing its role and acting as a broker on behalf of the industry'.[48] The intense debates over this new policy and strong local-level resistance spilt over into a series of clashes in which dozens of people died in 2007, many of them at the hands of the police at another site which was under consideration as the location for a new chemical hub, Nandigram in Medinipur District.[49]

Opposition to this new 'Chinese model' of industrialisation has focused on the rights of 'local' peasant farmers, and on the insecure and demeaning jobs in site construction that were made available to some long-term residents at Singur. There has been almost no mention of the reliance of seasonal migrant workers on work in transplanting and harvesting rice in Singur, which has vastly reduced in extent. Now 'outsiders' to the state are accused by the CPI(M) of stirring up trouble over industrialisation, a strategy involving the political use of scale to delegitimise protest against the land acquisition process.

How much negotiability will remain for temporary migrants and other workers in food production as large-scale capital is increasingly relied on in the countryside remains to be seen. Beyond Special Economic Zones the Indian government has now allowed the operation of multiple supermarket retailers and, encouraged by, among others, the British government, has begun to allow foreign capital some involvement in retailing food.[50] In her recent study of markets for agricultural produce in West Bengal, Barbara Harriss-White noted the state government's move towards the involvement of 'a much larger fraction of agri-business' in agro-commerce in the state than existed in the first three decades of the CPI(M)-led regime. This was likely to be in the interests both of the businesses concerned and the state, through workers being employed outside the remit of state regulation.

> The evidence in this book shows that market and environmental risks may be shifted onto independent out-workers, homeworkers or unprotected wage labour. Costs may be reduced by avoiding overheads, abandoning or never meeting employers' obligations, undercutting legal wage floors ... New kinds of low-cost labour may be incorporated, or old forms of low-cost labour may be re-incorporated (eg rural, female and child labour, and migrant workers). The labour process is controlled by avoiding the creation of conditions where it might be organized in unions through which it might grasp rights and exert some countervailing power.[51]

Jan Breman showed that when producer capital operates as a collusive block, as it did in the sugar industry of south Gujarat, where farmers had organised themselves into large processing co-operatives, workers had less room for manoeuvre.[52] In the UK case study that follows, oligopsonistic retailer capital has, with the help of the state, achieved a dominant position in relation to its suppliers in ways which have altered employment relations and created a demand for temporary international migrant workers. Because it does not make connections between different forms of capitalism and the relative power of seasonal migrant workers, the ILO report does not alert readers to the ways in which changing relations between agricultural growers and their markets in West Bengal may lead to more exploitative labour relations in the countryside.

UK

State involvement in West Bengal in the compulsory purchase of agricultural land in order to sell it on cheaply suggests that relations between fractions of capital—in this case large-scale industrial capital and peasant capitalists—are shaped by relations between capital and the state. In *A Brief History of Neo-Liberalism*, David Harvey argues that there have been:

> important structural changes in the nature of governance ... Businesses and corporations not only collaborate intimately with state actors but even acquire a strong role in writing legislation, determining public policies, and setting regulatory frameworks (which are mainly advantageous to themselves).

> Patterns of negotiation arise that incorporate business and sometimes professional interests into governance through close and sometimes secretive consultations.[53]

I have experienced the power of such relations first hand in the dissemination of research. In reporting on research work commissioned by the UK Department of Environment, Food and Rural Affairs (DEFRA) on temporary working in UK agriculture and horticulture, a research team I was part of was instructed to tone down parts of the draft which might have been considered to cast supermarkets in a negative light. The main bone of contention was our repeating details from the appendices of the Competition Commission report on supermarkets' relations with their suppliers that had been published in 2000. The government had never acted effectively to regulate supermarket–supplier relations which, I have argued elsewhere, have played an important role in the intensification of workplace regimes.[54]

The UK has a £2 billion horticulture industry primarily producing for the domestic market, and reliant on international migrant workers for its labour-intensive processes.[55] At the national level, horticultural growers are squeezed by the concentrated monopoly power of their main customers, the large retailers. The biggest four supermarkets between them account of three-quarters of UK retailing. So there are conflicts of interest between fractions of capital in the food supply chain.

Moreover, supermarket capital is interwoven with the workings of the British state. In her book *Not On the Label*, Felicity Lawrence has alleged that, following the Competition Commission report of 2000, tens of millions of pounds were spent lobbying against effective statutory regulation of super-market–supplier relations. She has also revealed the closeness of relations between top board members of Tescos and the then prime minister's office, as well as the cosy and informal welcome for Wal-Mart at the same level of government when it sought to buy then UK-owned supermarket Asda.[56]

Yet the state is not monolithic and can have protective effects for workers, whether or not those effects were originally intended. It does not always or only work in the interests of capital. In mid-20th century California it was the state, in the form of the La Fayette committee, which found for workers and against the interests of agrarian capital.[57] The opening of the UK labour market to the nationals of eight eastern European countries that acceded to the EU in May 2004 also had protective outcomes, as it enabled many workers, who were already resident and working without the legal right to do so, to improve their status and conditions. The UK Gangmaster (Licensing) Act is an example of a measure brought in by the state with the intention of protecting workers from abusive employment practices by labour-contracting intermediaries, known as gangmasters. The new licensing regime only opera-tes in agriculture and closely-related sectors. [58] Its extension to other sectors has been keenly opposed by parts of the UK government, which attributed 10 years of economic prosperity to its 'flexible' labour-market policy.

Supermarkets, mindful of their deteriorating public image following revelations of illegal practices by gangmasters in their supply chains, played a key role in supporting gangmaster licensing. However, the state in the UK has not so far been willing effectively to curb supermarket buyer power in relation to that other fraction of capital: agricultural and horticultural growers.[59] This is, in part at least, because the buying practices of large retailers have been perceived as helpful for meeting inflation targets.[60] Yet temporary migrant workers have in the past decade and a half become the major workforce in the sector,[61] and their living and working conditions have been found in some circumstances to fit the definition of forced labour: working under menace of a penalty and not being able to leave the job.[62] This was brought out vividly in Nick Broomfield's 2007 film, *Ghosts*, about the journeys, living and working experiences of the 23 Chinese cockle-pickers who drowned after being stranded by the fast-rising tides at Morecambe Bay in Lancashire in February 2004.

However, *Ghosts* also showed employment situations involving temporary migrant workers in food production which did not involve forced labour practices. Its apple harvest sequence, for example, portrayed the pressure growers' businesses were under because of supermarket power and showed the possibility for intimate and good-humoured relations to develop between a small-scale grower and group of temporary harvesters. Collaborative research with colleagues at Oxford University's Centre on Migration, Policy and Society (COMPAS), involving interviews with workers and growers as well as large-scale surveys, found evidence that migrant workers were often making trade-offs between short-term arduous work with little or no negotiability over workplace conditions, and longer-term goals such as working outside the sector or returning home with cash savings.[63] Moreover, for some, narratives of negotiability at workplaces came across too. For example, one temporary migrant worker from Lithuania told me in August 2004:

> it makes a big difference if you can speak English. If you talk English with people they will be happy. They will say morning and bye. You get better jobs. My boyfriend understands English—it is another thing to speak it [as I do]. He gets better jobs because of me. Some people have to work outside in the rain. At the break they are shivering. It is not a pleasure. But me and my boyfriend have been undercover in the rain.[64]

Conclusion

In the contemporary period of globalisation, the employment of migrant workers in agriculture on a seasonal or temporary basis may serve multiple interests simultaneously. Analysed at the level of the individual employer–worker relationship, it is possible to see how the interests of an individual worker may lie in an arrangement involving some degree of obligation to a particular employer. Moreover, workers may identify spaces of negotiability that make critical differences to the experience of working away in agriculture, even when, seen from a distance, they may seem to have no room for agency at all. Capital is not monolithic, and contains its own contradictory interests. The state at different levels—local, national and international—is a potential enabler and, at the same time, discipliner of capital. The state has discursive as well as material power. It lies within the means of the state to provide some protection for workers from the vulnerability associated with undocumented status, poverty and workplace abuse.

Reading the ILO report, for all its good intentions, forces me to question what purpose is served by lumping together forced labour, slavery and slavery-like conditions within such a broad continuum. The report explicitly subsumes large swathes of labour relations which contain elements of freedom as well as unfreedom, degrees of manoeuvrability, negotiation and contestation. Like the recent Joseph Rowntree Foundation report on modern slavery in the UK, the discourse of slavery and forced labour slips in too easily, while the larger, more complex causal apparatuses lying behind unfree labour relations hardly receive any analytical attention.

The report obscures actually existing power relations and contestations across different scales with multidirectional influences. Moreover, the language of 'victims' risks a descent into what Puwar has termed a 'politics of sympathy'.[65] There are of course politics in the production of reports of this kind. Member governments have seats on the ILO board and it was alleged by the *Guardian* in early 2005 that the UK board member strongly objected to the UK report on Forced Labour, because it drew attention to the relation between labour market deregulation and increasing employment abuse.[66]

By subsuming such a wide range of employment situations under the concept of forced labour exacted by 'private agents' for 'economic exploitation', GAAFL mistakenly includes under this umbrella situations which are not necessarily understood by workers themselves in that way. Moreover, by directing attention to the 'private agents' themselves, GAAFL seems to draw a veil over the role of contemporary forms of capitalism and their accommodation with states to produce both a lack of freedom and insecurity. States are rightly encouraged to tighten the means of prosecuting unscrupulous employers, but no space is given to discussion of the potential for state regulation of the market relations through which large-scale capital may be reshaping the conditions under which employment takes place. GAAFL also risks reducing the discursive space for programmes of critical analysis and action that can take into account the different and sometimes contradictory sets of interests that may need to be brought together at various scales to challenge the disempowering of workers in relation to capital.[67]

Notes

Thanks to Ronaldo Munck, Geert de Neve, Abdur Rafique, Kirat Randhawa, Janet Seeley and Pritam Singh for discussions about and/or comments on an earlier draft; to Bridget Anderson for an earlier collaboration on forced labour, ideas from which will have undoubtedly found their way into this article; to Andrew Herod and Jane Wills for access to their forthcoming papers; to participants in the panel on Migrant Workers: Geographical Perspectives at the Association of American Geographers (AAG) in April 2007 and at the seminar on Labour in the Global Political Economy at the University of Sussex in May 2007 for very helpful discussions, and to the respective pairs of organisers Jon May and Linda McDowell, and Kevin Gray and Jan Selby. I am also grateful to the British Academy for a conference attendance grant, which enabled me to travel to the AAG, and to the Development Research Centre on Migration,

Globalisation and Poverty for funding some of the research on which the paper draws. None of them are responsible for the views expressed here, nor for any errors.

1 J Lerche, 'A global alliance against forced labour? Unfree labour, neo-liberal globalization and the International Labour Organisation', *Journal of Agrarian Change*, 7 (4), 2007, pp 425–452.

2 D Massey, *Spatial Divisions of Labour: Social Relations and the Geography of Production*, Basingstoke: Macmillan, 1995.

3 G Hart, *Disabling Globalisation: Places of Power in Post-apartheid South Africa*, Berkeley, CA: University of California Press, 2002; JK Gibson-Graham, *A Post-capitalist Politics*, Minneapolis, MN: University of Minnesota Press, 2006; and P Dicken, *Global Shift: Mapping the Changing Contours of the World Economy*, London: Sage, 2007.

4 K Datta, C McIlwaine, Y Evans, J Herbert, J May & J Wills, 'From coping strategies to tactics: London's low-pay economy and migrant labour', *British Journal of Industrial Relations*, 45 (2), 2007, pp 404–432.

5 C Smith, 'The double indeterminacy of labour power: labour effort and labour mobility', *Work, Employment and Society*, 20 (2), 2006, pp 389–402.

6 DC Lier, 'Places of work, scales of organising: a review of labour geography', *Geography Compass*, 1 (4), 2007, pp 814–833.

7 Lerche, 'A global alliance against forced labour?', pp 430–431.

8 N Smith, *Uneven Development: Nature, Capital and the Production of Space*, Oxford: Blackwell, 1984; P Taylor, 'A materialist framework for political geography', *Transactions of the Institute of British Geographers*, 7, 1981, pp15–34; A Herod, 'Scale: the local and the global', in S Holloway, S Rice, G Valentine & N Clifford, *Key Concepts in Geography*, London: Sage (second edition), forthcoming; D Mitchell, 'Localist ideology, large-scale production and agricultural labor's geography of resistance in 1930s California', in Mitchell, *Organising the Landscape: Geographical Perspectives on Labor Unionism*, Minneapolis, MN: University of Minnesota Press, 1998, pp159–194; R Silvey, 'Power, difference and mobility: feminist advances in migration studies', *Progress in Human Geography*, 28 (4), 2004, pp 490–506; and S Marston, JP Jones & K Woodward, 'Human geography without scale', *Transactions of the Institute of British Geographers*, 30 (4), 2005, pp 416–432.

9 G Hart, *Disabling Globalisation*; and JK Gibson-Graham, 'Beyond the global versus local: economic politics outside the binary frame, in A Herod & M Wright (eds), *Geographies of Power: Placing Scale*, Oxford: Blackwell, 2002, pp 25–60.

10 Mitchell, 'Localist ideology, large-scale production and agricultural labor's geography of resistance in 1930s California'.

11 Marston *et al*, 'Without scale'.

12 *Ibid*, p 427.

13 H Leitner & B Miller, 'Scale and the limitations of ontological debate: a commentary on Marston, Jones and Woodward', *Transactions of the Institute of British Geographers*, 32, 2007, pp 116–125.

14 Lier, 'Places of work, scales of organising'.

15 Leitner & Miller, 'Scale and the limitations of ontological debate', p 122.

16 Silvey, 'Power, difference and mobility'.

17 Herod, 'Scale'.

18 D Mitchell, *The Lie of the Land: Migrant Workers and the California Landscape*, Minneapolis, MN: University of Minnesota Press, 1996; and K Morgan, T Marsden & J Murdoch, *Worlds of Food: Place, Power and Provenance in the Food Chain*, Oxford: Oxford University Press, 2006.

19 J Frances, S Barrientos & B Rogaly, *Temporary Workers in UK Agriculture and Horticulture*, Framlingham, UK: Precision Prospecting for DEFRA, 2005.

20 ILO, Forced Labour Convention, 1930, Article 2(1), cited in ILO, *A Global Alliance Against Forced Labour* (GAAFL), Geneva: ILO, 2005, p 5.

21 GAAFL, p 8.

22 G Craig, A Gaus, M Wilkinson, K Skrivankova & A McQuade, *Contemporary Slavery in the UK: Overview and Key Issues—Findings*, York: Joseph Rowntree Foundation, 2007, p 3, emphasis added.

23 This differs from Brass' conceptualisation. For Brass debt bondage is a quintessential form of continuing unfreedom in capitalist agriculture. Labour bonded by debt is unfree, even if there has been a cash advance–labour service tie which carries no explicit interest, is for a limited duration, and involves migrant workers. Forced labour, however, is something exacted by the state. T Brass, *Towards a Comparative Political Economy of Unfree Labour: Case Studies and Debates*, London: Frank Cass, 1999.

24 A Sharma, 'Agrarian relations and socio-economic change in Bihar', *Economic and Political Weekly*, 40 (10), 2005, pp 960–972.

25 *Ibid*, p 970.

26 G Rodgers & J Rodgers, *Semi-feudalism meets the Market: A Report from Purnia*, New Delhi: Institute for Human Development Working Paper, 2000, p 16.

27 The same is true of capitalism and slavery. As Graeber has shown, depending on how these are conceptualised, capitalism itself can be seen as slavery. D Graeber, 'Turning modes of production

214

inside out: or why capitalism is a transformation of slavery', *Critique of Anthropology*, 26 (1), 2006, pp 61–85.

28 Rodgers and Rodgers do not, however, present ethnographic data on the degree to which women have bought into male labour migration as a means of increasing *household* income.

29 V Lenin, *The Development of Capitalism in Russia: Collected Works*, Vol 3, Moscow: Progress Publishers, 1964, pp 240–254. See also B Rogaly, 'Dangerous liaisons? Seasonal migration and agrarian change in West Bengal', in B Rogaly, B Harriss-White & S Bose (eds), *Sonar Bangla? Agricultural Growth and Agrarian Change in West Bengal and Bangladesh*, New Delhi/London/Thousand Oaks: Sage, 1999, pp 357–380.

30 The two pieces cited are focused on Punjab as a destination area for bonded labourers from Bihar. M. Singh, 'Bonded migrant labour in Punjab agriculture', *Economic and Political Weekly*, 15 March 1997; and J Singh, 'Incidence and magnitude of bonded labour in Punjab', in M Singh & K Gopal Iyer (eds), *Migrant Labour and Human Rights in India*, New Delhi: Kanishka Publishers, 2003, pp 50–77. Interestingly both M Singh and K Gopal Iyer, co-editors of the book in which J Singh's chapter appears, are among the six people acknowledged as providing productive intellectual exchanges by Tom Brass in his major book on unfree labour, which elaborates the view that any form of prior payment to workers involving a future commitment to employment should be regarded as bonded labour.

31 A Herod, 'The production of scale in United States labour relations', *Area*, 23 (1), 1991, pp 82–88; and W Larner, 'A brief history of neoliberalism', *Economic Geography*, 82 (4), 2006, pp 449–451.

32 Smith, *Uneven Development*; and M Mann, *Workers on the Move: the Sociology of Relocation*, Cambridge: Cambridge University Press, 1973.

33 B Rogaly, 'Who goes? Who stays back? Seasonal migration and staying put among seasonal migrant workers in West Bengal, India', *Journal of International Development*, 15 (5), 2003, pp 623–632.

34 Brass, *Towards a Comparative Political Economy of Unfree Labour*, p 28.

35 V Gidwani, 'The cultural logic of work: explaining labour deployment and piece rate contracts in Matar Taluka, Gujarat—Parts 1 and 2', *Journal of Development Studies*, 38 (2), 2002, pp 57–74; H Bauder, *Labor Movement: How Migration Regulates Labor Markets*, New York: Oxford University Press, 2006; and A Rafique, D Massey & B Rogaly, 'Migration for hard work: a reluctant livelihood strategy for poor households in West Bengal, India', Development Research Centre on Migration, Globalisation and Poverty, Working Paper T17, 2006.

36 Gidwani, 'The cultural logic of work'; and Graeber, 'Turning modes of production inside out'.

37 Lerche, 'A global alliance against forced labour?', p 447.

38 S Mann, *Agrarian Capitalism in Theory and Practice*, Chapel Hill, NC: University of North Carolina Press, 1990.

39 J Guthman, *Agrarian Dreams: The Paradox of Organic Farming in California*, Berkeley, CA: University of California Press, 2004; and G Henderson, *California and the Fictions of Capital*, Philadelphia, PA: Temple University Press, 1998.

40 C Hahamovitch & R Halpern, 'Not a "sack of potatoes": why labor historians need to take agriculture seriously', *International Labor and Working-Class History*, 65, 2004, pp 3–10.

41 D Harvey, *A Brief History of Neoliberalism*, Oxford: Oxford University Press, 2005.

42 B Rogaly, D Coppard, A Rafique, K Rana, A Sengupta & J Biswas, 'Seasonal migration and welfare/illfare in eastern India: a social analysis', *Journal of Development Studies*, 38 (5), 2002, pp 89–115.

43 J Breman, '"Even dogs are better off": the ongoing battle between capital and labour in the cane fields of Gujarat', *Journal of Peasant Studies*, 17 (4), 1990, pp 546–608.

44 This interview took place as part of the project on Social Protection by and for Temporary Work Migrants in Bangladesh and West Bengal, which I directed along with Dr Janet Seeley of the University of East Anglia (funded by the Development Research Centre on Migration, Globalisation and Poverty).

45 B Rogaly, B Harriss-White & S Bose, 'Introduction: *Sonar Bangla?* Agricultural growth and agrarian change in West Bengal and Bangladesh', in Rogaly *et al*, *Sonar Bangla?*

46 B Rogaly, 'Containing conflict and reaping votes: management of rural labour relations in West Bengal', *Economic and Political Weekly*, 33 (42–43), 1998, pp 2729–2739.

47 Buddhadeb Bhattacharya, 'We cannot fail people's expectations', Public letter to Sumit Sarkar in response to Professor Sarkar's statement on conflicts over the acquisition the agricultural land for large-scale industry, 11 January 2007. More recently, West Bengal's Chief Minister has claimed that industrial growth does not need the involvement of the state except to ensure proper social responsibility. 'There is no need for any political interference in the process of industrialisation', cited in S Banerjee, 'Goodbye socialism', *Economic and Political Weekly*, 26 January 2008, p13. The national secretary of the CPI(M), Prakash Karat, reinforced the party's emphasis on large-scale units: 'If some argue that small and medium industries are sufficient, the CPI(M) does not agree. Large-scale units, particularly in manufacturing, are necessary'. *People's Democracy*, New Delhi, 24 March 2007.

48 EAS Sarma, 'Help the rich, hurt the poor: case of Special Economic Zones', *Economic and Political Weekly*, 26 May 2007, p 1901.

49 In one of the worst incidents, on 14 March 2007 at Nandigram, 14 people were killed and 162 people were injured when police fired on a crowd. Data extracted from West Bengal High Court Order in AST 205, 2007.

50 BBC News, 'Countdown to India's retail revolution', at http://news.bbc.co.uk/go/pr/fr/-/2/hi/business/4662642.stm, accessed 29 February 2008; and Mark Milner, 'UK urges India to welcome in supermarkets', *Guardian*, 15 November 2005. Similarly, two years earlier, the US Consulate-General had urged West Bengal to 'realize' its 'potential' by allowing 'groundbreaking investments' by US food processing companies and, following a report by McKinsey on the prospects for agribusiness in the state, accelerating moves towards reorganising parts of agriculture around contract farming. 'The shift in rural economic/political relations is still underway and it has encountered some resistance. That is natural, since all change involves some dislocation. But once the advantages have become clear, the prospects will open up for floriculture, horticulture, and animal husbandry. As the food processing industry grows, commercial possibilities will open up in areas like cold chain and logistics management.' Speech delivered by US Consul General George N Sibley to the Indo-American Chamber of Commerce, Kolkata, 11 December 2003, at http://calcutta.usconsulate.gov/121103.html, accessed 29 February 2008.

51 Barbara Harriss-White, *Rural Commercial Capital: Agricultural Markets in West Bengal*, New Delhi: Oxford University Press, 2008, pp 317–318.

52 Breman, '"Even dogs are better off"'.

53 Harvey, *A Brief History of Neoliberalism*, pp 76–77.

54 B Rogaly, 'Intensification of work-place regimes in British horticulture: the role of migrant workers', *Population, Space and Place*, forthcoming.

55 Promar International, 'The future of UK horticulture', UK National Horticulture Forum, 2006.

56 Felicity Lawrence, *Not on the Label*, London: Penguin, 2004.

57 Carey McWilliams, *Ill Fares the Land: Migrants and Migratory Labour in the United States*, London: Faber and Faber, 1945.

58 A Geddes, S Scott & K B Nielsen, 'Gangmasters Licensing Authority evaluation study: baseline report', Nottingham: Gangmasters Licensing Authority, 2007; and S Scott, A Geddes, K B Nielsen & P Brindley, 'Gangmasters Licensing Authority annual review', Nottingham: Gangmasters Licensing Authority, 2007. According to the authors of these studies, the legislation applies to roughly 10% of temporary agency workers in the UK.

59 Even the regulatory measures announced following the conclusion of the latest Competition Commission report on supermarket–supplier relations released on 15 February 2008 lacked teeth. See http://news.bbc.co.uk/2/shared/bsp/hi/pdfs/15_02_2008_Supply_Chain_Remedies%20.pdf, accessed 29 February 2008.

60 Mervyn King, Governor of the Bank of England, Speech at the Eden Project, Cornwall, 12 October 2004, available at http://www.bankofengland.co.uk/publications/speeches/2004/speech229.pdf, accessed 29 April 2008.

61 Audit Commission, *Crossing Borders: Responding to the Local Challenges of Migrant Workers*, London: Audit Commission, 2007.

62 B Anderson & B Rogaly, *Forced Labour and Migration to the UK*, London: Trades Union Congress, 2005.

63 B Anderson, M Ruhs, B Rogaly & S Spencer, *Fair Enough? Central and East European Migrants in low-wage Employment in the UK*, York: Joseph Rowntree Foundation, 2006.

64 Rogaly, forthcoming.

65 N Puwar, 'Speaking positions in global politics', *Multitudes*, 2004, available at http://multitudes.samizdat.net/article1321.html.

66 H Pai, 'Damning report on migrants delayed as government fears poll backlash', *Guardian*, 3 February 2005, at http://www.guardian.co.uk/politics/2005/feb/03/immigrationasylumandrefugees.immigrationandasylum.

67 Examples of such challenges include actions by contract cleaners in London, and cross-sectoral action by undocumented migrant workers in the USA. J Wills, 'Making class politics possible: organising contract cleaners in London', *International Journal for Urban and Regional Research*, forthcoming; and W Robinson, '"Aqui estamos y no nos vamos!" Global capital and immigrant rights', *Race and Class*, 48 (2), 2006, pp 77–91.

Towards a Theory of Illegal Migration: historical and structural components

MARTIN BALDWIN-EDWARDS

Illegal migration[1]— also known as clandestine, undocumented or irregular migration—appears frequently in contemporary popular and political discourses; yet there is relatively little theoretical literature on the phenomenon.[2] Nearly all academic and other discussions of the topic take as axiomatic that illegal migration is a 'problem', without pausing to question its rapid rise to prominence and the underlying issues that may be involved. It is the aim of this paper to search a little deeper into the historical and structural factors germane to the phenomenon: little attention will be paid to detailed empirical matters, since such information is available elsewhere.[3] I start with some definitional issues then, taking an overview of the history of migration controls, I proceed to a discussion of the complex structural factors that have contributed to the emergence of illegal migration as a putative 'crisis' in the developed world.

The nature of illegal migration

At one level, illegal migration is simple to define: it is migration that occurs outside of the legal–institutional frameworks established by states. It applies equally to emigration and immigration, although the right to leave one's country is now enshrined in international law as an asymmetrical principle (without the corresponding right to enter another).[4] Thus illegal migration is in the same class of problem as all non-legitimised private economic activities occurring across national territorial boundaries. It bears analogy with illegal flows of capital in the early 20th century, and with the smuggling of goods, which is a centuries-old activity and still flourishing.

Papademetriou identifies four common forms of illegal migration—namely, unauthorised entry, fraudulent entry (ie with false documents), visa overstaying, and violation of the terms and conditions of a visa.[5] Even these four broad categories are insufficient to cover all major aspects of illegal migration. Other types of illegal migrant are: rejected asylum seekers who are required to leave, but instead 'disappear' (this has been a major problem in Germany, in particular); formerly legal residents who are unable to renew their permits (this has been a massive problem in southern Europe); and those who are in technical violation of conditions of the visa or permit—for example, a change of employment that has not been authorised by the state. Many of these categories can be viewed as the result of excessive bureaucracy and over-management of protected labour markets, and perhaps are more accurately defined as illegal employment. To facilitate an historical overview, I focus principally on the four main categories of illegal migration listed above.

A brief history of migration controls

Recent advocates of open borders tend to view migration controls as a phenomenon of the 20th century:[6] this could hardly be further from the truth. Feudalism had exercised absolute control over its subjects. In Great Britain, for example, a 1662 Act of Elizabeth I established parish serfdom, which restricted movement even within the country. This was partially repealed in 1795, to be followed by the 1800 Act of Union which created common citizenship of the Irish in the UK and thus permitted mass migration of the Irish poor.[7] Similar restrictions on free movement had existed in the German lands since 1548, although in 1807 the Prussian peasantry were freed of hereditary servitude and other controls, paving the way towards a free market in labour.[8] The two guiding principles of the feudal period appear to be, at the local level, the retention of skilled workers (with restrictions on emigration) and restrictions on entry, to avoid mobility of the poor.

The great free trade debate was in full flow from the 1820s, especially in the UK, and led ultimately to the repeal in that country of the Corn Laws in 1846 and the beginning of a period of mass migrations, trade surge and large capital flows.[9] By 1856 the German *Länder* were still divided over the issue of granting the right of emigration, with two-thirds insisting on authorisation permits for would-be emigrants. However, relaxation of controls occurred over the next few years, both between German lands (including Holland) and also through reciprocal agreements with other European countries such as England, France, Belgium and the Scandinavian states.[10] By 1862 Switzerland, too, had abolished both entry and exit controls.

Yet the globalisation trend was neither universal nor sustained, and from 1870 onwards the USA, Canada, Australia, Argentina and Brazil gradually started to restrict immigration.[11] This culminated in the USA in a 1918 Act of Congress restricting both emigration and immigration, amended in 1919 to cover only immigration.[12] The knock-on effect was massive, since the USA was a major country of destination, and the 1920s saw almost universal adoption of immigration restrictions.[13] Britain, which had started its restrictionism as early as 1905 for fear of Jewish immigration from Eastern Europe, by 1930 had a foreign population of only 1%, even counting its Irish migrants. Simultaneous with the growing immigration restrictions of the interwar period, authoritarian regimes in the USSR, Germany, Italy, Spain and Portugal (among others) even resurrected emigration controls.[14]

Thus, by the eve of World War II, most countries of the world had come full circle with their management of migration—from feudal absolute restrictionism, through a short period of relatively free movement of labour, capital and goods in the late 19th century, back to a de-globalisation period of heavily-restricted mobility of trade, people and capital. However, the 20th century saw one irrevocable change in the management of migration: this was the changed locus of control—away from the local level and now vested with the national state. Accompanying this shift of authority was an apparently greater capacity for enforcement, and the increasing utilisation of modern technologies and documentation.[15] Coupled with rising nationalism and the growth of the modern welfare state for 'our' citizens, this new role of the state was to provide one of the cornerstones of contemporary migration management.

The postwar settlement of 1945 and the rapid emergence of human rights protection systems, including the European Court of Human Rights, are generally considered to be the basis of the current regime. Certainly the Geneva Conventions of 1949 remain as the guiding principles for the protection of refugees and stateless persons, along with the right to apply for political asylum, although Skran sees interwar refugee policies as the practical origin of the policy.[16] With regard to labour migration, the International Labour Organisation (ILO) produced in 1949 a Convention as a framework of labour recruitment policy for countries to follow: currently ratified by 45 countries, it provided a basic set of good practices in a period of economic expansion and substantial guestworker recruitment in northern Europe.[17] The New World 'settler societies' (Australia, Canada and the USA) chose permanent immigration over labour migration, and broadly followed this approach until the late 1980s.[18] The so-called 'Golden Age' of the booming late 1950s and 1960s was a period of labour shortages for most of the developed world, and of clearly identified economic need for immigration: the type of immigration varied, according to historical, cultural and geographical parameters. For example, postcolonial countries like France, The Netherlands and the UK had large inflows of their colonial citizens; Germany, Austria, Switzerland and Belgium relied heavily on what they envisaged as temporary labour (*Gastarbeiter*), while the New World encouraged permanent migration. Southern Europe was at this time an exporter of labour—primarily to Northern Europe.

The oil shocks of 1973 mark a clear turning-point in the history of migration policy.[19] Northern European countries stopped recruitment of guestworkers, and tried to repatriate those already there (without success); southern European countries began their transition away from labour export, initially with return of their own workers and later, in the 1980s, with labour immigration from elsewhere; and the Middle East and some 'Asian Tigers' found themselves with capital abundance and a labour shortage, so they quickly developed harshly controlled temporary guestworker programmes. Douglas Massey and his colleagues identify several characteristics of the new world migration system.[20] First, most immigrants come from countries with limited capital, poor job creation rates, and abundant reserves of labour; the imbalance of labour supply and demand in the developing world is far worse than had occurred during European industrialisation. Secondly, immigration countries are far more capital-intensive and much less land-intensive than in the past: international migrants now fill marginal niches in highly segmented labour markets. Thirdly, this economic marginalisation of immigrants has resulted in a sociopolitical perception that immigrants are no longer needed—despite persistent demand for their services. The final characteristic posited is the existence of five migratory systems in the world—North America, Western Europe, Asia and the Pacific, the Gulf region, and the Southern Cone of South America. The specific countries of emigration feeding into these regions are shaped by historical ties, trade, politics and culture; however, they are predominantly poor and in the South.

The emergence of mass illegal migration

As long ago as 1978, Alejandro Portes was able to write about illegal migration of Mexicans into the USA 'not as a problem, but as a solution to the problem'.[21] He was referring to the inability, or unwillingness, of the US authorities to manage the country's labour market needs with an appropriate immigration policy. A similar mismatch between economic need and government policy could be observed across the Western world, and especially in Europe. It was as if the political discourse had become 'frozen' in 1974, such that the state had lost its capacity to respond to national labour shortages with an effective management of immigration. A popular consensus began to emerge that there was a 'crisis of immigration', although it was more a crisis of political reaction to immigrants and minorities than about the management of migration flows.[22] The 1980s saw several new and distinct characteristics of immigration into Europe. These included, from 1982 onwards, the emergence of unprecedentedly large numbers of asylum seekers; extensive family reunification; and the beginning of a trend of mass illegal immigration.[23] Along with miniscule numbers of recruited temporary guestworkers, these new immigrants filled the gaps in northern European labour markets.

The 1980s also saw the emergence of southern European countries as new countries of immigration and this caught governments unawares.[24] In the absence of immigration infrastructure, and with significant black economy activity, illegal immigration and immigrant participation in informal employment came to predominate throughout southern Europe.[25] Portugal, Spain, Italy and Greece entered into apparently endless processes of legalisation of illegal migrants and/or workers; typically, more than 50% of those legalised lapsed back into illegality (for a variety of reasons), and yet more illegal immigrants continued to arrive. For most of southern Europe, the majority of illegal immigrants actually entered legally but overstayed or broke their visa conditions;[26] in the case of Greece the land border with Albania meant that illegal entry was the primary mode of entering Greece subsequent to the collapse of the Albanian socialist regime in 1991.[27] By 2005 the estimated number of immigrants in Italy was 2.5 million, in Spain 4.8 million (11.1% of total population) and in Greece 1.15 million (10.3% of total population).[28]

The phenomenon of illegal migration, primarily of Mexicans, into the USA continued unabated and by 2006 there were an estimated 11 million illegal aliens working in the US economy.[29] Stable or growing stocks of illegal aliens were easily visible throughout the world,[30] despite increased policy measures to combat illegal migration coupled with regularisation programmes. A 2005 study for the Global Commission on International Migration cites various estimates of the extent of illegal migration globally, with a somewhat bewildering range from 2–4.5 million (International Centre for Migration Policy Development) to 30 million (Council of Europe) illegal border crossings per year.[31] Smuggling of migrants has emerged as a profitable global business and has also partially transmuted into 'trafficking' and exploitation.[32] The international growth of both commercial forms[33] led in 2000 to two UN Protocols being opened for signature. The trafficking Protocol has, as of May 2008, 117 signatories, of which 119 countries have ratified as state parties; there are 112 signatories and parties to the smuggling Protocol. Both protocols are appended to the United Nations Convention against Transnational Crime of 2000, which itself has 147 signatories and 143 parties, as of May 2008. The Convention and these two Protocols have been in force since 2004.[34]

The latest aspect of illegal migrations into Europe, while not actually so large in scale, has created significant problems for receiving countries: this consists of clandestine arrivals by sea, principally into Spain and Italy and, to a lesser extent, into Greece, Cyprus and Malta. Starting with small-scale smuggling into Spain and Italy in the early 1990s, the smuggling of African immigrants into southern Europe by boat had become a major humanitarian crisis by 2005, worsened over 2006 and subsequently affected the Eastern Mediterranean. Although the total number of (known) illegal arrivals by boat in the region has remained fairly small, the arrival of immigrants in poor condition on small islands such as Lampedusa (Italy), Fuerteventura (Spain, Canaries) or Samos (Greece) presents massive problems for local management of proportionately large numbers. Furthermore, deaths at sea are now commonplace, and have been estimated at over 10% of known arrivals.

Structural parameters of illegal migration in advanced capitalism

Determinants of emigration and source countries

Afolayan identifies the reasons for emigration as population growth and population density, economic vulnerability and debt, sociocultural issues, ecological disasters, social networking, government migration policies and regional economic integration.[35] In the specific case of Africa, Adepojou considers the determinants of emigration to be categorisable under the headings of labour force growth, economic decline and debt, ethno-political conflict and ecological deterioration. In this context, emigration should be seen as a survival strategy by individuals and families.[36]

The older literature on migration,[37] along with some contemporary demographic literature, tended to assume that population growth had a direct correlation with the propensity to migrate. In other words, a high birth rate would lead (with lag) to high emigration, whereas low population growth would not (or might require immigration). This approach to migration has now been abandoned in the mainstream literature, with adequate empirical evidence to show that globally there is zero correlation. For countries with high fertility rates, which is most of the developing world, what matters is the ability of their economies to absorb the new workforce. Employment creation, rather than simple population increases, will be the crucial determinant of future emigration pressures.

Recent scholarship is inclined to see (voluntary) international migration as a stage of development, indicating a transition from a very low level of development to an upper-lower income level. According to this view, migration stems not from underdevelopment but from development itself. Generally the world's main labour exporters are upper-lower to lower-middle income countries such as North Africa or the Philippines.[38] Olesen names this range of low–middle income and high emigration countries as the 'migration band', above which emigration tends to diminish.[39] He posits the explanation as the reduced differential in income levels between emigration and immigration countries (measured in US dollars at purchasing power parity), citing ratios from 1:3 to 1:4.5. In a recent challenge to the current orthodoxy, Lucas suggests that poor data on migration are partly responsible for this analysis. While conceding that some very low-income countries in sub-Saharan Africa will probably show increased emigration with economic development, he points out that many supposedly zero-migration countries are clearly high nett emigration countries. UN data for the 1990s show 31 (out of 72) countries with zero nett migration, including Kazakhstan, Estonia, Burkina Faso, Mali and Lesotho.[40]

Illegal migrants and labour markets in Europe and North America

Almost unnoticed, at least in popular discourse, the informal sector in advanced economies has emerged as a mechanism for achieving increased competitiveness in the context of relatively fixed high wage costs. Portes and his colleagues identify three forms of informality in advanced capitalism: these are labelled survival, dependent exploitation and growth.[41] 'Survival' is a subsistence strategy of the individual or household through direct production or market sale of goods or services. 'Dependent exploitation' identifies the strategy of increasing managerial flexibility and decreasing labour costs through informal hiring and subcontracting.

'Growth' is explicitly a strategy for capital accumulation by small firms, using connections, greater flexibility and lower costs. The 'survival' strategy is known to us from economic study of the developing countries; the latter two are specific to capitalism and have become increasingly important as deregulation of markets has proceeded across the European Union.

As Williams and Windebank point out, orthodox opinion has long assumed that economic development leads to a shift away from informal employment and toward formal employment: this they call the 'formalisation thesis'.[42] In recent times the opposite has been taking place. As industrialised societies exclude more and more of their population from formal full-time work, informal work has increased in importance. Furthermore, the relationship between the informal sector and the formal has become increasingly complex (as shown by Portes et al[43]) with heterogeneous incidence and variable strategies even within narrow market sectors.[44] There is also some evidence from France and Italy that more prosperous regions have much higher incidences of informal employment[45]—again, suggesting that the informal sector is an important structural component of advanced capitalism.

The relationship of illegal immigration (or illegal employment of lawfully present immigrants) to informal employment in Europe and the USA is identified as a crucial factor in the growth of pre-existing informal sectors, as well as for the stimulation of illegal migrant labour flows.[46] A recent study of informal employment across the EU notes that 'information is sparse ... research on this topic is carried out in very few countries ... few countries are concerned with the exact definition of undeclared work'.[47] Clearly, if a phenomenon is not recorded or identified as a problem, in political terms it does not represent a problem. This is in marked contrast to the clearly identified 'problem' of illegal migration. The EC study identifies several economic sectors as exhibiting high degrees of informal employment—most notably construction, followed by agriculture, hotels and restaurants, and personal and domestic services.[48] It is precisely these sectors in which illegal (as well as legal) immigrants are to be found.[49]

Labour markets in advanced countries have become increasingly segmented, with clear division into primary, secondary and informal labour segments. Over the last two decades, illegal immigrants have taken up positions predominantly in the informal and secondary sectors—regardless of their skill levels or work experiences.[50] This labour market segmentation, and its importance for immigrants, was identified as long ago as the 1970s by Piore:[51] its relevance has increased, rather than diminished, and this is particularly true for southern Europe, where immigrants tend to occupy complementary roles in the labour market. Thus both legal and illegal immigrants have facilitated the upward mobility of indigenous workers, with minimal impact on unemployment rates.[52] These trends are more likely to continue than to disappear, with the implication of future increased need for immigration in the context of demographic change in the developed world.

Contemporary immigration policies in North America and Europe

As was noted above, most of the immigration policy options have apparently been more or less 'frozen' since 1974, with the partial exceptions of Canada, the USA and the UK.[53] However, even in the USA and the UK, the inflow of illegal migrants and asylum seekers has provided substantial cheap illegal labour. Thus formal immigration policies are only part of the story. The USA is often characterised as being shaped by client politics,[54] yet a relatively open immigration policy (though with a 'points system' favouring skilled workers and family migration) has been accompanied for decades by mass illegal immigration. In Europe, the southern European countries have admitted relatively few legal migrants: most immigration is effected through visa-overstaying, illegal work and illegal entry—eventually acquiring short-term legal status through legalisation programmes. Illegal immigration and illegal work are not confined to southern Europe, however, even if they are a larger proportion of both total immigration and total employment than in northern European countries or the wider Anglophone world.

The capacity of the state to implement restrictive immigration policies is a subject taken up by Massey, in an interesting attempt to theorise why illegal immigration has been consistently increasing across the world.[55] He posits a spectrum of state capacities, ranging from authoritarian Gulf states to traditional settler countries with their immigrant-supporting structures. The problem with this approach is that even the Gulf states have significant numbers of illegal immigrants—and, in fact, appear to have little idea of how many immigrant workers they have anyway.[56] An alternative approach is to question why state capacities to manage immigration according to labour market needs seem so inadequate. Two explanations can be offered. First, predicting economic needs for even the immediate future has proven too demanding for almost all countries, which frequently under- or over-estimate the need for temporary labour and cannot respond rapidly to changing market conditions. The results of inaccurate prediction are dire: employers find more reliability and flexibility in using illegal migrant labour. Secondly, a liberalisation of immigration policy has to be a political position; if the electorate is not convinced of the need for immigrant labour, or feels threatened in terms of job competition or wage rates, this policy is unlikely to be pursued.

The 'frozen' 1974 immigration policy appears at first sight puzzling in the light of increasing liberalisation of the factors of production in advanced capitalism. With increasing trade flows, capital flows and deregulation of state-owned companies (the latter within the EU), we might expect an accompanying freeing of the movement of labour. The analogous period of globalisation in the late 19th century might suggest this, too. What seems to have occurred, however, is that while governments have lost control of their currencies and capital flows, and have opened up markets to global trade, they have seized upon immigration policy—the protection of the country's borders—as the last bastion of sovereignty.[57] Originally placed as a rational response to economic crisis, restrictive immigration policies are now almost independent of economic imperatives: they are firmly embedded in essentially nationalist political discourses, which are ideological rather than pragmatic.[58] Each coming crisis, especially concerning national sovereignty, national security or anti-terrorism measures, can be linked with the need for tighter border controls and restrictive immigration policy.[59]

The result of this politicisation of immigration management is that illegal migration and illegal employment have emerged as fundamental structural components of modern capitalism.[60] Now, not only are entire sectors of the economy dependent on illegal labour, but the political management of national economies has to accept this as a reality. Simultaneously, potential migrants know, through networks of former migrants or hearsay, that illegal migration is an established and 'normal' route to a better life and employment in the world's richest countries. They also know that there is no easy way for unskilled or semi-skilled workers to migrate legally. Thus, at the beginning of the 21st century, the phenomenon of illegal migration can reasonably be described as structurally embedded. The non-stop arrival of boatloads of Africans in the small islands of the Mediterranean is a humanitarian crisis, but it is the logical outcome of nearly 30 years of mismanagement of world migration. Structural problems do not permit of easy solutions, and this is no exception. Like 'global warming' or other major issues, it seems that government policies are almost universally reactive, piecemeal and conservative. Never has the world been in more need of a visionary approach and major reform.

Notes

1 I use the term 'illegal migration' uncritically, and at variance with most contemporary literature. Although not all countries class illegal migration as a crime (the UK does, however), it is nevertheless in all cases migration outside of the rule of law.

2 Notable exceptions include A Portes, 'Toward a structural analysis of illegal (undocumented) immigration', *International Migration Review*, 12 (4), 1978, pp 469–484; B Ghosh, *Huddled Masses and Uncertain Shores*, The Hague: Kluwer Law International, 1998; B Jordan & F Duvell, *Irregular Migration*, London: Edward Elgar, 2002; and G Hanson, *The Economic Logic of Illegal Immigration*, CSR No 26, New York: Council on Foreign Relations, April 2007.

3 See, for example, M Jandl, 'The estimation of illegal migration in Europe', *Studi Emigrazione*, XLI (153), 2004, pp 141–155; and various studies of the International Centre for Migration Policy Development, Vienna.

4 Article 13 of the Universal Declaration of Human Rights, 1948. This right was not universally accepted, however, and in particular the communist bloc found it inimical to their political management of territory. The infamous 'Iron Curtain' was ultimately replaced after 1989 by a less tangible 'Wall around the West'. See P Andreas & T Snyder (eds), *The Wall around the West*, Oxford: Rowman and Littlefield, 2000.

5 D Papademetriou, 'The global struggle with illegal migration: no end in sight', *Migration Information Source*, 2005, at www.migrationinformation.org.

6 For example, N Harris, *Thinking the Unthinkable: The Immigration Myth Exposed*, London: IB Tauris, 2001; and T Hayter, *Open Borders: The Case against Immigration Controls*, London: Pluto, 2004.

7 J Torpey, *The Invention of the Passport*, Cambridge: Cambridge University Press, 2000, pp 66–67.

8 *Ibid*, p 59.

9 A Timmer & J Williamson, 'Immigration policy prior to the 1930s', *Population and Development Review*, 24 (4), 1998, pp 739–771.

10 Torpey, *The Invention of the Passport*, p 77.

11 Timmer & Williamson, 'Immigration policy prior to the 1930s', p 739.

12 J Torpey, 'The Great War and the birth of the modern passport system', in J Caplan & J Torpey (eds), *Documenting Individual Identity*, Princeton, NJ: Princeton University Press, 2001, p 264.

13 The great exception was France, which was primarily concerned with its population losses in World War I and its low population growth. See J Torpey, 'States and the regulation of migration in the twentieth-century North Atlantic world', in Andreas & Snyder, *The Wall around the West*, pp 31–54.

14 Torpey, 'States and the regulation of migration', p 38.

15 Torpey, 'The Great War and the birth of the modern passport system', p 269.

16 C Skran, *Refugees in Inter-war Europe: The Emergence of a Regime*, Oxford: Clarendon Press, 1995.

17 Migration for Employment Convention (1949), C 097, International Labour Organisation, Geneva.

18 G Freeman & B Birrell, 'Divergent paths of immigration politics in the United States and Australia', *Population and Development Review*, 27 (3), 2001, pp 525–551.

19 D Massey, J Arango, G Hugo, A Kouaouchi, A Pellegrino & JE Taylor, *Worlds in Motion*, Oxford: Oxford University Press, 1998, p 5.

20 *Ibid*, pp 6–7.

21 A Portes, 'Toward a structural analysis of illegal (undocumented) immigration', *International Migration Review*, 12 (4), 1978, p 470.

22 M Baldwin-Edwards & M Schain, 'The politics of immigration', *West European Politics*, 17 (2), 1994, pp 1–16.

23 M Baldwin-Edwards, 'Immigration after 1992', *Policy & Politics*, 19 (3), p 199.

24 M Baldwin-Edwards, 'Where free markets reign: aliens in the twilight zone', in M Baldwin-Edwards & J Arango (eds), *Immigrants and the Informal Economy in Southern Europe*, London: Routledge, 1999.

25 E Reyneri, 'Migrants' involvement in irregular employment in the Mediterranean countries of the European Union', *International Migration Paper 41*, Geneva: ILO, 2001.

26 M Baldwin-Edwards, 'Semi-reluctant hosts: Southern Europe's ambivalent response to immigration', *Studi Emigrazione*, 39 (145), 2002, p 33.

27 M Baldwin-Edwards, 'Albanian emigration and the Greek labour market: economic symbiosis and social ambiguity', *South East Europe Review*, 1, 2004, pp 51–65.

28 International Federation of Red Cross and Red Crescent Societies, *World Disasters Report*, Geneva, 2006; and M Baldwin-Edwards, *Statistical Data on Immigrants in Greece*, Athens: Mediterranean Migration Observatory and Migration Policy Institute, Ministry of the Interior.

29 D Papademetriou, 'The global struggle with illegal migration'.

30 P Martin, *Bordering on Control: Combating Irregular Migration in North America and Europe*, Migration Research Series No 13, Geneva: International Organisation for Migration, 2003, p 6.

31 K Koser, 'Irregular migration, state security and human security', paper prepared for the Policy Analysis and Research Programme of the Global Commission on International Migration, 2005, at www.gcim.org.

32 J Salt & J Stein, 'Migration as a business: the case of trafficking', *International Migration*, 35 (4), 1997, pp 467–494.

33 Trafficking is defined as 'the recruitment, transportation, transfer, harbouring or receipt of persons, by means of the threat, or use of force or other forms of coercion, of abduction, of fraud, of deception, of the abuse of power or of a position of vulnerability or of the giving or receiving of payments or benefits to achieve the consent of a person having control over another person, *for the purpose of exploitation*'. Smuggling is defined as 'The procurement, in order to obtain, directly or indirectly a financial or other material benefit, of the *illegal entry of a person into a state Party* of which the person is not a national or a permanent resident'. Emphasis added.

34 See http://www.unodc.org/unodc/en/treaties/CTOC/signatures.html.

35 AA Afolayan, 'Issues and challenges of emigration dynamics in developing countries', *International Migration*, 39 (4), 2001, p 10.

36 A Adepojou, 'Trends in international migration in and from Africa', in D Massey & JE Taylor (eds), *International Migration: Prospects and Policies in a Global Market*, Oxford: Oxford University Press, 2004, p 65.

37 Notably EG Ravenstein, 'The laws of migration', *Journal of the Royal Statistical Society*, 48, 1885, pp 167–227.

38 H de Haas, 'Morocco: from emigration country to Africa's migration passage to Europe', *Migration Information Source*, 2005, at www.migrationinformation.org.

39 H Olesen, 'Migration, return and development', *International Migration*, 40 (5), 2002, pp 125–150.

40 R Lucas, 'International migration to the high income countries', mimeo, 2004, p 7, available from www.worldbank.org.

41 A Portes, M Castells & L Benton (eds), *The Informal Economy: Studies in Advanced and Less Developed Countries*, Baltimore, MD: Johns Hopkins University Press, 1989.

42 C Williams & J Windebank, *Informal Employment in the Advanced Economies*, London: Routledge, 1998, pp 174–175.

43 Portes *et al*, *The Informal Economy*.

44 T Jones & M Ram, 'Shades of grey in the informal economy', *International Journal of Sociology and Social Policy*, 26 (9–10), 2006, pp 357–373.

45 Williams & Windebank, *Informal Employment in the Advanced Economies*, p 101.

46 WA Cornelius, 'Controlling "unwanted" immigration: lessons from the United States, 1993–2004', *Journal of Ethnic and Migration Studies*, 31 (4), 2005, pp 775–794; E Reyneri, 'Migrants' involvement in irregular employment'; and Baldwin-Edwards & Arango, *Immigrants and the Informal Economy*.

47 P Renooy, S Ivarsson, O van der Wusten-Gritsai & R Meijer, *Undeclared Work in an Enlarged Union: Final Report*, Brussels: European Commission, DG Employment, May 2004, pp 25–26.

48 *Ibid*, p 9.

49 Reyneri, 'Migrants' involvement in irregular employment'; Baldwin-Edwards & Arango, *Immigrants and the Informal Economy*; and R King & R Black (eds), *Southern Europe and the New Immigrations*, Brighton: Sussex Academic Press, 1997.

50 W Boehning, 'Top-end and bottom-end labour import in the United States and Europe', in H Van Amersfoort & J Doomernik (eds), *International Migration: Processes and Interventions*, Amsterdam: IMES and Het Spinhuis Publishers, 1998.

51 M Piore, *Birds of Passage*, New York: Cambridge University Press, 1979.

52 E Vidal, F Gil & A Domingo, 'Participation of immigrants in the European Union's national labour markets in a context of complementarity', paper presented to the EAPS European Population Conference 2006, Liverpool, 21–24 June 2006; and M Baldwin-Edwards, 'Southern European labour markets and immigration: a structural and functional analysis', in *The Greek Labour Yearbook 2001*, Athens: IAPAD, Panteion University (in Greek). English version available as *Mediterranean Migration Observatory Working Paper No 5*, at www.mmo.gr.

53 I am excluding from this discussion the issue of asylum seekers and refugees, on the grounds that such policy is not intended to increase labour supply, even though such is the inevitable result of refugee flows. Furthermore, as the UN High Commissioner for Refugees (UNHCR) concedes, a very high proportion of asylum seekers have no real claims under the Geneva Convention and arguably are economic migrants. Thus the borderline between illegal migrant and asylum seeker is often blurred.

54 Freeman & Birrell, 'Divergent paths of immigration politics in the United States and Australia'.

55 D Massey, 'International migration at the dawn of the twenty-first century: the role of the state', *Population and Development Review*, 25 (2), 1999, pp 303–322.

56 M Baldwin-Edwards, *Migration in the Middle East and Mediterranean*, Regional Study prepared for the Global Commission on International Migration, 2005, at www.mmo.gr and www.gcim.org.

57 M Baldwin-Edwards & M Schain, 'The politics of immigration', p 15. The symbolic role of border controls in the Schengen area is also noted in K Groenendijk, 'Reinstatement of controls at the internal borders of Europe: why and against whom?', *European Law Journal*, 10 (2), 2004, pp 150–170.

58 F Pastore, 'Europe, migration and development: critical remarks on an emerging policy field', *Development*, 50 (4), 2007, pp 56–62.

59 F Adamson, 'Crossing borders: international migration and national security', *International Security*, 31 (1), 2006, pp 165–199.

60 S Palidda, 'Migration between prohibitionism and the perpetuation of illegal labour', *History and Anthropology*, 16 (1), 2005, pp 63–73.

Index

Note: page references in *italics* indicate tables, those in **bold** indicate figures.
EU = European Union
UK = United Kingdom
UN = United Nations

industrialisation 209-10
inequality 10, 11
    Mexico 155, *155*; South Africa 102
informal employment 220, 222, 223
    and illegal immigration 223
information, for migrants 41
insecurity 5, 7, 147, 158
Institute for Public Policy Research
    (IPPR) 25
Inter-American Court of Human Rights
    28-9
International Conference on Migrant
    Remittances 163, 165
International Convention of Migrant
    Workers (ICMW) 28, 33, 72
International Forum on Remittances 165, 166
international labour market 21-35
    migrant rights 26-35
international labour migration 21-35
International Labour Organisation (ILO)
    8-9, 23, 28, 33, 201, 204, 219
    board 213; *Global Alliance Against
    Forced Labour* (GAAFL) 200-13;
    global remittance trend 163, 164;
    Multilateral Framework on Labour
    Migration 30, 33-4; *Stopping Forced
    Labour* report 8; and UK report on
    Forced Labour 213
international migration **3**
    rise in 131, 161
International Organisation for Migration
    (IOM) 1, 3, 5, 33, 99
    global remittance trend 163, 164
interventionalism 113, 116, 118, 126
irregular migration 6, 18, 22, 26-9, 196
    Africa 77-91; amnesties 28; Asia 66,
    67; criminalisation 27; Europe 26, 81;
    females 66; Filipino 44; and illegal
    work 26; policy approaches to 81-2;
    regularisation 28; regularisations 88;
    reliance on 31; USA 6, 26, *see also*
    illegal migration
Italy 81, 82, 220, 221, 223
    arrivals by sea 221

Jacinto, Dr Elmer 53
Japan 68, 69

Jones, J.P., K. Woodward and S. Marston
    202-3
Jordan 71
Joseph Rowntree Foundation 204, 213

Kapur, D. 118
Knowles, Caroline 8
Korea 68
Kouaouci, A., A. Pellegrino, J.E. Taylor,
    D.S. Massey, J. Arango and G.Hugo
    117, 220

labour
    cheap illegal 224; laws 32, 87;
        restrictions 13; shortages 219, 220
labour markets
    EU deregulation 223; Europe 222-3;
        Filipino 52-4; liberalisation 23;
        migrant rights 21-35; North America
        222-3; northern Europe 220; shortages
        24, 42-3, 51, 52-3, *see also*
        international labour market
labour-capital relations 206, 207, 208
Latin America 7, 165, 204
Lawrence, Felicity 211
Leitner, H. and B. Miller 203
Lerche, J 201, 204-5, 207
Levitt, Peggy, social remittances 170
Levitt, Peggy and Ninna Nyberg-Sorensen 11
live-in caregiver programme (LCP) 47-8,
    58-9
living conditions 187, 191, 196
India 205; UK temporary workers 212
low-skilled workers 22, 23-6, 51, 52, 225
    East Asia 68; programmes 32, *see also*
        unskilled workers
Lucas, R. 222

MacDonald, M. 102
Mahler, Sarah 173
maids
    Filipino 46, *see also* domestic service
male migration 65, 158
    India 205; Philippines 44, 45; reasons
        151-2, *152*, *see also* gender; return
        migration
males